D1163748

WITHDRAWN

THE UNITED IRISHMEN

THE UNITED IRISHMEN

Popular Politics in Ulster and Dublin,
1791–1798

NANCY J. CURTIN

CLARENDON PRESS · OXFORD

1994

Oxford University Press, Walton Street, Oxford OX2 6DP
Oxford New York Toronto
Delhi Bombay Calcutta Madras Karachi
Kuala Lumpur Singapore Hong Kong Tokyo
Nairobi Dar es Salaam Cape Town
Melbourne Auckland Madrid
and associated companies in
Berlin Ibadan

Oxford is a trade mark of Oxford University Press

Published in the United States
by Oxford University Press Inc., New York

British Library Cataloguing in Publication Data
Data available

Library of Congress Cataloging in Publication Data
Curtin, Nancy J.
The United Irishmen: popular politics in Ulster and Dublin,
1791–1798 / Nancy J. Curtin.
p.   cm.
Includes bibliographical references (p.   ) and index.
1. United Irishmen.   2. Ulster (Northern Ireland and Ireland)—
Politics and government.   3. Ireland—Popular culture—
History—18th century.   4. Ireland—History—Rebellion of 1798—
Causes.   5. Ireland—Politics and government—1760–1820.   6. Dublin
(Ireland)—Politics and government.   I. Title.
DA948.5.C87 1994 93-32522 941.507—dc20
ISBN 0–19–820322–5 (acid-free paper)

1 3 5 7 9 10 8 6 4 2

Set by Hope Services (Abingdon) Ltd.
Printed in Great Britain by
Bookcraft (Bath) Ltd
Midsomer Norton, Avon

Acknowledgements

For permission to quote from the collections in their possession I would like to thank the Centre for Kentish Studies, the National Army Museum, the Council of Trustees of the National Library of Ireland, Keele University, the British Library, the Board of Trinity College Dublin, the Royal Irish Academy, the Public Record Office of Northern Ireland, Mrs R. V. T. Edie, Michael Duffin, R. C. Lytton White, the Ulster Museum, and the Director of the National Archives of Ireland.

Funding for my research abroad was provided by a Social Science Research Council grant, a Fulbright fellowship, a bursary from Queen's University of Belfast. My research experience was enriched by my affiliation with the Institute of Irish Studies at Queen's. I would like to thank the former Director, Dr R. H. Buchanan, and the fellows of the Institute who provided me with countless forms of assistance and inspiration. For support in seeing the project through its final stages I must thank Fordham University. This included the services of Christopher Bellitto, Andre Cizmarik, and Tom Horan as research assistants.

My research in Ireland, north and south, was made all the more pleasurable owing to the many personal friendships I enjoyed. I would like to single out Jonathan Bell, Anne O'Dowd, and Stewart Roulston who happily tore me away from the archives and introduced me to the land and the people of the country I was studying.

I wish to render my thanks as well to the staff of Oxford University Press, and especially to Nicola Pike for her impressively meticulous copy-editing.

The community of historians of late eighteenth-century Ireland is a particularly generous and stimulating one. Professor Marianne Elliott was especially giving with her time and encouragement in transforming the dissertation into a book. Dr Julia Adams, Dr Maryanne Kowaleski, and Dr D. M. C. Worzala gave a careful and critical reading of certain chapters. My greatest intellectual debt is owed to my much-esteemed mentor, Professor James S. Donnelly, jun. Not only did he initiate me into the study of Irish history and the United Irishmen in particular, but with his own work he has set standards for scholarship which I shall always strive to emulate. If I fail in this task, it will not be because his own patient and careful attention to my work has been wanting.

Finally, I would like to thank my family, especially my parents, Don and Marilyn Curtin, whom I can never adequately thank for the material and emotional support they have given me over the years.

Bibliographical note: since the completion of my research the Public Record Office of Ireland and the State Paper Office of Ireland were amalgamated to form the National Archives. I have opted to use the former citations in the bibliography and footnotes.

CONTENTS

LIST OF TABLES

ABBREVIATIONS

BL	British Library
BNL	*Belfast News-Letter*
FDJ	*Faulkner's Dublin Journal*
FJ	*Freeman's Journal*
JHCI	*Journals of the house of commons of the kingdom of Ireland*
Kent CAO	Kent County Archive Office
NAM	National Army Museum, London
NLI	National Library of Ireland
NS	*Northern Star*
PROHO	Public Record Office, Home Office
PROI	Public Record Office, Ireland
PRONI	Public Record Office of Northern Ireland
RIA	Royal Irish Academy
SPOI	State Paper Office, Ireland
TCD	Trinity College Library, Dublin

INTRODUCTION

UNTIL recently the United Irish movement had received relatively little attention from historians.[1] Perhaps this was because the story seemed so familiar, with the names of Tone, Drennan, O'Connor, and Fitzgerald reverberating throughout the subsequent course of Irish history.[2] Also, W. E. H. Lecky's multivolume, scrupulously researched, and elegantly narrated account of eighteenth-century Ireland (over half of which dealt with the decade of the 1790s) seemed to have said it all.[3] But Lecky, an expert practitioner of 'history from above', begged many questions about the actual United Irish movement in terms of its aims, its personnel, and the reasons for its emergence in the 1790s. Basically, he saw Irish republicanism as a product of the French revolution, which polarized public opinion in Ireland between radicals and conservatives, destroying in the process a much-admired moderate whiggism represented by Henry Grattan and his party. E. P. Thompson, among others, has directed our attention away from this notion of popular political mobilization as significant only to the extent that it demanded the attention of the governing élites, and he has pushed the popular classes themselves to the centre of the stage. *The making*

[1] Exceptions to this assertion include an important body of research conducted in the 1930s on the reformist phase of the movement. See e.g. Rosamund Jacob, *The Rise of the United Irishmen* (London, 1937); Frank MacDermot, *Theobald Wolfe Tone and his times* (first published, 1939; Tralee, 1968); R. B. McDowell, 'The personnel of the Dublin Society of United Irishmen, 1791–4', *Irish Historical Studies*, 2/5 (Mar. 1940), 12–53; T. W. Moody, 'The political ideas of the United Irishmen', *Ireland To-Day*, 3/1 (Jan. 1938), 15–25; Revd Patrick Rogers, *The Irish Volunteers and Catholic emancipation, 1778–1793* (London, 1934); Edward Sheehy, 'Tone and the United Irishmen', *Ireland To-Day*, 2/12 (Dec. 1937), 37–42. Recent contributions to the historiography of the movement are discussed below.

[2] For Theobald Wolfe Tone, see Henry Boylan, *Theobald Wolfe Tone* (Dublin, 1981); Nancy J. Curtin, 'The Belfast uniform: Theobald Wolfe Tone', *Eire-Ireland*, 20/2 (Summer 1985), 40–69; Tom Dunne, *Theobald Wolfe Tone, colonial outsider: an analysis of his political philosophy* (Cork, 1982); Marianne Elliott, *Wolfe Tone: prophet of Irish independence* (New Haven, Conn., and London, 1989); MacDermot, *Tone*; Sheehy, 'Tone and the United Irishmen'. For treatments of other United Irishmen, see A. T. Q. Stewart, '"A stable unseen power": Dr William Drennan and the origins of the United Irishmen', in John Bossy and Peter Jupp (eds.), *Essays presented to Michael Roberts* (Belfast, 1976), 80–92; Frank MacDermot, 'Arthur O'Connor', *Irish Historical Studies*, 16/57 (Mar. 1966), 48–69; Rupert Coughlan, *Napper Tandy* (Dublin, 1976); C. J. Woods, 'The place of Thomas Russell in the United Irish movement', in Hugh Gough and David Dickson (eds.), *Ireland and the French revolution* (Dublin, 1990), 83–108. For collections of the biographies of various United Irishmen, see W. T. Latimer, *Ulster biographies relating chiefly to the rebellion of 1798* (Belfast, 1897); R. R. Madden, *Antrim and Down in '98* (Glasgow, n.d.); id., *The United Irishmen, their lives and times*, 3rd. ser. (7 vols., London, 1842–5). For memoirs of individual United Irishmen, see e.g. John Binns, *Recollections of the life of John Binns* (Philadelphia, 1854); Valentine Lawless, Lord Cloncurry, *Personal recollections of the life and times, with extracts from the correspondence, of Valentine, Lord Cloncurry* (Dublin, 1849); Thomas Russell, *Journals and memoirs of Thomas Russell, 1791–5*, ed. Christopher Woods (Dublin, 1992).

[3] W. E. H. Lecky, *A history of Ireland in the eighteenth century* (5 vols., London, 1898).

of the English working class has inspired a generation of historians, and its impact on the practice of Irish history is unquestionable.[4] Not only did Thompson revive interest in popular political mobilization and mentalities in general, but he also quite directly provoked a new interest in the United Irishmen by uncovering an underground of English revolutionary Jacobins in the late 1790s with Irish connections.[5] This led to a fuller examination of both movements, culminating in Marianne Elliott's commanding *Partners in revolution*, and Roger Wells's far less convincing *Insurrection*.[6] Elliott has gone even further and explored the connections between the United Irishmen and France.

The history of Ireland's first republicans is thus being rescued from a rather parochial nationalist hagiography as historians have begun to place them in a general context of late eighteenth-century European or transatlantic radicalism. But the dynamics of the organization within Ireland—its aims, its social bases, and the reasons why it adopted or discarded certain strategies of mobilization—remain blurred. This study seeks to sharpen our vision by focusing on the internal organization and development of the United Irish movement. It concerns itself primarily with popular politicization and mobilization, its approach analytic rather than narrative or biographical.

Recent scholarship tended to focus on the leadership within the United Irish organization, slighting the more elusive lower echelons and the achievement of building a mass movement under trying circumstances. R. B. McDowell has offered a precise analysis of the social composition of the Dublin Society of United Irishmen from 1791 to 1794, but no comparable study is available on the social bases of the revolutionary organization of the later 1790s.[7] The mobilization of the United Irish movement, and the reactions that this provoked from the governing class, have received the lion's share of historiographical attention. Lecky remains the starting-point

---

[4] E. P. Thompson, *The making of the English working class* (New York, 1963); id., 'The moral economy of the English crowd in the eighteenth century', *Past and Present*, 50 (Feb. 1971), 76–136. For Irish historians working in a broadly defined Thompsonian tradition, see e.g. Tom Bartlett, 'An end to moral economy: the Irish militia disturbances of 1793', *Past and Present*, 99 (May 1983), 41–64; James S. Donnelly, jun., 'Hearts of Oak, Hearts of Steel', *Studia Hibernica*, 21 (1981), 7–73; S. J. Connolly, *Priests and people in pre-famine Ireland, 1780–1845* (Dublin, 1982).

[5] See e.g. Albert Goodwin, *The friends of liberty: the English democratic movement in the age of the French revolution* (London, 1979); Malcolm I. Thomis and Peter Holt, *Threats of revolution in Britain, 1789-1848* (London, 1977); Gwyn Williams, *Artisans and sans-culottes: popular movements in France and Britain during the French revolution* (New York, 1969).

[6] Marianne Elliott, *Partners in revolution: the United Irishmen and France* (New Haven, Conn., and London, 1982); Roger Wells, *Insurrection: the British experience, 1795–1803* (Gloucester, 1983).

[7] McDowell, 'Personnel of the Dublin Society'. For a less satisfactory discussion of the social base of the republican movement in rural Antrim and Down in the late 1790s, see Peter Gibbon, 'The origins of the Orange Order and the United Irishmen: a study in the sociology of revolution and counter-revolution', *Economy and Society*, 1 (1972), 134–63.

for any understanding of the government's response to republican activities. McDowell's *Ireland in the age of imperialism and revolution* is also marked by the clarity and perceptiveness with which it presents the political and administrative history of the 1790s.[8] Indeed, the much-abused Anglo-Irish ascendancy receives sympathetic treatment from McDowell and from A. P. W. Malcomson in his biography of John Foster, reflecting a trend in recent Irish historiography to rehabilitate the once universally denigrated landed élite.[9]

This reassessment of the Castle and loyalist dilemma in confronting smouldering popular rebellion at home and the threat of invasion from abroad is certainly understandable considering the chief archival sources on the United Irishmen. They mobilized as a secret society, after all, and the historian's understanding of their movement must be filtered through the lens of magistrates, office-holders, and informers, who provide the great bulk of documentary material consulted in this study. The picture presented in these sources is often tainted with bigotry and paranoia, but one can also see sincere and well-meaning men engaged in a life and death struggle to preserve liberty and property from the threat of anarchic social disruption represented by the republican movement. From 1796 the threat grew to formidable proportions. United Irish terror paralysed the normal judicial and peace-keeping processes. The authorities responded with counter-terror, brutal and repressive to be sure, but, under the circumstances, perhaps not excessive in the light of the obstacles they confronted in re-establishing the rule of law in Ireland. Civil wars are, after all, a messy business.

Indeed, a cycle of provocation and reaction was established by 1793 and culminated in the rebellion of 1798. The United Irishmen would constitute a threat to the established order; the government would respond. The United Irishmen would then regroup, reconsider their strategy, and adapt to a more repressive political climate, an adaptation which generally led to a more extreme position and a new campaign of provocation. And so the government would react yet again in its counter-campaign. One side was struggling to assert the rights of individuals and citizens; the other to preserve the social order. Both sides were self-interested and idealistic; both were excessive in their zeal.

It is a conventional republican piety that the struggle of the 1790s was between Britain and patriotic Irishmen. But it is often forgotten that the United Irishmen and the Catholic Committee regarded the British ministry as a potential ally against ascendancy misgovernment and exclusivity. This explains the euphoric reception of Earl Fitzwilliam in Ireland in 1795 and

[8] R. B. McDowell, *Ireland in the age of imperialism and revolution* (Oxford, 1979).
[9] A. P. W. Malcomson, *John Foster: the politics of the Anglo-Irish ascendancy* (Oxford, 1978). For another sympathetic portrayal of the ascendancy, see J. C. Beckett, *The Anglo-Irish tradition* (Ithaca, NY, 1976).

the bitter disappointment triggered when Pitt recalled him. The policy of severe repression of the republican movement was advocated most strenuously by loyalist Irishmen, not by imperial policy-makers. It was the ascendancy that was most endangered in the 1790s, and it reacted accordingly.

The United Irishmen secured a mass following with their promises of civil and political equality, their assurances that traditional grievances would be removed by a republican government, and their confident claims that French aid would bring them certain victory. But such an agenda was liable to repel as many Irishmen as it attracted, both among the governing élites and among the lower and middle ranks. It was not only the forces of a defensive, militant, popular protestantism that arrayed themselves against the republicans. The Catholic church found the United Irishmen equally repugnant. The republicans pinned many hopes on the disaffection of the militia, but the soldiers, too, sided with the loyalists in 1798. Britain secured Ireland in the 1790s because it also had a popular mass following. The issue was not exclusively a contest between the people and a corrupt government, as the United Irishmen claimed, but a civil war over the kind of government and society that Ireland should have.

One of the more important contributions to our understanding of the mobilization of the United Irish movement comes from Marianne Elliott.[10] Her main interest, however, is with the alliance between the Irish republicans and revolutionary and Napoleonic France. It is hardly surprising, then, that she sees United Irish mobilization and strategy largely through the prism of the fluctuating fortunes of this alliance.[11] Elliott has not ignored other troublesome allies of the United Irishmen. In a provocative but seminal article she has claimed that the middle-class, cosmopolitan republicanism of the United Irishmen was overwhelmed by the surging Catholic nationalism of their Defender allies.[12] A particularly elusive secret society which appeared in parts of Ireland as a sectarian faction, in others as a further refinement of Whiteboy agrarian protest, and still in others as a movement of radical artisanal democrats, the Defenders have recently received some needed attention.[13] But their relationship with the United Irishmen,

[10] Elliott, *Partners in revolution*.

[11] In fact, she argues that the most important achievement of the United Irishmen was the negotiation of this alliance (Marianne Elliott, 'The United Irishman as diplomat', in Patrick J. Corish (ed.), *Radicals, rebels, and establishments* (Belfast, 1985), 69–89).

[12] Marianne Elliott, 'The origins and transformation of early Irish republicanism', *International Review of Social History*, 23/3 (1978), 405–28.

[13] See Thomas Bartlett, 'Select documents, XXXVIII: Defenders and Defenderism in 1795', *Irish Historical Studies*, 24/95 (May 1985), 373–94; L. M. Cullen, 'The political structures of the Defenders', in Gough and Dickson (eds.), *Ireland and the French revolution*, 117–38; Nancy J. Curtin, 'The transformation of the Society of United Irishmen into a mass-based revolutionary organisation, 1794–6', *Irish Historical Studies*, 24/96 (Nov. 1985), 463–92; Elliott, 'Origins and transformation'; Tom Garvin, 'Defenders, Ribbonmen, and others: underground political networks in pre-famine Ireland', *Past and Present*, 96 (Aug. 1982), 133-55; David W. Miller, 'The Armagh troubles, 1784-95', in Samuel Clark and James S. Donnell, jun. (eds.), *Irish*

and the extent to which they coalesced with the republican cause, require further investigation. It was with the aid of the Defenders, after all, that the United Irish movement became a national one.

Elliott thus set an agenda which other historians are following in looking more closely at the popular dimensions of United Irish and Defender mobilization. This is reflected not only in the concerns of this book, but also in three recently published works: the essays in David Dickson and Hugh Gough's *Ireland and the French revolution*, another collection edited by Dickson, Dáire Keogh, and Kevin Whelan, *The United Irishmen: republicanism, radicalism and rebellion*, and Jim Smyth's, *The men of no property*.[14] Smyth especially addresses the question of popular political mobilization, his focus primarily the Defenders in Dublin and County Armagh.

Little has been done to explore the sources of the nationalism and republicanism which all agree that the United Irishmen espoused, but which few have bothered to trace. Indeed, United Irish republicanism is equated simply—and wrongly—with a desire for total separation from Britain. In general, there has been little effort to place these republicans within a cultural and intellectual tradition; the prevailing tendency, on the contrary, has been to regard them as having emerged, *sui generis*, from the storming of the Bastille in 1789, the example of which provided an irresistible stimulus to the revival of Ireland's dormant reform movement.[15] Consequently, early Irish republicanism increasingly took on the character of French Jacobinism. While this view helps to explain the radical aims of the revived reform movement, which far outdistanced the demands of the Volunteers, as well as the subsequent contagion of Francophilia which infected many lower-class adherents to the republican cause, it minimizes the influence of pre-existing radical and republican ideas on the founders and leaders of the United Irish movement. Thus, other historians have searched within Ireland for the origins of revolutionary republican tendencies.[16] Here the trend is to

peasants: violence and political unrest, 1780–1914 (Madison, Wis., 1983), 155–91; James Smyth, 'Popular politicisation, Defenderism and the Catholic question', in Gough and Dickson (eds.), *Ireland and the French revolution*, 109–16.

[14] Gough and Dickson (eds.), *Ireland and the French Revolution*; David Dickson, Dáire Keogh, and Kevin Whelan (eds.), *The United Irishmen: republicanism, radicalism, and rebellion* (Dublin, 1993); Jim Smyth, *The men of no property: Irish radicals and popular politics in the late eighteenth century* (New York, 1992).

[15] See J. C. Beckett, *The making of modern Ireland, 1603-1923* (New York, 1973), 246-67; R. F. Foster, *Modern Ireland, 1600–1972* (Harmondsworth, Middlesex, 1988), 259–60; Jacob, *United Irishmen*; W. Benjamin Kennedy, 'The Irish Jacobins', *Studia Hibernica*, 16 (1976), 109–21; Lecky, *History of Ireland*, iii. 4–16; McDowell, *Ireland*, 351-89.

[16] J. M. Barkley, *A short history of the Presbyterian church in Ireland* (Belfast, 1960), 25–44; Terence Brown, *The whole protestant community: the making of a historical myth* (Field Day pamphlet 7; Belfast, 1985); Marianne Elliott, *Watchmen in Sion: the protestant idea of liberty*, (Field Day pamphlet 8; Belfast, 1985); J. L. M. Haire (ed.), *Challenge and conflict: essays in Irish Presbyterian history and doctrine* (Antrim, 1981); R. L. McCartney, *Liberty and authority in Ireland* (Field Day pamphlet 9: Belfast, 1985); David W. Miller, 'Presbyterianism and

stress the peculiar affinity of Ulster Presbyterianism with democratic, representative systems of government. While this approach is useful in directing our attention to part of the intellectual and cultural milieu which gave rise to early Irish republicanism, it restricts the scope of investigation to one confessional community. Furthermore, such an identification of Presbyterianism with liberal political thought tends to lead to the historical myth described by Terence Brown as the 'theory of Ireland's last chance', in which an enlightened north was betrayed by a crudely nationalist and Catholic south in the 1790s, forcing Ulster protestants to look to themselves and to Britain to preserve their liberties.[17]

Certainly, a tradition of Presbyterian radicalism and the trigger of the French revolution helped to launch a resurgent reform movement in Ireland. But a political vocabulary already existed in the lexicon of the civic humanist or commonwealth tradition, with its emphasis on public virtue, the subordination of self-interest, and the rights and, even more important, the responsibilities of citizens to secure the good state, the *res publica*. That this was a vocabulary that was adopted by supporters of protestant ascendancy in Ireland such as whig moderates and anti-Catholic civic politicians makes it no less relevant to the origins of Irish republicanism. A recent history of the French revolution is entitled *Citizens*, an ironic comment by the author, to be sure, considering that his citizens are depicted as violent and irrational.[18] Nevertheless, this should not obscure the point that popular politicization of the late eighteenth century was precisely about citizenship. Words are flexible, and the United Irish embraced a nation with the word 'citizen', while the moderate whig tradition comprehended only property.

The inclusiveness with which the United Irishmen connoted such words as 'citizen' and 'nation' reflects the exclusiveness with which these words were used by their adversaries.[19] Examining the Chartist movement, which adopted a political programme almost identical to that of the United Irishmen, Gareth Stedman-Jones has described radicalism as the public language of envy, the political vocabulary of the excluded.[20] A sense of exclu-

"modernization" in Ulster', *Past and Present*, 80 (Aug. 1978), 66-90; Stewart, '"A stable unseen power"'; id., 'The transformation of Presbyterian radicalism in the north of Ireland, 1792–1825', MA thesis, (Queen's University of Belfast, 1956). For the roots of this radical tradition, see e.g. J. C. Beckett, *Protestant dissent in Ireland, 1687-1780* (London, 1948); Michael Walzer, 'Puritanism as revolutionary ideology', *History and Theory*, 3/1 (1963), 59–70.

[17] Brown, *The whole protestant community*, 13–14.

[18] Simon Schama, *Citizens: a chronicle of the French revolution* (New York, 1989).

[19] Such inclusiveness, however, did not include advocation of the civic rights of women: see Nancy J. Curtin, 'Women and eighteenth-century Irish republicanism', in Margaret MacCurtain and Mary O'Dowd (eds.), *Women in early modern Ireland* (Edinburgh, 1991), 133–44.

[20] Gareth Stedmen-Jones, 'Rethinking Chartism', in *Languages of class: studies in English working-class history, 1832-1982* (Cambridge, 1983), 90–178.

sion pervades all the political imbroglios which afflicted eighteenth-century Ireland. Certainly, the rise of a colonial nationalism reflected the Anglo-Irish ascendancy's feeling that they were excluded from important policy-making decisions in Ireland. The socio-political basis of the ascendancy's dominance was based on the exclusion of Catholics and, to a lesser extent, Presbyterians from a civic polity defined by religion and property.[21] The United Irish politics of inclusion reached across class barriers, inviting participation by the artisan, the farmer, and the labourer in the direction of the country. The excluded in Ireland were numerous.

The dissemination of these radical republican ideas in Ireland has received some attention from historians. The Young Ireland historian R. R. Madden collected United Irish ballads, songs, and other popular literary productions, but he was strongly inclined to regard such productions both as objective descriptions of historical events and republican aspirations and as examples of the cultural nationalism and literary taste and sensitivity of the United Irishmen.[22] A more rigorous and scholarly, but none the less similar, approach was taken by R. B. McDowell in his study of Irish pamphlet literature in the second half of the eighteenth century.[23] But James S. Donnelly, jun., has drawn our attention to a wider array of United Irish literary productions which served as propaganda exercises designed to attract a mass following. Because the United Irishmen tailored these productions to suit the popular classes, they also provide reflections of popular mentalities in Ireland in the 1790s.[24] Tom Dunne, however, has questioned the extent to which the middle-class United Irishmen succeeded in adapting their bourgeois agenda to traditional aspirations. At best, he suggests, republican literary propaganda offers 'dim and constricted reflections of what some contemporaries thought popular political mentalities were, or ought to be'.[25] It will be argued here that propagating the cause was one of the essential and defining activities of the United Irishmen. They possessed a genius for propaganda evidenced not only in their wide-ranging literary productions (newspapers, pamphlets, handbills, ballads, songs, and poems), but also in their carefully planned demonstrations and riots and the calculated use of the symbols and rituals of their mobilization. Moreover, at a fundamental level, United Irish propaganda represented the union of republican theory and revolutionary practice. The radicals ultimately sought 'to

[21] Maureen Wall, *The penal laws, 1691–1760* (Dundalk, 1976).

[22] R. R. Madden, *Literary remains of the United Irishmen of 1798 and selections from other popular lyrics of their times, with an essay on the authorship of the 'The exile of Erin'* (Dublin, 1887).

[23] R. B. McDowell, *Irish Public opinion, 1750–1800* (London, 1944).

[24] James S. Donnelly, jun., 'Propagating the cause of the United Irishmen', *Studies*, 69/273 (Spring 1980), 15–23.

[25] Tom Dunne, 'Popular ballads, revolutionary rhetoric and politicisation', in Gough and Dickson (eds.), *Ireland and the French revolution*, 140.

make every man a politician', and devised an imaginative and extensive system of political education which conferred citizenship upon all its students, a status which carried with it not only the privileges of self-government, but also the responsibility to secure good government.

At another level, of course, United Irish propaganda represented a compromise with the avowed aim of promoting a brotherhood of affection, since it relied on the exploitation of class and sectarian resentments to attract new recruits to the cause. The extent to which the United Irishmen failed or succeeded in reflecting and reshaping popular political culture, however, is extremely difficult to resolve. To be sure, republican propaganda was calculated to attract recruits, and recruits flocked to the United Irish standard in droves. But it does not necessarily follow that these new members were impelled into insurrectionary behaviour by a few pithy verses. Rather, such verses, along with the wide array of literary and symbolic expressions of the United Irishmen, served to define an alternative political culture designed to supplant traditional mentalities. It is as an exercise in political self-definition rather than as a reflection of political culture that United Irish propaganda must be examined. In these efforts to refashion popular political culture, the United Irishmen both took advantage of, and contributed to, a growing print industry and what one historian has called a 'revolution in *English*-language literacy' in the 1790s carried on by itinerant schoolmasters in rural Ireland, often ardent radical ideologues themselves.[26]

This is a study of popular politicization and mobilization, and I maintain that the two are intricately connected. United Irish readiness to accord full civil and political rights to all Irishmen was clearly demonstrated not only in their propaganda, but also in the structure of their organization. An underground, democratic mass movement, open to all who would swear the oath of allegiance to the republican cause, represented both a strategy of mobilization and a civic polity poised to assume power.

This concern to analyse the aims, social composition, and mobilization of Irish republicans throughout the 1790s justifies the restriction of the study to Ulster (especially the north-east) and Dublin, where the republican movement originated and where it achieved its greatest support. The revolutionary movement was national, though uneven in scope, by 1798, but it was not necessarily a united republican one, although recent work has certainly overturned the conventional view of a sectarian Jacquerie in Wexford.[27] It was within Ulster and Dublin that the aims of the United Irishmen were

---

[26] David Dickson, *New foundations: Ireland, 1660–1800* (Dublin, 1987), 195–6.

[27] For the most recent statements of the conventional view, see e.g. Foster, *Modern Ireland*, 279–82; R. B. McDowell, 'The age of the United Irishmen: revolution and the Union, 1794–1800', in T. W. Moody and W. E. Vaughan (eds.), *A new history of Ireland*, iv. *Eighteenth-century Ireland, 1691–1800* (Oxford, 1986), 355; for a persuasive reassessment of this view, see Kevin Whelan, 'Politicisation in County Wexford and the origins of the 1798 rebellion', in Gough and Dickson (eds.), *Ireland and the French revolution*, 156–78.

expressed in their purest form and where the propaganda mills were lodged, where the relations between leaders and followers can be examined most closely, where the changing nature of the movement from radical reformism to insurrectionism can be most effectively charted, and where the government first employed its arsenal of repressive weapons to undermine revolutionary determination. Furthermore, these two centres of radical activity offer contrasts which illuminate the questions of politicization and mobilization examined in this work.

'I confess I am quite proud of this club,' declared Thomas Russell shortly after the founding of the Society of United Irishmen in 1791. 'It is the first ever instituted in this kingdom for the removal of religious and political prejudices. I think [of] it as an event in the history of the country and, if properly managed, as the dawning of liberty.'[28] The United Irishmen failed to establish this new age of liberty. Instead of removing religious prejudices, they exacerbated them. But despite these failures—indeed, because of them—the United Irish movement remains one of the most significant chapters in the tortured history of Ireland. In the largest context, the mobilization of Irish republicans in the 1790s can be seen as part of the general democratic revolution described by R. R. Palmer.[29] To a great extent, these radical Irishmen saw themselves as part of this general movement towards bourgeois and national liberty, and when they came to justify their mobilization, they borrowed heavily from an intellectual legacy shared by radical Frenchmen, Americans, and Englishmen. Through them, we can also see how the vocabulary of classical republicanism was adapted to an emerging liberalism. On a second level, the United Irishmen posed a considerable threat to British security interests, not only by threatening to sever Ireland's connection to Great Britain, but also by encouraging and plotting with British republicans to bring down the state.[30] Lastly, these first Irish republicans are of interest because of the historical and mythological legacy that they bequeathed, unwittingly to be sure, to subsequent generations.

The United Irishmen came to be regarded as the forerunners of modern physical-force nationalism, the first in a line that extended to the Young Ireland revolutionaries of 1848, the Fenians of 1867, the Irish Republican Brotherhood of 1916, and, of course, the Irish Republican Army of today. At the same time, these first Irish republicans have been claimed by many of today's unionists in northern Ireland. As Terence Brown has observed:

In this almost unconscious memory of the past, the '98 rebellion is recalled as the moment when radical, just ideals and demands rooted in the achieved identity of

---

[28] [Thomas Russell] to ——, [Oct. or Nov. 1791] (PROHO 100/34/41–2).

[29] R. R. Palmer, *The age of democratic revolution: a political history of Europe and America, 1760–1800* (2 vols., Princeton, NJ, 1959).

[30] See e.g. Marianne Elliott, 'The "Despard conspiracy" reconsidered', *Past and Present*, 75 (May 1977), 20-54; Wells, *Insurrection*.

the northern Presbyterian people were overwhelmed by forces of atavistic racial nationalism. Ever since that time this memory has meant that protestant ideas of liberty have taken second place to *realpolitik*.[31]

Consequently, the Ulster Presbyterian, who, according to A. T. Q. Stewart, 'is happiest when he is being radical', was forced to repress his natural democratic, libertarian instincts in the face of a Catholic nationalist threat.[32] Thus, later generations have defined early Irish republicanism in two different ways. Irish protestants have tended to glory in the liberal, democratic, and contractual components of United Irish republicanism, whereas later republicans have focused on what they interpret as the United Irishmen's nationalist aim to break Ireland's connection to Great Britain. Thus the bedrock of modern Irish republicanism remains Theobald Wolfe Tone's conviction 'that the influence of England was the radical vice of our government, and consequently that Ireland would never be free, prosperous, or happy until she was independent, and that independence was unattainable whilst the connection with England existed'.[33]

In fact, early Irish republicanism contained both these elements—a secular, democratic liberalism and a nationalism that quickly became defined in racial and religious terms. The United Irish movement was riddled with contradictions, stemming largely from the fact that it started in Ulster among middle-class, radical Presbyterians who eventually sought to enlist the support of an aggrieved Catholic peasantry throughout the rest of Ireland. While the urban radicals and the rural insurgents occupied common ground in their hatred of the Anglo-Irish ascendancy and its social, economic, and political dominance, they viewed their oppressors in different ways. To the middle-class radical, the ascendancy represented illiberal government, the exercise of unmerited privileges, and a collection of renegade Irishmen, but Irishmen nevertheless, who subordinated the interests of their country to the rewards offered to them by English ministers. To the rural Catholic poor and especially to the secret societies known as Defenders, the ascendancy simply represented the descendants of conquerors and confiscators. To many Catholic United Irishmen, Irish protestants were foreigners. As the Catholic physician and United Irish leader William James MacNeven told a committee of the Irish parliament in 1798, 'in his language the Irish peasant has but one name for protestant and Englishman, and confounds them; he calls both by the name of

---

[31] Brown, *The whole protestant community*, 14.

[32] A. T. Q. Stewart, *The narrow ground: aspects of Ulster, 1609–1969* (London, 1977), 83. For a discussion of this protestant libertarianism and its anti-Catholic themes, see Elliott, *Watchmen in Sion*.

[33] William Theobald Wolfe Tone (ed.), *Life of Theobald Wolfe Tone* (2 vols., Washington, DC, 1826), i. 32. (Hereafter cited as Tone, *Life*.)

Sassanagh.'[34] The middle-class United Irishman saw the source of his oppression as rooted in the government's deviation from the principles of the British constitution and representative government, and consequently he strove for constitutional and political change. The Catholic peasant sought a reversal of the conquest and dispossession of previous centuries as the cure for social and economic ills.

Thus the United Irishmen, who desired above all a union of Catholic and protestant, unwittingly contributed to further division among their countrymen. Yet their achievements were remarkable, though admittedly ephemeral. A relatively small collection of middle-class radicals was able to secure, largely on its own terms, an alliance with the greatest military power on the Continent, revolutionary France.[35] Even more astonishing, the United Irishmen were able to mobilize thousands of their countrymen— urban and rural, middle-class and peasant, Catholic and protestant—into the most formidable revolutionary movement to confront a besieged Great Britain in the turbulent decade of the 1790s. Whereas later Irish republicans have often been dismissed as romantic visionaries whose feeble revolts were tactically pathetic but mythologically powerful, the United Irishmen represented a potent threat to British rule in Ireland.[36] To be sure, the United Irish movement possessed its share of idealistic adventurers, but it also displayed a hard-headed pragmatism and a genius for mass mobilization, achieved largely through an extremely effective and multifaceted propaganda campaign. The ultimate failure of the movement can be attributed to a number of factors—internal divisions and dissensions, a formidable counter-revolutionary campaign waged by the government, and just bad luck—but this should not disguise its remarkable successes. The French attempted to invade Ireland and assist the republicans on three separate occasions in the late 1790s. Bad weather and bad timing thwarted these ventures, but the enterprise itself was scarcely foolhardy. The United Irishmen claimed that, by 1798, they possessed half a million members in a country with about five million inhabitants. Tens of thousands of Irishmen rose in rebellion under the republican standard in 1798, when their efforts were defeated largely by a lack of co-ordination and central direction,

[34] Thomas Addis Emmet, Arthur O'Connor, and William James MacNeven, *Memoire or detailed statement of the origin and progress of the Irish union, delivered to the Irish government by Messrs Emmet, O'Connor, and M'Nevin, together with the examinations of these gentlemen before the secret committees of the houses of lords and commons in the summer of 1798* (Dublin, 1798), 25.

[35] For the United Irish mission to France and the French alliance, see Elliott, *Partners in revolution*; ead., 'The United Irishman as diplomat'. For a less positive view of the diplomatic achievements of the Irish republicans, see W. B. Kennedy, '"Without any guarantee on our part": the French Directory's Irish policy', in Lee Kenneth (ed.), *The consortium on revolutionary Europe, 1750–1850: proceedings, 1972* (Gainesville, Fla., 1973), 50–64.

[36] Arguments for the seriousness of this revolutionary threat are most strenuously made by Wells, *Insurrection*.

owing to the mass arrest of their leaders on the eve of the planned rising. A national rising assisted by a successful French invasion might well have secured Ireland's independence from Britain and led to the creation of a secular, democratic republic. But the United Irishmen failed to achieve their objectives. The reasons for this failure as well as for their partial successes will be explored in the following chapters.

1

Ideology and Aims

THE dominant ideological influence on United Irish leaders was the British radical whig tradition. This itself was a blend of classical republicanism as articulated by Caroline Robbins's eighteenth-century 'commonwealthmen', country tory critiques of the established whig oligarchy, and John Locke's views on the nature and function of government.[1] Whereas this eclectic intellectual heritage spurred British radicals to demand reform of the existing system, it was eventually transformed first by American colonists and then by Irish patriots into full-fledged republicanism.

The label 'republican' is an ambiguous one in the late eighteenth century. Essentially, the confusion revolves around whether one is referring to the spirit or to the form of government. The classical republican tradition, derived from Aristotle's notion of the best form of government as a perfect balance of monarchy, aristocracy, and democracy (the one, the few, and the many), accommodated hereditary institutions, provided that these did not degenerate into despotism or oligarchy. Political arrangements were thus evaluated in moral terms. That government was best, regardless of its form, which promoted republican virtue, defined as the subordination of private interest to the public good. To ensure the dominance of virtue in government, lawmakers had to be responsive and accountable to the public will.

[1] For the Lockian tradition, see Joyce Appleby, *Capitalism and a new order: the republican vision of the 1790s* (New York, 1984); Richard Ashcraft, *Revolutionary politics and Locke's two 'Treatises of government'* (Princeton, NJ, 1986); John Dunn, *The political thought of John Locke: an historical account of the argument of the two 'Treatises of government'* (Cambridge, 1969); Isaac Kramnick, 'Republican revisionism revisited', *American Historical Review*, 87 (June 1982), 629–64; For the civic humanist or classical republican tradition, see Bernard Bailyn, *The ideological origins of the American revolution* (Cambridge, Mass., 1976); J. G. A. Pocock, *The ancient constitution and the feudal law: a study of English historical thought in the seventeenth century: a reissue with a retrospect* (Cambridge, 1987); id., *The Machiavellian moment: Florentine political thought and the Atlantic republican tradition* (Princeton, NJ, 1975); id., 'Radical criticisms of the whig order in the age between revolutions', in Margaret and James Jacob (eds.), *The origins of Anglo-American radicalism* (London, 1984), 33–57; id., *Virtue, commerce, and history: essays on political thought and history, chiefly in the eighteenth century* (Cambridge, 1985); Caroline Robbins, *The eighteenth-century commonwealthman: studies in the transmission, development, and circumstances of English liberal thought from the restoration of Charles II until the war with the thirteen colonies* (New York, 1968); John Robertson, 'The Scottish Enlightenment at the limits of the civic tradition', in Istvan Hont and Michael Ignatieff (eds.), *Wealth and virtue: the shaping of political economy in the Scottish Enlightenment* (Cambridge, 1983), 137–78; Gordon S. Wood, *The creation of the American republic, 1776–1787* (New York, 1972). For the French version of the civic humanist tradition, see Carol Blum, *Rousseau and the republic of virtue: the language of politics in the French revolution* (Ithaca, NY, and London, 1986).

To the extent that the much-applauded British constitution accommodated democratic as well as monarchical and aristocratic institutions, Great Britain and Ireland could be said to be republican in spirit. Towards the end of the eighteenth century, the definition of republicanism shifted to one concerning the form of a government, in which hereditary institutions like the monarchy and the aristocracy were replaced by popularly accountable representative structures. Increasingly, republicans began to see hereditary institutions as tending towards the corruption of the body politic. The United Irishmen used the term 'republican' in both its moral and its formal sense, a usage that was determined by the strategies available to them in restoring their 'ancient constitution' to the basic principles of a fair and equal representation. Thus, to the extent that they could hope to implement their programme through peaceful constitutional reforms, the United Irishmen were republicans in spirit. But when the road to reform was blocked by British and ascendancy intransigence, the United Irishmen became republicans in practice. Furthermore, by exploiting this ambiguity between formal and moral republicanism, the United Irishmen were able to recruit reformers as well as revolutionaries into their organization.

The earliest issues of Samuel Neilson's *Northern Star*, the voice of the Belfast United Irishmen, highlighted the civic humanism which informed this brand of Irish republicanism.[2] 'The public will our guide—the public good our end': this was the motto of the *Northern Star*, founded in January 1792.[3] The public will was indivisible, a comforting thought to radicals who sought to eradicate sectarian tensions in Ireland, the persistence of which they attributed to the illiberal machinations of a 'divide and rule' imperial policy. The *Northern Star* sought to make the Irish people aware of their common interests so that they might act together 'with one heart and with one voice to assert their freedom and endeavour by all constitutional means to shake off the badges of slavery which yet disgrace them as a nation'.[4] To bring them to a sense of their obligations as citizens, to recall them to the principles of civic virtue which alone guaranteed their liberties and made nations great, the *Northern Star* exhorted its readers to hasten towards the day 'when *every Irishman shall be a citizen, every citizen an Irishman*'.[5]

Virtue in public life was the more urgently desired because Ireland was teetering dangerously on the precipice of despotism. Corruption in government was rampant, and corruption, in classical republican terms, was the cancer which invaded the body politic and brought it to the death agonies of tyranny. The years after the so-called constitutional revolution of 1782 saw only the acceleration and intensification of this disease. The vocabulary of the *Northern Star*'s political analysis was clearly derived from the classi-

[2] See Ch. 8 for a full discussion of the *Northern Star*.   [3] *NS*, 4 Jan. 1792.
[4] *NS*, 11 Feb. 1792.   [5] *NS*, 27 June 1792.

cal republican tradition, which opposed corruption with virtue and regarded political arrangements in organic terms. The government—indeed, the constitution—was a diseased body in need of a cure, in this case a strong dose of radical reform. The public will presupposed an organic whole, an indivisible people whose individual concerns must be subordinated to the public good. 'If you would true happiness learn,' declared a poet in the *Northern Star*, 'it is to be virtuous and free.'[6] Virtue was the guarantor of liberty.

Classical republicanism provided the United Irishmen with the language that they used to expose the inadequacies of their government, but John Locke gave them the justification for that government's dissolution. Civic virtue was a prerequisite for the enjoyment of liberty, but the *Northern Star* defined liberty in Lockian terms—civic liberty was submission to laws of one's own making. 'Liberty, or freedom,' maintained the *Northern Star*, 'consists in having an actual share in the appointing of those who frame the laws and who are to be the guardians of every man's life, property, and peace.'[7] 'There can be no security for liberty', the editors declared, 'in any country that is not fairly represented.'[8] Popular consent to the laws required what Locke termed a 'fair and equal representation' of the people, a phrase which repeatedly found its way into United Irish oaths, declarations, and other literary productions.[9]

Classical republicans used the litmus test of virtue and the interests of the public good to evaluate the legitimacy of any given government. Locke maintained that governments fulfilled the people's trust to the extent that they upheld the individual's natural and inalienable rights to life, liberty, and property. Though the former tradition emphasized the needs of an organic community, Locke focused on the liberty of the individual. The tensions between these two paradigms, however, did not prevent the first Irish republicans from incorporating both of them into their critique of ascendancy rule. Their obsession with wasteful, expensive, and corrupt government was informed by the classical republican tradition. Their concern to establish representative government as a corrective to these abuses was derived from Locke.

Locke himself shied away from embracing the democratic republicanism which was implicit in his views of representative legislatures as the guarantors of natural liberties, but he gave the United Irishmen the rationale not only for their reform campaign, but for their revolutionary mobilization as well. Governments act as trustees to secure the people's liberties. When governments breach this trust, 'they forfeit the power the people had to put into their hands for quite contrary ends, and it devolves to the people to

---

[6] *NS*, 7 Apr. 1792. [7] *NS*, 28 Jan. 1792. [8] *NS*, 10 Mar. 1792.
[9] For Locke's coinage of this phrase and its adoption by late 18th-cent. British radicals, see Kramnick, 'Republican revisionism revisited', 638.

resume their original liberty, and by it the establishment of a new legislature'.[10] As the *Northern Star* put it: 'the king of a free people is only the first magistrate, holding a great public trust, and subject to the majesty of the people. . . . The compact between the people and their first magistrate is mutual, and a departure on either side dissolves the obligation. . . . Loyalty . . . is conditional.'[11] Irishmen had no difficulty in recognizing Locke's king who 'acts contrary to his trust when he either employs the force, the treasure, and offices of the society to corrupt the representatives and gain them to his purpose'.[12]

Armed with a Lockian analysis, the *Northern Star* proclaimed that the government was in danger of breaking its trust with the people. The terms of that trust were outlined in the glorious British constitution which Irish patriots also claimed as their political heritage. The United Irishmen professed themselves to be friends of the constitution, 'according to its original spirit; but should it ever degenerate into a system of corruption, artifice, and oppression,' declared a correspondent to the *Northern Star*, 'I should avow my execration'.[13] But when did the constitution originate? In 1688? In 1215 with Magna Carta? Or must the origins of the constitution be sought during the so-called golden age of Anglo-Saxon liberty? Adopting the antiquarianism of the classical republicans, the *Northern Star* included all these landmarks, and concluded that the original constitution must therefore enshrine annual parliaments, the exclusion of placemen and pensioners from the legislature, and the abolition of rotten boroughs. It was during the century following the Glorious Revolution that the constitution entered upon a period of degeneracy and deformation, eventually reaching its present sorry state.[14] 'I think it is generally allowed', declared one correspondent to the *Northern Star*, 'that our government is administered as badly as it can [be], consistently with the preservation of the constitution.'[15] In the early 1790s United Irish reformers were reluctant to assert that the governmental compact had been broken. Rather, Ireland was then veering dangerously towards despotism, a despotism confirmed in later years by such violations of the constitution as the gunpowder and convention acts of 1793, which abrogated the people's rights to arms and assembly, and later by the imposition of martial law and the suspension of habeas corpus in 1796. By then the United Irishmen had clear evidence that Ireland's government had dissolved its trust with the people, and in Lockian terms the true rebels in Ireland were the corrupt, self-interested representatives sitting in College Green.

The constitutional whiggism which informed the emerging republicanism of the *Northern Star* in the early 1790s also animated the revolutionary

---

[10] John Locke, *The second treatise of government* (Indianapolis, 1952), 124.
[11] NS, 4 Apr. 1792.   [12] Locke, *Second treatise*, 124.   [13] NS, 7 Apr. 1792.
[14] NS, 4 Feb. 1792.   [15] NS, 28 Apr. 1792.

republicanism defended by the United Irish leaders in their examinations before the Irish parliament in 1798. The United Irishmen, claimed Arthur O'Connor, did not aim to destroy the constitution, the essence of which he defined as representative government and public accountability. Indeed, it was the gentlemen whom he was addressing and their backers in the British ministry who had overturned the constitution of Ireland. 'All we wanted', O'Connor maintained, 'was a house of commons which should represent the whole of the people of Ireland.' When the United Irishmen mobilized, 'it was not to destroy this vital principle of the constitution, it was to put down a parliament of self-constituted men, who first destroyed every vestige of the constitution and then committed every outrage and cruelty to support their usurpation'.[16] O'Connor did not quote Locke directly, but clearly he presented his analysis of the causes of Irish discontent in contractual, Lockian terms. The government had broken its compact, leaving the United Irishmen, the champions and interpreters of the public will, free to withdraw their allegiance and establish a new government based on popular support.

A blend of classical republicanism and Lockian ideas thus provided the United Irishmen with the vocabulary to challenge ascendancy rule—or misrule, as they would have put it—in Ireland. United Irish leaders and propagandists in fact shared a common set of political assumptions. So widespread were these assumptions among Ireland's commercial and professional classes that they rarely needed elucidation. The *Northern Star*, O'Connor, and the authors of countless United Irish literary productions alluded to Locke and the key figures of the radical whig canon, confident of an audience well versed in these classic texts. The educated Irish middle classes acquired their education in these matters in a variety of ways. Irishmen, especially in Ulster, took a keen interest in the Americans' campaign to sever their connection to what was regarded as an increasingly corrupt and decadent Britain.[17] There was scarcely a family in the north of Ireland which did not have relatives living in the colonies.[18] Furthermore, American criticisms of a self-interested, unresponsive, and increasingly despotic British ministry and parliament struck a chord of recognition in the ears of Irish patriots. John Caldwell, the son of a Ballymoney merchant, recalled that

[16] Thomas Addis Emmet, Arthur O'Connor, and William James MacNeven, *Memoire or detailed statement of the origin and progress of the Irish union, delivered to the Irish government by Messrs Emmet, O'Connor, and M'Nevin, together with the examinations of these gentlemen before the secret committees of the houses of lords and commons in the summer of 1798* (Dublin, 1798), 70–4.

[17] For the ideological roots of the American revolt, see Bailyn, *Ideological origins*, and Wood, *American republic*, 1–124. For the impact on Ireland, see M. R. O'Connell, 'The American revolution in Ireland', *Eire-Ireland*, 11/3 (1976), 3–12.

[18] For a discussion of the Irish in America in this period, see David Noel Doyle, *Ireland, Irishmen, and revolutionary America, 1760–1820* (Dublin and Cork, 1981).

in early childhood certain ideas of liberty were under various circumstances instilled
on my mind, which, as I increased in years, increased with my age and strengthened
my strength. Thus on the news of the battle of Bunker Hill, my nurse Ann Orr led
me to the top of a mount on a midsummer eve, where the young and the aged were
assembled before a blazing bonfire to celebrate what they considered the triumph of
America over British despotism.[19]

Further down the social scale, James Hope, a Templepatrick weaver,
remembered the profound impact that the American revolution had on himself and his neighbours: 'The American struggle taught people that industry
had its rights as well as aristocracy, that one required a guarantee as well
as the other, which gave extension to the forward view of the Irish
leaders.'[20] To a future United Irish leader, the Presbyterian minister Dr
William Steele Dickson, the American war was a 'mad crusade, and while I
regretted its folly, I execrated its wickedness'.[21] And as sympathetic
Irishmen avidly followed the arguments and the course of the American
revolution, they imbibed the emergent republicanism of the colonists, itself
an amalgam of Lockian individualism and contractualism, civic humanism,
and a conviction that divine providence supported a special destiny for the
inhabitants of the new world.[22]

The fact that Ulster in particular was mesmerized by the stirring events
in America is easily explained. First, ties of kinship drew northern Irishmen
to the cause of the colonists. Secondly, the war itself caused special distress
in the linen-manufacturing north, directing Irish resentment towards the
government which unjustly waged the war. Thirdly, Ulster Presbyterians
had no difficulty in recognizing and applauding the aim of many American
Dissenters to establish a new Jerusalem on their continent, a godly republic
sanctioned by the deity. And, fourthly, the Presbyterian middle class of the
north had already accepted the radical whig canon, especially as this was
mediated through key figures of the Scottish Enlightenment.

Barred on account of their religion from receiving degrees from Trinity
College in Dublin, Irish Dissenters made their way to the more congenial
universities of Scotland. There they became immersed in a vibrant intellectual movement preoccupied with the relationship between good government
and the progress of civilization, particularly its material advances.[23] A. T. Q.
Stewart has already noted the profound influence of Francis Hutcheson's

---

[19] John Caldwell, jun., 'Particulars of the history of a north country Irish family' (PRONI,
Caldwell papers, T3541/5/3, fo. 4).

[20] 'Autobiographical memoir of James Hope', in R. R. Madden, *Antrim and Down in '98*
(Glasgow, n.d.), 94 (hereafter cited as Hope, 'Autobiographical memoir').

[21] William Steele Dickson, *A narrative of the confinement and exile of William Steele
Dickson, DD, formerly minister of the Presbyterian congregation of Ballyhalbert and Portaferry
in the county of Down* (Dublin, 1812), 7.

[22] For this republican synthesis, see Bailyn, *Ideological origins*, 22–54.

[23] Dickson, *Narrative*, 3–4.

moral philosophy on the radicalism of Dr William Drennan.[24] The library of the Belfast merchant and United Irishman William Tennent was filled with the works of the Scottish *philosophes*—Hutcheson, Hume, Robertson, Ferguson, Smith, Beatty, Stewart, and Millar.[25]

Such influences were not confined to Ulster Presbyterians. Arthur O'Connor was a devoted disciple of Adam Smith. 'He talked well enough,' Lord Wycombe observed after dining with this County Cork gentleman and barrister, 'and in a manner which convinced me that he had applied himself assiduously to that dullest of all studies, the study of political economy.'[26] Even Trinity College, that bastion of the Anglo-Irish ascendancy, was entrenched with an ethos of 'liberal whiggery', in which Locke's two *Treatises of government* were avidly scrutinized by students.[27] A similar spirit animated the civic politicians of Dublin corporation in the last quarter of the eighteenth century.[28]

Irish radicals were strongly influenced by the example of English reformers as well.[29] Englishmen tended to regard their own history as sufficient justification for demanding what they felt to be the lost rights of free-born Britons. In 1776 Major John Cartwright wrote his famous pamphlet *Take your choice*, in which he urged radical reform of parliament and cited Anglo-Saxon precedent. Cartwright's proposals, which became the core of radicalism for the next century, found full expression in the Chartist programme of the late 1830s and the 1840s. The advocacy of such measures as annual parliaments, equal electoral districts, payment of legislators, the secret ballot, and universal manhood suffrage was revolutionary by

[24] A. T. Q. Stewart, '"A stable unseen power": Dr William Drennan and the origins of the United Irishmen', in John Bossy and Peter Jupp (eds.), *Essays presented to Michael Roberts* (Belfast, 1976), 83–4.

[25] Catalogue of books belonging to William Tennent, 1 Jan. 1807 (PRONI, Tennent papers, D1748/A/403).

[26] Lord Wycombe to Lord Holland, 24 Dec. 1797 (BL Add. MS 51683). On a later occasion Wycombe complained that 'Arthur O'Connor has behaved like an imbecile, if not worse. When he is in company, by the aid of a good memory he talks a few pages out of Adam Smith in lieu of conversation' (Lord Wycombe to Lady Holland, 6 Mar. 1798 (BL Add. MS 51682)).

[27] See Marianne Elliott, *Wolfe Tone: prophet of Irish independence* (New Haven, Conn., and London, 1989), 20–1.

[28] See Jacqueline Hill, 'The politics of Dublin corporation, 1760-1792', in David Dickson, Dáire Keogh, and Kevin Whelan (eds.), *The United Irishmen: republicanism, radicalism, and rebellion* (Dublin, 1993), 88–101.

[29] For British radicalism in this period, see Colin Bonwick, *English radicals and the American revolution* (Chapel Hill, NC, 1977); John Cannon, *Parliamentary reform, 1640–1832* (Cambridge, 1973); Carl B. Cone, *The English Jacobins: reformers in late eighteenth-century England* (New York, 1968); H. T. Dickinson, *Liberty and property: political ideology in eighteenth-century Britain* (London, 1977); Albert Goodwin, *The friends of liberty: the English democratic movement in the age of the French revolution* (London, 1979); J. Ann Hone, *For the cause of truth: radicalism in London, 1796–1821* (Oxford, 1982); Edward Royle and James Walvin, *English radicals and reformers, 1760–1848* (Lexington, Mass., 1982); *Selections from the papers of the London Corresponding Society, 1792–1799*, ed. and introd. Mary Thale (Cambridge, 1983).

implication. In effect, these measures would mean the transfer of political power from the landed oligarchy to the mass of the people. Cartwright argued that the enactment of such proposals would restore the Anglo-Saxon democracy that had been lost with the Norman conquest. A national association of reformers constituting a convention would act if parliament refused to reform itself.[30] Cartwright's programme went further than most English reformers wished to go. The aristocratic Friends of the People called for the addition of more county seats and the elimination of some rotten boroughs, a programme similar in spirit to the reform act of 1832. Middle-class reform associations such as the Society for Constitutional Information were comfortable with household suffrage. Although talking of universal suffrage, these reformers, like the Levellers before them, advocated the concept of free agency, in which servants and labourers were barred from the franchise because they were a dependent class and therefore unable to exercise freely the privilege of voting. Working men's associations, such as the London Corresponding Society, composed of artisans, tradesmen, and small merchants, were quick to adopt Cartwright's proposals. What all these groups had in common, aside from demanding a certain degree of reform, was their insistence on a return of lost rights. Moderate reformers tended to regard the Glorious Revolution as the starting-point from which to urge a restoration of rights. The more radical the organization, the greater was the emphasis placed on the restoration of Anglo-Saxon rights. In this sense, the English radicals saw reform as restoration rather than innovation. They needed no French example when it came to formulating and justifying their demands. The French revolution served only to spur them to renewed activity.

The idea of reform as restoration had pervaded the Volunteer agitation in Ireland in the early 1780s, when the return of the independence of the Irish legislature was demanded. The United Irishmen themselves occasionally used the Anglo-Saxon past and the revolution of 1688 in their own rhetoric.[31] But unlike the English radicals, Irishmen did not find much comfort in reviewing the history of their divided and troubled country, marked as it was by outbreaks of vicious sectarian hatred. To raise the standard of William III and the Glorious Revolution in Ireland, for example, was only to remind Catholics of how their civil and political liberties had been

---

[30] E. P. Thompson, *The making of the English working class* (New York, 1963), 84; Cone, *English Jacobins*, 51–2. For a discussion of this notion of lost rights, see Christopher Hill, 'The Norman yoke', in *Puritanism and revolution: studies in interpretation of the English revolution of the seventeenth century* (New York, 1964), 50–122. For a discussion of the use of an extra-parliamentary convention as a means to secure reform and good government, especially as advocated by James Burgh, see Kramnick, 'Republican revisionism revisited', 639–40; Robbins, *Eighteenth-century commonwealthman*, 366–7.

[31] *NS*, 24 Feb. 1794; Rosamund Jacob, *The rise of the United Irishmen, 1791–1794* (London, 1937), 186.

crushed by triumphant protestantism. When William Drennan drafted the prospectus for a new political society uniting Catholic and protestant, he urged that Irishmen look to the future and not to the past. The new society would not force mankind 'back into the lanes and alleys of their ancestors. It will have an eye provident and prospective, a reach and amplitude of conception commensurate to the progressive diffusion of knowledge.'[32] In a circular letter issued in December 1791, the Dublin United Irishmen announced:

In thus associating, we have thought little about our ancestors—much of our posterity. Are we forever to walk like beasts of prey over fields which these ancestors stained with blood? In looking back, we see nothing on the one part but savage force succeeded by savage policy; on the other, an unfortunate nation. . . . But we gladly look forward to brighter prospects—to a people united in the fellowship of freedom—to a parliament the express image of the people—to a prosperity established on civil, political, and religious liberty.[33]

This anti-historical attitude on the part of the United Irishmen was further expressed in their November 1792 address to the reformers in Scotland. Applauding the intellectual achievements of the Scottish nation, the Dublin United Irishmen suggested that the genius which had been applied to the writing of history should now be engaged in the making of it.[34] The United Irishmen thus eschewed arguments from history as compelling reasons for the introduction of radical reform in Ireland. Rather than calling for a return to an idealized golden age of Irish liberty, Irish radicals drew inspiration from innovative concepts of reform, based on reason and justice rather than tradition. Such inspiration was readily available to anyone following the events in France.

For the United Irishmen, France was the 'temple of universal liberty'.[35] They consistently pointed to the example of France not only as an inspiration for their own mobilization, but as a lesson to an intransigent government and aristocracy. Above all, the French revolution had proved to the 'people of every country . . . that when they are oppressed, they have the *power* to obtain redress'.[36] In adopting France as their revolutionary model, the United Irishmen made an ideological turn to the left. Englishmen might worship together at the shrine of the revolution of 1688, but in Ireland the invocation of the Glorious Revolution would have proved too divisive. 'Of all revolutions,' asserted the *Northern Star*, 'that of France is the most

---

[32] 'Idem Sentiere, Dicere Agere, June 1791', in *The report of the secret committee of the house of commons, with an appendix* (Dublin, 1798), 87 (hereafter cited as *Rep. secret comm.*).

[33] 'Circular letter from the Society of United Irishmen of Dublin, 30 Dec. 1791', in *Rep. secret comm.* 94.

[34] 'Address from the Society of United Irishmen in Dublin to the delegates for promoting a reform in Scotland', in *Rep. secret comm.* 97.

[35] *NS*, 4 Jan. 1792. [36] *NS*, 3 Mar. 1792.

glorious. That of England is not to be put in competition with it. It was neither so just in its principle nor so glorious in its effect.'[37] United Irish support for France was steadfast throughout the September massacres of 1792 and the execution of Louis XVI and his queen, events which served to discourage support for the revolution in other quarters. 'I ever thought that if they did not execute the king,' Drennan maintained, 'they murdered the nation.'[38] The *Northern Star*, though regretting that such measures were necessary, reminded its readers that the members of 'the French Convention are not only much better acquainted with, but also much more interested in their country's welfare than we can possibly be, and it would appear that a *regal faction* imposed on them the *necessity* of taking away the life of the *ci-devant* king as the only mode of protecting internal tranquillity.'[39] The newspaper later expressed the hope that the king's execution would 'not be made the pretext, by the slaves of a corrupt system, for exciting the indignation of the ignorant against the friends of freedom and the promoters of the happiness of mankind'.[40] By their unequivocal enthusiasm for the French revolution, the United Irishmen invited government repression. By 1793 the French revolution meant formal republicanism, nationalism, and democracy, principles utterly inimical to British rule in Ireland.

Although the victory of republicanism in France helped to sustain the growing radicalism of the United Irishmen, the popularization of revolutionary principles was primarily the work of Tom Paine. Paine's influence on Irish radicals is difficult to overstate. The first part of his *Rights of man* appeared in March 1791. By the time that Theobald Wolfe Tone journeyed to Belfast to assist in the foundation of the first society of United Irishmen, the book was so widely and enthusiastically read that he called it the 'Koran of Belfast'.[41] Nevertheless, Paine's powerful polemics only confirmed rather than inspired the educated, middle-class founders of the Irish republican movement in their adherence to their radical agenda. But because of Paine's ability to write trenchantly and accessibly, the dissemination of his principles became a major concern of the United Irishmen in their efforts to rally popular support for their programme of parliamentary reform and Catholic emancipation.

In part I of his *Rights of man*, Paine's main objective was to discredit the monarchical, traditional, and hereditary system of government advocated by Edmund Burke in his *Reflections on the revolution in France*. Since Burke's tradition was a dubious criterion for justifying political arrangements, Paine replaced it with reason. It was 'evident' that monarchy was a

---

[37] *NS*, 7 Apr. 1792.

[38] William Drennan to Anne Lennox Drennan, 24 Jan. 1793 (PRONI, Drennan letters, T765/378).

[39] *NS*, 26 Jan. 1793.   [40] *NS*, 2 Feb. 1793.   [41] Tone, *Life*, i. 142.

bad institution.[42] Paine needed no Anglo-Saxon precedents to support his political principles; his own rational power, unclouded by superstition and received authority, would suffice. Sovereignty lay in the nation, not in any individual defined as 'king'. But since every citizen of the nation was a member of the sovereignty, he was subject only to the authority of the laws of his own making. Borrowing from Locke and Rousseau, Paine maintained that if any government did not guarantee the rights and sovereignty of the citizen, and therefore of the nation, the nation had a right to overthrow it. It is small wonder that Paine held the British system of king, lords, and commons in contempt. In France the National Assembly was a representative body originating 'in and from the people by election, as an inherent right in the people'. But the representative system in England sprang not from the people, but from the monarchy: 'The house of commons did not originate as a matter of right in the people, delegate or elect, but as a grant or boon.'[43] In comparing English and French legislators, Paine pointedly remarked that the latter had 'sprung not from the filth of rotten boroughs, nor are they the vassal representatives of aristocratical ones'.[44] The house of lords was a 'hereditary aristocracy assuming and asserting indefeasible, irrevocable rights and authority wholly independent of the nation'.[45] Monarchy was 'human craft to obtain money from a nation under specious pretences'.[46] None of these institutions derived any authority from the people; rather, their authority was confirmed in the name of hereditary government and tradition. At worst, such institutions were irrational and tyrannical. At best, they were expensive. Here Paine struck perhaps his most appealing note to the tens of thousands of skilled workers and tradesmen who read his book: 'The enormous expense of governments have [*sic*] provoked people to think by making them feel, and when once the veil begins to rend, it admits not of repair.'[47]

In the second part of *Rights of man*, which appeared in February 1792, Paine was concerned less with refuting Burke and more with elaborating his own political principles. His attacks upon the institution of monarchy and the professed constitution of Britain became more vitriolic, and eventually provoked government prosecution.[48] Though fostering the illusion of representative government, the British legislature was essentially despotic. Whatever else it might be, the so-called constitution of Great Britain was, for Paine, 'the most productive machine of taxation that was ever invented'.[49] The enormous expense of such despotic and irrational systems of government was one of the main reasons why Paine sought their

---

[42] Thomas Paine, *Rights of man* (Harmondsworth, Middlesex, 1976), 165.

[43] Ibid. 111. [44] Ibid. 112. [45] Ibid. 152. [46] Ibid. 146. [47] Ibid. 140.

[48] For treasonous excerpts of Paine's work, see T. B. and T. J. Howell (comps.), *A complete collection of state trials and proceedings for high treason and other crimes and misdemeanours* (34 vols., London, 1811–26), xxii. 357–79.

[49] Paine, *Rights of man*, 216.

overthrow. War was the primary buttress of monarchical despotism. It provided the justification for increased government expenditure and therefore
heavy taxation. Indeed, it was a favourite, if historically untenable, notion
of republicans that rational, popular government contributed to international peace. As the *Northern Star* put it: 'One of the happiest effects of a
republican government over a monarchical one is that it is not so prone to
make war with other states.'[50] Exorbitant taxes had a deleterious effect
upon internal as well as foreign commerce. Markets contracted, and the
commercial and manufacturing sectors within the nation became unneces-
sarily burdened. In this way, Paine argued, the 'uncivilised state of
European governments is injurious to commerce'.[51] Paine urged international economic co-operation, since 'there can be no such thing as a nation
flourishing alone in commerce'.[52]

Although Paine's economic arguments may have been unsophisticated,
the spirit behind his theories proved infectious. He spoke for the industrious classes of society—the merchants, manufacturers, tradesmen, and artisans who were so strongly attracted to political radicalism. Their efforts
created the wealth of the nation and therefore contributed to its general
happiness. But this was not the reason why they should share in political
power; rather, the rights of citizenship were inherent in all men. Not only
was Paine demanding the inclusion of the commercial and manufacturing
sectors in government, but he was also justifying his demand on the basis
of abstract political principles, without reference to historical precedent.

In December 1792 the Dublin United Irishmen turned their attention to
formulating a specific political programme by appointing a committee of
twenty-one members to draft a plan for the reform of parliament.[53]
Drennan had urged in the previous year that such a document be drafted,
but James Napper Tandy successfully persuaded the Dublin society that
they should 'attend to those things in which we agree, to exclude from our
thoughts those in which we differ'.[54] Such caution was not ill-founded, as it
turned out, for there were some profound disagreements among the members as to what constituted a 'fair and adequate' representation of the
people. The first division within the committee was over the issue of the
extent of the suffrage. By a close vote of eleven to nine, the members
rejected property qualifications as a condition for the exercise of the

[50] NS, 18 Apr. 1792.   [51] Paine, *Rights of man,* 235.   [52] Ibid. 236.
[53] The members of the committee were Thomas Addis Emmet, Simon Butler, Leonard
McNally, George Powell, William Drennan, John Burke, Thomas Ryan, James Napper Tandy,
Simon Maguire, Malacky C. O'Connor, John Chambers, Theobald Wolfe Tone, Thomas
Russell, Edward Sweetman, Owen McDermot, Thomas Rainey, Archibald Hamilton Rowan,
Oliver Bond, Henry Jackson, Hampden Evans, and Richard McCormick. See R. B. McDowell,
'Select documents: United Irish plans of parliamentary reform, 1793', *Irish Historical Studies*,
3/9 (Mar. 1942), 39.
[54] *Rep. secret comm.* 94.

franchise.[55] Thus the United Irishmen adopted the very radical principle of universal manhood suffrage. Middle-class reformers had much to fear from the full exercise of the rights of citizenship by the lower classes. In his own plan of reform, committee-member Whitley Stokes, a fellow of Trinity College, recommended a small property qualification as more likely to promote a virtuous, independent, and responsible electorate: 'Liberty is only a good as the means of virtue and happiness, and more may be lost than these than gained in the point of liberty by the voting of the very lowest class.'[56]

The ardent democrats won on the issue of the franchise, but were forced to concede on the question of the secret ballot. The committee recommended viva voce voting. This issue was again debated in a meeting of the whole society in January 1794. The democrats moved that this procedure should be replaced by voting by ballot. Thomas Addis Emmet, Simon Butler, Leonard McNally, and John and Henry Sheares successfully defended the committee's recommendation, arguing that the secret ballot 'would only corrupt the morals of the people by holding out a mode of deception'.[57] The very real fear of Irish radicals was that any substantial reform might be undermined by the powerful influence that the landed interest exerted over their tenantry. This fear had informed Theobald Wolfe Tone's proposal in his famous *An argument on behalf of the Catholics of Ireland* that the property qualification for the franchise be raised rather than lowered, in order to exclude 'that disgrace to our constitution and our country, the wretched tribe of forty-shilling freeholders whom we see driven to their octennial market by their landlords, as much their property as the sheep and bullocks which they brand with their names'.[58] The unequivocal desire of all United Irishmen was that the general will should be expressed through the election process, free from the special interests of a few individuals, and that the overwhelmingly disproportionate share of political influence wielded by the landed class should be considerably reduced. Both the ballot and open voting, though diametrically opposed at one level, were similar strategies to achieve this end. Proponents of viva voce voting felt that the open and public exercise of the franchise would prove a guarantee against secret tampering with a voter's independence. Under the open gaze of one's friends and neighbours, a voter was more likely to act in the interests of his community. Those who favoured the ballot, of course, rejected this notion that peer pressure would ensure

[55] McDowell, 'Select documents', 39.

[56] 'A plan of parliamentary reform', drafted by Whitley Stokes (SPOI, Rebellion papers, 620/53/33).

[57] Quoted in McDowell, 'Select documents', 41.

[58] Theobald Wolfe Tone, *An argument on behalf of the Catholics of Ireland . . . by a northern whig* (Dublin, 1791), 361 (repr. in Tone, *Life*, i. 341–66). See Ch. 2 for the contribution of Tone and his pamphlet to the founding of the Society of United Irishmen in Belfast.

independent and responsible voting. Indeed, advocates of secret voting tended to esteem the natural tendency towards virtue and independence that they observed in the lower orders. It was the northerners who were, as Drennan described them, 'foolishly fond' of the ballot.[59] And, not surprisingly, the northerners were famous in Ireland for exercising their civic responsibilities independently of their landlords. James Stewart, a landowner in County Tyrone, expressed concern that his tenants regarded consultation with him on political matters 'as a surrender of their right to think and a mark of vassalage'.[60] Lord Mountjoy also complained that 'my tenantry are of such a description that in the best of times they would not submit to be dictated to by any landlord, and at this levelling period I question whether a recommendation from me might not induce a certainty of an opposite decision.'[61]

The third major issue to divide the Dublin United Irishmen was the question of the frequency with which the reformed legislature should meet. The committee, perhaps in a compromise with those moderates who had submitted to universal manhood suffrage, recommended that each parliament should convene for two years. The full assembly of Dublin United Irishmen, however, opted for a duration of one year, in order to ensure the greater accountability of representatives to their constituents.[62]

In January 1794 the Dublin United Irishmen presented their plan for a representation of the people to the public. This programme was very much in the vanguard of European radicalism in the late eighteenth century.[63] In the twenty-three articles finally adopted, the United Irishmen called for 300 electoral divisions, based as nearly as possible on equal population. Within each electoral unit, there were to be subdivisions in which all men over the age of 21 could vote for a 'deputy returning officer'. The electors of each unit were then to vote for the unit's representative to a unicameral legislature. Representatives were required to be at least 25 years old. They need not be residents of the district; residency 'within the kingdom' was sufficient. Nor were representatives required to meet any property qualification as a condition of taking office. All placemen and pensioners were ineligible for elective office. Representatives were to be paid, and parliaments elected annually.[64]

In their plan, the United Irishmen adhered strictly to their cherished principles of popular representation and legislative accountability. All adult

---

[59] William Drennan to Samuel McTier, 17 Jan. 1794 (PRONI, Drennan letters, T765/461).

[60] [James Stewart] to Dr John Reynolds, 31 Dec. 1792 (PRONI, Stewart of Killymoon papers, D3167/2/83).

[61] Viscount Mountjoy to James Stewart, 17 July 1797 (ibid., D3167/2/131).

[62] McDowell, 'Select documents', 40.

[63] T. W. Moody, 'The political ideas of the United Irishmen', *Ireland To-Day*, 3/1 (Jan. 1938), 25.

[64] *Rep. secret comm.* 105–6.

men were considered entitled to vote, at least indirectly, for representatives to the national legislature. Even men from the humblest levels of society, if they secured the approval of their communities, might become representatives themselves, their sustenance and independence assured by an adequate salary. Here was the career open to talents, even if it was unlikely that agricultural labourers would edge out lawyers and merchants on the benches of the new assembly. Annual parliaments assured that the legislature would be continually accountable to the people's will. Nor was a superior chamber representing any special interest or class envisaged as a needed check on the exercise of the public will in the legislature. Although the United Irishmen proposed a system of indirect representation in order to minimize possible abuses in the full and complete exercise of the franchise by the lower orders, they came out decisively in favour of political democracy.

The timing of this plan of reform is interesting. The decision in December 1792 to devise a plan of representation was partly informed by the fact that the whigs were planning to introduce their own reform proposals, which focused on the limitation of crown influence by placing restrictions on placemen and pensioners in the Irish house of commons. Radicals clearly sought to outbid the whigs for the support of the people, hoping to establish the Society of United Irishmen as the true party of reform in Ireland. But, more important, the year 1793 brought to the United Irishmen a series of defeats and set-backs. The government outlawed extra-parliamentary political assemblies. Volunteer mobilization was prohibited. And the commencement of war with revolutionary and republican France placed the United Irishmen in a situation in which their adherence to the French cause cost them sympathy and support. Painted by the administration as an irresponsible crew of malcontents determined to undermine Irish security, the United Irishmen were forced to tread carefully in their opposition to the war. Thus in April 1793, when the committee had agreed upon a plan of reform, the United Irishmen chose to delay consideration of it, 'as individual representation is the basis of it, [and] . . . at present it would be imprudent to send it forth while there is such a charge of republicanism against the society'.[65] By January 1794 the United Irishmen had little membership or public credibility to lose. Indeed, the society in Dublin was approaching its nadir, and the decision to issue its plan of reform was a desperate attempt to revive the radicals' fortunes. The United Irishmen then took a greater interest in shaping the opinion of the public, the definition of which they had enlarged in scope. Having failed to arouse sufficiently the 'decent and respectable' middle classes in favour of radical reform, the radicals now looked to the lower orders. 'To you, the poorer

---

[65] Quoted in McDowell, 'Select documents', 40.

classes of the community, we now address ourselves,' the Dublin United Irishmen declared in a statement attached to their reform proposals.

Do you find yourselves sunk in poverty and wretchedness? Are you overloaded with burdens you are little able to bear? Do you feel many grievances which it would be tedious and might be unsafe to mention? Believe us, they can all be redressed by such a reform as will give you your just proportion of influence in the legislature, AND BY SUCH A MEASURE ONLY. . . . Hang this plan up in your cabbins [*sic*]; think on it over and over again; do not throw it by in despair, as being impossible to be carried into effect, FOR NOTHING, WE HOPE, IS IMPOSSIBLE THAT IS JUST.[66]

To call the United Irish proposals a plan of reform is something of an understatement. Clearly, such a radical restructuring of the Irish system of representation would not be effected by Ireland's governors except under duress. Insurrection, or the very real threat of it, could alone induce the Anglo-Irish ascendancy and its British backers to commit such political suicide. The United Irishmen were in fact calling for a major political revolution which would transfer power and influence from the landed class to the industrious members of society—themselves. But, to bring about this revolution, the United Irishmen needed the dangerous support of the mass of the Irish people. Consequently, their strategic objective—the full and successful exercise of the popular will in Ireland on behalf of radical political change—happily coincided with their most cherished political principle, that every man had a right and duty to participate in public life. The genius of the United Irishmen was their ability to translate such abstract principles into concerns of real interest to the Irish lower classes whom they sought to mobilize. When, during his interrogation before the Irish house of lords in 1798, Dr William James MacNeven was asked whether Catholic emancipation or parliamentary reform really animated the lower classes, he replied: 'I am sure they do not . . . they do not understand it. What they very well understand is that it would be a very great advantage to them to be relieved from the payment of tythes and not to be fleeced by their landlords.'[67] Emmet, responding to the same question, maintained that the lower classes did not think of parliamentary reform 'until it was inculcated to them that a reform would cause a removal of those grievances which they actually do feel'. What grievances would a reformed legislature redress? 'In the first place,' Emmet maintained,

it would cause a compleat abolition of tythes; in the next, by giving the common people an encreased [*sic*] value in the democracy, it would better their situation and make them more respected by their superiors; the condition of the poor would be ameliorated; and what is perhaps of more consequence than all the rest, a system of national education would be established.[68]

---

[66] 'The Society of United Irishmen to the people of Ireland', in *Rep. secret comm.* 108–9.
[67] Emmet, O'Connor, and MacNeven, *Memoire*, 26.   [68] Ibid. 47–8.

Thus, when it became clear that a reformed legislature could only be secured through insurrection or the threat of it, the United Irishmen actively sought the support of the lower classes by asserting that radical political change would lead to meaningful social and economic reform. But despite the addition of the populist dimension, the ideology of the insurrectionary United Irishmen remained very much the same as that of the earlier reformers. 'I believe in the Irish Union, in the supreme majesty of the people, in the equality of man, in the lawfulness of insurrection and of resistance to oppression,' declared the preamble of the widely distributed catechism of the revolutionary United Irishmen.[69] This catechism, given to all potential United Irish recruits, contained numerous references to a redistribution of land and the redress of real economic grievances. But its analysis of the causes of Irish discontent relied very much on the vocabulary of the civic humanist tradition, especially as employed by the men of commerce who led the United Irish movement. The emancipation of Ireland would mean 'deliverance from the odious influence of England, and that domestic tyranny it generated, which is calculated to corrupt our morals, impoverish our people, and retard our industry'. How were 'Irish morals' injured by England? 'By monopolizing the trade of the world and confining us to deal only with her.'[70] Unlike many other adherents to the classical republican tradition, the United Irishmen happily reconciled virtue and commerce; indeed, they closely identified the two.[71] And, as economic individualists, the United Irishmen firmly rejected any notion of an equality of property. Although they sought to lure the lower classes to the republican standard with promises of a 'fair division' of the land confiscated from the established church and recalcitrant loyalists, any idea of 'an equality of property' was 'too absurd to imagine'.[72]

The United Irishmen adapted a populist appeal to their classical republican and Lockian programme for propagandist and recruitment purposes. But this invitation to the masses to participate actively in political life was not exclusively instrumental. It also accorded well with the radicals' extensive definition of the general will and with another bedrock of republican principle—that the general will could assert itself with the greatest virtue

---

[69] 'The union doctrine, or the poor man's catechism', 3 (SPOI, Rebellion papers, 620/43/6).

[70] Ibid. 4.

[71] For the classical republican concern that commercial wealth could corrupt civic virtue, see Pocock, *Machiavellian moment*, 423–505; id., *Virtue, commerce, and history*. For the compatibility of republicanism with bourgeois economic individualism, see Appleby, *Capitalism and a new order*; Kramnick, 'Republican revisionism revisited'.

[72] 'The union doctrine, or the poor man's catechism', 7. Jim Smyth, at pains to resist the motion that the United Irishmen were social conservatives, highlights the 'social-radical elements' of this document, but concludes that it is 'not quite the proto-socialist manifesto it might at first appear'. Rather, he notes its 'commitment to such classic bourgeois nostrums as unrestricted commerce and the career open to talents' (Jim Smyth, *The men of no property: Irish radicals and popular politics in the late eighteenth century* (New York, 1992), 167–8).

and legitimacy when it was armed. Republicans cherished the notion of a citizen militia, in which the private interests of many individuals would be subordinated to the general good of society. Such an ideal seemed to have been realized in Ireland in the late 1770s and the early 1780s with the Irish Volunteers. This armed body of Irish patriots provided the United Irishmen with both a strategic and an ideological legacy. The United Irishmen regarded the right to bear arms as a badge of citizenship. The people, MacNeven testified in 1798, 'never considered it a crime to have arms, nor do I; on the contrary, they have been taught and know it is a right of theirs to possess them'.[73] Indeed, Drennan attributed the sectarian disturbances in County Armagh in the mid-1790s to 'an instinctive desire for arms'.[74] The assumption was that all citizens had a right to bear arms not only to protect their personal property, but also to guard their interest in the state. Thus, citizenship was partly defined by the right to bear arms. That Catholics were prohibited from possessing arms throughout much of the eighteenth century was a very deliberate means of excluding them from any political status.

Not only did the citizen have the right to bear arms in defence of the state, but the state also had a right to expect that its citizens would rally to its defence. The republican tradition stressed a preference for a civilian militia as opposed to a professional standing army. The United Irishmen regarded the Volunteers as the perfect expression of an armed citizenry prepared to defend Ireland from foreign and domestic enemies. The government-controlled militia which the Irish legislature created in 1793 was interpreted by the radicals as a means 'to invest an ever-grasping administration with an enormous and alarming patronage, to extend its influence wide beyond the walls of parliament, and to diffuse corruption through all classes of the people'. Furthermore, the newly created militia was designed to supplant the Volunteers, 'to which we again look, almost exclusively, for the protection of ourselves and of our constitution'.[75] This was not only a political move to suppress Irish patriotism and radicalism, but also an attempt to undermine Irish civic morality. The militia provided the government with further patronage resources for the exercise of corruption, and, by restricting the right of the citizen to defend his country, the government was sapping the moral fibre and civic virtue of the individual. It was an

[73] William James MacNeven, *Pieces of Irish history illustrative of the condition of the Catholics of Ireland, of the origin and progress of the political system of the United Irishmen, and of their transactions with the Anglo-Irish government* (New York, 1807), 209; see also *The duty of armed citizens at this awful period examined* (Dublin, 1797).

[74] William Drennan, *A letter to his excellency Earl Fitzwilliam, lord lieutenant, etc., of Ireland* (Dublin, 1795), 24.

[75] 'Report on the war, the militia, and the gunpowder act', 10 Feb. 1793, in *Society of United Irishmen of Dublin, established November IX, MDCCXCI: 'Let the nation stand'* (proceedings) (Dublin, 1794), 62–7.

axiom of history as read by the civic humanists that the Roman republic went into decline once its citizens transferred their military responsibilities to mercenaries and professionals.[76] The Volunteers of Ireland, then, represented a counter to English and ascendancy corruption, by cultivating a sense of patriotism and civic responsibility. 'The military ardour which this institution [the Volunteers] inspired', Drennan recalled in 1795, 'advanced the civilisation of Ireland more in five years than in half a century before, and that merely by connecting the public interest with a kind of personal ambition.'[77] Here was a Hutchesonian notion that individual happiness could only be achieved in pursuing the public good.

The principle that an armed citizenry provided the greatest guarantee for liberty and freedom as well as for the promotion of civic virtue accorded well with the practice of the United Irishmen as reformers and as revolutionaries. 'To your *formation*', the United Irishmen addressed the Volunteers, 'was owing the peace and protection of this island, to your *relaxation* has been owing its relapse into impotence and insignificance, to your *renovation* must be owing its future freedom.'[78] The *Northern Star* observed that when the Volunteers were in their full vigour, they 'had only to ask and our free trade and independency as a nation followed'.[79] Internal divisions alone, according to the United Irishmen, prevented the Volunteers from following up their triumphs by securing parliamentary reform. The assumption was that the British and Irish governments could not ignore the will of the people once it was expressed by an armed citizenry united behind a compelling demand. Thus United Irish practice in the early 1790s focused on reviving the Volunteers. This strategy was frustrated early in 1793, when the Volunteers were suppressed. But it was revived once again when the United Irishmen opted for insurrectionary mobilization in the mid-1790s. Then the United Irishmen transformed the loose affiliation of reform clubs into a centrally co-ordinated, paramilitary organization intent on mobilizing the masses, arming and training them in military procedures, and generally preparing them to rise in rebellion when summoned. The mass nature of the United Irish conspiracy, the perhaps misguided and contradictory attempt to construct a democratic and representative revolutionary organization, and the consequent security problems which plagued the republican movement can all be explained by the radicals' tendency to regard the citizen as a soldier, the soldier as a citizen. The political principles of the United Irishmen thus required the full participation of adult Irishmen not only in their civic rights, but also in their civic obligations.

[76] See Pocock, *Machiavellian moment*, 183–218, 401–22; Robbins, *Eighteenth-century commonwealthman*, 88–133.

[77] Drennan, *Letter to Fitzwilliam*, 10.

[78] 'The Society of United Irishmen, at Dublin, to the Volunteers of Ireland', 14 Dec. 1792, in *Rep. secret comm.* 100.

[79] *NS*, 8 Sept. 1792.

'The crime, as well as misery, of our civil society in Ireland', observed
Drennan,

are clearly traceable to the corruptions of our political constitution—for it appears
to me a truth that the full and free enjoyment of our rights is absolutely necessary
to the performance of our duties, and [that] the unequal distribution of the former,
preventing the accomplishment of the latter, the freedom of the public must be necessarily connected with their virtue as well as their happiness.[80]

To what extent did the public will in Ireland and the virtue exercised by
its armed citizenry express the genius of the Irish nation? In other words, to
what extent were these first Irish republicans nationalists? Some historians
have painted the middle-class United Irishmen as true cosmopolitan children of the Enlightenment. Their allies, the Defenders, espoused a crude,
primitive nationalism, predicated on the assumption that adherence to the
Catholic religion and a Gaelic heritage marked one off for membership in
the Irish nation. This Catholic nationalism soon overshadowed the republican internationalism of the United Irish leaders, leaving an unfortunate
legacy which polarized the inhabitants of Ireland along religious and racial
lines, dividing them into natives and settlers, Catholics and protestants,
Irishmen and transplanted Britons.[81] It is certainly clear that the Defenders
regarded the liberation of Ireland as a matter of destroying the economic
and social basis of protestant ascendancy in Ireland. They envisaged the
return of lands owned by protestants to their so-called 'original' Catholic
possessors. The French alliance was the means by which such deliverance
from protestant and British dominance could be secured. For the Defenders,
then, the Irish nation was defined in social, economic, cultural, and racial
terms, and the triumph of the Irish nation would mean 'the world turned
upside down'—the replacement of the Anglo-Irish protestant ascendancy
with a Gaelic Catholic one, the reversal, in effect, of the conquest of
Ireland by England.[82]

The protestant middle-class United Irishmen were, in a sense, descendants of the conquerors of Ireland, though they preferred to think of their
ancestors as settlers who carried with them the ancient rights of true
Britons. Their sense of national consciousness, which was indeed quite
marked, was strongly informed by colonial dissatisfaction with the policies
of the metropolis. The United Irishmen, like the Volunteers and patriots

---

[80] Drennan, *Letter to Fitzwilliam*, 18.
[81] See D. George Boyce, *Nationalism in Ireland* (Dublin, 1982), 123-33; Marianne Elliott,
'The origins and transformation of early Irish republicanism', *International Review of Social
History*, 23/3 (1978), 405–28.
[82] See Thomas Bartlett, 'Select documents, xxxviii: Defenders and Defenderism in 1795',
Irish Historical Studies, 24/95 (May 1985), 373–94; Nancy J. Curtin, 'The transformation of
the Society of United Irishmen into a mass-based revolutionary organisation, 1794–6', *Irish
Historical Studies*, 24/96 (Nov. 1985), 476–84.

before them, and like Swift and Molyneux early in the eighteenth century, avoided the label 'colonial' to describe Ireland's relationship to Britain. Ireland was not, nor had she ever been, a colony of England's; rather, she was a sister kingdom, an independent and, to these settler patriots, unconquered nation, voluntarily tied to England by a common crown and ties of kinship and affection. What Irish patriots from Molyneux onwards resented was the increasing tendency to treat Ireland as a colony of subject people, deprived of rights which they regarded as their heritage.[83]

Two consequences attended Britain's insistent treatment of Ireland as a British dependency. First, to secure the submission of the nominally independent Irish legislature, the British government sanctioned and encouraged widespread political patronage and corruption. It was to counteract this demoralizing trend, by making the Irish legislature accountable to the people, that the radicals demanded parliamentary reform. The second consequence, of equal importance to the middle-class United Irishmen, was the restrictions which such dependency placed on the prosperity and expansion of Irish commerce and manufacturing. This point was confirmed over and over again by the United Irish leaders who were examined before the secret committee of the Irish parliament in 1798. If Ireland were to be separated from Britain, Emmet maintained,

her trade would be infinitely encreased [*sic*]. One hundred and fifty years ago, when Ireland contained not more than one million and a half men . . . the connexion might be said to be necessary; but now that she contains five millions, and America is the best market in the world, and Ireland the best situated country to trade with that market, she has outgrown the connexion.[84]

O'Connor, an amateur political economist, described at length the economic and commercial inequities attendant on Ireland's subservience to Britain:

If you would correct all these evils, restore to the Irish nation its just rights—then wealth must flow in from every quarter—thousands of means of exercising industry will present themselves—wages will be liberal—rents will be moderate—and it will be as impossible to disturb the public mind, when the reign of justice shall be established, as it will be to tranquillise it as long as the actual system of usurpation, plunder, and tyranny shall be continued.[85]

Thus, separation from Britain would liberate the Irish economy, deliver it from English restrictions, and place it under the guidance and protection of

---

[83] For a discussion of this dimension of early Irish nationalism, see Boyce, *Nationalism*, 94–122. See also Sean Cronin, *Irish nationalism: a history of its roots and ideology* (Dublin, 1980); L. M. Cullen, 'The cultural basis of modern Irish nationalism', in Rosalind Mitchison (ed.), *The roots of nationalism: studies in northern Europe* (London, 1980), 91–106; Tom Garvin, *The evolution of Irish nationalist politics* (Dublin, 1981).

[84] Emmet, O'Connor, and MacNeven, *Memoire*, 42.   [85] Ibid. 71–2.

the industrious classes, whose private interests happily coincided with the national good of pursuing general prosperity. The middle class viewed the liberation of Ireland in political and economic rather than racial or cultural terms. Separation from Britain would give the Irish middle class the political power and influence denied them by the landed élite. This same middle class would govern in the popular interest and would thus enjoy popular support, because it would pursue policies which would overturn the old mercantilist restrictions imposed by Britain and encourage the expansion of the Irish economy. The national consciousness of the middle-class United Irishmen was thus, to a certain extent, class-based.[86]

To be sure, the United Irishmen also opted for separation from Britain in order to secure an alliance with revolutionary France. When it appeared that reform would not be conceded by Ireland's governors and that insurrection might be necessary, the United Irishmen looked to Britain's enemy France for assistance.[87] But France would not exert itself on behalf of a mere reform movement. The new French republic might, however, extend its assistance and protection to a movement which sought to sever the connection with Britain, thus weakening Britain in its war against France.[88] But these pragmatic considerations should not obscure the fervent desire of the United Irishmen for national independence. This independence, however, need not be fulfilled only through the creation of a formal Irish republic. The unfettered, popularly accountable legislature which United Irish reformers demanded in the early 1790s would have satisfied the great majority of United Irish revolutionaries in the late 1790s.[89] Of course, what the reformist United Irishmen wanted was a republic in all but name. They were willing enough to accept the connection with Britain as long as Ireland could pursue its own interests. Thus the United Irish reform plan of 1794 was strongly utopian. It is scarcely conceivable that either the landed élite in Ireland or the ministry in Britain would ever have countenanced such a scheme, designed as it was to place real political power in the hands of the middle class, accountable only to an unruly peasantry. In demanding a total restructuring of the political system, the United Irishmen, wittingly or not, were already treading down the road to revolution.

The national consciousness of the middle-class United Irishmen, fed by

[86] For a discussion of the class-based dimensions of English nationalism, see Linda Colley, 'Whose nation? Class and national consciousness in Britain, 1750–1830', *Past and Present*, 113 (Nov. 1986), 97–117.

[87] For the United Irish alliance with France, see Marianne Elliott, *Partners in revolution: the United Irishmen and France* (New Haven, Conn., and London, 1982); W. Benjamin Kennedy, '"Without any guarantee on our part": the French Directory's Irish policy', in Lee Kennett (ed.), *The Consortium on revolutionary Europe, 1750–1850: proceedings, 1972* (Gainesville, Fla., 1973), 50–64.

[88] Emmet, O'Connor, and MacNeven, *Memoire*, 5–6.

[89] For the protests of United Irish leaders that substantial reform would have satisfied their ambitions even as late as 1798, see ibid. 16–17, 23, 73–4.

their exclusion from political life and by their resentment of the commercial inequities which existed between Britain and Ireland, was very much colonial in nature.[90] For the most part, protestant middle-class Irishmen willingly shared a common cultural and intellectual heritage with educated Britons.[91] They would happily have entered into an equal partnership with Britain in promoting a vibrant commercial empire. MacNeven reassured his parliamentary interrogators in 1798 that even if Ireland were formally separated from Britain, ties of cultural affinity, affection, and mutual interest would continue to bind the two nations.[92] If Britain would respect the rights of Irishmen to popular self-government and the unfettered pursuit of their own economic interests, the sister kingdoms would coexist in harmony and prosperity.

The United Irishmen were petty-bourgeois revolutionaries. Their chief aims were popular self-government and economic liberation from England. To a certain extent, nationalism and formal republicanism were the means to attain these ends rather than ends in themselves, adopted in the face of government refusal to concede the radicals' demands. They had an abiding confidence in the fact that they represented the will of the mass of the Irish people, and that if such support could be adequately marshalled and demonstrated, they would secure a swift and relatively bloodless political revolution in Ireland. Such a revolution was necessary because current political practices were sapping the moral fibre of the Irish nation and contributing to general economic distress. The Americans of 1776 had exposed the tyrannical tendencies and civic vices of the British state. The French of 1789 and 1792 had demonstrated how the popular will of the nation could exert itself. The colonial abuse of Ireland by Britain suggested to Irish patriots that their country was no better off than pre-revolutionary America or France. Rural distress, commercial and industrial stagnation, and the apparent alienation of Ireland's governors from the people created the con-

---

[90] For a discussion of this type of colonial nationalism, see Benedict Anderson, *Imagined communities: reflections on the origin and spread of nationalism* (London, 1983), 50–65; John Lynch, *The Spanish American revolutions, 1808–1826* (New York, 1986).

[91] The colonial, class-based nationalism of the United Irishmen, however, did not preclude an interest in the ancient heritage of Ireland. Thomas Russell, for example, took a keen interest in Gaelic culture, learned the Irish language, and became involved with Whitley Stokes in publishing an Irish dictionary. For this Gaelic revival of the late 18th cent., see John Hutchinson, *The dynamics of cultural nationalism: the Gaelic revival and the creation of the Irish nation state* (London, 1987), ch. 2; Norman Vance, 'Celts, Carthaginians, and constitutions: Anglo-Irish literary relations, 1780–1820', *Irish Historical Studies*, 22/87 (Mar. 1981), 216–38. Russell was also involved in organizing the famous Belfast harpers' festival of 1792 (Mary McNeill, *The life and times of Mary Ann McCracken, 1770–1866: a Belfast panorama* (Dublin, 1966), 78–85; Robert M. Young, 'Edward Bunting's Irish music and the McCracken family', *Ulster Journal of Archaeology*, 4/3 (Apr. 1898), 175–8). Not all United Irishmen were interested in such cultural nationalism. Tone derided the festival with 'Strum, strum and be hanged' (Tone, *Life*, i. 157).

[92] Emmet, O'Connor, and MacNeven, *Memoire*, 23–4.

text in which radical Irishmen launched their movement for political and
economic liberation. In doing so, the original Irish republicans adapted the
cultural and intellectual heritage which they shared with Britain. They
turned to the commonwealth tradition of Harrington, to the analyses of
political corruption of Trenchard and Gordon, to the moral and economic
philosophy of the Scottish Enlightenment, and, above all, to Locke's
notions about the right of citizens to overthrow tyranny. In 1795, in a pamphlet addressed to the new viceroy, Earl Fitzwilliam, Drennan declared:
'You are told that the people of the north of Ireland are deeply infected
with what are called French principles. My Lord, I do believe them most
obstinately attached to the principles of Locke.'[93] The United Irishmen,
whom some have claimed as the first nationalist republicans in Ireland,
showed themselves to be deeply immersed in British radical whig culture.

But antipopery often accompanied this radical whig tradition. The
Catholic church seemed to represent all the illiberal forces of arbitrary
despotism, privilege, and tradition, and the ignorance and superstition
which retarded the progress of rational and virtuous government. Even one
of their most ardent champions, Samuel Neilson, described the Catholics as
'bigots to monarchy'.[94] But such prejudices were suppressed, if not entirely
eradicated, in the effort to create a political movement based on the union
of all Irishmen. This union was necessary for both theoretical and tactical
reasons. 'Our efforts for reform hitherto have been ineffectual,' Neilson
proclaimed in 1791, 'and they deserve to be so, for they have been selfish
and unjust, as not including the rights of Catholics in the claims we put
forward for ourselves.'[95] Catholics deserved equal civil and political rights
because such rights were natural and inalienable. But expediency as well as
principle militated for a union of Catholic and protestant. The previous
decade had proved that middle-class protestants alone could not pressure
an intransigent government into reforming itself. But if Catholics could be
persuaded to rally behind the reform campaign, public opinion might well
triumph over the self-interested ascendancy. The price of Catholic support
could be no less than full civic and political equality with protestants. 'Let
them [the protestant reformers] cry *reform and the Catholics*, and Ireland is
free, independent, and happy,' Tone predicted in his influential pamphlet
An argument on behalf of the Catholics of Ireland.[96]

The radical whig protestants who formed the ideological core of the
United Irish movement were willing (indeed, they found it necessary) to
court middle-class Catholic and, later, Defender participation. The rights of

[93] Drennan, *Letter to Fitzwilliam*, 41.

[94] Information of John Smith (alias Bird), 1795–6 (SPOI, Rebellion papers, 620/27/1).

[95] Quoted in R. R. Madden, *The United Irishmen, their lives and times*, 3rd ser. (7 vols.,
London, 1842–5), i. 79.

[96] Tone, *Argument*, 366.

man required it, as did the strategy of mass mobilization. But sectarianism, not unity, underlay these ephemeral alliances. The radicals fanned the flames of Catholic resentment towards a political and landed ascendancy that defined itself as protestant.[97] How, then, could middle- and lower-class Catholics see their struggle with their governors in anything but sectarian terms? Radical Dissenters, to be sure, resented the Anglican church establishment in Ireland, but their animus was directed primarily against a parasitical landed élite which provided the support for illiberal government. It was their common enemy, not common sympathy, that brought Catholics and radical protestants, peasants and merchants together in the 1790s.

---

[97] For the origins and use of this term, 'protestant ascendancy', see Jacqueline Hill, 'The meaning and significance of "protestant ascendancy", 1787–1840', in *Ireland after the union: proceedings of the second joint meeting of the Royal Irish Academy and the British Academy, London, 1986*, introd. Lord Blake (Oxford, 1989), 1–22; James Kelly, 'The genesis of "protestant ascendancy": the Rightboy disturbances of the 1780s and their impact upon protestant opinion', in Gerard O'Brien (ed.), *Parliament, Politics and People: essays in eighteenth-century Irish history* (Dublin, 1989), 93–127; W. J. McCormack, *Ascendancy and tradition in Anglo-Irish literary history from 1789 to 1939* (Oxford, 1985), 61–96.

2

From Reform to Revolution

THE United Irishmen were the direct descendants of the Volunteer and patriot agitation of the late 1770s and early 1780s.[1] In those years the efforts of an aroused Irish protestant nation secured favourable trade legislation from Britain and, as the crowning glory, the legislative independence of the Irish parliament in 1782. But this independence was merely nominal, as many Irish patriots were quick to perceive. No longer able to legislate directly for Ireland or to amend Irish bills, British ministers secured a submissive parliamentary majority in Ireland through the methods of patronage and corruption.

The constitutional revolution of 1782 proved to be a major turning-point for Ireland. However limited the victory, it had nevertheless been achieved by the near unanimous exertions of the protestant nation. But then these self-proclaimed patriots began to fall out. One party remained satisfied with what had been accomplished, and offered their support to the Irish executive. Another faction, inspired by the Rockingham whigs in Britain, saw the need for administrative reform—a reduction in the number of placemen, and pensioners in the Irish house of commons, for example—to make the executive more responsible to public opinion as represented in parliament. A more radical wing extended the reform programme to include franchise reform which might make the Irish house of commons representative of a wider segment of the Irish people than the narrow ascendancy class. And even this group was divided on the question of whether Catholics should be included in the broadened definition of the political nation. The parliamentary reform movement, however, experienced a temporary eclipse after the failures of 1784 and 1785, and it was not until 1789 that the Irish whigs formally became a parliamentary party, complete with organization and programme.

The Regency crisis of 1788–9 underlined the subservience of Grattan's

---

[1] For the Volunteer movement of the late 1770s and early 1780s, see R. B. McDowell, *Ireland in the age of imperialism and revolution* (Oxford, 1979), 209–326; Maurice O'Connell, *Irish politics and social conflict in the age of the American revolution* (Philadelphia, 1965); Revd Patrick Rogers, *The Irish Volunteers and Catholic emancipation, 1778–1793* (London, 1934); P. D. H. Smyth, 'The Volunteers and parliament, 1779–84', in Thomas Bartlett and D. W. Hayton (eds.), *Penal era and golden age: essays in Irish history, 1690–1800* (Belfast, 1979), 113–36. For the general political environment of the period, see J. L. McCracken, *The Irish parliament in the eighteenth century* (Dublin, 1971); Gerard O'Brien, *Anglo-Irish politics in the age of Grattan and Pitt* (Dublin, 1987).

parliament to the British ministry, indicating that Irish legislative independence was merely a sham. The defeated Irish whigs entered into formal opposition on a party basis. The organization of the party was confirmed with the establishment of the Whig Club in Dublin in 1789, which adopted for its programme the reduction of executive influence by administrative reform (a place and pension bill), and a responsibility bill designed to make the treasury accountable to the Irish rather than the British parliament. The ultimate aim of the Whig Club was to secure the real independence of the Irish legislature by making the *executive* responsible to the parliament, a circumstance which would considerably reduce English influence in the government of Ireland. As such, the Whig Club was anticolonial, but hardly revolutionary and democratic. Although such popular heroes as Henry Grattan and the earl of Charlemont, the commanding general of the Irish Volunteers, belonged to the club, they were joined by an archbishop, a bishop, and eleven other peers. These élite moderates placed their greatest emphasis on the reduction of Castle patronage, and, as a body, eschewed the issues of Catholic emancipation and extensive parliamentary reform. The administrative reform of the Irish whigs was designed to make government more responsive to public opinion, but the public whose opinion counted was the ascendancy itself. The fundamental difference between the whigs and the radical reformers was that the former sought to unshackle the Irish parliament from English interference while leaving the governing class intact, but the latter sought not only to establish real as well as nominal independence, but also to broaden the governing class and to establish government on a popular basis.

Interest in reform, of course, had not died out in the second half of the 1780s, after the failure of the Volunteers to secure meaningful changes in the Irish representation system. But as the Volunteers declined during this period, there was no longer a national organization to focus and channel reformers' activity.[2] After 1789, however, Irish radicals could draw inspiration from the impressive spectacle of revolution in France. Henry Joy, editor of the *Belfast News-Letter*, recalled its impact: 'Encouraged by the success of these glorious efforts of the French nation, the friends of liberty in this country once more turned their undivided attention to the salutary measure of reform and renewed those efforts from which they had been so ingloriously compelled to desist.'[3]

These two events in 1789—the formation of the Whig Club and the French revolution—laid the basis for the regeneration of a national reform movement within Ireland. The Irish whigs, hardly a popular party,

[2] For political clubs formed in different parts of Ulster in the decade, see e.g. *BNL*, 17 Sept., 5 Oct., 30 Nov., 24 Dec. 1784; Rogers, *Irish volunteers*, 62.

[3] Henry Joy, *Historical collections relative to the town of Belfast from the earliest period to the union with Great Britain* (Belfast, 1817), 325–6.

nevertheless hoped to court popular support for the upcoming general election in 1790 by calling for modest reform. But the influence of radical ideas emanating from revolutionary France inspired Ireland's politically excluded middle class to expect a more meaningful restructuring of the Irish system of government. Ultimately, their diverging responses to the drama unfolding in France would drive the whigs and the radicals further and further apart. As Tone later remarked: 'The French revolution became the test of every man's political creed.'[4]

But in the mean time, no sooner had the whigs launched their party in Dublin than they sought to extend it to that stronghold of reform and anti-colonial sentiment in Ireland—Ulster. Charlemont was especially interested in co-opting northern reformers and Volunteers, and hoped to harness the resentment of Belfast's Presbyterian merchants against the current policies of the government. Yet he also feared that such resentment might be directed into radical channels unless moderating controls were exercised.[5] He entrusted the delicate task to Dr Alexander Haliday, a prominent Belfast physician and a close personal and political friend. But Haliday and Charlemont were to meet with some difficulty in influencing the northern liberals. Their timid counsels were little suited to the political climate of this self-proclaimed Athens of the north.

Belfast experienced phenomenal commercial and demographic growth in the last half of the eighteenth century. With a population of 8,500 in 1757, the town boasted over 18,000 inhabitants by 1791, reflecting its enhanced importance as an industrial and commercial centre.[6] A town dominated by Presbyterians, Belfast was characterized by an emphasis on civic and cultural self-help, with constant activity on the part of educational, charitable, and political organizations. Yet Belfast was virtually unrepresented in the Irish parliament, since it was a 'pocket borough' controlled by Lord Donegall. Dr Haliday wrote to Charlemont from Belfast in April 1789, during the height of the Regency crisis, that 'the spirit of commerce, here as elsewhere, monopolizes the human mind, and most of our merchants are infinitely more anxious about their own credit than that of parliament or the nation'.[7] But Haliday underestimated the political consciousness of the Belfast merchants. Perhaps the feeble efforts of one faction within the ascendancy to secure control over the Irish administration did not fire their political imaginations. But their former involvement in the Volunteer movement and their later participation in the United Irish societies suggest that they were businessmen who resented the dominance of the Anglican landed interest in the economic, social, and political arrangements of Ireland, and thought that the time had come for a redistribution of power.

---

[4] Tone, *Life*, i. 43.   [5] Joy, *Belfast*, 334.   [6] *BNL*, 28 Oct. 1791.
[7] Dr Alexander Haliday to earl of Charlemont, 11 Apr. 1789 (HMC, *The manuscripts and correspondence of James, first earl of Charlemont* (2 vols., London, 1891–4), ii. 96).

Although Belfast reformers would have preferred more extensive reforms than those advocated by the Irish whigs, they nevertheless supported the Northern Whig Club when it was established by Haliday, at Charlemont's instigation, in March 1790. There were sixty original members, twelve from the town proper and the remainder from the surrounding neighbourhood. Among these members were men later notable for their involvement in the United Irish societies, such as Samuel Neilson and Archibald Hamilton Rowan. The club was composed overwhelmingly of landed gentlemen; the Belfast merchants and professional men were the exceptions.[8]

Nevertheless, their activities extended to political campaigning during the general election of 1790. In Dublin the whigs managed a victory, when Grattan and Lord Henry Fitzgerald defeated the Castle nominees. The whig triumph was largely the work of the untiring efforts of the radical Dublin merchant James Napper Tandy, reputedly the darling of the Dublin 'mob' and a future organizer of the Dublin Society of United Irishmen. The campaign in the north was even more heatedly fought, as reformers in Antrim and Down, representing the 'independent interest', successfully worked for the election of two standard-bearers, one for Antrim, John O'Neill, a moderate reformer and widely respected landlord who was to become a victim of his former supporters eight years later when he fell at the battle of Antrim, and Robert Stewart, later Lord Castlereagh, returned for County Down and universally regarded at the time as the reformers' brightest hope for the future. Samuel Neilson, another future United Irish organizer, served as Stewart's election agent.[9]

Reformers recovering from the doldrums of the late 1780s were initially cheered and easily wooed by the patriotic exertions of the anticolonial whig party in parliament, and lent their enthusiastic support, which seemed to reach its apex during the election campaigns of 1790. Dr William Drennan was an enthusiastic witness to this alliance in Dublin, where he saw

Grattan advancing [to the hustings] on his light fantastic toe, hope elevating and joy brightening his crest, his eyes rolling with that fine enthusiasm without which it is impossible to be a great man . . . while at some distance behind walks Napper Tandy, in all the surliness of republicanism, grinning most ghastly smiles, and as he lifts his hat from his head the many-headed monster raises a shout that reverberates through every corner of the castle. . . . Let me take another glimpse at Grattan [wrote the irrepressible poet]. When all that mighty multitude shall be dead and forgotten as if they had never been . . . his name shall live as a redeemer of Ireland.

The father of Thomas Addis and Robert Emmet was in attendance, and asked the great man where he stood on the vexatious question of parliamentary reform. Grattan proclaimed that he was 'by no means adverse to a

---

[8] For a complete list of the original members, see Joy, *Belfast*, 341.
[9] Charles Dickson, *Revolt in the north: Antrim and Down in 1798* (Dublin, 1960), 83.

reform in Parliament'. Emmet then proclaimed: 'The people then are enlisted under you as a party, that people, who were once the principals and the nation, is become a Ponsonby party.'[10]

But they were not to remain a Ponsonby party for long. This euphoric conjunction between politicians and people did not endure once the heady days of electioneering were over. In February 1791 Drennan complained that the Whig Club in Dublin 'literally does nothing more than eat and drink'.[11] And in the following May the radical doctor opined that the Whig Club was nothing more than an 'aristocratical society without any fellow-feeling with the commonality. When the people come forward, these men draw back, and when they come forward, the People are lifeless and there is no strength in them.'[12]

The people were not so lifeless, however, as to refrain from forming their own associations. The Whig Club in Dublin represented the political élite, and, consequently, less exalted reformers, among them James Napper Tandy, were thrown to their own devices. They formed the Whigs of the Capital in 1791, 'a body', according to Drennan, 'made of good honest men but not so honourable as of the Whig Club, and not so genteel as to gain admission there, so were obliged to tack the shreds of whiggism together to make an association for themselves.'[13] In July 1791 the Whigs of the Capital published a cheap edition of Paine's *Rights of man*, attesting to the radical spirit which infused the new association.[14] Similarly, the gentry-dominated Northern Whig Club proved both too exclusive and too moderate for many Belfast radicals, who, in imitation of the Whigs of the Capital, formed a new association, the Whigs of Belfast, a body quickly subsumed within the United Irish organization.[15] Indeed, the formation of the Societies of United Irishmen in Belfast and Dublin in the autumn of 1791 represented the displacement of moderate, élitist whig leadership by the radical middle class in a revived Irish reform movement. Jerome Fitzpatrick attended a meeting of the Dublin Society of United Irishmen in November 1791 and informed the government of his impressions: 'If I dare presume to give an opinion, I should be induced to say from my knowledge of this kingdom that the society called *whigs* are nearly at an end. . . . By them [the United Irishmen] I am pretty certain the *whigs* must fall.'[16]

Interest in forming a new and more radical political society to replace the timid and aristocratically dominated Whig Club came from literary radical circles in Dublin and remnant radical Volunteers in Belfast. In the winter of

[10] Dr William Drennan to Samuel McTier, 3, 27 May 1790 (*The Drennan letters*, ed. D. A. Chart (Belfast, 1931), 51–2).
[11] Drennan to McTier, 5 Feb. 1791 (ibid. 53–4).
[12] Drennan to McTier, 21 May 1791 (PRONI, Drennan letters, T 765/2/300).
[13] Ibid.					[14] *FJ*, 16 July 1791.
[15] Haliday to Charlemont, 16 June 1791 (HMC, *Charlemont manuscripts*, ii. 140).
[16] Jerome Fitzpatrick to government, 30 Nov. 1791 (PROHO 100/34/25–7).

1790-1 Theobald Wolfe Tone, an ambitious young barrister, founded a political literary club in Dublin, designed to accommodate advanced political opinion. The society quickly degenerated into a mere social club, or, as Tone called it, 'an oyster club', and within three or four months it ended as a result of internal dissensions.[17] The effort to create a new political club was renewed by one of the members of the dissolved society, Dr William Drennan, in May 1791. Drennan, the son of a Presbyterian minister in Belfast, and a physician then residing in Dublin, was a true son of the Scottish Enlightenment. His father's close friend was the renowned moral philosopher Francis Hutcheson, and William himself, like so many other Irish Presbyterians, attended university in Edinburgh.[18] Drennan was also a veteran of the Volunteer agitation of the early 1780s, and the ignominious defeat of the reform campaign led him to entertain the idea of a new and radical departure in Irish popular politics.[19]

In May 1791 Drennan proposed to his brother-in-law, Samuel McTier of Belfast, that advanced radicals should form a secret society, 'the Brotherhood its name—the rights of man and the greatest happiness of the greatest number its end—its general end real independence to Ireland, and republicanism its particular purpose'.[20] The following month a paper outlining Drennan's proposal was circulated. The new club would exert itself in three areas: first, the propagation of the principles of freedom and toleration; second, the establishment of a national convention of the people of Ireland; and, third, communication with similar organizations in France, England, and Scotland.[21]

Early in July 1791 McTier responded to Drennan's proposal. He had discussed the idea with some of Belfast's leading reformers, most of whom warmly approved: 'If your club Brotherhood takes place, we will immediately follow your example.'[22] Drennan's brother-in-law was a member of a secret committee of Volunteers who constituted an advanced democratic party in the radical town of Belfast. The leader of this group of eleven radical Dissenters was Samuel Neilson, a prosperous linen merchant and also the son of a Presbyterian minister.[23]

The French revolution was a source of inspiration for radical Irishmen in

[17] Tone, *Life*, i. 38–40. For Tone's activities in this club, see Marianne Elliott, *Wolfe Tone: prophet of Irish independence* (New Haven, Conn., and London, 1989), 103–7.

[18] For Drennan, see A. T. Q. Stewart, ' "A stable unseen power": Dr William Drennan and the origins of the United Irishmen', in John Bossy and Peter Jupp (eds.), *Essays presented to Michael Roberts* (Belfast, 1976).

[19] See e.g. William Drennan, *Letters of Orellana, an Irish helot, to the seven northern counties on a more equal representation of the people in the parliament of Ireland* (Dublin, 1785).

[20] Drennan to McTier, 21 May 1791 (*Drennan letters*, 54–5). McTier was married to Drennan's sister Martha.

[21] *Rep. secret comm.* 91.   [22] McTier to Drennan, 2 July 1791 (*Drennan letters*, 55–6).

[23] Tone, *Life*, i. 142; Rosamund Jacob, *The rise of the United Irishmen, 1791–4* (London, 1937), 54.

many ways, but its impact on protestant perceptions of Catholics was profound. The revolution took place in a Catholic country by Catholics who
placed the national good before sectarian interests. Astonishingly, these revolutionaries abolished tithes and disestablished the church. If the Catholics
of France could place their duties as citizens above their religious inclina-
tions, were not the Catholics of Ireland able to do the same? Samuel
Neilson and his secret committee of Belfast Volunteers thought that they
could, and he too began to pursue Drennan's proposal for a new political
club uniting Catholic and protestant in Ireland. Neilson and his comrades
hoped that a Volunteer celebration of Bastille day to be held in Belfast in
1791 would be the occasion for the realization of this new political initiative. Thomas Russell, an army officer stationed in Belfast and a member of
Neilson's circle, invited his friend Theobald Wolfe Tone to send a declaration and resolutions for adoption on the occasion. But when Tone offered a
resolution merely insinuating the necessity as well as the desirability of
Catholic emancipation, it was rejected by the majority of those Volunteers
attending. Tone bitterly recorded his disappointment in his diary:

I am on this day, July 17, 1791, informed that the last question [on Catholic eman-
cipation] was lost. If so my present impression is to become a red-hot Catholic, seeing that in the party apparently and perhaps really most anxious for reform, it is
rather a monopoly than an extension of liberty which is their object, contrary to all
justice and expediency.[24]

Tone consequently turned his considerable talents towards propagandizing
the Catholic cause.

The result was his masterful *An argument on behalf of the Catholics of
Ireland*, which he wrote in August and which appeared in September 1791.
Essentially, Tone urged a union of Catholic and protestant in Ireland to
overthrow British and ascendancy domination. 'The misfortune of Ireland is
that we have no *national government*.'[25] His modest proposal was that only
a popular movement based on the unity of the Irish people could counteract the influence of England in the governance of Ireland. The will of the
people could be established peaceably and constitutionally through the
reform of parliament, but no reform would be 'honourable, practicable, or
efficacious' that did not extend the franchise to Catholics.[26]

The pamphlet was a phenomenal best seller for the time, with sales
reaching 6,000 by early 1792.[27] Tone's effort did much to overcome prejudices in Belfast, and the pamphlet took pride of place, second only to
Paine's *Rights of man*, in the canon of Belfast radicalism. But we should not

---

[24] Tone, *Life*, i. 140.
[25] Theobald Wolfe Tone, *An argument on behalf of the Catholics of Ireland . . . by a northern
whig* (Dublin, 1791), 344 (repr. in Tone, *Life*, i. 341–66).
[26] Ibid. 348.   [27] Elliott, *Wolfe Tone*, 129.

exaggerate the claim that this conversion was deeply felt or even sincere, that northern Dissenters at one instant began to look upon their Catholic brethren with unprecedented warmth and affection and earnestly sought to establish their political rights. Essentially, Tone persuaded the Dissenters that the enemy of their enemy was their friend. The common enemy was clearly an illiberal Anglo-Irish ascendancy backed by British power. It was expedient as well as just, therefore, that Catholics should be included in any demands made to alter this undesirable state of affairs.

By October Neilson's committee had found that the time was ripe for the institution of a new political body to unite all Irishmen in patriotic action, and they invited Tone to Belfast for the occasion.[28] On 18 October, with thirty members present, including Tone, Thomas Russell, and the eleven members of Neilson's secret committee, the Society of United Irishmen held its first meeting, with Samuel McTier in the chair and Robert Simms, a wealthy tanner, serving as secretary. Six new members were proposed, bringing the total membership of the club to thirty-six.[29]

Three resolutions, written by Tone, were passed unanimously and formed the cornerstone of the United Irish movement:

First, that the weight of English influence in the government of this country is so great as to require a cordial union among *all the people of Ireland* to maintain that balance which is essential to the preservation of our liberties and the extension of our commerce.

Second, that the sole constitutional mode by which this influence can be opposed is by the complete and radical reform of the representation of the people in parliament.

Third, that no reform is practicable, efficacious, or just which shall not include Irishmen of every religious persuasion.

The declaration framing these resolutions concluded with a call for the formation of 'similar societies in every quarter of the kingdom for the promotion of constitutional knowledge, the abolition of bigotry in religion and politics, and the equal distribution of the rights of men through all sects and denominations of Irishmen'.[30] Dublin followed suit on 9 November 1791, when the radical merchant and civic agitator James Napper Tandy convened the Dublin Society of United Irishmen.

The significance of this explosive new political departure was not lost on the government. 'I may be a false prophet,' Home Secretary Grenville observed to the lord-lieutenant, the earl of Westmorland, two days after the foundation of the new club, 'but there is no evil that I should not prophesy if that union [between Dissenters and Catholics] takes place at the present

---

[28] Tone, *Life*, i. 141.   [29] Ibid. 141–4.   [30] Joy, *Belfast*, 359.

moment, or on the principles on which it is endeavoured to bring it about.'[31]

The powder-keg from which the Catholic question exploded into the centre of Irish political consciousness in 1792 and 1793 was lit by two fuses. First, by extending their offer of a mutually beneficial alliance, the United Irishmen raised the value of Catholic loyalty in the eyes of the British government. And, secondly, the Catholics themselves, spurred on by the radicals' *bête noire* Edmund Burke and by radicals among their own brethren, stepped up their own campaign to achieve the abolition of the penal laws. The result was a fissuring of traditional allegiances in Ireland which transcended a simple confessional or radical–conservative dichotomy. The whig opposition divided on whether Catholics ought to be awarded immediate or gradual relief and, further, over the extent of that relief—total or partial. The politicized protestant middle classes differed, as did reformers in Belfast, over similar questions, fissuring into pro-Catholic and anti-Catholic factions. In the countryside the Catholic question served to undermine deferential patterns of authority. The Catholics themselves were divided between their own conservatives and radicals. And, finally, the Irish government fell out with its British masters.[32]

The British government had realized during the agitation of the protestant Volunteers in the late 1770s that the rising Catholic middle class might become warm supporters of the British connection and a counter to Anglo-Irish patriotism if they were played right. Thus the government forced the first major Catholic relief act on the Irish parliament in 1778 and began the process of removing the hated penal laws. Anglo-Irish protestant nationalism had partly been informed by the assumption that the ruling class in Ireland existed in a state of mutual dependence on the government of Britain. Thus the Anglo-Irish felt free to extort concessions from a beleaguered British ministry in 1782 with impunity. Yet such an assumption of mutual dependence was conditional, as the British demonstrated through

---

[31] Lord Grenville to earl of Westmorland, 20 Oct. 1791 (SPOI, Westmorland correspondence, 22).

[32] See e.g. Thomas Bartlett, 'An end to moral economy: the Irish militia disturbances of 1793', *Past and Present*, 99 (May 1983), 41–64; Elliott, *Wolfe Tone*, 151–200; Jacqueline Hill, 'The meaning and significance of "protestant ascendancy", 1787–1840', in *Ireland after the union: proceedings of the second joint meeting of the Royal Irish Academy and the British Academy, London, 1986*, introd. Lord Blake (Oxford, 1989), 12–16; ead., 'The politics of privilege: Dublin corporation and the Catholic question, 1792–1823', *Maynooth Review*, 7 (Dec. 1982), 17–36; W. E. H. Lecky, *A history of Ireland in the eighteenth century* (5 vols., London, 1898), iii. 22–186; A. P. W. Malcomson, *John Foster: the politics of the Anglo-Irish ascendancy* (Oxford, 1978), 65–70; James Smyth, 'Popular politicisation, Defenderism and the Catholic question', in Hugh Gough and David Dickson (eds.), *Ireland and the French revolution* (Dublin, 1990); id., *The men of no property: Irish radicals and popular politics in the late eighteenth century* (New York, 1992), ch. 3; Thomas Bartlett, *The fall and rise of the Irish nation: the Catholic question, 1690–1830* (Savage, Md., 1992), chs. 8–9.

their espousal of Catholic relief in Ireland, reminding the erstwhile protestant patriots that there were, as A. P. W. Malcomson has put it, 'elements outside the ascendancy to whom it might be profitable for the British government in the future to make a direct appeal'.[33]

In 1789 the Catholic Committee, an élite and conservative body established in 1773 to promote the gradual relaxation of the penal laws, resolved to step up its campaign.[34] It was not, however, until early 1791 that a steering committee of thirteen was formed, dominated by Dublin businessmen and professionals, who succeeded in wresting control of the movement from the more cautious Catholic gentry. This change in leadership in the committee, connoting a more aggressive and radical spirit, also encouraged the northern Presbyterians to regard Catholics as suitable and reliable allies in the cause of parliamentary reform. By the summer of 1791 the Catholic Committee had informed the government that it intended to petition for relief in the next parliamentary session. Irish Chief Secretary Hobart received the Catholic delegation, but declined to commit himself on the question of relief, maintaining that such a momentous issue must be considered by the British cabinet. He did imply, however, that the good behaviour and loyalty of Irish Catholics would not go unnoticed by the British and Irish governments, a warning to the Catholics not to associate with the radical Presbyterians if they looked to Britain for eventual emancipation.[35]

The times looked propitious for the final abolition of the penal laws. The relief acts of 1778 and 1782 repealed most of the laws affecting the holding and inheritance of land by Catholics. They were still, however, denied access to the legal profession and the exercise of political rights, particularly onerous restrictions for the rising Catholic middle class.[36] From 1778 on, it was clear to Irish Catholics that Britain might well court and reward their loyalty with liberal legislation. The possibility of an alliance between Catholics and radical protestants in Ireland ranged against British executive influence, combined with the dread that Great Britain might once again find itself at war with France, raised the value of Catholic good will in ministerial eyes. Dundas, the new home secretary, was convinced that the sure way

[33] Malcomson, *John Foster*, p. xxi.
[34] For the Catholic Committee's campaign, see Patrick J. Corish, *The Catholic community in the seventeenth and eighteenth centuries* (Dublin, 1981), 116–39; R. B. McDowell, 'The age of the United Irishman: revolution and the Union, 1794–1800', in T. W. Moody and W. E. Vaughan (eds.), *A new history of Ireland*, iv. *Eighteenth-century Ireland, 1691–1800* (Oxford, 1986), 302–22. For documentary sources on the Catholic agitation, see Revd John Brady, *Catholics and Catholicism in the eighteenth-century press* (Maynooth, 1965); R. Dudley Edwards (ed.), 'The minute book of the Catholic Committee, 1773–92', *Archivium Hibernicum, or Irish Historical Records*, 9 (1941), 3–172.
[35] McDowell, *Ireland*, 390–5.
[36] For the growing economic power of Catholics, see Maureen Wall, 'The rise of a Catholic middle class in eighteenth-century Ireland', *Irish Historical Studies*, 9/42 (Sept. 1958), 91–115; Bartlett, *Fall and rise of the Irish nation*, 44–50; T. P. Power and Kevin Whelan (eds.), *Endurance and emergence: Catholics in Ireland in the eighteenth century* (Dublin, 1990).

to keep Catholics loyal to the British connection was to give them the vote.
'The protestant interests in Ireland run a greater risk by adhering to a total
exclusion of the Roman Catholics from the privilege of electing than they
do by admitting them to a moderate and qualified participation of that
privilege.'[37] Despite the protests of the ascendancy and of its champion, the
viceroy himself, the British ministry was adamant that something be done
for the Catholics to secure them to the constitution.[38] The Catholic relief
act of 1792, however, fell far short of the expectations of the Catholics and
their Presbyterian radical allies. Catholics were admitted to the bar, and all
remaining restrictions on education were removed, but they were still
excluded from the exercise of significant political rights.

'To grant them liberties by piecemeal is but to whet their appetite,'
claimed Drennan, and the Catholic Committee redoubled its efforts to
secure final repeal of the remaining penal laws.[39] In July 1792 the Catholic
Committee acquired the services of their most ardent protestant advocate,
Theobald Wolfe Tone, who was hired by John Keogh to serve as the committee's secretary. Despite Tone's involvement, the Catholic Committee
remained aloof from the United Irish movement, though individual
Catholics certainly participated. The committee reasoned, as Drennan
noted, that the mere threat of a Catholic–Dissenter alliance could be a useful tool in the attainment of legislative relief. 'The Catholics wish to have
two strings to their bow—a part to deal with government, a part to ally
with us—and if one string cracks, why, try the other.'[40] Nevertheless, the
Catholics were not so confident of English support as to relinquish the
hand of partnership extended to them by radical protestants.

Indeed, the Catholics operated as something of a conservative force
within the United Irish movement during these early years. 'We are scarcely
able to keep them from altering the very character and spirit of our society,' Drennan complained. They 'are exerting all their power in and out of
the society to impose a milk-and-water spirit or to water down every resolution'.[41] Drennan reported with some disgust a debate which occurred in
the Dublin club when the Catholics and their supporters, led by Emmet and
Simon Butler, sought to adopt a resolution 'expressing attachment to the
established constitution, which is said to be the bargain [undertaken by the
government] with the Catholics for their emancipation'. Drennan succeeded
in opposing this resolution, which in fact denied the necessity for meaningful parliamentary reform.[42] Dr Alexander Haliday of Belfast delighted in
informing his whig patron, the earl of Charlemont, that a delegation of

---

[37] Henry Dundas to earl of Westmorland, 26 Dec. 1791 (PROHO 100/33/205–14).
[38] For these protests, see Westmorland to [Dundas], 21 Jan. 1792 (ibid. 100/36/120–5).
[39] Drennan to McTier, [Nov. 1791] (*Drennan letters*, 64).
[40] Drennan to McTier, 17 Dec. 1791 (ibid. 70).
[41] Drennan to McTier, 31 Dec. 1792 (ibid. 115).
[42] Drennan to McTier, 28 Jan. 1792 (PRONI, Drennan letters, T 765/2/321*b*).   ·

Catholic Committeemen 'gave some marks of their good sense as they passed through this town [Belfast], condemning the extreme violence of the *Northern Star* [the United Irish newspaper] as being more likely to injure them than serve the common cause'.[43] Nevertheless, Catholics were not insensitive to agitation sustained on their behalf in the north by Presbyterian reformers. In late March 1792 Edward Byrne, chairman of the Catholic Committee, sent an address of gratitude to the people of Belfast for their favourable pronouncements on Catholic emancipation.[44]

Drennan was certainly disappointed that the Catholics did not come out aggressively in favour of parliamentary reform. They 'dread us republican sinners and don't like to have much communication with us'.[45] But while the United Irishmen on the Catholic steering committee may have been radically inclined themselves, they nevertheless represented a generally conservative body which relied on clerical and gentry support, and Drennan showed little patience with their difficulties.[46]

Many of the other protestant United Irishmen, however, understood and accepted the Catholic dilemma. 'Belfast is decided on the Catholic question,' observed Catholic leader John Keogh after a visit to the north in July 1792, 'and its neighbourhood daily converting. Gentlemen who had opposed us last year are now amongst our warmest advocates.'[47] It was generally believed that emancipation might be easier to achieve than reform, and that if Catholics gained political rights, they would hasten the advent of a fair and adequate system of representation. Thus Tone, for one, felt that the interests of reform and independence could best be served by advancing the Catholic cause. 'Reform seems a long way off,' he wrote in his diary in September 1792, but Catholic emancipation seemed imminent.[48] A real concern of the protestant radicals, however, was that their Catholic allies would allow themselves to be bought off by the British ministry and would abandon the cause of reform.

This concern became particularly acute during the months preceding the passage of the Catholic relief act of 1793, demonstrating how tenuous and easily strained the union between Catholic and protestant was in Ireland. Early in December Catholic delegates from all over the country held a convention in Dublin, with the idea of demonstrating their determination to secure final relief. This extraordinary political initiative created what was, in effect, a sort of anti-parliament, a representative assembly based on republican commonwealth assumptions. The election of delegates encour-

---

[43] Haliday to Charlemont, 16 Dec. 1792 (HMC, *Charlemont manuscripts*, ii. 208–9).

[44] *NS*, 4 Apr. 1792.   [45] Drennan to McTier, 8 Dec. 1792 (*Drennan letters*, 87).

[46] For a discussion of the activities of the Catholic Committee at this time, see Elliott, *Wolfe Tone*, 151–207.

[47] Extract of a letter from Ireland, Mount Jerome (Keogh's residence), 26 July 1792 (PROHO 100/38/266–8).

[48] Tone, *Life*, i. 166.

aged the extension of the Catholic question deep into the Irish countryside, further politicizing and polarizing inhabitants.[49]

United Irish societies in Dublin and Belfast used the opportunity of the convention to urge Catholics to accept nothing less than full political and civil rights.[50] The fact that such urging was deemed necessary illustrates the radicals' distrust of the Catholics. A small inner circle of the Belfast United Irishmen, called the 'select society', which included Neilson and McTier, pushed this demand for complete emancipation by summoning Luke Teeling, a wealthy Lisburn merchant and a delegate, from County Antrim. In urging Teeling to press the demand for full emancipation, they reasoned that Catholic claims should be kept as high as possible. If frustrated, the Catholics would still need the support of radical protestants; if their demands were granted, and Catholics regained the right to sit in parliament, it would virtually assure the passage of reform measures.[51] The *Northern Star* was at pains to discredit a widespread rumour (which Drennan believed) that the Catholics had made a deal with the government by which relief would be granted if the Catholics 'would engage to stand by government in support of the constitution *as it is* against all reformers'.[52]

Though it was in the interest of reformers to stand firmly behind the Catholic convention, their misgivings were not allayed by its proceedings. A small delegation of Dublin United Irishmen, led by Archibald Hamilton Rowan and James Napper Tandy, attended the convention in order to deliver a declaration from the society expressing its continued support for complete Catholic relief. But they were refused admittance to the convention floor, and although 'many plausible reasons' were given for this refusal, Drennan believed that 'their real reason was the fear of showing any *public* communications with United Irishmen in the present stage of the business, and I suppose the Belfast advice was hushed up as quietly as our own resolutions have been'.[53] Nevertheless, Drennan grudgingly admitted that the convention's resolutions in favour of parliamentary reform indicated a 'decided and honest mind'.[54]

The Catholic convention snubbed the unsympathetic Irish government and sent its delegates directly to London to petition the king and his government for relief. The desire to pre-empt the Catholic–Dissenter alliance, along with the necessity of placating Catholics in the light of an impending war with revolutionary France, persuaded Pitt's government into granting concessions.[55] The relief act passed in April 1793 granted Catholic 40s. free-

---

[49] Smyth, 'Popular politicisation'.
[50] Martha McTier to William Drennan, 3 Dec. 1792 (*Drennan letters*, 102).
[51] Maureen Wall, 'The United Irish movement', *Historical Studies*, 5 (1965), 132.
[52] *NS*, 5 Dec. 1792.
[53] Drennan to Samuel and Martha McTier, 10 Dec. 1792 (*Drennan letters*, 106–7).
[54] Drennan to McTier, [Dec.] 1792 (ibid. 114).
[55] For these negotiations, see Elliott, *Wolfe Tone*, 199–205.

holders the right to vote and allowed Catholics to hold all but the highest offices in the state and parliamentary seats.[56] But if the government hoped to stem the tide of public criticism, the Catholic relief act of 1793 was only of limited utility. The greatest limitation of the act was its failure to satisfy the restive Catholic middle class which the protestant radicals courted. Furthermore, the protestant ascendancy felt abandoned, betrayed, and besieged, accounting in part for the bitter resurgence of sectarian hostility in Ireland during the remaining years of the decade.

The United Irishmen were more than mere spectators watching the Catholic drama unfold. Their activities between 1791 and 1793 were largely concerned with mobilizing public opinion behind not only Catholic emancipation, but also radical parliamentary reform. In the early years of the movement, therefore, the United Irishmen operated as an open, constitutional society, its function largely propagandist—to disseminate political information and, whenever possible, to co-ordinate the activities of other like-minded reform groups.[57]

The United Irishmen constituted the radical wing of the Volunteers, and used their influence to revive these old companies and create new ones. 'The patriotic spirit of volunteering daily increases,' the *Northern Star* proclaimed in July 1792. 'There appears a general resurrection of the Volunteer body throughout the counties of Antrim and Down.'[58] Formerly, the Volunteers had been composed of farmers, tradesmen, and merchants led by the local gentry and patriot leaders, a phalanx of the protestant Anglo-Irish ascendancy, feeling besieged by both an unsympathetic British ministry and Ireland's Catholic majority. Though the social composition of the revived organization is not always clear, there were suggestions that members of lower social status and even Catholics were now encouraged to join.[59]

There were also suggestions that many members joined for confused or ill-defined reasons, or that they were simply carried away by the general enthusiasm for volunteering itself. George Knox reported to Lord Abercorn that though Volunteer corps were established daily, there seemed to be no consistent reason for enlisting. When Knox asked one Volunteer why he had joined, the man replied: 'Is not it time to arm when three million of our fellow subjects are in chains?' This remark could easily have been extracted from any article in the *Northern Star* endorsing Catholic emancipation. But another member of the same corps, when asked the same

---

[56] For the passage of this act, see Lecky, *History of Ireland*, iii. 133–78; McDowell, *Ireland*, 408–21.

[57] For the organizational history of the United Irish societies, see Ch. 4.

[58] *NS*, 28 July 1792.

[59] See e.g. Charlemont to Haliday, 14 Mar. 1785 (RIA, Charlemont papers, MS 12 R 26/10); *FJ*, 28 Oct. 1790; *NS*, 5, 12, 15 Dec. 1792: R. R. Madden, *Antrim and Down in '98* (Glasgow, n.d.), 96.

question, responded that he did not want to see Ireland become a 'popish country'.[60] It would seem that the radicalism and non-sectarianism which characterized many of the leaders of the Volunteer revival were not reflected uniformly among the ranks. And then there were reasons of sociability, recreation, or personal vanity which impelled many erstwhile reformers into the Volunteer movement. As Thomas Prentice of Armagh confessed to Charlemont: 'most of us are rather fond of the showy than the substantial part of the business.'[61] If some of the rank and file associated for non-political or even reactionary motives, their adherence itself lent at least the appearance of a popular outcry for radical political measures.

Throughout the summer and autumn of 1792 resolutions in favour of Catholic emancipation and parliamentary reform filled the columns of the Belfast newspapers. But the Volunteers did not confine themselves to political pronouncements alone; they were equally interested in arming and drilling in the event that their services might be needed.[62] The *Northern Star* reported in December 1792 that 'a plan is in agitation in this town [Belfast] for procuring a quantity of the very best firelocks, of the newest and most durable construction,' for by this means the 'armed citizens of Ireland will be able to act with *effect* when it becomes necessary to step forward in support of their country against foreign or domestic foes.'[63]

The formation of a new brand of Volunteers, called the National Guard, in Belfast, Derry, Newry, and Dublin proved equally alarming to the administration. In the autumn of 1792 some Dublin United Irishmen, under the direction of Archibald Hamilton Rowan, James Napper Tandy, Oliver Bond, and Henry Jackson, launched a project for the establishment of a new Volunteer body inspired by French example and espousing republican principles.[64] Although the National Guard aspired to a membership of 6,000–10,000, it fell drastically short of the mark, with only '200 select men'.[65] Thomas Addis Emmet attributed this failure to the blatant radicalism of the corps: 'Republicanism had not then stricken root [*sic*] in the capital.' Moderate reformers were reluctant to become involved in such an overtly provocative association.[66] Small the National Guard may have been, but the government felt sufficiently provoked to call for its dissolution. 'It is very dangerous to attempt to stop volunteering,' maintained Westmorland, 'and difficult to pass it by.'[67] On 8 December the viceroy issued a procla-

---

[60] George Knox to marquis of Abercorn, 14 Feb. 1793 (PRONI, Abercorn papers, T2541/IB1/4/12).

[61] Thomas Prentice to Charlemont, 28 Apr. 1791 (HMC, *Charlemont manuscripts*, ii. 138–9).

[62] See e.g. *NS*, 15 Dec. 1792; R. B. McDowell, 'The proceedings of the Dublin Society of United Irishmen', *Analecta Hibernia*, 17 (1949), 29; *Rep. secret comm.*, 40–1.

[63] *NS*, 5 Dec. 1792.   [64] Lecky, *History of Ireland*, iii. 102.

[65] Drennan to Martha McTier, 25 Nov. 1792 (*Drennan letters*, 98); McDowell, 'Proceedings', 40.

mation against 'divers ill-affected persons' associated 'to withstand lawful authority and violently and forcibly to redress pretended grievances and to subvert the established constitution of his majesty's realm'.[68] The proclamation clearly referred to the National Guard and other recently formed Volunteer companies of a similar description. As Hobart informed Downshire, the 'old' Volunteers had been exempted from the proclamation because 'it was considered expedient to do so; first, because they are a body which we did not think it prudent under all the circumstances of the times to offend, and secondly because we hope to mould some of them into a militia'.[69]

Drennan saw the proclamation as an attempt by the administration to cause dissension within Volunteer ranks. As he warned his sister in Belfast: 'The proclamation aims really at the north, though it hopes to strike the first panic into the capital. God direct you all for the best, but if you do not act with spirit and determination, the protestant cause [i.e. the reform of parliament] is lost.'[70] The *Northern Star* also urged the Volunteers, as the traditional saviours of Ireland, to stand firm against the government's challenge: 'Be it remembered that proclamations are not law, and that every freeman is enjoined by law to carry arms.'[71] In general, the northern Volunteers continued their political agitation undeterred by—and, indeed, denouncing—the viceroy's proclamation against the new National Guard.[72]

But in Dublin the government's challenge proved more effective, though at first it merely bred defiant contempt. An address issued by the United Irishmen of Dublin to the Volunteers of Ireland called on the armed nation to exert itself in defence of the liberties of the subject. 'Citizen soldiers,' the manifesto began, 'you first took arms to protect your country from foreign enemies and from domestic disturbances. For the same purposes it now becomes necessary that you should resume them.' Citing the lord-lieutenant's proclamation, Drennan, the author of the address, pointed out the imminent danger to Irish liberties and called upon the Volunteers to remain resolute.[73]

---

[66] William James MacNeven, *Pieces of Irish history illustrative of the condition of the Catholics of Ireland* (New York, 1807), 35.

[67] Westmorland to Dundas, 18 Dec. 1792 (PROHO 100/38/175–6).

[68] *NS*, 12 Dec. 1792.

[69] Robert Hobart to Lord Hillsborough (later marquess of Downshire), 9 Dec. 1792 (PRONI, Downshire papers, D607/B/380); see also Westmorland to [Henry Dundas], 29 Nov. 1792 (PROHO 100/38/105–8).

[70] Drennan to Samuel and Martha McTier, 10 Dec. 1792 (*Drennan letters*, 107–8).

[71] *NS*, 12 Dec. 1792.

[72] For Volunteer denouncements, see Henry Joy, *Belfast politics, or a collection of the debates, resolutions, and other proceedings of that town in the years 1792 to 1793* (Belfast, 1794), 92–4, 98–9.

[73] *Rep. secret comm.* 100. This manifesto brought many United Irishmen into the dock, including its author Drennan, who was acquitted, various newspaper publishers who printed it (including the proprietors of the *Northern Star*), and Archibald Hamilton Rowan, who was found guilty and imprisoned for distributing it. But the government delayed taking action on

Except for the Merchants' Corps, the Volunteers in Dublin greeted the address from the United Irishmen with approval.[74] The first significant challenge to the government occurred when the Goldsmiths' Corps assembled on 27 January 1793 to attest their loyalty to the constitution and their willingness to serve the city's magistrates in the preservation of public order, but at the same time to proclaim their desire for parliamentary reform and Catholic emancipation. A zealous public servant dispersed the assembly, though, as a long-established Volunteer company, the Goldsmiths' Corps was technically immune from the proclamation.[75] The problem for the government, however, was that the radicals had only withdrawn from the National Guard to enrol in established Volunteer corps. Dublin Castle therefore thought it necessary to extend the proclamation to cover all Dublin Volunteer bodies.[76]

'I shall not think ourselves safe', Cooke wrote to the home office, 'until the Volunteers be completely put down by law and militia. They are kept under in Dublin but they spread in the north.'[77] The government proceeded cautiously against the northern bodies. Hobart confirmed the serious state of the north: 'The levelling system under the mask of reform is spreading furiously in that part of the country,' abetted by the Volunteers.[78] Wise policy dictated that the government wait before attempting to extend the proclamation to the north, and, as Westmorland argued, 'not to hazard any general measure before a force was prepared for preventing resistance to its execution'. Consequently, the viceroy dispatched General Whyte into Ulster and reinforced the military establishment there, especially in the neighbourhood of Belfast.[79]

Among the reinforcements sent by Westmorland to Whyte in Belfast was the 17th Regiment of Light Dragoons. No sooner had these British troops arrived in the town, on 9 March 1793, than they collided with the Belfast radicals. According to General Whyte, a corporal and a private of the regiment were strolling through the streets when they encountered a crowd of people parading behind a fiddler 'playing "Ça ira"', or, as the dragoons termed it, 'some rascally outlandish, disloyal tune'. The dragoons demanded that the fiddler change his tune to 'God save the king', but the crowd would not allow it, 'damning the king and all his dirty slaves'. The soldiers claimed that the people then began pelting them with stones; in

the address until its position was strengthened in 1793. As Hobart told Lord Hillsborough: 'You may be assured, but this is in strict confidence, because we *may* have reasons for not letting our intentions be known *yet*, that proper care will be taken of the treasonable publication to the Volunteers from the United Irishmen' (Hobart to Hillsborough, 18 Dec. 1792 (PRONI, Downshire papers, D607/B/381)).

[74] Drennan to McTier, 19 Dec. 1792 (*Drennan letters*, 108–9).   [75] 30 Jan. 1793.
[76] Westmorland to Dundas, 29 Mar. 1793 (PROHO 100/43/145–51).
[77] Edward Cooke to Evan Nepean, 26 Feb. 1793 (ibid. 100/43/15–17).
[78] Robert Hobart to Evan Nepean, 29 Dec. 1792 (ibid. 100/42/9–12).
[79] Westmorland to Dundas, 29 Mar. 1793 (ibid. 100/43/145–51).

self-defence, the dragoons drew their sabres, were 'immediately joined by a dozen of their comrades, drove all the town before them, immediately proceeded and cut down the famous sign of Gen. Dumourier, and broke the windows and compleatly [*sic*] terrified some of the most noted democrats before their officers could get to them'. Whyte was hardly disturbed by this breach of discipline among his troops, and expected that the riot would prove beneficial by frightening the radicals into submission.[80]

The *Belfast News-Letter* offered a very different interpretation of the incident. The newly arrived troops, with little provocation, 'rushed from their quarters and drove furiously through most of the principal streets with their sabres drawn, wounding and maiming some of the unoffending inhabitants and attacking houses'. As to the cause of the riot, the *Belfast News-Letter* reported that there was proof that, on their arrival, some of the troopers had 'avowed their intention of committing outrage against certain individuals who had been represented to them as disaffected'.[81]

Although the Belfast Volunteers mobilized to protect the town from further military outrage, General Whyte succeeded in persuading them to disband, threatening to call out the troops again if they declined. 'It has given the death blow to these Volunteers,' he boasted.[82] Two days later, on 11 March 1793, the lord lieutenant issued a proclamation declaring all Volunteer assemblies unlawful, thus extending his original proclamation to the north.[83] A letter from Whyte to Hobart on that same day suggests that the riot, which so conveniently suited the administration's purpose, might well have been planned by the general himself.

Everything has succeeded to my wishes. The Volunteers have given up their nightly meetings by stipulation. Not a man of the 17th is to be prosecuted. . . . They were in a scrape from their loyalty . . . The men are charming boys . . . The great leading men of situation are compleatly [*sic*] humbled and we are all well-disposed friends to the king and constitution.[84]

'The Dublin Volunteers seem to have entirely given up the game,' a satisfied Hobart could write to the home office, 'and the steps taken to check the spirit of rebellion at Belfast have been attended with a success beyond our expectations.'[85] The success of the government's proclamations against the Volunteers was only temporary and superficial, however. Many Volunteer corps in the north merely went underground and continued in existence as political clubs until they were finally absorbed in 1795 by the revived and reconstituted revolutionary Society of United Irishmen.

[80] Gen. Richard Whyte to Robert Hobart, [Mar.] 1793 (ibid. 100/43/152–4).
[81] *BNL*, 9 Mar. 1793.   [82] Whyte to Hobart, [Mar.] 1793 (PROHO 100/43/152–4).
[83] Hobart to Whyte, 11 Mar. 1793 (ibid. 100/43/157).
[84] Whyte to Hobart, 11 Mar. 1793 (ibid. 100/43/103–4).
[85] Hobart to Nepean, 19 Mar. 1793 (ibid. 100/43/117–19).

The reform impulse generated by the United Irishmen and Volunteers also found its way into Irish freemasonry. Little is known about the freemasons. In a letter to the *Northern Star* one freemason insisted that the object of the association was 'to meet together as brethren for the promulgation of knowledge, the advancement of morality, the exploding of bigotry, by removing all the prejudices of education and drawing as it were the whole universal family of mankind into a holy bond of union, peace, and concord'.[86] As carriers of such Enlightenment notions, masonic lodges could reinforce acceptance of a radical or republican ideology.[87] Though masons were officially forbidden to engage in political controversy, many soon found themselves unable to resist entering the general debate over the adequacy of the Irish system of representation. The first masonic political pronouncements of this period, however, were conservative in tone. The *Freeman's Journal* reported in December 1792 that delegates from twenty-five lodges had assembled in Armagh in order to express their loyalty to the government and their satisfaction with the established order.[88] Similar loyal declarations were passed by freemasons in Dublin and at Bellaghy and Castledawson, County Derry.[89] Such displays of subservience to the administration provoked reform-minded lodges into passing counter-resolutions asserting the necessity for a reform of parliament and Catholic emancipation.

The most eloquent challenge to the Armagh resolutions came from an important assembly in Tyrone representing 1,432 masons, seeking to correct the impression that masons complacently accepted the existing order with all its abuses and excesses. While expressing their loyalty to the constitution in theory, the Tyrone masons called for practical reforms to alleviate the stark condition of the Irish lower classes:

How could any of you, whose benevolence should be [as] extensive as the habitations of man, behold two-thirds of your countrymen miserable, oppressed, naked, literally living on *potatoes* and *point*, labouring under sanguinary penal laws, taxed without being represented, unable in sickness to procure assistance, and obliged annually to desert their hovels at the approaching ravages of the hearth collector.

The remedies for these evils were parliamentary reform and Catholic emancipation. The masons thanked the Volunteers for their exertions on behalf of these causes, and invited all masons to share in the promotion of these measures and to subscribe to the following declaration: 'I solemnly promise and declare that I will by all rational means promote the universal emancipation and adequate representation of *all* the people of Ireland, and will not be satisfied until these objects have been unequivocally obtained.' The

---

[86] NS, 19 Dec. 1792.

[87] For freemasonry and radicalism, see Margaret Jacob, *Living the Enlightenment: free-masonry and politics in eighteenth-century Europe* (Oxford, 1991).

[88] FJ, 22 Dec. 1792   [89] NS, 23 Jan. 1793.

Tyrone resolutions concluded with an appeal that the reform party be 'peaceable but powerful. Let every lodge in the land become a company of citizen soldiers. Let every Volunteer company become a lodge of masons.'[90]

Pro-reform declarations by Volunteers and freemasons formed only part of the wave of political excitement which swept over Ulster during the winter of 1792–3. Presbyterian ministers and their congregations contributed lustily to the general cry for reform and emancipation. In November 1792 the United Irishman and freemason John Caldwell of Magherafelt, County Derry, submitted a set of resolutions to the Presbyterian congregations of Ulster calling for immediate reform of parliament on a democratic and non-sectarian basis and proposing a national convention to achieve this end. Though there was no direct response to Caldwell's revolutionary proposal, Presbyterian congregations nevertheless met to discuss the political questions of the day and they published their conclusions in the newspapers. At the same time, several parishes in the counties of Derry, Tyrone, and Down called for a day of thanksgiving 'on account of the rapid progress of civil and religious liberty through Europe and the amazing success of the glorious friends of freedom in France, aided by the *King of kings*, against the tyrannical combinations of unprincipled despots'.[91] In January 1793 resolutions from congregations throughout the north-east calling for parliamentary reform and Catholic emancipation appeared in newspapers.[92] These pronouncements were given official sanction when the Synod of Ulster held its annual meeting at Lurgan in June 1793. United Irishman Dr William Steele Dickson was elected moderator and led the assembly of divines in calling for immediate reform of the abuses of government.[93]

But the United Irishmen could not content themselves with such local successes. The whole thrust of their propaganda campaign and their efforts to politicize and mobilize other organizations was directed towards displaying the full force of the popular will. One means adopted to this end was the convention, a forum used successfully by the Volunteers in 1782 and by the Catholics in 1792.[94] A County Down correspondent to the *Northern Star* recommended that the effort should begin with a provincial convention in Ulster, to be held on 15 February at Dungannon, a most suitable time and place, with the anniversary of the Volunteer convention of 1782 clearly in mind.[95] In the end, five counties—Antrim, Down, Derry, Tyrone, and Donegal—sent delegates to the Dungannon convention, which claimed to represent 1,250,000 citizens.[96]

---

[90] *NS*, 16 Jan. 1793.   [91] *NS*, 28 Nov. 1792.
[92] *BNL*, 8 Jan. 1793; *NS*, 16–30 Jan. 1793.
[93] *NS*, 29 June 1793.
[94] Drennan to McTier, 25 Apr. 1792 (*Drennan letters*, 87–8); *NS*, 3 Dec. 1792.
[95] *NS*, 12 Dec. 1792.
[96] *NS*, 20 Feb. 1793; R. R. Madden, *The United Irishmen, their lives and times*, 3rd ser. (7 vols., London, 1842–5), iii. 81.

Though the government feared the meeting, the convention was as moderately whiggish in its proceedings and resolutions as it was ominous in its symbolic aspect.[97] The delegates endorsed Catholic emancipation and parliamentary reform, but they failed to condemn the war and they denounced republicanism in Ireland, while applauding the British constitution.[98] The Dungannon convention failed to produce that great chorus of support for radical remedies to Ireland's ills. Indeed, as Marianne Elliott has argued, the proceedings 'reflected the moderate reaction against the United Irishmen, even in the north'.[99]

Whether the United Irishmen could have improved on their performance at a national convention which they proposed to hold at Athlone in the summer of 1793 is a moot point. The government, still smarting from the successful use of the method by the Catholic Committee, took the weapon out of the radicals' hands by passing the convention act. Part of a series of repressive measures directed at radical activity, the act prohibited any further extra-parliamentary representative assemblies in Ireland and was passed by a large majority.[100]

This prohibition against convening in extra-parliamentary and representative assemblies, along with the suppression of the Volunteers, effectively undermined the reform strategy of the United Irishmen. Denied the means to express the popular will through conventions or the Volunteer movement, the United Irishmen increasingly constituted a radical fringe group, their numbers declining, their members subject to judicial harassment, and their influence at its lowest ebb. During the bleak months following the outbreak of war and the passage of the government's anti-radical legislation, the United Irish movement reached its nadir.

The most disabling weakness of the United Irishmen in the early 1790s, however, was their failure to resist the government's efforts to isolate and contain them. The administration clearly overestimated the strength of the radical movement, an assessment which accounted in part for its cautious delay in confronting this challenge to ascendancy and British dominance. No one was perhaps more surprised, for example, at the success in suppressing the Volunteers than the government itself. Three reasons account for the lack of resistance which greeted the government's anti-radical measures. First, although the radicals had succeeded in mobilizing impressive numbers on behalf of reform and emancipation, they failed to rouse their allies beyond certain limited demands. There was perhaps more posturing than principles behind the resolutions, assemblies, and demonstrations of the early 1790s. Since the principles were not deeply held, their sacrifice in the face of a show of strength from the government was no great matter. A

[97] Drennan to McTier, [Feb.] 1793 (*Drennan letters*, 137).
[98] *NS*, 20 Feb. 1793; Martha McTier to Drennan, 16 Feb. 1793 (*Drennan letters*, 137).
[99] Elliott, *Wolfe Tone*, 216.   [100] Lecky, *History of Ireland*, iii. 189–90.

second reason for the submission of the reform movement to the government's anti-radical measures was the consequent timidity of the middle-class radicals. If playing the role of a virtuous citizen required hazarding life and property, most of the reformers preferred to call a halt. A third reason for the government's success was simply its willingness to confront the radicals. By their actions in the face of what seemed to be a widespread cry for political change, Dublin Castle and its ministerial backers in England were decisively asserting that they would not give in to popular pressure, that they would not, in the radicals' terms, heed the popular will. It was clear that the government would only be moved by force, or at least by a credible threat of it. Thus the failure of the reform campaign led to the adoption of an insurrectionary strategy.

In spite of the failure of conventional extra-parliamentary pressure and the defection of moderate reformers from their ranks, however, the United Irishmen continued to pursue their goals in the face of open government hostility and apparent public apathy. Revolutionary France symbolized their twin goals of popular government and the abolition of all religious dis-qualifications, and espousal of the French cause had played a prominent part in the propaganda of the society from its inception. Thus, with the commencement of war in 1793, the United Irishmen heartily assumed the role of an anti-war party.

The looming war was first discussed by the Dublin United Irishmen shortly before its outbreak in early February 1793. 'Whatever pretexts may be held out,' they declared, 'the real objects of the war about to be declared against France appear to this society to be not merely to punish crimes but to persecute principles.' It would be a war 'entered into by tyrants and abettors of tyranny, when France had committed no crime, unless the emancipation of 24 million men be one'. Furthermore, the conflict would have unfortunate practical implications, for the war 'can scarcely be main-tained except to the ruin of commerce'.[101] Nevertheless, the war served to strengthen the government's position in Ireland. Even Grattan, speaking for the whig opposition, declared in parliament: 'We must rise and fall with Britain.'[102]

Isolated as they were, the radicals were easy targets for persecution by the administration. With their popularity among the middle classes approaching its nadir, the government could more easily prosecute the radicals without outraging public opinion. 'Their great aim', Drennan told McTier, 'is to get rid of us by prosecution, persecution, or the terror of it.'[103] The most celebrated of these prosecutions was the indictment of Archibald Hamilton Rowan for publishing and distributing the inflamma-

---

[101] *NS*, 20 Feb. 1793.   [102] *NS*, 27 Jan. 1794.
[103] Drennan to McTier, 14 July 1794 (*Drennan letters*, 211).

tory address to the Volunteers and for circulating it at an armed assembly.[104] Though this manifesto had been issued in December 1792, the government waited until February 1794 to bring Rowan to trial in the hope of gathering sufficient evidence to ensure a capital conviction. Marcus Beresford observed to his father John, one of the most powerful men in the administration, that 'government are determined to hang Rowan'.[105] The *Northern Star*, admittedly a biased source, reported that Joseph Corbally, a Defender incarcerated in Kilmainham, had been offered a 'place in the revenue' if he would swear that Tandy and Rowan were leaders of the Defenders.[106] If the government actually harboured such a plan for judicial murder, it was aborted by Rowan's dramatic escape early in May 1794.[107]

Rowan's colleagues in the movement were also placed in the dock. Tandy was to have been indicted in April 1793 for 'publishing a libel', but he failed to appear and subsequently left the country.[108] Drennan was tried as the author of the Volunteer address in the summer of 1794, but he was acquitted. 'I think their disappointment in my case', declared Drennan, 'is [in] not having frightened me away before the trial.'[109] The experience was a traumatic one, however, and henceforth Drennan resided on the margins of the radical movement in Ireland. The proprietors of the United Irish newspaper, the *Northern Star*, were twice tried and acquitted for propagating sedition. This policy of the government hardly constituted a general purge of known radicals. Basically, it was designed to discredit the United Irish leaders and, if possible, to keep them out of circulation for a while. Moreover, such a policy might discourage further participation in the society.

Government harassment and the ineffectuality of the reform campaign combined to undermine support for the radicals. The Castle finally delivered the *coup de grâce* in the spring of 1794, to a Dublin society with a greatly depleted membership and no specific plans as to how to regenerate the movement.[110] But even if the United Irishmen offered no immediate threat to the government, they might prove more of a nuisance in the future. In March 1794 the informer Thomas Collins warned the government: 'If we are let to proceed quietly, all the evil consequences which have heretofore arose from our productions are but trifling to what may be expected in future.'[111] The arrest of the Revd William Jackson, an Anglican minister and agent sent by the French to assess the revolutionary climate in Ireland,

---

[104] See William Wenman Seward, *Collectanea politica, or the political transactions of Ireland from the ascension of George III to the present time* (3 vols., Dublin, 1801–4), ii. 111.
[105] Marcus Beresford to John Beresford, 28 Apr. 1794 (*The correspondence of the right hon. John Beresford*, ed. William Beresford (2 vols., London, 1854), ii. 26).
[106] *NS*, 3 Mar. 1794.   [107] *FJ*, 3 May 1794.
[108] *BNL*, 16 Apr. 1793.   [109] Drennan to McTier, 14 July 1794 (*Drennan letters*, 211).
[110] Drennan to Martha McTier, 3 July 1794 (ibid. 211).
[111] McDowell, 'Proceedings', 118.

in April 1794 gave the government the pretext that it needed to suppress the Dublin Society of United Irishmen. Among the members implicated in Jackson's mission to assess the revolutionary potential of Ireland were Rowan, Tone, and Leonard McNally, a barrister.[112] In May 1794 the Dublin police raided a United Irish meeting, dispersed its members, and confiscated the society's papers, thus marking the virtual end of the reformist phase of at least the society in the capital.

Jackson's arrest served to publicize the favourable disposition of France towards a possible Irish rebellion. Though the possibility of an alliance between Irish radicals and the French had existed since the beginning of the war, that prospect had never been dramatized more openly than with Jackson's arrest and trial.[113] After war was declared in February 1793, the French occasionally sent agents to Ireland to offer support against the common enemy, England. The reformist Society of United Irishmen, while applauding the principles of the French decree of November 1792 offering assistance to peoples in need of liberation, declined these overtures until the reform campaign itself reached its nadir.[114] Thus, when Jackson arrived in Ireland in the spring of 1794, he was warmly received by individual United Irishmen. The French, however, would not ally with a mere reform movement. The United Irishmen had to adopt separatist goals and commit themselves to mass revolutionary mobilization. But the Jackson affair and the possibility of a French alliance was only one factor in driving the United Irishmen down the road to insurrection. Equally significant was the frustration engendered by the brief lord-lieutenancy of Earl Fitzwilliam in the winter of 1794–5.[115]

In July 1794 the Portland whigs were brought into the Pitt ministry, apparently under the assumption that one of them would be given the administration of Ireland.[116] It was well known that the Portland whigs were favourably disposed towards the reform party led by Henry Grattan in the Irish house of commons.[117] It was therefore possible to infer from this ministerial shuffle that the policies of Grattan's party—parliamentary reform and the final abolition of the penal laws—would soon be implemented. Catholic hopes were raised to the point of certainty. Fitzwilliam, the new viceroy recruited from the Portland party, was, on his arrival in

---

[112] Ibid. 124.　　　　[113] See *The trial of Revd William Jackson* (Dublin, 1795).

[114] See Marianne Elliott, *Partners in revolution: the United Irishmen and France* (New Haven, Conn., and London, 1982), 51–7.

[115] See R. B. McDowell, 'The Fitzwilliam episode', *Irish Historical Studies*, 16/58 (Sept. 1966), 115–30; Lecky, *History of Ireland*, iii. 238–324; Rex Syndergaard, 'The Fitzwilliam crisis and Irish nationalism', *Eire-Ireland*, 8/2 (1973), 34–41; E. A. Smith, *Whig Principles and party politics: Earl Fitzwilliam and the whig party, 1748–1833* (Manchester, 1975).

[116] Edmund Burke to William Windham, 16 Oct. 1794 (*The correspondence of Edmund Burke*, ed. R. B. McDowell (10 vols., Chicago, 1958–78), viii. 37–9).

[117] Earl Fitzwilliam to Henry Grattan, 23 Aug. 1794 (*Memoirs of the life and times of the right hon. Henry Grattan*, ed. Henry Grattan, jun. (4 vols., London, 1842), iv. 18).

Ireland early in January 1795, 'decidedly of the opinion that it [Catholic emancipation] ought no longer be deferred', and he prepared to give the measure government support.[118] To facilitate this effort, he dismissed several stalwart supporters of the protestant ascendancy, notably John Beresford, the influential commissioner of the revenue. In these activities Fitzwilliam had exceeded his instructions and he was promptly recalled late in February 1795. Without government support, the measure for Catholic emancipation failed.

Fitzwilliam's administration raised many hopes, and his departure left Irish Catholics and reformers more frustrated than ever, further alienating Irish radicals from their government. Reform by conventional and legal methods appeared impossible under the existing system. Faced with a corrupt and unresponsive administration, reformers became revolutionaries. Many Catholics who had optimistically and patiently looked to the eventual removal of their grievances by the government now turned to the United Irishmen and sought redress through rebellion. According to McNally, Catholic leaders 'declared that though there was a time when they looked no further than a reform in parliament and a full emancipation of the Catholic body, yet now their interests were general and not confined to themselves; the question to be determined was no longer a Catholic question but a national question—the freedom of Ireland'.[119] The Catholics had become patriots.

While the early 1790s offered many opportunities for the open expression of political criticism, the coming of war in 1793 closed many of these channels. No longer could the radicals hope to give the popular will its most awesome expression through the medium of the convention. Nor could they exploit the public spectre of the armed citizen militia embodied in the Volunteers to carry out their threat to ascendancy government. Their initial strategy of mobilizing public opinion through a loose network of reform clubs, culminating in a convention of the people's representatives which would effect change peacefully, was no longer practical.

And yet the revolutionary strategy which succeeded these reform aims employed a similar model for overcoming ascendancy refusal to accept the popular will. The loose affiliation of clubs was replaced by a more or less centrally co-ordinated, hierarchical system, meeting in secret, but nevertheless actively and publicly courting a mass following. The contradictions involved in coupling secrecy with mass recruitment plagued the United Irish movement throughout its so-called revolutionary phase, leaving it open to infiltration by government agents at all levels of the organization, and

---

[118] William Wentworth Fitzwilliam, 4th earl, *Second letter . . . to the earl of Carlisle* (2nd edn., London, 1795), 8–9. For Fitzwilliam's account of his viceroyalty, see this and id., *First letter . . . to the earl of Carlisle* (3rd edn., London, 1795).

[119] Quoted in Lecky, *Ireland*, iii. 458.

requiring an opportunistic mode of enlistment which heightened class and sectarian tensions rather than diffusing them. But underlying this strategy was the old commitment to represent the popular will. When popular representative assemblies were outlawed in 1793, the radicals were forced to enrol the masses directly into their organization, which was thus legitimized as a popular assembly of sorts, a representative body led by the people's tribunes, expressing the popular will and, when ready, assuming power in the name of the people.

The mass-based, national, revolutionary organization which the United Irishmen set out to build after 1795 required that the middle-class republicans expand their base among the lower classes of Ireland. Thus the United Irishmen launched an energetic recruitment drive, particularly, but not primarily, geared towards enlisting the loose association of Catholic agrarian rebels and plebeian radicals known as the Defenders into the republican organization. The Defenders had developed out of lower-class sectarian conflict in County Armagh in the mid-1780s as a sort of Catholic protection society. But as Defenderism spread from Ulster to Leinster and northern Connacht, it increasingly took on the character of traditional agrarian secret societies. In Dublin, however, Defenderism assumed a more political, republican complexion, attracting workers and artisans excluded from the more élitist society of United Irishmen in the capital. The value of the Defenders to the United Irishmen was not only that they provided the republicans with an entrée into rural, Catholic Ireland, but that the Catholic insurgents had also infiltrated the largely Catholic Irish militia, created in 1793 to provide for Ireland's defence in the event of a French invasion. By securing a significant body of militiamen to the republican cause, the United Irishmen might well be assured of a victory if and when it became necessary to raise the standard of insurrection.

But the United Irishmen had reason to fear these new allies, actuated as they were by social and economic grievances underscored by a violent sectarianism. The middle-class radicals ran the risk of themselves becoming victims of the popular fury that they were attempting to unleash against an intransigent government. The United Irishmen would not have enrolled the masses in their insurrectionary movement if they had not believed that the middle class would remain in control of the revolution that they were trying to effect. For this belief, there were several reasons. By recruiting the lower classes, and especially the militia, the United Irishmen hoped to preempt an armed contest with the government. The establishment would realize that resistance to the national will was futile, and would therefore concede the radicals' demands for popular, representative government. But if the government proved intransigent and an insurrection was required, then the United Irishmen hoped to make it as bloodless and orderly as possible. To do this, they tore a page from the Glorious Revolution of 1688 and sought aid from a foreign power. Republican France would not only assist the United Irishmen in liberating their country, but would also protect them from the kind of class warfare that might follow the fall of the old regime in Ireland. Thus the middle-class republicans required the Defenders to enhance United Irish credibility with the French, and they needed the French to protect themselves against the Defenders.

In voluntary exile because of his involvement in the Jackson affair, Theobald Wolfe Tone undertook the mission to France. With no credentials to speak of, representing a mass revolutionary organization that barely existed, and seeking a major intervention on the part of the French, Tone's mission succeeded beyond his expectations.[120] The Directory, impressed by Tone's picture of an Ireland ready for a revolution and needing only the spark of an invasion by France, agreed to Tone's request. In December 1796 the first fruits of Tone's negotiations appeared off the southern Irish coast at Bantry, but inclement weather and the failure of the Cork peasantry to rally to the French invaders led to the failure of the expedition. Nevertheless, the Bantry Bay incident confirmed both the willingness of the French to aid Irish rebels and the vulnerability of Ireland to an invasion attempt, and thousands of recruits subsequently flocked to the republican standard.

The problem with the French alliance, however, was that it required the United Irishmen to commit themselves to an insurrectionary, separatist strategy before they possessed a national organization capable of backing up their claims to represent an armed people determined on its own liberation. By pinning their hopes on a successful French invasion as a preliminary to a mass insurrection, the United Irish leaders lost some control over the revolutionary momentum of their mobilization. Having built up a mass organization quickly, partly on the strength of the expectation that French assistance would be forthcoming, these leaders then found it necessary to contain the revolutionary enthusiasm that they had generated, causing discontent and suspicion among the ranks. The repeated failure of the French to launch a successful invasion at an appropriate time and place contributed further to demoralization, while in the mean time republicans were becoming increasingly vulnerable to the government's rigorous counter-insurgency campaign. When the United Irishmen finally decided to act independently of their French allies in May 1798, they found themselves seriously weakened in the north and victims of the defections of half-hearted revolutionaries who had counted on French aid as the only guarantee of success.

The alliances contracted by the United Irishmen in the cause of revolution were thus a source of anxiety as well as of strength. Middle-class

[120] For an assessment of Tone's mission, see Marianne Elliott, 'The United Irishman as diplomat', in Patrick J. Corish (ed.), *Radicals, rebels, and establishments* (Belfast, 1985).

republicans hoped to steer a course through the hazardous waters of a potentially predatory French ally on the one side and a militantly Catholic Defender association on the other. Both allies were necessary to make the United Irishmen a formidable revolutionary organization, but, taken together, these alliances contributed to disunity among the leaders, demoralization within the ranks, and an ugly explosion of sectarian hostility in Ireland.

Some United Irish leaders, however, were concerned by the influx of such vast numbers of recruits, secured through the republican campaign of recruitment and propaganda. Henry Joy McCracken lamented to James Hope that 'what we had latterly gained in numbers we lost in quality'.[121] United Irish success at home and the prospect of French assistance convinced the moderate, the wavering, and the opportunistic that the days of the ascendancy were numbered, and that those who wished to pursue their own self-interest should quickly jump on the republican bandwagon. The result, according to James Hope, was that the organization had become suffused with informers and traitors who repented their hasty decision to side with the United Irishmen once the government commenced its counter-offensive. Furthermore, the movement itself, by becoming so strategically dependent on France, had lost its ability to act effectively and purposively in the face of government repression. 'The majority of the leaders', lamented Hope, 'became foreign-aid men and were easily elevated or depressed by the news from France, and amongst their ranks spies were chiefly found.'[122] Hope regarded the French alliance as lending the Irish republican movement merely the illusion of strength: 'Their plausible pretensions soon lulled the people into confidence.'[123] But Hope had travelled around the country as a United Irish emissary. He doubted that the sight of a French tricolour would persuade a majority of shrewd Irish peasants to rally around the green flag, unless, of course, they were already adequately organized within the republican movement. And if they were well organized, what need was there for the French to land? 'The seeds of corruption', declared Hope in true republican analysis, 'were sown in our society' as a consequence of this reliance on the French.[124]

Nevertheless, the alliance and the heartening success of French arms did draw thousands of recruits, timid though they might be, to the United Irish cause. 'Count not on our loyalty,' Edward Cooke, secretary at the Castle, sardonically observed. 'We follow the strongest.'[125] But, fortunately for Cooke and his fellow loyalists, United Irish strength was, as Hope maintained, illusory. Internal dissensions, an effective counter-revolutionary campaign, and the failure of the French alliance to deliver the goods

---

[121] Hope, 'Autobiographical memoir', 106. [122] Ibid. 105. [123] Ibid.
[124] Ibid. 107.
[125] Edward Cooke to Lord Auckland, 9 Feb. 1797 (PRONI, Sneyd papers, T3229/2/22).

contributed to the erosion of the strength of the republican movement. Furthermore, the uneasy combination of different religious and social groups within the movement and a mode of recruitment that exacerbated class and sectarian tensions and relied on a mixture of terror and reward were much less able to withstand a vigorous government assault.

3

Mobilization and Counter-Revolution

ALTHOUGH the appearance of a French fleet in Bantry Bay in 1796 convinced the government that the United Irishmen, especially when allied to a belligerent foreign power, posed a formidable threat to the British–Irish connection, Castle officials had enjoyed little success in crushing or even containing the republican movement throughout the previous year. County Antrim was, as one correspondent put it, 'the principal source of the present treasonable practices'.[1] In the early months of insurrectionary mobilization Antrim provided the greatest number of United Irishmen, but Down was not far behind. In August 1796 one Down magistrate reported that three-quarters of the people of that county were 'up'.[2]

A flood of reports poured into Dublin Castle from all parts of the province of Ulster in 1796 and 1797 expressing alarm at the emboldened activities and growth of the United Irish movement.[3] Having established so quickly and firmly this base of support in the north-east of Ulster, the United Irishmen soon extended the movement westward. Camden reported to Portland in December 1796 that the most disturbed counties then were Tyrone and Derry.[4] Throughout the previous several months the lord lieutenant had been inundated with magistrates' reports from these two counties lamenting the intrusion of the United Irish system into their neighbourhoods. 'Matters are growing worse in the neighbourhood of Cookstown,' declared Thomas Knox in November 1796. 'The reign of terror is completely established here.'[5] James Stewart of Killymoon confirmed the deteriorating condition of that area: 'The situation of this neighbourhood is become alarming. . . . After a day or two there will not remain any magistrates . . . to assist me.'[6] John Richardson of Coleraine observed that his neighbourhood 'continues hourly to shew still stronger symptoms of insurrection and the danger appears fast approaching'.[7] 'A most dangerous

---

[1] —— to Isaac Corry, 12 May 1796 (SPOI, Rebellion papers, 620/23/102).
[2] Andrew Newton to Dublin Castle, 30 Aug. 1796 (ibid. 620/23/9).
[3] For the claim that the United Irishmen possessed insignificant support in the other Ulster counties besides Antrim and Down, see Charles Dickson, *Revolt in the north: Antrim and Down in 1798* (Dublin, 1960); Peter Gibbon, 'The origins of the Orange Order and the United Irishmen', *Economy and Society*, 1 (1972), 134–63.
[4] Earl Camden to duke of Portland, 21 Dec. 1796 (PROHO 100/65/177–8); see also Conway Blizard to Dublin Castle, [?] 1796 (SPOI, Rebellion papers, 620/27/7).
[5] Thomas Knox to Dublin Castle, 27 Nov. 1796 (SPOI, Rebellion papers, 620/26/83).
[6] James Stewart to Dublin Castle, 5 Nov. 1796 (ibid. 620/26/20).
[7] John Richardson to Dublin Castle, 26 Oct. 1796 (ibid. 620/25/189).

conspiracy exists and is rapidly spreading' through the district of Dungannon, reported W. C. Lindsay.[8] And the contagion spread westward in the succeeding months. From Omagh, a clerical magistrate confessed that his area had 'fallen entirely under the domination of the disaffected'.[9] Reports from the Derry–Donegal border in February 1797 confirmed that the United Irish movement had extended through the northern half of the province of Ulster.[10] In March 1797 General Knox described the geographical strength of the United Irish movement as follows: 'In the counties of Down, Antrim, Derry, and parts of Donegal and Tyrone the whole people are ill-disposed . . . but in the counties of Armagh, Cavan, Monaghan, Fermanagh, and part of Tyrone . . . a proportion of the people are hostile to the United Irishmen.'[11]

Magistrates' reports provide only partial evidence for the spread of the United Irish organization. The problem with relying solely on these accounts as an indicator of the geographical mobilization of the United Irishmen is that many of the local authorities preferred to forsake their duty in order to preserve their lives. Isolated, vulnerable, and constantly threatened with assassination if they exerted themselves in opposition to the United Irishmen, many magistrates either left the country or suffered the conspiracy in silence and inactivity. Thus, while the reports of active magistrates regarding the expansion of the United Irish system give some indication of the geographical distribution of the movement, the silence of those from other parts of the country cannot be interpreted as evidence of United Irish weakness there. Indeed, where the United Irishmen were strong and well organized, the magistracy was weak and the occasion for disturbance limited. Consequently, as Camden complained to Portland in August 1796, 'that part of the country whence most danger is to be apprehended is apparently most quiet and peaceable'.[12] The government's dilemma is shared by the historian of the United Irish movement: does the absence of disturbance in a neighbourhood indicate widespread loyalty or entrenched disaffection?

The returns of membership made available to the United Irish leadership demonstrate that the numerical strength of the movement lay in the north-east. Table 3.1 presents these returns for the province of Ulster for October 1796 and February and May 1797. Here we can see the extent to which the movement spread from the north-east after 1796, while at the same time

[8] W. C. Lindsay to Dublin Castle, 22 Oct. 1796 (SPOI, Rebellion papers, 620/25/182).
[9] Revd James ——— to bishop of Clogher, 9 May 1797 (ibid. 620/30/40).
[10] See e.g. Sir George F. Hill to John Beresford, 5 Feb. 1797 (ibid. 620/28/217); Revd William Hamilton to Edward Cooke, 19 Feb. 1797 (ibid. 620/28/259); abstract of information regarding the state of the north during the last 6 months, 13 Feb. 1797 (ibid. 620/28/280).
[11] Gen. John Knox to Gen. Gerard Lake, 11 Mar. 1797 (BL, Pelham papers, Add. MS 33103/265–6).
[12] Camden to Portland, 6 Aug. 1796 (PROHO 100/64/168–72).

noting the persistence of Antrim and Down as containing the solid core of United Irish strength. In October 1796 the United Irishmen clearly had a significant presence in Tyrone and Derry as well, the returns for these counties (4,855 and 3,696 respectively) reflecting a fairly accurate count. But the returns for Armagh, Donegal, and Monaghan are clearly wishful estimates and were probably inflated in an attempt to encourage supporters; at least we can presume that the organization in those counties was not sufficiently advanced to produce an accurate return of membership.

TABLE 3.1. *United Irish membership returns in Ulster, 1796–1797*

County	Oct. 1796	Feb. 1797	May 1797
Antrim	15,000	20,940	22,716
Armagh	1,000	4,500	17,000
Cavan	n/a	1,000	6,880
Derry	3,696	10,000	10,500
Donegal	2,000	5,050	9,648
Down	11,016	15,000	26,153
Fermanagh	n/a	2,000	2,000
Monaghan	1,000	3,200	9,020
Tyrone	4,855	7,500	14,000
TOTAL	38,567	69,190	117,917

Note: n/a = not available.
Source: PRO HO 100/62/333–4; SPOI, Rebellion papers, 620/28/285, 297, 620/30/61.

The steep rise in membership in all the Ulster counties by February 1797 indicates not only the success of the United Irish recruiting drive, but also the boost given to United Irish fortunes by the Bantry Bay invasion attempt, which attracted so many new members to the organization. Again, however, casual estimates took the place of actual returns for the southern counties of Ulster, while the returns for the northern counties, though possibly exaggerated, indicate a significant and potentially formidable presence. Furthermore, the rise in membership in southern Ulster for both February and May 1797 also reflects the forging of the alliance between the United Irishmen and the Defenders.[13] One can safely assume that the huge leap in the figures for Armagh, Donegal, Monaghan, Cavan, and Fermanagh—and, indeed, for Down, Tyrone, and Derry as well—indicates a substantial influx of Defenders into the United Irish system. But it should be remembered that these Defenders were rather loosely associated with the United

[13] For the Defenders and the United Irishmen with them, see Ch. 6.

Irishmen, and although the returns of membership for May 1797 suggest extensive numerical strength in Ulster (117,917 were supposedly enrolled in the movement), they do not tell us much about the actual strength of the organization. In other words, numbers alone, contrary to the assumption of the United Irish leadership, do not indicate a formidable republican movement ready to be mobilized for insurrectionary activity.

An effective United Irish organization in the counties of Fermanagh, Cavan, Monaghan, and much of Donegal and Armagh seems to have been more of a fantasy among the republicans than an actuality. The reports of magistrates in Derry and Tyrone frequently attested to the growing United Irish threat, more formidable, to be sure, in the eastern part of both counties adjacent to County Antrim, but also strong in the west as well. What can be said in conclusion is that United Irish participation extended persistently beyond Antrim and Down after 1796, but that the system of organization weakened the further one went from Belfast. United Irish activists plagued magistrates and other loyalists all over Ulster, but such occurrences tended to reflect lack of discipline and control over the rank and file rather than deliberate republican policy.

Contributing to the disturbances was the emergence of the Anglo-Irish ascendancy's own popular base of support. Many lower-class protestants, attached by ties of deference to the landed élite, or simply alarmed by the relief measures accorded to Catholics in the past two decades, began to mobilize as champions of the establishment. In Ulster, and especially in Armagh, these protestant militants reacted to resurgent Defenderism and spreading republicanism by forming the Orange Order, often with gentry acquiescence if not encouragement. By late 1795 Armagh once again became the scene of vicious sectarian warfare between Defenders and Orangemen.

The process of pacifying Ulster had been proceeding for a few months prior to the abortive French invasion attempt in December 1796. Noting with alarm the spread of the United Irish movement in Ulster, as well as the revival of sectarian hostility in Armagh, the viceroy, Earl Camden, initiated a legislative assault against rural disorder and sedition during the parliamentary session in the spring of 1796. The first order of business was to pass an indemnity act to prevent the prosecution of Commander-in-Chief Carhampton and his imitators, who had used extraordinary and illegal measures to suppress Defenderism in Connacht.[14] But the cornerstone of the government's strategy to defeat sedition at home was the insurrection act, a severe and comprehensive measure which recognized that, in many parts of the country, the judicial system had broken down under intimidation and coercion by the insurgents. The act made it a capital offence to

[14] W. E. H. Lecky, *A history of Ireland in the eighteenth century* (5 vols., London, 1898), iii. 449. For these disturbances, see Ch. 6.

administer an illegal (i.e. United Irish or Defender) oath, and the taking of such an oath was made punishable by transportation for life. Registration of arms was demanded. The lord lieutenant and privy council were empowered to declare districts in a state of disturbance upon the supplication of local magistrates. Inhabitants were prohibited from leaving their homes from one hour after sunset to one hour before sunrise. Justices of the peace could search all houses during prohibited hours, and might demand the surrender even of registered arms. Clauses were introduced concerning daytime assemblies, nocturnal meetings in public places, and the circulation of seditious papers. Magistrates in proclaimed areas were permitted to send to the fleet all persons whom they considered disorderly.[15]

Camden's chief secretary, Thomas Pelham, warned Portland: 'If this bill . . . does not restore peace and give the laws and constitution their necessary operation, we must have recourse to the sword.'[16] The strategy was to bend the constitution to save the constitution, but the danger was that the ministers would pervert and distort the law to such an extent that it would no longer command the respect or the allegiance of the people of Ireland. In a sense, the insurrection act was something of a turning-point. It signified the administration's failure to suppress the United Irishmen through normal judicial channels. This failure initiated the resort to government terror in order to counteract the equally ruthless violence of the United Irishmen and their Defender allies.

An extreme and costly measure, the insurrection act was employed only when traditional methods proved ineffective. The first area to be proclaimed was east Down in November 1796, a district noted for its linen manufacture.[17] Later in that month the northern part of Armagh received the same treatment. This area, adjacent to the proclaimed district in Down, shared its association with the linen industry.[18] In early December the neighbourhoods of two key urban centres, Newry and Armagh, were added to the list.[19] Towards the end of December the district around Dungannon in County Tyrone found itself subjected to these harsh measures.[20] The first five months of 1797 saw central and west Derry, east Donegal, and northwest Tyrone join the swelling number of proclaimed districts.[21]

Generalizations about a pattern of distribution of disturbed districts are difficult to make. Yet it is most striking that the proclaimed districts were concentrated within the so-called 'linen triangle', an area characterized by the advanced development of the linen industry. The triangle extended roughly from Dungannon to Newry to Lisburn. According to the historian of the Irish linen industry, Conrad Gill, linen manufacturing in this area

[15] R. B. McDowell, *Ireland in the age of imperialism and revolution* (Oxford, 1979), 552–3.
[16] Thomas Pelham to duke of Portland, 31 Mar. 1796 (PROHO 100/62/94–8).
[17] *BNL*, 21 Nov. 1796.   [18] *BNL*, 25, 28 Nov. 1796.   [19] *BNL*, 5, 16 Dec. 1796.
[20] *BNL*, 30 Dec. 1796.   [21] *BNL*, 13 Jan., 6, 13, 20 Feb., 2 May 1797.

was characterized by advanced capitalist concentration, leading to the pro-
letarianization of former weaver craftsmen.[22]

Of course, the linen triangle was also infamous for the persistence of sectarian hostilities, and the proclamations to a great extent reflected the
difficulties encountered by local magistrates in dealing with that situation.
Early in November 1796 a west Down magistrate, Robert Waddell, urged
the government to proclaim certain adjacent parishes in County Armagh in
which the victims of outrages included both protestant and Catholic
weavers who 'dare not put their webs into their looms lest they should
have it cut to pieces. . . . There is not a night almost [that] passes without
breaking, robbery, burning of houses, sometimes murder, and very often
near it.' United Irish victims tended to be more substantial members of the
community, and in fact Waddell dissociated these insurgents from the disturbances that he was reporting. In closing, he remarked: 'As to the United
Irishmen, they are going on in their own accursed and evil way,' implying
that, odious as the republicans were, they were not responsible for the sectarian hostilities plaguing the neighbourhood.[23]

Within a few months, however, the United Irishmen became prominent
fixtures in the disturbed areas of the Armagh countryside. As one loyalist
informed the government: 'The United work is drawing very near us, and
which is composed of Scotch and Irish, and they certainly would think it
God's service to sacrifice Orangemen.' Around Newry, 'whole bodies of
Orangemen turned over to the United men'.[24] Although the social status of
these insurgents remained unclear, their religious affiliations were scrutinized by concerned observers. The assertion that the 'Scotch and Irish', or
Presbyterians and Roman Catholics, formed the basis of the United Irish
movement was confirmed in August 1796 by the Revd Thomas Higginson,
an Anglican clergyman in west Down. It was Higginson's belief that the
United Irishmen were chiefly Dissenters, supported by Catholic Defenders.
Though the movement was increasing rapidly, it was as yet rather
restrained in its operations. But if the harvest proved bountiful, Higginson
feared that, with the 'means of subsistence for another year' in their hands,
the United Irishmen would try their strength in a more aggressive and, perhaps, decisive manner. He was in no doubt that they would sway much of
the population to the cause: 'They will make the supporters of the government like the loyalists of the Vendée.'[25]

The absence of proclaimed districts in County Antrim certainly does not
mean that the countryside around Belfast remained immune to sedition
emanating from that town. On the contrary, Antrim, after Down, furnished

[22] Conrad Gill, *The rise of the Irish linen industry* (1st edn., 1925; Oxford, 1964), 273.
[23] Robert Waddell to Edward Cooke, 8 Nov. 1796 (SPOI, Rebellion papers, 620/26/29).
[24] Revd M ——— ll to Dublin Castle, 29 Mar. 1797 (ibid. 620/29/205).
[25] Revd Thomas Higginson to John Foster, 22 Aug. 1796 (ibid. 620/24/156).

more recruits to the United Irish cause than any other county in Ireland. Aside from the western part of the county adjacent to Armagh, Down, too, was notably free from the onerous insurrection act. In a perverse way, this situation reflected the greater strength of the movement in these two north-eastern counties. The United Irishmen there were more disciplined and better organized than elsewhere in Ulster. Only in these two counties, after all, did United Irishmen participate in any significant numbers in the rebellion of 1798. Arms raids were less frequent there than in west Ulster, perhaps because many United Irishmen in Down and Antrim had already acquired weapons during their Volunteer days.

Different conditions prevailed along the Donegal–Derry border in west Ulster. Here was another concentration of proclaimed districts. United Irish bodies of up to 800 men roamed the region in search of arms. William Rae, a Donegal magistrate, attributed the rise of rural disorder to the absence of resident landlords, 'for where they are settled on their estates and have been active, the country round them is quiet'.[26] A more precise analysis was forwarded to the government by the Revd William Hamilton in February 1797. He described the most disturbed area as a ten-mile semicircle extending into Donegal, with the city of Derry as its centre, a region which constituted the wealthiest part of the county. The further away from this area a neighbourhood lay, the less likely it was to be disaffected. In addition, there were distinct demographic features in the geography of disturbances. Within Hamilton's semicircle of disaffection Presbyterians dominated, while in the more peaceable areas to the south the established church held sway, and to the west Catholics were preponderant.[27] Earlier in the year Hamilton had boasted to the government of his success in detaching Anglicans, and especially Catholics, from the seditious influence of the radical Dissenters.[28] Catholics appeared to be less prominent in the United Irish movement in west Ulster than in Armagh and Down, though in both areas Presbyterians clearly stood out as the driving force behind the movement.

But the Donegal–Derry border did share one feature with the proclaimed districts in the east, and that was involvement in the linen industry. Although the industry in the west was not characterized by Gill as particularly advanced, it nevertheless played an important role in the rural economy, with the city of Derry being the chief point of entry for flax-seed.[29] The United Irishmen made great inroads among participants in the industry there. Sir Richard Musgrave maintained that in County Derry 'the great bleachers were almost universally obliged to countenance the conversion of

---

[26] William Rae to Sackville Hamilton, 27 Mar. 1797 (ibid. 620/29/116).
[27] Revd William Hamilton to Dublin Castle, 15 Feb. 1797 (ibid. 620/28/269).
[28] Hamilton to Dublin Castle, 14 Jan. 1797 (ibid. 620/28/99).
[29] William Vaughan Sampson, *Statistical survey of the county of Londonderry* (3rd edn., Dublin, 1802), 347.

their overseers and workmen to the United cause, that they might continue their business; but some did so from pure attachment to it. Such of them as were steadfast in their loyalty were under a necessity of discontinuing their bleaching for the season.'[30]

Alarmed northern magistrates continued to inform the Castle of the latest outrages committed by the republicans, particularly their intimidation of jurors and witnesses, which rendered the judicial system ineffective in dealing with the disturbances or the conspiracy behind them. Assassinations of informers and active opponents of the movement were becoming the order of the day. As early as March 1796 the normally cool-headed William Pollock of Newry informed the government that a general rising was expected daily, and that the loyal inhabitants of his neighbourhood were so ill-prepared to defend themselves that they might hold back the rebel tide for 'ten minutes and then we must submit to be butchered'.[31] The country 'is teeming with treason', declared another magistrate, 'and what is worse, treason methodised'.[32] Most frustrating to those responsible for maintaining law and order was the fact that, although the identities of the United Irishmen were frequently well known, there was insufficient evidence available to bring them successfully to trial. Although many informers kept the government well apprised of the development of the conspiracy, 'it will be difficult', one magistrate observed, 'to get one to come forward and prosecute, as they think there is no part in the three kingdoms they could be assured safe in.'[33] Even the victims of United Irish outrages were reluctant to prosecute their tormentors publicly: 'No man gives evidence because they say it is no use risking themselves when no one gets hanged.'[34]

By the autumn of 1796 the government and its allies were at a loss as to how to proceed in attacking the republican conspiracy. Initially reluctant to employ the full vigour of the insurrection act, frustrated in bringing insurgents to justice, unable to count on the terrorized magistracy, placed under the double threat of foreign invasion and internal rebellion, and forced to scatter its military force ineffectively throughout the country, the government once again resorted to extremely controversial legislation. Confident that his measures would soon become law when parliament was summoned in October 1796, Camden adopted the twin strategy of establishing a yeomanry and arresting republican chiefs.

Informers readily reported on the actions of Samuel Neilson, Henry Joy McCracken, Thomas Russell, and others, but refused to repeat their allegations in a public court. From September 1796, however, the government

[30] Sir Richard Musgrave, *Memoires of the different rebellions in Ireland* . . . (3rd edn., 2 vols., Dublin, 1802), i. 236.
[31] William Pollock to Dublin Castle, 4 Mar. 1796 (SPOI, Rebellion papers, 620/23/41).
[32] Knox to Dublin Castle, 4 July 1796 (ibid. 620/24/16).
[33] Andrew Macnevin to Edward Cooke, 27 June 1796 (ibid. 620/23/197).
[34] James Waddell to Robert Ross, 14 June 1796 (ibid. 620/23/174).

issued warrants for the arrest of the known northern leaders. As Pelham noted: 'Nothing can be done till the heads of the United Irishmen can be taken up.'[35] Completing this coup of arresting the United Irish leaders, Camden summoned parliament in October to suspend habeas corpus in cases of high treason, thus acquiring the right to detain the state prisoners indefinitely.[36]

The government thus demonstrated its resolve to deal with the current crisis, thereby encouraging the reluctant and timid magistrates. In one respect, the arrests of the United Irish leaders were very successful, in that few eluded the warrants issued against them. But the government had hoped to throw the movement into disorder and confusion by removing the leadership. In this, the Castle was frustrated, for new leaders, though perhaps not of the same calibre as those arrested, were chosen, and the organization seemed to have survived the government assault intact. In fact, however, the centre of the conspiracy began to shift from Belfast to Dublin.

The immediate response of the United Irishmen to the arrest of their leaders was one of boldness and, indeed, impudence. It seemed as if the republicans were intent on taunting and embarrassing the government, and their response took on an almost playful aspect. Over the next few months the newspapers and magistrates reported the assembly of massive gatherings of country people to raise the state prisoners' crops. This was a traditional way of showing popular respect for a local leader, but, under the circumstances, it appeared as a United Irish challenge to the government. The republicans were demonstrating their numbers and their discipline to great effect, and thus scored a propaganda victory of sorts.[37]

Stronger exertions might be required of government. In the same session of parliament Camden had received legislative approval to create a yeomanry force. The viceroy was, of course, reluctant to institute this auxiliary volunteer army, recalling, as he did, the politicization of the Volunteers in the late 1770s and early 1780s and not wishing to spawn yet another armed association in Ireland, legal or illegal. The inability of the British to send sufficient troops to Ireland, however, made the creation of such a force a necessity.[38] The government was determined to keep the yeomanry firmly under its control. Its officers were to be appointed by the viceroy and placed under the command of the general in charge of the district. Arms and ammunition would be supplied by the government, but their

[35] Edward Cooke to Thomas Pelham, 14 July 1796 (BL, Pelham papers, Add. MS 33102/68–71).

[36] Lecky, *History of Ireland*, iii. 459.   [37] See Ch. 9 for these potato diggings.

[38] For Camden's concerns, see Camden to Portland, 6 Aug. 1796 (PROHO 100/62/63). 'I do not like to resort to yeomanry cavalry or infantry or armed associations if I can help it— but I see no other resource in the present times. The army must be withdrawn from many of its quarters and must be drawn together to act in larger bodies than it has lately done' (Earl Camden to Thomas Pelham, 28 Aug. 1796 (BL, Pelham papers, Add. MS 33102/115–17)).

distribution would be strictly supervised. It was hoped that the yeomanry would provide an impartial police force, but, under the circumstances, it was doomed to become yet another sectarian association.[39]

The demand for a yeomanry came from active local magistrates, who wished to create a counter-force to United Irish terror and intimidation.[40] The plan was to enrol the loyal and well-affected into an armed defence association proclaiming its devotion to the king and the constitution. This would all have been quite innocuous in itself, and was in fact reminiscent of the origin of the Volunteers in 1778, but during a time of radically polarized political opinions and sectarian hostility, such a force was bound, as Camden feared, to be seen as a politicized, sectarian association of Irish reactionaries, let loose upon an innocent and injured people whose only crime was a desire for equal political and civil rights. 'By arming the property I shall be construed as arming the protestants against the papists.'[41] And this was how the United Irishmen painted the new yeomanry as they launched their campaign to discourage recruitment to it. The major and inescapable problem with the yeomanry was that it was a sectarian band, and, as warm supporters of the government, the yeomen were implicated in the administration's intransigent and ruthless policies.[42] As Grattan maintained in opposing the measure: 'Under an administration that was sent here to defeat a Catholic bill, a protestant mob very naturally conceives itself a part of the state.'[43]

The republicans threatened potential enlistees with dire consequences should they enrol, and those who left such warnings unheeded were frequent targets of nocturnal visits by the United Irishmen, who confiscated their arms and warned them sternly against any further activity. As a consequence, enrolment in the yeomanry was rather disappointing during the first few months of its formation.[44] In Orange-dominated areas in Armagh and Tyrone, however, the government enjoyed some success, but this only confirmed the identification of the new force with the protestant ascendancy. Although disaffection was by no means universal in other parts of Ulster, the loyal were far too intimidated to come forward and enlist in the corps, and waited to see which way the wind was blowing before they committed themselves. When the protestant wind blew over Bantry Bay in December 1796, however, enlistments increased rapidly.

Just as the appearance of the French fleet in Bantry Bay confirmed the

[39] McDowell, *Ireland*, 557–9.

[40] See e.g. Knox to Dublin Castle, 4 July 1796 (SPOI, Rebellion papers, 620/24/16).

[41] Camden to Portland, 3 Sept. 1796 (PROHO 100/62/208–14).

[42] See e.g. the United Irish handbill, 'Portrait of a soldier yeoman' (SPOI, Rebellion papers, 620/28/249).

[43] Quoted in Lecky, *History of Ireland*, iii. 461.

[44] See e.g. John Boyd to Hugh Boyd, 5 Oct. 1796 (SPOI, Rebellion papers, 620/25/148); Andrew Newton to Revd Dr —— O'Connor, 6 Nov. 1796 (ibid. 620/26/26).

growing power of the United Irishmen, so too it convinced timid loyalists that their only defence against internal rebellion on the one hand and foreign invasion on the other was their own exertions. Those magistrates who had chosen to remain in the country to counter United Irish activity redoubled their efforts and worked avidly to arouse their loyal tenants into bold defiance of the republicans. While United Irish threats cowed many into submission, they convinced many more that the time had come for harsh reaction. The Orangemen led the way into the yeomanry corps, but they were quickly followed by moderate reformers who, while uncomfortable with the government's anti-reform and anti-Catholic policies, none the less dreaded the spectre of popular insurrection which the United Irishmen were raising. Indeed, the seeming unanimity of even Belfast's reform sentiment was broken when, early in January 1797, ninety-seven persons enlisted in the first corps of yeoman infantry and cavalry in Belfast.[45] Martha McTier had some sympathy for the new yeomen, pointing out that many of them, as former Volunteers, were uneasy about swearing loyalty to the present laws and constitution, especially since so many of them found some of those laws—the convention act, the gunpowder act, and the insurrection act, to name the most glaring—offensive and contrary to their political principles.

These indeed are trying times, and the *right* path becomes complex. Oaths are taken and reconciled in the usual way by mental reservation, and I pity the brave and honourable men who must either decline arming against a foreign foe or swear to support the present government. . . . About a hundred have agreed to arm . . . yet there is enough apparent spirit in this enrolment to make it appear honourable to some. God forbid that any should ever be in a situation too feelingly to repent it.[46]

In fact, Martha McTier suggested that yeomanry enrolment was working out exactly as the government had hoped. The men of property were realizing that, regardless of their differing political opinions, they had to stand or fall with the present government. 'In this same town I hardly know what is called a gentleman who is not enrolled. . . . The moneyed [*sic*] men are subscribing.'[47] In other parts of the north as well, the invasion attempt had a sobering effect on the men of property. W. C. Lindsay of Dungannon reported to Pelham that

in consequence of the French appearing on our coasts, the spirit of loyalty and true patriotism has been excited in persons of all denominations in my neighbourhood. . . . I am fully of opinion that if this was now followed up by the exertions of

---

[45] John Brown to Thomas Pelham, 4 Jan. 1797 (ibid. 620/28/31).

[46] Martha McTier to William Drennan, 13 Jan. 1797 (*The Drennan letters*, ed. D. A. Chart (Belfast, 1931), 247).

[47] Martha McTier to Drennan, 30 Jan. 1797 (ibid. 249).

gentlemen of landed property, the principles of the United Irishmen that have hitherto prevailed might be so thoroughly counteracted as to be no longer worth
notice.[48]

On 3 March 1797 Chief Secretary Thomas Pelham wrote to General
Lake, commanding general of the northern district, detailing the sorry state
of Antrim, Down, Tyrone, Derry, and Donegal, where 'secret and treasonable associations still continue to an alarming degree'. Pelham ordered Lake
to disarm the agitators with the help of the yeomanry, to disperse seditious
assemblies, and to take action 'without waiting for the sanction and assistance of civil authority'. Lake was to consider the areas involved as, in
effect, under martial law.[49] This communication was followed on 13 March
by an order of Lake's demanding the surrender of all arms and ammunition
by non-military personnel.[50] Parties of militia, regulars, and yeomen
scoured the countryside over the succeeding months to enforce this order.
By the end of May 1797 some 8,000 regulars, sent to the north from
Scotland, had been added to this already imposing force.[51]

In conjunction with this military onslaught, Camden issued a proclamation on 17 May 1791 offering a pardon to all those who came forward and
recanted their United Irish oaths, surrendered their arms, and swore allegiance to the king's government.[52] These policies eventually proved successful, and by the end of the year the French traveller De Latocnaye was able
to summarize the results thus:

The United Irishmen, who for long had been accustomed to obey no orders but
those of their leaders, and to despise the soldiers and the government, paid no
attention at first to these commands; but finding soon that the government had serious intentions, and seeing that their houses were burned and that imprisonments
followed illegal assembling, they broke up immediately, passing, it may be said, in
the winking of an eye, from audacity to fear, most of them hurrying to make submission and to do what was required of them.[53]

General Lake, the officer in charge of this 'dragooning' of Ulster, was perhaps the most brutal and insensitive man on the Irish general staff after
Lord Carhampton. His zealous repression of sedition made him the darling
of the most reactionary wing of the Anglo-Irish ascendancy. He regarded the
disturbances in the north as a problem to be addressed only with unrelenting force, 'which I trust will wear those wretches out'.[54] Pelham assured
Lake that any excesses on his part would receive government sanction, thus

[48] W. C. Lindsay to Thomas Pelham, 5 Jan. 1797 (SPOI, Rebellion papers, 620/28/43).
[49] Thomas Pelham to Gen. Gerard Lake, 3 Mar. 1797 (NLI, Knox papers, MS 56/32).
[50] *BNL*, 13 Mar. 1797.   [51] *FJ*, 13 Mar. 1797.   [52] *BNL*, 19 May 1797.
[53] De Latocnaye, *A Frenchman's walk through Ireland, 1796–7*, trans. John Stevenson
(Belfast, 1917), 262.
[54] Gen. Gerard Lake to Thomas Pelham, 13 Mar. 1797 (BL, Pelham papers, Add. MS
33103/220–1).

encouraging an already sanguinary and brutal temperament.[55] Within the first week of the implementation of the disarming policy, however, even Castle officials were beginning to wonder if Lake was not going too far. Reports were pouring into Dublin, complaining of the excesses and outrages committed by the military. Pelham urged Lake to use his authority to curb these breaches of proper discipline. 'I really do not know of any excesses committed by the military,' an ingenuous Lake replied.[56] Indeed, the general argued that even stronger measures would be required to bring the north to submission: 'I am convinced that the contest must lay between the army and the people,' though he conceded with perfunctory regret that among those people there were a number of innocent bystanders.[57]

In the first few weeks of their implementation in March 1797 Lake's Draconian measures had some effect in depriving the disaffected of their weapons. But this was largely because of the element of surprise involved in this offensive against the United Irishmen. Early reports in the conservative papers proclaimed the success of the policy, but such boasting was, in reality, premature.[58] Once the United Irishmen realized what was happening, they attempted to undermine Lake's campaign. Greater care was taken in hiding arms, and if suspected of disaffection, many United Irishmen would merely offer old, rusty, and unusable guns to the authorities, while feigning repentance and loyalty by swearing the oath of allegiance. Whereas many republicans regarded an oath as a solemn compact, others rationalized that swearing to a false and corrupt government was no breach of their integrity and in no way undermined their fundamental allegiance to the United Irish cause. The result was that the real victims of the government's coercive policy were often loyalists themselves, who were deprived of their arms and then left defenceless against the more cunning United Irishmen.[59] Eventually, however, in the summer of 1797, Lake redoubled his already vigorous exertions, and by the end of the year his policy showed signs of real success. Charles Teeling accurately described the state of the north under this repression: 'The gaols were now crowded with prisoners. Many private houses were turned into military provosts, floating prisons had been established, and the loathsome tenders stationed around the coasts received the surplus of the victims which the land prisons were unable to

---

[55] Pelham to Lake, 3 Mar. 1797 (NLI, Knox papers, MS 56/32).
[56] Lake to Pelham, 17 Mar. 1797 (BL, Pelham papers, Add. MS 33103/240–1).
[57] Lake to Pelham, 19 Mar. 1797 (ibid. 33103/254–5).
[58] See e.g. *FDJ*, 16 Mar. 1797; *BNL*, 17 Mar. 1797.
[59] See e.g. Alexander Stewart to Dublin Castle, 14 Mar. 1797 (SPOI, Rebellion papers, 620/29/69); C. M. Warburton to Edward Cooke, 17 Mar. 1797 (ibid. 620/29/85); marquess of Downshire, 26 Mar. 1797 (ibid. 620/29/114). As Downshire explained: 'The papist, the United Irishman, the turbulent, the disaffected, [and] the vagabonds concealed and denied their arms and are left now in the liberty of destroying the property and plundering the innocent and good subject'—who surrendered his.

contain.'[60] It appeared that, as a result of this unrelenting repression, peace and stability of a sort were returning to the turbulent and disaffected north.

Defections occurred in all ranks of the movement. Even as early as March 1796 many northern magistrates were happily observing daily desertions from the revolutionary party among gentlemen, prosperous farmers, and substantial tradesmen, along with increasing moderation in political views as the movement spread among the lower classes.[61] A Derry magistrate remarked that middle-class United Irishmen, 'having thus embarked in one vessel with a populace who look only to plunder . . . already quarrel at the helm. It is not the interest of the rich to encourage predatory outrage, and the lower orders are too impatient for the revolutionary advantages of constitutional innovations.'[62]

The picture at the other end of the social scale was equally pleasing to the eyes of loyalists. Popular reaction to the arrest of many republican leaders in Belfast in September 1796 should have served as a warning to the United Irishmen that their followers were not necessarily the committed and determined republicans required to overturn the regime. As Pelham remarked to the duke of York, a number of arrests occurred on fair-day,

and consequently an immense crowd of country people was collected. . . . The common people seemed in general well satisfied [with the arrests], and many expressed themselves so, which induces me to believe what I have heard represented by gentlemen in the country, namely that many of the lower class of people have taken oaths and entered societies and associations through fear.[63]

This apparent indifference—indeed, approval—with which the lower classes witnessed the arrest of their tribunes was confirmed by a magistrate in County Derry, who contemptuously observed that 'the lower class, with their usual inconsistency, praise the vigour of government in seizing their mock champions with the utmost *sang-froid*.'[64] Clearly, loyalists preferred to think that the people were merely deluded or coerced into supporting the republicans, and that a strong show of strength by the government would recall them to a sense of duty and submission. These same lower classes, interested in preserving themselves from the wrath of magistrates and landlords, may have merely feigned repentance and complacency about the arrest of their leaders. But whether these defections from the republican cause were real or fabricated is not the point. As Cooke proclaimed, 'We

---

[60] Charles Hamilton Teeling, *The history of the Irish rebellion of 1798 and sequel to the history of the Irish rebellion of 1798* (1st edn., 1876; Shannon, 1972), 50.

[61] See e.g. William Bristow to Dublin Castle, 31 Mar. 1796 (SPOI, Rebellion papers, 620/23/58).

[62] Henry Alexander to Dublin Castle, 24 Dec. 1796 (ibid. 620/26/150).

[63] Thomas Pelham to duke of York, 22 Sept. 1796 (BL, Pelham letter-book, Add. MS 33113/47–52).

[64] Henry Alexander to Edward Cooke, 26 Sept. 1796 (SPOI, Rebellion papers, 620/25/122).

follow the strongest,' or, as one magistrate asserted, the people 'want only encouragement and protection to become loyal and give up those who deluded them into their late improprieties'.[65] Encouragement and protection essentially meant a vigorous demonstration of government power which would undermine the United Irish contention that a republican victory was inevitable. Consequently, the rapid but unstable expansion of the United Irish system, the provocative acts of local republican societies, and the ever-present danger of a French invasion forced the government into a policy of ruthless coercion.

The state of Ulster in the winter of 1796–7 both demanded government intervention and gave the authorities the opportunity to be most effective in rousing loyalist opinion and suppressing the United Irishmen. The disturbed nature of the country and the emboldened activities of the constantly growing republican movement so alarmed the well-affected in the north as to initiate a surge of loyalism, which appeared most gratifying to a besieged government. The administration alone could not suppress the republican conspiracy in the north. It did not have enough troops, and, even if these had been available, they could not have acted effectively without local guidance. Thus the steady rise in yeomanry enrolment and the frequently published expressions of loyalty indicated that at last the government might be able to take the hitherto dangerous course of pacifying Ulster.[66]

On 9 March 1797 Camden delivered another of his pessimistic reports to Portland:

The state of the north has become more alarming, and the conduct of the ill-disposed has been more outrageous. Murder has accompanied robbery, and such a system of terror has been established that those persons who are well-inclined to support the laws and to range themselves with the friends of good order and government, have in many instances been alarmed into adoption of the system of the United Irishmen from an apprehension of not receiving efficient and speedy assistance from the exertions of magistrates and the support of the troops.

After describing in some detail the latest outrages and assassinations, Camden went on to discuss United Irish strategy, which was

to prevent the magistrate from acting and the yeomanry from assembling, and by these means to deprive the country of the services of both descriptions of persons. It is therefore become absolutely necessary, in order to keep that part of Ireland in any degree of good order, to assure the well-disposed that they will be protected and that the arm of government is strong enough to shield them from the execution of any threats they receive.

Actions must be undertaken, therefore, which would not 'suffer the cause of justice to be frustrated by the tendency of most of the local authorities

[65] Andrew Newton to Revd Richard Bourne, 4 Feb. 1797 (ibid. 620/28/206).
[66] For these loyalist resolutions, see e.g. *BNL*, 2 Jan. 1797.

to respect the delicacies of constitutional proprieties'.[67] In other words, it was time for the government to get down to the serious business of meeting terror with terror.

With loyalism beginning to reassert itself under the banner of the yeomanry corps, and with the insurrection act already in force in parts of Ulster, the government girded itself for a final struggle with the northern republicans. All resources were to be exploited, and all excesses countenanced. But it took the greater part of the year for these actions to bear fruit and to uproot that troublesome tree of liberty which had been so firmly planted in Ulster. In the judicial arena, the authorities forged for themselves the powerful weapon of the right to detain suspected traitors without the burden of bringing them to trial. Yet it was in the courts, operating under normal procedures, that the government sought to re-establish its authority and discredit republican claims to ascendancy.

When the United Irishmen dominated a neighbourhood, they often managed to paralyse the system of law enforcement through the intimidation of active magistrates, informers, and witnesses. The informer Edward Newell maintained that when he was a United Irishman, he was in fact a member of an assassination committee, and the government wasted no time in publicizing the existence of this sanguinary tool of the republican organization.[68] While James Hope and such United Irish leaders as O'Connor, Emmet, and MacNeven denied that any committee of assassination was ever officially sanctioned by the republican organization, the fact of numerous assassinations remains.[69] Individuals may have acted in self-defence. Local societies may well have felt particularly hounded and threatened by an active magistrate. When the threatening letter, which was a commonplace of United Irish activity, proved ineffectual, the insurgents felt obliged to follow up the warning. The victims were rarely innocent bystanders. Targets of assassination were either violently opposed to the movement or dangerous to it as a result of their betrayal.[70]

---

[67] Camden to Portland, 9 Mar. 1797 (PROHO 100/69/132–8).

[68] See the notebook of Denis Browne for Newell's testimony before a parliamentary secret committee set up to investigate reports of a United Irish committee of assassination, 2 May 1797 (SPOI, Rebellion papers, 620/30/6).

[69] For these denials, see Thomas Addis Emmet, Arthur O'Connor, and William James MacNeven, *Memoire or detailed statement of the origin and progress of the Irish union* (Dublin, 1798), 8–9; Hope, 'Autobiographical memoir', 112–13.

[70] For an example of the assassination of an informer against the United Irishmen, see the report of George Stephenson on the death of Daniel Morgan, who was found with part of his head shot off and 10 stab wounds in his back (Stephenson to marquess of Downshire, 19–20 Mar. 1796 (SPOI, Rebellion papers, 620/26/140)). For the assassination of active magistrates, see John Goddard to marquess of Downshire, 2 Sept. 1796 (PRONI, Downshire papers, D607/26/149); Thomas Lane to marquess of Downshire, 23 Sept. 1796 (ibid. D607/D/199); Revd William Hamilton to Thomas Pelham, 22 Dec. 1796 (SPOI, Rebellion papers, 620/26/146); earl of Cavan to Thomas Pelham, 3 Mar. 1797 (ibid. 620/29/13).

Significantly, at the Derry summer assizes in 1796 numerous United Irishmen were brought to trial, but all escaped conviction.[71] This success apparently gave considerable momentum to the movement. The Tyrone magistrate Andrew Newton reported that 'since Derry assizes, when all the United Irishmen were tried and acquitted, everyone that will not instantly join that set is threatened with destruction.'[72] Another Tyrone magistrate, Richard Griffith, described the fate of one poor creature who had dared to give evidence against the United Irishmen: his tongue and ears were cut off.[73] Such incidents became commonplace as the republicans gained ascendancy. C. M. Warburton, a County Armagh magistrate, despairingly cried in April 1797:

The game is nearly up in the north—no juries, no prosecutions, no evidence against any person under the denomination of *united man*! The men of property and clergy completely alarmed and, instead of resistance, are all flying away into garrison towns—the mobs plundering every gentleman's house. . . . Every young tree has been cut down in this neighbourhood for handles of pikes.

Having exhausted all means of quieting the countryside and finding himself deserted by his fellow magistrates, the despondent Warburton informed the government of his intention to join the exodus.[74] The collapse of traditional methods of maintaining order was confirmed early in 1797, when the spring assizes in the counties of Monaghan and Armagh saw further mass acquittals of United Irishmen.[75]

Table 3.2 shows the number of those tried for all crimes in the five north-eastern counties of Ulster between 1796 and 1798. The percentage of those convicted is also given. In most of these Ulster counties the rate of conviction was lower than the national average, which suggests that United Irish methods of obstructing justice were fairly successful. Of course, the meaning of these figures is obscured by the existence of martial law in these counties since 1796. Especially with regard to 1798, the figures do not indicate the frequency with which insurgents were brought before a tribunal of some sort. Despite this qualification, these five counties together accounted for more trials and a lower conviction rate than the national average for all jurisdictions, as Table 3.3 demonstrates. In fact, it was the extreme difficulty of convicting United Irishmen that led to the adoption of Draconian measures by the government. The United Irishmen had frequently bested the government in the courts in late 1796 and early 1797. Such sweeping victories, often won by assassinating would-be prosecutors,

---

[71] *BNL*, 12 Aug. 1796.
[72] Newton to Bourne, 15 Aug. 1796 (SPOI, Rebellion papers, 620/24/120).
[73] Richard Griffith to Edward Cooke, 20 Aug. 1796 (ibid. 620/24/117).
[74] C. M. Warburton to Dublin Castle, 12 Apr. 1797 (ibid. 620/29/223).
[75] Marcus Beresford to Edward Cooke, 11 Apr. 1797 (ibid. 620/29/216).

TABLE 3.2. *Trials and convictions in Ulster, 1796–1798*

Country	1796		1797		1798	
	No.	%	No.	%	No.	%
Antrim	63	17.5	87	19.5	60	30.0
Armagh	143	23.1	106	26.4	142	14.1
Derry	34	26.5	79	20.0	43	32.6
Down	87	19.5	168	16.1	60	16.7
Tyrone	142	15.5	132	13.6	56	26.8
ALL IRELAND	2,675	25.6	2,991	24.0	2,470	31.4

Source: *JHCI* xvii. 213–14, 1, 182–3; xviii. 348–9.

TABLE 3.3. *Conviction rates for Ireland and Ulster, 1796–1798*

Year	Average no. of trials		Average conviction rate (%)	
	In each jurisdiction	In Ulster	In each jurisdiction	In Ulster
1796	72.3	93.8	25.6	20.4
1797	80.8	114.4	24.0	19.1
1798	66.8	72.2	31.4	24.0

Source: *JHCI* xvii. 213–14, 1, 182–3; xviii. 348–9.

prompted the government to include a clause in the insurrection act allowing information from murdered witnesses to be used as evidence in a trial.[76]

The odds were against the government at first. The Castle's main problem was in securing and then protecting crown witnesses against the United Irishmen. Another barrier was the reluctance of local juries to convict if the death penalty was involved. In many cases, the government indicted United Irishmen for lesser offences, punishable by a term of transportation, in the hope of overcoming the qualms of jurymen. And greater care was taken in preparing the cases against those brought to trial, which meant that the number of prosecutions for political crimes may have dropped, but that the number of convictions began to rise.[77] The revived efficiency of the courts was finally achieved by the end of 1797, when, in conjunction with the strong military repression unleashed in the north, the authorities seemed to be succeeding in pacifying Ulster, at least temporarily. As a signal that the rule of law was once again returning to the north, the summer assizes in

[76] Lecky, *History of Ireland*, iii. 464, 484.   [77] McDowell, *Ireland*, 543–7.

1797 proved most encouraging. In early October a jubilant Camden reported to Portland on the assizes that had just been concluded in the north: 'The event has been most satisfactory—between forty and fifty capital convictions have taken place, and most of them have been for those crimes connected with the conspiracy which had so formidably spread itself in that part of the kingdom.' The judges could not, as Camden reported, fault an over-anxious desire on the part of the juries to punish these offenders. 'The conspiracy certainly exists in that part of the kingdom, but their spirits are much depressed and the system which had spread so rapidly is out of fashion.'[78]

Though defeated in the courts, the United Irishmen were not to be denied a propaganda victory of sorts, however dearly purchased. One of the most notorious and controversial cases of judicial prosecution occurred at the Antrim summer assizes of 1797.[79] William Orr, a young Presbyterian farmer of some property, with significant local influence and popularity, was indicted for administering the United Irish oath to two soldiers, named Wheatley and Lindsay. Under the insurrection act, of course, this was a capital offence. The prosecution of Orr was, to some extent, a test case, for it was the first time that a prisoner has been tried for the offence. The government clearly felt confident that it was strong enough to pass the test and to make of Orr a terrible example to his comrades.

The evidence against Orr was indeed damning. Wheatley and Lindsay testified that Orr had delivered the oath to them at a baronial meeting in the presence of a number of other United Irishmen, many of them named by the witnesses. It did not help Orr's case that none of these bystanders was able to come forward and refute the testimony. Attempts were made by the United Irishmen to discredit Wheatley and Lindsay, with some success in the case of the former. Wheatley was of notoriously bad character, but Lindsay was irreproachable. The jury reluctantly pronounced Orr guilty, but urged mercy in his sentencing.[80] They were not alone, and the viceroy soon received memorials from many respectable gentlemen in County Antrim, including a former MP, Lord O'Neill, and William Bristow, an earlier sovereign of Belfast, who urged Camden to commute the death penalty.[81] Orr's judge, Lord Yelverton, famous for his patriotic exertions in 1782, conveyed the jury's request for mercy to Camden, but declined to reinforce the plea with one of his own: 'Being perfectly satisfied with the conviction, I am sorry that neither the state of the country here

---

[78] Camden to Portland, 6 Oct. 1797 (Kent CAO, Pratt papers, U840/C31/1).

[79] See *A brief account of the trial of William Orr of Farranshane in the country of Antrim, to which are annexed several interesting facts and authentic documents connected therewith* (Dublin, 1797).

[80] See Lecky, *History of Ireland*, iv. 103-16, for an account of Orr's trial and execution.

[81] See the collection of memorials to the viceroy requesting mercy for Orr (Kent CAO, Pratt papers, U840/031/9–11).

nor the nature of the case will warrant me in adding my own recommendation to that of the jury.'[82] Camden chose to overrule the wishes of the
jurors and the county gentlemen of Antrim. 'The question seems to be
reduced to one of mere policy,' Pelham observed.[83] Under the circumstances, and given the continuing disturbed state of the country, what policy would have more effect in inducing good order—mercy or severity? It
was Pelham's and Camden's opinion that an example of the full terror of
the law was necessary.

The matter did not end there, however, and the United Irishmen
embarked upon a propaganda campaign designed to discredit the trial.
John Philpot Curran, the foremost barrister in Ireland and a committed
whig, had conducted Orr's defence. He secured affidavits from some of the
jurors claiming that undue or unusual pressure had been applied in order to
produce a guilty verdict. One juror claimed that two bottles of very strong
whiskey had been given to the jurors as they conducted their deliberations,
and that at least some of them were intoxicated when they reached their
final verdict.[84] Almost immediately, plots were hatched to rescue the unfortunate prisoner from Carrickfergus gaol, all of which were frustrated when
news of them reached General Lake.[85] An affidavit was then voluntarily
sworn by a Presbyterian minister, the Revd James Elder of Finroy Park—
oddly enough, not himself a United Irishman—maintaining that he had
been called to attend a suicidal Wheatley, who lamented that he was
guilty of swearing false evidence. Elder's evidence was corroborated by the
local magistrate, Alexander Montgomery, but to no avail.[86] Since Lindsay's
testimony had proved unimpeachable, it was assumed that Wheatley was
referring to another case. The execution of Orr was fixed for 7 October, but
in order to consider the many pleas for clemency Pelham respited it until 14
October. This produced a wave of exultation among Orr's supporters,
which prompted Colonel Lucius Barber in Belfast to warn the government:
'If Orr is pardoned, you'll find no jury to convict again.'[87]

On 14 October Orr met his fate with courage and dignity. He acknowledged his profound faith in the doctrines of Presbyterianism, and on his
way to the gallows he distributed his dying declaration: 'If I have loved my
country, to have known its wrongs, to have felt the injuries of the persecuted Catholics, and to have united with them and all other religious persuasions in the most orderly and least sanguinary means of procuring

---

[82] Lord Yelverton to Earl Camden, 19 Sept. 1797 (Kent CAO, Pratt papers, U840/031/1).
[83] Thomas Pelham to Lord Yelverton, 20 Sept. 1797 (ibid. U840/031/2).
[84] Lecky, *History of Ireland*, iv. 106–7.
[85] Lake to Pelham, 3 Oct. 1797 (BL, Pelham papers, Add. MS 33105/122–3).
[86] Examination of Revd James Elder, [Sept. or Oct.] 1797 (Kent CAO, Pratt papers,
U840/031/4–6).
[87] Col. Lucius Barber to Edward Cooke, 10 Oct. 1797 (SPOI, Rebellion papers, 620/32/160).

redress—if these be felonies, I am a felon, but not otherwise.'[88] His execution ignited a powder-keg of indignation throughout Ireland and even in England. Charles James Fox offered a toast at an English political banquet 'to the memory of the martyred Orr', a sentiment echoed by another British politician, who proposed 'that the Irish cabinet may soon take the place of William Orr'.[89]

The declining fortunes of the United Irishmen in the courts, the embodiment of the yeomanry spearheaded by an emboldened magistracy, and the apparent success of Lake's campaign to disarm the disaffected provided ample evidence that the government was capable of protecting the loyal and punishing the rebellious. This state of affairs kept rank-and-file United Irishmen in eager anticipation for orders to resist, to rise in open rebellion with or without French aid. It was better, they reasoned, to risk themselves in open conflict than to wait sheepishly for a nocturnal visit from a band of yeomen. If Ulster was allowed to continue in such a state, United Irish support there would erode so much as to render the province ineffective in a national rising. As James Hope bitterly recalled: 'The people were in daily expectation of being called to the field by their leaders, an intention, as it appeared afterwards, which the leaders had little intention of putting into execution.'[90]

But the United Irish movement was only partially organized on a national basis. There was no clear way of knowing how seriously Lake's campaign in Ulster had undermined insurrectionary commitment in the province. The northerners had wanted to rise in the autumn of 1797, but the Leinster directory refused to co-operate, on the grounds that the southern organization was incomplete.[91]

The republican leadership in Dublin was not immune to the pleas of the northerners to stage an immediate rising, but the committee was deeply divided on the question. Arthur O'Connor and Lord Edward Fitzgerald, initially among the most enthusiastic for a French alliance, now advocated an early rising—if necessary, without French aid—before government repression further eroded United Irish support. The two aristocrats were opposed by a more moderate group led by Thomas Addis Emmet and William James MacNeven. Emmet argued that the military arm of the movement was not strong enough and that experienced leaders were too rare; social anarchy might be let loose upon the country if an undisciplined army of vengeful peasants were allowed to take the field. The only wise course was to wait for a French expeditionary force, which would provide the discipline, strategy, and experience necessary to wage a successful insurrection.

---

[88] Quoted in Lecky, *History of Ireland*, iv. 114.   [89] Ibid. 103–4.
[90] R. R. Madden, *The United Irishmen, their lives and times*, 3rd ser. (7 vols., London, 1842–5), ii. 443.
[91] Francis Higgins to Dublin Castle, 17 Oct. 1797 (SPOI, Rebellion papers, 620/18/14).

Emmet's party carried the directory when news arrived in February 1798 that the French were promising an invasion for that spring.[92]

Emmet's resistance to the idea of an immediate and independent rising was based not on the fear that Lord Edward's motley army would be defeated, but rather on his anxiety that it would succeed only too well. Social radicalism and militant Catholic nationalism, if unleashed in such a victorious way, could dash the leaders' hopes for a rational, secular, capitalist and middle-class republic. Not only their dreams, but their very lives might be at risk. As students of the French revolution, Emmet's party was well aware that one of the first casualties of uncontrolled popular fury was moderate leadership. French troops would discipline United Irish followers and protect United Irish leaders. They would pre-empt the social revolution which might otherwise follow upon the heels of the bourgeois political revolution.[93]

The Dublin leaders may have been correct to assume that a partial rebellion in Ulster and portions of Leinster would fail without the spark of a French invasion. Nevertheless, such caution underscored several weaknesses in the United Irish movement. The refusal of the Leinster directory to accede to the northerners' wish to rise in 1797 or early 1798 demonstrates vividly the chasm between the leaders and the rank and file in the organization. First, those in charge of that area in which the organization was strongest, Ulster, had lost their commanding influence in the central leadership. This turn of events could only discourage those in the ranks, who now saw their leaders being disregarded by remote directors in Dublin. Secondly, the caution of the leadership contrasted starkly with the adventurism, or at least the desire for decisive action, among the rank and file. This is a constant theme in James Hope's memoirs, but other participants in the United Irish movement confirmed it. Leonard McNally observed as early as 1796 that the 'men of B[elfast] are wealthy, wily, and avaricious. They are too conscious of life and property to move themselves, whatever they may effect by means of others, and however they may *bravado*, they will never dare to act decisively till they are aided by the French.'[94] Furthermore, local societies often simply ignored central directives when they did not like the orders. During the period of severe government repression, they found more reason to be dissatisfied with remote middle-class leaders. Since 1796 they had been told to ready themselves for an imminent rising which would free them from the burdens of tithe, high rents and

[92] For a full discussion of these divisions among the United Irish leaders, see Marianne Elliott, *Partners in revolution: the United Irishmen and France* (New Haven, Conn., and London, 1982), 189–213.

[93] For Emmet's views that popular mobilization must be accompanied by restraining and moderate leadership, see his testimony before the house of lords in 1798 (Emmet, O'Connor, and MacNeven, *Memoire*, 44–9).

[94] 'J. W.' to ———— , 24 July 1796 (PROHO 100/62/137–8).

taxes, the ascendancy, and illiberal government. But unexplained delays bred impatience and distrust. 'People will not pay up subscriptions,' observed one Dublin informer, 'saying they are imposed on and will give up the business if something is not done.'[95]

The problem with the leadership's strategic dependence on the French was that it was both a benefit and a handicap. The promise of French aid, apparently confirmed by the Bantry Bay invasion attempt, induced many to join the movement, and thus considerably facilitated United Irish recruitment efforts. The problem was that the timing of the insurrection was taken out of the hands of the United Irish leaders, and often they were left as much in the dark as the rank-and-file complainers. Even more damaging, while the United Irish association with the French made the movement more threatening to the government, the authorities had been assured that the republican leaders were unlikely to act before the French arrived. There might be time—how much time was uncertain—to destroy the United Irish movement before it had a chance of linking up with French arms and probably overwhelming the forces of loyalism in Ireland. Thus the government was compelled to step up its campaign of repression, no matter what the cost, to neutralize the United Irish threat at home in order to confront more effectively the danger from abroad. 'Everything must be done directly, before the French come,' Beresford insisted to Cooke in March 1798. 'They [the United Irishmen] will never unite cordially until the *French* do come. They can therefore be suppressed.'[96]

So, Lake's reign of terror in Ulster had been given full licence, and a similar campaign was soon to harry the United Irishmen in Leinster and parts of Munster. Pitt, distracted by his continental war, placed complete trust in Camden's government. The policy—indeed, the system—of government in Ireland was to be one of unrelenting assault against the United Irish conspiracy. British troops became much more numerous as the crisis became more acute. Ireland was quickly becoming what Pelham said it should be, a garrison state.[97] 'It is not to be denied', an uneasy and defensive Camden proclaimed to Pitt, 'that government meant to strike terror.'[98] 'If we treat rebellion as rebellion,' Cooke declared, 'we are safe.'[99]

---

[95] Thomas Boyle to ———, 16 Apr. 1798 (SPOI, Rebellion papers, 620/18/3). As early as July 1797 Boyle reported to the government that the Dublin members were accusing their leaders of 'keeping the country in the dark' (Boyle to ———, 1 July 1797 (ibid.)).

[96] John Beresford to Edward Cooke, 24 Mar. 1798 (PRONI, Sneyd papers, T3229/2/31).

[97] Pelham to Portland, 29 Sept. 1797 (PROHO 100/70/146–9).

[98] Earl Camden to William Pitt, 3 Nov. 1797 (NLI, Lord-Lieutenants' correspondence, MS 886/165–81).

[99] Edward Cooke to Lord Auckland (PRONI, Sneyd papers, T3229/2/32).

4

Organization

IF the United Irishmen adopted one persistent and fundamental strategy to alter existing political arrangements in Ireland, it was to apply the force of public opinion where it would be felt most effectively by an intransigent administration and its supporters in the British government. The theory behind the organization of the United Irishmen from 1791 to 1798 was to provide a mechanism for the expression, and hence the triumph, of the popular will in Ireland. In this, the radicals remained true to their republican ideals, even if the leaders might disagree about how the people's will should be mediated, channelled, and controlled by their middle-class tribunes.

Models for the expression and embodiment of the popular will were readily available to the United Irishmen. Throughout their existence from 1791 to 1798 they employed—in varying degrees, depending on the circumstances of their mobilization—three such models, which I have termed the polemical, the masonic, and the paramilitary models of organization.

At the beginning of their mobilization the radicals adopted the polemical model. The purpose of the organization was to provide the public with a political education, to disseminate radical ideas, and to promote the full expression of these ideas among an audience which was not required to participate directly in the institution. Irish radicals had only to look at the corresponding societies in revolutionary America, the Jacobin clubs in France, or, closer to home, the Society for Constitutional Information in England. Here were loose, decentralized networks of affiliated clubs sharing a common name and common aims. Since the purpose of these societies was polemical and didactic, it was not deemed necessary to promote mass participation in the clubs themselves, though participation was not discouraged. Thus the early United Irishmen were content to keep their own numbers relatively small as long as they could use the Volunteer corps, the Catholic Committee, masonic lodges, Presbyterian congregations, and town, parish, and county meetings to pronounce critically on current political arrangements.[1] They could direct and manipulate political education in

---

[1] For the Volunteer revival and the United Irish influence within it, see *NS*, 23 May, 23 June, 28 July, 7 Nov. 1792; *Rep. secret comm.* 40–1; William Drennan to Samuel McTier, [?] Feb. 1793 (*The Drennan letters*, ed. D. A. Chart (Belfast, 1931), 128–9). For radical pronouncements by Irish freemasons, see *NS*, 16 Jan. 1793. For reform declarations passed by Presbyterian congregations, see *NS*, 28 Nov. 1792, 8–30 Jan. 1793, 29 June 1793.

Ireland and even offer their own public pronouncements, but ultimately they were content to allow other organizations of a more representative nature to conduct the challenge to government.

Although this polemical model of organization dominated the early years of the United Irish societies, it also faced competition from the other two models. Drennan took pains to introduce masonic trappings into the Dublin society, which adopted a test binding all members to the causes of reform and emancipation in brotherly affection.[2] But the masonic model emphasized secrecy and ritual, both of which, while certainly represented in the reformist phase of the United Irishmen, were hardly prominent. More influential was the paramilitary model, the legacy that was given to the United Irishmen by the Volunteers and provided the cornerstone of the civic humanist tradition. In the paramilitary model, the popular will was expressed awesomely by an armed citizen militia representing disinterested but often excluded members of the polity who banded together in the cause of patriotism and civic virtue. The Volunteer conventions of 1782, 1783, and 1793 all pitted themselves against the ascendancy-controlled and British-dominated parliament, which was accused of excluding the civic participation of the respectable, propertied middle classes of Ireland. When the public will in Ireland could represent itself as unified and armed, it must surely overawe a corrupt government into conceding timely reforms. It was just such a fear of these armed conventions that drove the government into outlawing all such rival assemblies in 1793 and suppressing the Volunteers. As an organization, the United Irishmen at this period did not engage directly in such activity. It did, however, work through existing Volunteer corps, and, more ominously, at least from the government's point of view, some United Irishmen themselves engaged in the formation of the National Guard.

All three models of organization persisted in the revolutionary phase of the United Irish movement, but after the harassment and repression of 1793 and 1794 the emphasis shifted. The polemical model still suited the purpose of the republicans to arouse public opinion on their behalf. Committees of correspondence linked societies together, and propaganda was disseminated through local branches. But the masonic and paramilitary models of organization now combined to produce that secret but mass-based system which characterized the movement in the late 1790s. These models not only proved compatible with United Irish strategy, but they were also pressed on a lower-class population which could easily graft them on to its own peculiar form of collective insurrectionary organization—the agrarian secret societies. Whiteboys, Rightboys, Hearts of Steel, Defenders, and Peep o' Day Boys had all organized themselves into oath-bound collectivities on a

[2] Drennan to McTier, 21 May 1791 (*Drennan letters*, 54).

military model, led by 'captains' and sporting some form of a recognizable uniform or insignia.[3] Masonic oaths, symbols, and rituals most certainly influenced these agrarian organizations, and the obsession of the Defenders and Peep o' Day Boys in particular with the right to bear arms indicates an aspiration towards the civic rights and obligations accorded to an armed polity.

The organizational history of the early United Irishmen is hardly impressive. The first society appeared in Belfast in October 1791, and in the following month a similar club was established in Dublin. Within the first year of their formation the United Irishmen succeeded in extending their organization into three of the four provinces of Ireland, but outside Ulster their numbers were hardly significant.[4] It was in the Presbyterian north-east that the new movement took deepest root, and even there it was unimpressive. I have found references to only nine societies in the north outside of Belfast.[5] But the purpose of the society was not really to replicate itself throughout the countryside. Rather, its function was largely propagandist—to disseminate political information and, whenever possible, to co-ordinate the activities of other like-minded reform groups. The radicals successfully exploited the existing reform sentiments in Volunteer companies and masonic lodges. Resolutions passed by county, parish, and town meetings reflected the principles and aims of the United Irishmen. The energy and optimism of these reformers proved infectious, and other political clubs felt the general impulse for political change which swept over the north of Ireland. In addition, many newly established Volunteer corps in the north acted as United Irish clubs in all but name.[6] The influence of the clubs was far greater, therefore, than the mere number of individual societies might indicate.

[3] For these secret societies, see M. R. Beames, 'The Ribbon societies: lower-class nationalism in pre-famine Ireland', *Past and Present*, 97 (1982), 128–43; Gale E. Christianson, 'Secret societies and agrarian violence in Ireland, 1790–1840', *Agricultural History*, 46 (1972), 369–84; James S. Donnelly, jun., 'Hearts of Oak, Hearts of Steel', *Studia Hibernica*, 21 (1981), 7–73; id., 'Irish agrarian rebellion: the Whiteboys of 1769–76', *Proceedings of the Royal Irish Academy*, 83C/12 (1983), 293–331; id., 'The Rightboy movement, 1785–8', *Studia Hibernica*, 17–18 (1977–8), 120–202; id., 'The Whiteboy movement, 1761–5', *Irish Historical Studies*, 21/81 (Mar. 1978), 20–54; Tom Garvin, 'Defenders, Ribbonmen and others', *Past and Present*, 96 (Aug. 1982), 133–55; W. A. Maguire, 'Lord Donegall and the Hearts of Steel', *Irish Historical Studies*, 21/84 (Sept. 1979), 351–76; David W. Miller, 'The Armagh troubles, 1784–95', in Samuel Clark and James S. Donnelly, jun. (eds.), *Irish peasants: violence and political unrest, 1780–1914* (Madison, Wis., 1983), 155–91; T. Desmond Williams (ed.), *Secret societies in Ireland* (Dublin, 1973).

[4] For United Irish societies outside of Ulster, see R. B. McDowell, 'The proceedings of the Dublin Society of United Irishmen', *Analecta Hibernia*, 17 (1949), 8, 40, 51; *BNL*, 3 Apr. 1792.

[5] There was 1 society in the town of Armagh, 2 in County Down, and 6 in County Antrim. See *NS*, 11, 16 Jan., 1, 4 Feb. 1792; *BNL*, 21 Dec. 1792; Samuel McSkimin, *Annals of Ulster from 1790 to 1798*, ed. E. J. McCrum (Belfast, 1906), 5; R. B. McDowell, *Irish public opinion, 1750–1800* (London, 1944), 147; id., 'Proceedings', 40.

[6] See *NS*, 23 May, 23 June, 28 July, 7 Nov. 1792, for the resolutions of the Downpatrick, Larne, Ballynahinch, Ballyclare, Ballyeaston, Connor, and Kircubbin Volunteers corps.

There was no organizational unity among the early United Irishmen. Each local society adopted what it wanted from the models provided by the Belfast or Dublin clubs. The Sixmilewater Society of United Irishmen, for example, borrowed the resolutions of the Dublin club, 'except that they [more] fully and unequivocally avow the *principles* of the *French revolution as their own*'.[7] In Belfast the United Irishmen were divided into many societies. There were at least four such clubs in the town by the autumn of 1792. Each of these societies could contain no more than thirty-six members.[8] The Dublin society, however, was open to anyone who would swear the test and submit to approval by the existing members. There may have been as many as 425 persons admitted to the club between 1791 and 1794, though only about 200 can be described as active members; regular attendance at meetings rarely surpassed ninety, and even then only at times of acute political interest, such as during the sitting of the Catholic convention late in 1792.[9]

Of these two poles in the radical sphere, the Dublin society clearly surpassed the Belfast clubs in visibility and prominence, owing to the more exalted social status of some of its leading members and to the greater public activity of the radicals of the capital. A very respectable mercantile and professional element dominated the Dublin club, and, of course, at its very centre was that famous popular member of the corporation and merchant, James Napper Tandy, the darling of the Dublin crowd.[10] In addition, representatives from the landed élite participated in the society in the capital, notably Simon Butler, the son of Lord Mountgarret, and Archibald Hamilton Rowan. As the reports of the government informer Thomas Collins show, the main function of the Dublin Society of United Irishmen was to produce, approve, and disseminate political information. Two important committees captured most of the Dublin radicals' attention—a committee to consider appropriate publications and a committee of correspondence.[11]

'Tandy likes rather too much to publish,' complained that famous political man of letters, William Drennan, and the activities of the Dublin United Irishmen surely gave full scope to the radical merchant's propensity.[12] Much of the information on United Irish meetings submitted by Thomas Collins focused on the reports of the publications committee. Its members were responsible for considering 'what publications it may be necessary to republish and what others may require to be confuted as injurious to the

---

[7] McDowell, 'Proceedings', 23.   [8] *NS*, 20 Oct. 1792.
[9] R. B. McDowell, 'The personnel of the Dublin Society of United Irishmen, 1791–4', *Irish Historical Studies*, 2/5 (Mar. 1940), 14–15.
[10] For Tandy, see Rupert J. Coughlan, *Napper Tandy* (Dublin, 1976).
[11] McDowell, 'Proceedings', 8.
[12] Drennan to McTier, [Dec. 1791] (*Drennan letters*, 69).

public good'.[13] This meant that members of the committee had to keep abreast of the plethora of pamphlets which poured off the presses in Dublin and London. The committee also recommended the republication and mass distribution of literature, in either pamphlet or handbill form, written by the United Irishmen themselves or by their fellow-travellers.

The committee of correspondence, as its name suggests, received all the addresses, foreign and domestic, which were sent to the Dublin society, and framed suitable responses. The committee of twelve was kept quite busy with the frequent communications from and to various reform societies in Scotland and England, and they were also responsible for maintaining contacts with the other United Irish societies in Ireland. This committee thus had a great deal of power in outlining and defining the political stance of the United Irishmen, but on some issues its members felt obliged to refer to the society as a whole. In January 1793, for example, the committee of correspondence reported that it had received a letter from the Lisburn Society of United Irishmen 'of so serious a nature that they could not determine on it; therefore [they] referred it to the society at large'. The Lisburn club had asked the Dublin society to supply them with funds to purchase arms. Such a request naturally produced heated debate in a radical club which included some militant republicans as well as mild reformers. The society settled on a compromise. Rather than disavow the propriety of acquiring arms, which some moderates urged, the committee was instructed to refuse Lisburn's request for aid, on the grounds that the Dublin society's financial resources were too depleted by the 'number of *heavy lawsuits* that we are engaged in'.[14]

The publications and correspondence committees were an ongoing concern of the Dublin United Irishmen. Special committees were created to serve particular purposes—legal defence, relief of prisoners, and, most important, the committee of twenty-one proposed by Thomas Addis Emmet to produce 'a plan for the full representation of all the people in parliament'.[15]

The Dublin Society of United Irishmen, which met fortnightly at Tailors' Hall in the capital, was open to all who, upon approval of the membership, agreed to take Drennan's test of resolve to work for a fair and adequate representation of all Irishmen, Catholic and protestant, in parliament. Each meeting opened with the balloting of new members, each of whom had to be nominated by two members in good standing. All attending members then cast either a white bean, marking approval of the candidate, or a black bean, denoting disapproval. One vote against the candidate was sufficient to bar him from the society, but this rarely happened.[16] When the summons for a United Irish meeting was sent to members, a list of nomi-

[13] McDowell, 'Proceedings', 8.   [14] Ibid. 57–8.   [15] Ibid. 57, 98, 104–5.
[16] Drennan to McTier, 24 Dec. 1791 (PRONI, Drennan letters, T765/318).

nees with their sponsors was also included.[17] Successful candidates would swear the test before the assembly and formally sign their names in the society's roll. Regular attendance, of course, was not required, and membership was often conferred on leading radicals as a token of honour and esteem. Tom Paine and Thomas Muir of Scotland, for example, were so honoured, as were William Sinclaire and Robert Simms, the chairman and secretary of the first Society of United Irishmen in Belfast. The publishers of the *Northern Star*, when in Dublin facing trial for seditious libel, were also invited to join the Dublin society.[18]

There was little continuity of formal leadership in the Dublin club. The posts of chairman and secretary rotated among active and willing members every three months. Tandy certainly provided the driving force behind the society in its early phase, though the United Irishmen, implacable democrats that they were, were delighted to make Simon Butler, the son of a viscount, their first president. Hamilton Rowan, Drennan, and the Sheares brothers all served as president. Tandy, Tone, Russell, and Oliver Bond were among those who served as secretary at various times.[19]

The United Irishmen in Dublin aimed to be more than the kind of political eating and drinking society so prevalent in the capital. The reports of Collins show that substantive issues were hotly debated, particularly those dealing with the progress towards Catholic emancipation and the harassment that several United Irish leaders endured at the hands of the government. It was a serious undertaking to preside over a United Irish meeting. If such a meeting produced what the government deemed to be an inflammatory publication, the president and secretary were subject to prosecution for seditious libel. Thus Simon Butler and Oliver Bond found themselves serving a short and, thanks to the largesse of their comrades, a rather commodious term in prison for insulting the dignity of a parliamentary officer.[20] Such publications, as Drennan observed, 'would be as good a mode of joining issue with government as any other'.[21]

The importance of the Dublin club was due not only to its extensive publication activities, its well-known leaders, or even to its rather modest efforts in co-ordinating the activities of other clubs. Its key significance lay

[17] See e.g. McDowell, 'Proceedings', 44.   [18] Ibid. 20–4, 87, 130–42.
[19] See *Society of United Irishmen of Dublin . . . 'Let the nation stand'* (proceedings) (Dublin, 1794).
[20] For this incident, see R. B. McDowell, *Ireland in the age of imperialism and revolution* (Oxford, 1979), 439–40. Drennan was particularly outraged by the lavish style in which the Dublin Society of United Irishmen was keeping Butler and Bond during their imprisonment. They 'are living at too great a rate in prison for our finances. I shall not subscribe one farthing more' (Drennan to McTier, 4 May 1793 (*Drennan letters*, 160)). Drennan even proposed that 'a resolution of economy' be submitted by the society to their imprisoned comrades, listing the accounts of their expenses, which included a £100 wine bill (Drennan to McTier, [Apr. or May 1793] (ibid. 158–60)).
[21] Drennan to McTier, [Nov. 1791] (ibid. 62).

in the fact that it was located in the capital itself, where the society could keep abreast of political developments and have easy access to the latest offerings in press and pamphlet. Dublin was the political hub of Ireland. The radicals there could meet leading members of the whig opposition and the Catholic Committee, forging, as northerners could not do, that potential alliance of discontented whigs, middle-class protestant radicals, and militant, enlightened Catholics which would, it was hoped, bring sufficient pressure to bear on an intransigent and exclusive ruling élite. Furthermore, Dublin already enjoyed a rich tradition of local political activism at various levels. The city was a relatively open borough, its government heatedly contested by well-organized Castle and popular parties, and, of course, its citizens frequently took to the streets in support of popular tribunes from Charles Lucas to Grattan.[22]

Oddly enough, however, the other key component of the United Irish coalition, the Presbyterian radicals of the north, was scarcely represented in the capital. The Belfast and Dublin Societies of United Irishmen seem to have had little official contact with one another. Thomas Russell gravitated towards both centres of radical activity, being part of the inner circle of Belfast radicals and, in Dublin, closely associated with Tone and the Catholic Committee. Drennan, a Belfast native carrying on a frequent correspondence with his sister and brother-in-law in the north, nevertheless complained persistently that he did not know what the northern clubs were doing.[23] Northerners who visited Dublin were readily accepted into the society in the capital, but they did not participate actively. When one of them tried to intervene in the policy of the Dublin club, he was quickly but politely dismissed for his alien ways.

Nothing, perhaps, illustrates the difference between the Dublin and Belfast societies more vividly than this attempt by Samuel Neilson to impose some central discipline on the club in the capital. In January 1794 Neilson attended a meeting of the Dublin Society of United Irishmen. He acknowledged that he was a stranger in the town, and a stranger to almost every member in the room. He was, of course, far too modest. Everyone present would have known of the famous Neilson, the oft-proclaimed leader of the northern United Irishmen and the editor and publisher of that voice of a free people, the *Northern Star*. Neilson went straight to the

---

[22] See e.g. Jacqueline Hill, 'The politics of Dublin corporation, 1760–1792', in David Dickson *et al.* (eds.), *The United Irishmen: republicanism, radicalism, and rebellion* (Dublin, 1993), 88–101; Sean Murphy, 'Charles Lucas and the Dublin election of 1748–9', *Parliamentary History*, 2 (1983), 93–111; id., 'The Dublin anti-union riot of 3 December 1759', in Gerard O'Brien (ed.), *Parliament, politics and people* (Dublin, 1989), 49–68; M. R. O'Connell, 'Class conflict in pre-industrial society: Dublin in 1780', *Duquesne Review*, 9/1 (Autumn 1963), 43–55; James Smyth, 'Dublin's political underground in the 1790s', in O'Brien (ed.), *Parliament and people*, 93–127; Jim Smyth, *The men of no property: Irish radicals and popular politics in the late eighteenth century* (New York, 1992), ch. 6.

[23] See e.g. Drennan to McTier, 2 Aug. 1794 (PRONI, Drennan letters, T765/519).

point. He had evidence that the Dublin society was lodging a traitor in its midst who provided the Castle with detailed information on the club's proceedings. Neilson urged his Dublin comrades to follow the example of the northern clubs in order to guard against the effects of treachery. The Dublin society, he suggested, should establish a committee of public safety, with a membership of twelve, which would transact all the society's business and determine when it was necessary and safe to call a meeting of the whole society. Real control, though Neilson hardly put it this way, would pass into the hands of twelve men.[24]

The Dublin radicals were appalled by Neilson's suggestion that a small committee should secretly direct the activities of the society. Neilson was proposing a conspiratorial body, which particularly outraged the sensibilities of the gentlemen among the Dublin radicals. Simon Butler declared that 'he wished the hall to be uncovered and all the people of Dublin, of all Ireland, to be present at their debates, as he knew of nothing having ever been agitated but what was perfectly constitutional.' John Sheares, famous for his sanguinary and premature revolutionary proclamation of 1798, echoed Butler: the society's transactions 'could not be too public'.[25]

This incident is significant in underscoring not only the open, constitutional nature of the Dublin Society of United Irishmen, but also the conspiratorial nature of the Belfast clubs. Much is known, thanks to the informer Collins, of the personnel and proceedings of the United Irishmen in the capital. Despite the detailed reports supplied by Collins, however, the government still could find no reason to suppress the Dublin society. The pretext, when it came, was provided by the Jackson affair. The radicals' imprudent dealings with this French spy gave the government the excuse that it needed to close down the Society of United Irishmen in the capital in May 1794.

The Belfast societies, on the other hand, were cloaked in secrecy. The historian may only infer, from bits and fragments of evidence, the nature, social composition, organization, and goals of these clubs. Neilson's proposal to the Dublin society is one of these suggestive morsels. We know that a secret committee directed Volunteer reform activities in Belfast and was responsible for staging the celebration of the French revolution in that town in July 1791.[26] Tone was invited to this celebration with the express purpose of assisting in the launching of a new reform group espousing Catholic emancipation. The initiative failed that summer, only to be revived

---

[24] McDowell, 'Proceedings', 108–9.   [25] Ibid.

[26] Tone, *Life*, i. 142; Rosamund Jacob, *The rise of the United Irishmen, 1791–4* (London, 1937), 54. The members of this committee within the 1st company of Belfast Volunteers were Samuel Neilson, William Sinclair, William McCleery, Henry Haslett, William Tennent, Samuel McTier, Thomas McCabe, Gilbert McIlveen, William and Robert Simms, and John Campbell (see Marianne Elliott, *Partners in revolution: the United Irishmen and France* (New Haven, Conn., and London, 1982), 22).

by Tone's *Argument on behalf of the Catholics of Ireland*. In the following
October this same secret committee, led by Neilson, invited Tone once
again to Belfast, where he assisted in the establishment of the first Society
of United Irishmen. Thereafter, the history of the Belfast United Irishmen
becomes fragmentary. Their major activities involved working with radical
Volunteer corps and other organs to express political criticism. Like their
comrades in Dublin, the Belfast radicals seemed chiefly interested in propagating the cause of reform and emancipation. But they did this less through
the vehicle of official club publications than through the medium of their
own newspaper, the *Northern Star*. The northern clubs, unlike that in
Dublin, enjoyed limited enrolment. Only thirty-six members were allowed
in each, and when a society exceeded this number, it was split into two
separate clubs. Each club was then numbered for purposes of identification.
Resolutions of the individual societies were rarely published. The northern
radicals were apparently content to let sympathetic cover organizations and
the *Northern Star* itself convey the will of the northern people, a process
culminating in the Dungannon convention in February 1793. There was, at
least on the surface, no central co-ordination of these activities.

But Neilson's espousal of the institution of a committee of public safety
in Dublin to transact and direct all the society's business suggests that he
was already familiar with such a body. In fact, he was probably the leader
of just such a committee in Belfast. In a letter to Drennan in March 1792
Sam McTier mentioned a 'committee of our three societies' which directed
radical activity in Belfast.[27] The existence of this committee is confirmed by
the regrettably fragmentary but nevertheless suggestive evidence concerning
the transition of the Society of United Irishmen from an open, constitutional reform club into a mass-based, secret, revolutionary organization in
1794 and 1795.[28]

Indeed, there is evidence to suggest that a foundation for the transformation of the reform clubs into a revolutionary organization had been laid
within months of the society's origin in 1791, under the direction of
Neilson's committee of public safety in Belfast. In his testimony before the
Irish house of lords in 1798 Neilson was asked when the 'present' or revolutionary organization of the United Irishmen began. As editor and proprietor of the *Northern Star* and an active Belfast radical leader, he was
clearly familiar with the United Irish system in the north. He replied to the
committee's question by saying that the 'affiliated system' had been established in the spring of 1792 and had gradually increased since that time.[29]

[27] Samuel McTier to William Drennan, [Mar. 1792] (PRONI, Drennan letters, T765/333).
[28] For a discussion of the continuities between the reformist and revolutionary United Irish
organization, see Nancy J. Curtin, 'The transformation of the Society of United Irishmen into
a mass-based revolutionary organisation, 1794–6', *Irish Historical Studies*, 24/96 (Nov. 1985),
468–76.
[29] *Rep. secret comm.* 48.

The northern clubs confined their public activities in the early 1790s to the occasional publication of resolutions, unlike the Dublin club, which opened its meetings to all comers and courted public attention. The United Irishmen in Ulster, however, were already engaging in rather secret, advanced, sometimes seditious, and certainly militant activity, including the acquisition of arms for their members in the event that force should become necessary to implement their demands. As early as July 1792 a northern correspondent reported to the government that 'the patriots' were arming themselves.[30] Chief Secretary Hobart responded to this and to numerous additional reports by banning the import of arms into Ireland unless the shipment secured privy council approval.[31] We have already seen that the Lisburn United Irishmen requested financial assistance from the Dublin club to purchase arms and ammunition. Undoubtedly, much of this activity reflected the revival of Volunteer corps in the north under the impetus of United Irish radicalization. Hugh White suggested to John Wright of the Ballyclare Independent Volunteers in February 1793 that the corps should equip some pikemen in the event of 'real action'.[32] In Belfast, as one United Irishman later informed the government, 'they were ready to unsheath the sword' as early as 1792, but the Dublin club refused to co-operate with, or even countenance, such proposals.[33] In March 1793 a magistrate near Coleraine, County Derry, complained of 'daily incursions of disaffected people . . . disseminating the most seditious principles and assaulting even peaceable inhabitants'.[34] Evidence that the United Irishmen constituted an insurrectionary threat at this time is not abundant, and most magistrates failed to note or to comment on their activities. But the available material does suggest a militancy about the early United Irishmen in the north that has generally been overlooked.

Neilson's contention that the United Irishmen continued in existence in the north through the early 1790s and through their insurrectionary period is confirmed by other evidence. As early as March 1794 a weaver in south Antrim, John Mitchell, was recruited into a secret society of United Irishmen dedicated to overthrowing the 'present government', by force if necessary. Mitchell also claimed that the activities of this local club were supervised by a central committee in Belfast.[35] This suggests that an insurrectionary strategy was considered by some northern United Irishmen even before the Dublin society was suppressed in May 1794 and long before the maddening recall of Earl Fitzwilliam. William Drennan, lamenting the

---

[30] William Fork to ——, [July] 1792 (PROHO 100/34/66–8).

[31] Robert Hobart to John Beresford, 20 Dec. 1792 (SPOI, Rebellion papers, 620/19/124).

[32] Hugh White to John Wright, 26 Feb. 1793 (ibid. 620/20/11).

[33] Patrick Kennedy to bishop of Ossory, 9 Oct. 1796 (ibid. 620/25/157).

[34] Robert Graham to Dublin Castle, 28 Mar. 1793 (ibid. 620/20/15).

[35] Examination of John Mitchell of Ballynashee, Co. Antrim, *c.*1796 (PROI, Frazer papers, IA 40/111*a*/16).

inactivity of the Dublin club to his brother-in-law McTier, applauded the persistence of the northern societies, which had continued to meet and plot throughout the frustrating summer of 1794.[36]

Indeed, new societies were formed in the north at this time. In November 1794 an address by the Loughmore United Irishmen to one newly formed club proclaimed:

It is the internal divisions amongst Irishmen that gives [sic] an opportunity to our profligate, audacious, and self-making lawgivers to prey upon our vitals and carry away our substance without equity. . . . Let us join heart and hand to purify our constitution, which by being too long neglected, is grown intolerable—if revolution must be tried, let us endeavour to have it as bloodless as possible.[37]

This implies that the northern United Irishmen, while espousing a constitutionalist approach to political change, kept in reserve a revolutionary strategy which might be required if reformist methods failed. Rather than an abrupt shift from reform to revolution triggered by official repression or by Fitzwilliam's recall, the northern United Irishmen experienced an erosion of their early constitutionalism and the emergence of this latent militancy. The recall of Fitzwilliam and the dashing of reformers' hopes accelerated, but did not initiate, a development that was already under way long before 1795. As Charles Teeling, himself deeply involved in the movement at this time, observed: 'Prior to Lord Fitzwilliam's appointment to the government of Ireland in 1795, the United Irish societies, though progressive, had been slow in march and comparatively limited in numbers, but on the removal of that popular viceroy and the nomination of Lord Camden as his successor, the system immediately assumed a more general and imposing appearance.'[38]

Teeling concurred with Neilson that the United Irish societies enjoyed an uninterrupted existence throughout the 1790s, that radicalization came from within the organization, under the direction of the Belfast leadership, and that the societies were restructured primarily to accommodate the new revolutionary strategy which emerged from the frustrated former constitutionalism. The claims of leaders like Emmet, William James MacNeven, and Arthur O'Connor that ministerial folly in recalling the popular viceroy initiated the development of a revolutionary movement in Ireland require some qualification.[39] Clearly, the base of support for the movement expanded considerably after Fitzwilliam's recall, requiring organizational readjust-

---

[36] Drennan to McTier, 30 Oct. 1794 (PRONI, Drennan letters, T765/532).

[37] Address from Loughmore Society of United Irishmen, 8 Nov. 1794 (BL, Pelham misc. state papers, Add. MS 33118/247).

[38] Charles Hamilton Teeling, *The history of the Irish rebellion of 1798* (1st edn., 1876; Shannon, 1972), 5.

[39] William James MacNeven, *Pieces of Irish history: illustrative of the condition of the Catholics of Ireland* (New York, 1807), 176–7, 180.

ment. But revolutionary recruitment also coincided with the early weeks of his administration, a time of great expectations for reformers.[40] And it should be remembered that these recruits were joining existing United Irish clubs as well as forming new ones in the north. Thus a small network of revolutionary societies operated well before and during Fitzwilliam's viceroyalty. Emmet and his colleagues accurately noted that enrolment increased with phenomenal rapidity after Fitzwilliam's recall, but this, too, coincided with the conscious determination of the old revolutionary network to increase its base.

In the summer of 1794 the Belfast leaders met frequently in secret cabal, prompting the frustrated curiosity of William Drennan.[41] It was this secret committee which initiated the restructuring of the United Irish system in the north. The transformation concerned not so much the aims and personnel of the republican movement as its organizational structure, which was readjusted to suit the needs of a growing mass-based movement. In a digest on United Irish activity and organization sent to Portland in July 1795 Camden maintained: 'The general committee of the society meet at Belfast and is the centre of motion to the whole machine.' A committee of public welfare was also located there, having been set up 'in order to constitute an executive power, whenever an opportunity may offer, of bringing forward their forces; and in the meantime, to order and arrange every matter for that purpose'.[42]

'Evil, cunning, and artful means is [*sic*] now in force to excite nothing less than *rebellion* in these parts,' wrote one government correspondent in April 1795. 'The shopboys, etc., of Belfast and Lisburn are traversing the country on various pretences to diffuse the poison.'[43] They carried with them, at the direction of the general committee in Belfast, copies of the revised constitution, which had been drafted by United Irish leaders late in 1794.[44] By May 1795 there were only about 5,000 members in the northern United Irish organization, and these were concentrated in clubs within a twenty-mile radius of Belfast.[45] In Belfast alone, however, there were as many as sixteen societies at this time.[46] If the United Irishmen were to move from their narrow base of support in the Belfast neighbourhood to become the provincial and, eventually, national movement that their strategy required, they had to devise an organizational structure which would

[40] Examination of Michael Lowry, 19, 26 Aug. 1796 (PROI, Frazer papers, IA 40/111/49); examination of Andrew Agnew (ibid. IA 40/111*a*/8).

[41] Drennan to McTier, 2 Aug. 1794 (PRONI, Drennan letters, T765/519).

[42] Earl Camden to duke of Portland, 25 July 1795 (SPOI, Rebellion papers, 620/22/19).

[43] Michael Thompson to John Pollock, 12 Apr. 1795 (Kent CAO, Pratt papers, U840/0144/8).

[44] Note on the history of the constitution of the United Irishmen (TCD, Russell correspondence, MS 868/1[N.4.2]/1).

[45] Robert Johnston to John Lees, 8 May 1795 (Kent CAO, Pratt papers, U840/0146/3).

[46] Camden to Portland, 25 July 1795 (SPOI, Rebellion papers, 620/22/19).

provide for the proliferation of new societies all over the country under centralized leadership. The revised constitution offered the means to achieve these ends.

The constitution of the United Irishmen in the late 1790s replicated the one which had preceded it. The same declaration of principles that Tandy had penned for the Dublin club in 1791 introduced the document. Tone's three resolutions, adopted in October 1791 and calling for parliamentary reform, Catholic emancipation, and a union of all Irishmen to achieve these two aims, formed the centrepiece of the so-called revised constitution. What was changed, however, was the organizational framework in which the United Irishmen were to operate. Previously, the Belfast and Dublin radicals had advocated the creation of similar societies throughout the country, but they provided no institutional mechanism by which their activities could be co-ordinated, apart from the work of the committees of correspondence. In Belfast, of course, Neilson's secret committee of public welfare attempted to direct the activities of the local northern clubs. But the Belfast leaders probably relied more on their reputation and personal standing with country members than on a formal, institutionalized process. Now, so read the constitution,

the societies of United Irishmen, ardently desiring that the *unawed, unhired,* and *honest* part of the community should become one great Society of United Irishmen, are of opinion that a general code of regulations is absolutely necessary to accomplish that important end. For this purpose they have, after mature deliberation, adopted the following *constitution* and *test,* the adoption of which is necessary for such societies as wish to enter into communication and correspondence with those already established.[47]

Each local club or Volunteer corps was urged to affiliate itself with the United Irishmen and to register with the Belfast committee. The committee would then provide each affiliated club with an identification number. When any local society reached a total membership of thirty-six, the society was to split into two, a senior and a junior society, applying to Belfast for a new number. 'When a new society is intended in any place,' reported the informer John Smith (alias Bird), 'printed instructions are given by the Belfast committee—constitutions, copies of the test, etc. When the society is full, they give notice to the Belfast committee and are then empowered to form other clubs.'[48] Each town or half-baronial society was to send three elected representatives to the baronial committee. When more than eight local societies were represented in this superior committee, the committee itself would split. Once three or more baronial committees were established within a county, the baronial representatives would elect delegates to a

---

[47] Constitution of the Society of United Irishmen (ibid. 620/34/59).
[48] Information of John Smith (alias Bird), 1795–6 (ibid. 620/27/1).

county committee, and when two or more county committees had been formed in a province, delegates from them would create a provincial committee. A national committee would be established once five persons from each of at least two provincial committees were so delegated.[49]

On 10 May 1795, in Belfast, the United Irishmen officially approved the new constitution. Numerous delegates were present from Antrim and Down, representing seventy-two local societies.[50] By August an Ulster provincial committee had been formed, serving over 8,000 United Irishmen from the counties of Antrim, Down, Armagh, and Tyrone.[51]

Local societies met monthly, generally on a Sunday evening. All members were required to pay dues: a shilling on being sworn and a shilling every month thereafter, though reductions based on ability to pay could be arranged.[52] A secretary and a treasurer constituted the chief officers of each local club, appointed for a term of three months. The treasurer and two or three elected representatives formed the committee of finance, responsible for collecting and dispersing the society's funds, the bulk of which were passed on to superior committees in order to finance United Irish emissaries, defray publication costs, purchase arms, and provide legal fees. Each local society was also required to have a committee of public safety, the chief purpose of which was to correspond with other clubs and to oversee the conduct of members. This committee was not elected: the first four persons on the seniority list of members took on the task, and every fortnight the two most senior members would give way to the next two on the list.[53] At any rate, this was how it was supposed to work; in practice, membership on the committees tended to be of much longer duration.[54] The election of delegates to superior committees was entrusted to 'two confidential men' who were chosen to count the ballots and had sworn to inform only those elected of the results, thus preserving secrecy as far as possible.[55]

All members were required to take an oath pledging themselves to promote 'a brotherhood of affection among Irishmen of every religious persuasion' and to persevere to obtain 'an equal, full, and adequate representation of *all* the people of Ireland'. Members were also bound not to reveal the

---

[49] Constitution of the Society of United Irishmen (ibid. 620/34/59).

[50] Andrew Macnevin to John Pollock, 9 May 1795 (Kent CAO, Pratt papers, U840/0146/7); McSkimin, *Annals*, 29.

[51] Robert Johnston to John Lees, 8 Aug. 1795 (SPOI, Rebellion papers, 620/22/28); Camden to Portland, 25 July 1795 (ibid. 620/22/19); Capt. —— Johnson to John Lees, 2 July 1795 (Kent CAO, Pratt papers, U840/0147/17).

[52] Camden to Portland, 25 July 1795 (SPOI, Rebellion papers, 620/22/19).

[53] Ibid.; Andrew Macnevin to Thomas Pelham, 6 July 1795 (Kent CAO, Pratt papers, U840/0148/2/1).

[54] Information of John Edward Newell, 15 Apr. 1797 (PROHO 100/69/202–5).

[55] 'The unfortunate Robert McCormick's discoveries of the plans and views of the United Irishmen, so far as known to him, and the history of his connections with them' (PRONI, McCance papers, D272/6).

secrets of the society.[56] One concerned parent, the Revd John Tennent, a Presbyterian minister, attempted unsuccessfully to wean his sons away from involvement in the United Irish movement: 'Oaths of secrecy can be no sufficient security for any society, especially among those of loose principles and licentious practices.'[57] Neilson, however, complacently applauded the caution and secrecy of the reconstituted United Irish organization. 'We have a very strong test and are as cautious as possible' in recruiting new members, 'nor have we yet been betrayed by anyone.' Ironically, Neilson was addressing his remarks to the informer John Smith.[58] The oath of secrecy may have served to reinforce the resolve of members to achieve United Irish aims, but it could hardly protect the society from infiltration by informers. James Hope lamented that 'we should shrink from an open declaration of our views into conspiracy'. This was even more regrettable, since such secrecy was, at best, illusory. Committed radicals and sincere patriots, whether oath-bound or not, would never betray their comrades; but 'oaths would never bind rogues. . . . I would rather act openly,' Hope maintained, 'in which way of proceeding there was but one danger.'[59]

The enrolment of new members formed the first order of business at each local meeting. New members were required to swear the test and oath of secrecy before the assembled United Irishmen, who stood at attention, their hats off in recognition of this solemn ceremony. After the secretary had read the minutes of the previous meeting, the main business was undertaken—committee reports. These came not only from the internal committees of finance and public safety, but, more importantly, from the superior committees in the United Irish organization.[60] Special attention was paid to the county returns of men and arms available to the organization, designed to encourage members with somewhat overstated accounts of the rapid advance of the movement.[61] Local United Irishmen could then ask their officers for further information, or they could raise questions which would be referred to the superior committee for consideration. But in many ways these local meetings served merely to rubber-stamp decisions that had already been taken by the leadership.

Nevertheless, the submissiveness of the local societies should not be exaggerated, for these clubs would often ignore the instructions of their superior committees. An example of such insubordination was provided when the United Irishmen committed themselves to grafting a military organization on to their civil one late in 1796. Again, the system was representative in

[56] Constitution of the Society of United Irishmen (SPOI, Rebellion papers, 620/34/59).
[57] Revd John Tennent to William Tennent, 6 Feb. 1796 (PRONI, Tennent papers, D1748/A/331/7).
[58] Information of John Smith (alias Bird), 1795–6 (SPOI, Rebellion papers, 620/27/1).
[59] Hope, 'Autobiographical memoir', 96.
[60] Constitution of the Society of United Irishmen (SPOI, Rebellion papers, 620/34/59).
[61] *Rep. secret comm.* 71.

theory. A local society would elect a sergeant. Three such societies would elect a captain, and ten captains, representing thirty societies which constituted a regiment, would elect their superior officers.[62] A military committee was established in Belfast by the leaders. One of its members, the infamous informer Edward Newell, complained that it had 'done little but consider plans for discipline'. In overseeing the implementation of the military organization, Newell and his comrades were pleased with the progress under way in County Down, but they ran into obstacles in Belfast and in County Antrim. In Belfast, Newell observed, 'the idea is that discipline is not necessary—that they need only give one fire and rush out with the bayonet.'[63] The independent-minded artisans and merchants of Belfast may well have bridled at this attempt to regiment them under military discipline, but some local leaders in the Antrim countryside were alarmed at the insurrectionary militancy implicit in such an initiative. 'The report of the last county committee abounds with contradiction, absurdity, and nonsense,' complained one baronial society. 'We are called upon to march well as if a knowledge of military tactics could be acquired in a closet or by night. We look upon such a report as unworthy of men who are fit to represent a county and as offering an insult to our understanding.' Furthermore, the Antrim local leaders regarded the imposition of a military system as 'premature and highly improper . . . because it would be attended with the utmost danger, for there is nothing but a pretext wanting to declare us out of the king's peace'. Not only would such a plan call forth the severest repression from the government, but it was clearly 'evident that a few counties in Ulster would be unable by force of arms to accomplish an object of such magnitude until our principles are more generally known and better understood'.[64] In this case the leadership was being condemned for being too militant.

The drilling and disciplining of the motley civilian army so assiduously recruited by the United Irishmen was entrusted largely to deserters and those republicans who had served in Volunteer corps. United Irishmen in Ballynahinch, County Down, for example, offered deserters 6*d.* a day to drill local troops.[65] But drilling was not the only form of military discipline necessary to mould an effective fighting force. An underground revolutionary army required strict secrecy from its members, a condition that was often difficult to satisfy among people prone to frequent visits to the public house, often in the service of the movement itself. The indiscreet babbling of drunken United Irishmen posed a formidable threat to the United Irish

---

[62] William Torney to Col. —— Johnson, 2 Sept. 1797 (BL, Pelham papers, Add. MS 33105/73).

[63] Information of Edward Newell, 15 Apr. 1797 (PROHO 100/69/202–5).

[64] United Irish committee report, 1796 (BL, Pelham papers, Add. MS 33104/330).

[65] Marquess of Downshire to Edward Cooke, 17 Jan. 1797 (SPOI, Rebellion papers, 620/28/109).

army. Efforts to impose sobriety on their troops enjoyed some success, and an astonished magistrate observed in June 1797: 'About nine months ago I would see more people in a state of intoxication at a market than I will perceive now in a year.'[66]

Discipline alone could not make an army formidable, and the United Irishmen also devoted much effort to securing arms and ammunition for their followers. Smuggling provided one solution. The United Irishmen in Dublin managed to supply gunpowder to their northern comrades, and weapons were smuggled out of Belfast in coffins for distribution in the countryside. American gunpowder was also shipped into Derry in flax-seed casks.[67] In addition, the Antrim United Irishmen enjoyed the services of two professional smugglers, James Morrow and Gibson Campbell, both delegated to secure arms from France.[68] Blacksmiths exercised their trade in the production of that formidable weapon, the pike, a long-handled instrument which proved remarkably effective against cavalry. Oliver Bond's father-in-law, Henry Jackson, an iron-founder in Dublin, manufactured pikes on a large scale while being employed by the government on public works projects.[69]

One of the widest chasms between theory and practice was opened when members were prohibited from participating in arms raids. The leaders rightly reasoned that such activity would only call attention to the movement from the local authorities. It was vitally important to preserve the secrecy and energy of the movement until membership and organization were sufficiently advanced to take the initiative and either to coerce the government into granting reform and emancipation or to carry through these objectives in one swift and relatively bloodless rising. The leadership assured its followers that arms would be available to all when the time came to use them. Unfortunately, the rank and file were often too impatient to heed such promises and the accompanying pleas for caution and discretion.[70]

Nocturnal raids for arms were a constant feature of United Irish activity in many parts of Ulster. Lord Cavan reported that, in the neighbourhood of Derry city, over 400 families had been robbed of their weapons in a single night.[71] Matthew Hood, land-agent to the marquis of Abercorn, laconically informed his employer of similar activity by the United Irishmen in the

[66] Revd Clotworthy Soden to Thomas Pelham, 3 June 1797 (SPOI, Rebellion papers, 620/31/22).
[67] See e.g. Macnevin to Pelham, 24 Feb. 1796 (ibid. 620/23/36); Col. James Durham to Revd Clotworthy Soden, 29 May 1796 (ibid. 620/23/129); Francis Brooke to Dublin Castle, 2 Mar. 1797 (ibid. 620/29/6).
[68] Revd James Matthew MacCarry to William Williams, 29 Mar. 1797 (ibid. 620/29/129); Andrew Macnevin to Edward Cooke, 23 May 1797 (ibid. 620/30/167).
[69] 'Left Hand' to Thomas Pelham and Edward Cooke, [1797] (ibid. 620/30/211).
[70] MacNeven, *Pieces of Irish history*, 183.
[71] W. E. H. Lecky, *A history of Ireland in the eighteenth century* (5 vols., London, 1898), iv. 13.

vicinity of his estate in west Tyrone: 'As they keep their excursions a profound secret, I have little hopes of procuring any previous intelligence in
case of a visit; as the greatest part of the arms are now taken up, their
excursions have become less frequent.'[72] James Stewart, another of
Abercorn's correspondents, observed that although every house on his lordship's Donegal estate had been robbed of arms, nothing else had been
taken.[73] This circumstance suggests an almost congenial relationship
between the United Irishmen and their victims. Many, no doubt, gladly
offered their arms to the United Irishmen out of sympathy for the cause, or,
at the very least, because of a desire to avoid confrontation with the insurgents. The United Irishmen, however, often consciously restricted their
plundering to weapons alone. As would-be revolutionaries needing mass
support, they could ill afford to alienate the country people by unnecessary
acts of aggression. The republicans aimed their more violent assaults at
parsons, zealous magistrates, and informers—those clearly hostile to the
movement. Although robbery of money as well as arms was a feature of
many United Irish raids, the financial needs of the movement were largely
supplied through subscriptions from its members.

But the rank and file also proved restive under central direction when it
came to the question of finances. Rumours abounded, clearly triggered by
the repeated requests for subscriptions from the superior committees, that
the leaders were misappropriating the society's funds. No doubt there were
a number of treasurers at all levels in the organization who pocketed a few
shillings for themselves. But the accusations became so widespread, at least
in Down, that the county committee felt obliged to issue a formal declaration in May 1797:

We are astonished that they [the rank and file] can trust us with their lives and cannot with a penny or two pence. We have had a great deal of trouble this last assizes
and the expense has been immense—our affairs in consequence has [*sic*] been rather
deranged. However, you may depend upon a regular account being given at the
next county meeting. At present we urge you, as you value the cause you are
engaged in, not to withhold the usual subscription.[74]

Despite these fitful challenges from the rank and file, the central leadership remained in control of the organization, at least to the extent that control was possible over the increasingly vast network of clubs. This central
leadership was embodied not in the provincial committee, but within an
executive directory, referred to at various times as the 'grand committee',

---

[72] Matthew Hood to marquess of Abercorn, 20 Feb. 1797 (*An introduction to the Abercorn
letters (as relating to Ireland, 1736–1819)*, ed. John H. Gebbie (Omagh, 1972), 346).

[73] James Stewart to marquess of Abercorn, 3 Mar. 1797 (PRONI, Abercorn papers,
T2541/IB2/2/6).

[74] United Irish handbill forwarded by Roger Parke to Col. —— Cooper, 22 May 1797
(SPOI, Rebellion papers, 620/30/144).

the 'committee of elders' (suggestive of the Presbyterian predominance in the movement), or the 'committee of public welfare' in Belfast, which passed orders to the local clubs through the provincial and county committees.[75] It was this committee which managed and financed United Irish emissaries to carry the system to the rest of the country. The executive directory also approved the formation of new societies and generally oversaw all organizational matters relating to the movement. It sent out representatives to local clubs to collect money and 'to examine the societies and to confirm them in their republican career'.[76] Most important, the Belfast committee decided all major policy and tactical questions confronting the organization. 'All business of the greatest importance originated in an executive directory, who communicated with their provincial committee,' reported a County Down informer in August 1797.[77] Negotiations with the French, for example, were supervised by the executive directory.[78] And in the summer of 1797, when Lake's troops were ravaging the countryside, rooting out sedition wherever they could find it, the executive directory ordered all committees, from the provincial down to the local societies, temporarily to cease meeting.[79] The provincial committee elected five members to the executive directory, but the directors themselves were empowered to co-opt additional members if needed.[80] This meant that the directory was only partially accountable to the network of clubs and committees which they represented and directed. If the collective wisdom of the inferior societies failed to push forward men of talent and ability (at least in the judgement of the Belfast leaders), the executive directors could rectify the error as well as ensure a continuity of leadership which, though disrupted by government arrests, would be immune from the interference of the lower committees. As Camden observed to Portland in June 1797, the originators of the United Irishmen 'still remain in great degree the directors'.[81]

By October 1796 the United Irish system had expanded beyond Ulster and into Leinster, where a provincial committee was formed.[82] By the following December a national executive had been established.[83] The centre of

[75] Information of Francis Higgins (SPOI, Rebellion papers, 620/18/14); William Bristow to Dublin Castle, 24 May 1796 (ibid. 620/23/122); John Macarra to Gen. George Nugent, 8 Aug. 1797 (BL, Pelham papers, Add. MS 33105/14–15); Macnevin to Pelham, 6 July 1795 (Kent CAO, Pratt papers, U840/0148/2/1).
[76] Information of John Smith (alias Bird), 1795–6 (SPOI, Rebellion papers, 620/27/1); see also Macnevin to Pelham, 6 July 1795 (Kent CAO, Pratt papers, U840/0148/2/1).
[77] Macarra to Nugent, 8 Aug. 1797 (BL, Pelham papers, Add. MS 33105/14–15).
[78] Francis Higgins to Dublin Castle, 19 Aug. 1796 (SPOI, Rebellion papers, 620/18/14).
[79] Viscount Castlereagh to Thomas Pelham, 11 Nov. 1797 (BL, Pelham papers, Add. MS 33105/204).
[80] Information of Samuel Turner (PROHO 100/70/339–49).
[81] Camden to Portland, 17 June 1797 (ibid. 100/69/397–9).
[82] Camden to Portland, 13 Nov. 1796 (ibid. 100/62/333–4).
[83] Earl of Londonderry to Dublin Castle, [1] Jan. 1797 (SPOI, Rebellion papers, 620/28/2).

the Leinster organization, obviously, was in Dublin, where the United Irish society had been suppressed in 1794. In fact, however, the activists had never ceased to meet in Dublin. In July 1794 the Sheares brothers hosted a United Irish meeting to receive addresses from radical societies in Dundee and Glasgow.[84] A few months later, Drennan wrote to McTier:

Our society met last night at [Henry] Jackson's in Church Street. . . . There were about fifty present . . . About 250 are now members . . . Sheares proposed a new plan of organizing the society into sections, which may meet in different parts of the city, never more than fifteen in number, each section returning weekly a deputy to a council or central committee. . . . I suppose this will be adopted, though I don't like it much for myself, as I shall not attend these petty, private, plotting meetings which, though they may multiply numbers, will not, I think, add real power and will annihilate or disorganise, as the term is, the society itself.[85]

It is not clear whether Sheares's plan was adopted in Dublin. There is no mention of official United Irish meetings in the capital in the documentary sources until the autumn of 1796.[86] But there was, nevertheless, a great deal of republican activity in Dublin at this time. It seems that, by the early months of 1795, the Dublin United Irishmen, or at least a radical rump, had reorganized themselves, meeting under the banner of the Strugglers' Club, a change in name, but not in personnel.[87] One Dublin informer claimed that the most important republican club in Dublin in 1795 and 1796 was simply called the 'Committee', which may have been the Strugglers. The 'Committee' consisted of about seventy members, 'mostly men of great property and extremely cautious of whom they admit. They imitate all the forms of the Jacobin society of France', addressing one another as 'citizen' on penalty of a fine, and even addressing waiters in the same manner.[88] According to information collected by Francis Higgins, editor of the pro-government *Freeman's Journal*, the Catholic Committee was also active in pursuing republican principles and in corresponding with the Belfast United Irishmen.[89]

Because they mobilized under the watchful eye of the local authorities, the Dublin radicals had to be extremely cautious throughout the late 1790s. 'They now resort to publick tea houses evening and morning and take a few women with them,' reported one informer. 'They sit at different tables

---

[84] Sackville Hamilton to Evan Nepean, 14 July 1794 (PROHO 100/52/159).

[85] Drennan to McTier, [Oct. 1794] (*Drennan letters*, 214–15). Henry Jackson was a wealthy iron-founder.

[86] Higgins to Dublin Castle, 27, 30 Sept. 1796 (SPOI, Rebellion papers, 620/18/14).

[87] John Pollock to Thomas Pelham, 16 Apr. 1795 (Kent CAO, Pratt papers, U840/0143/7); J. Sheridan to John Crawford, 21 Apr. 1795 (ibid. U840/0143/9); 'J. W.' to ——, 22 Apr. 1795 (ibid. U840/0143/11); Thomas Boyle to ——, n.d. (SPOI, Rebellion papers, 620/18/3); Higgins to Dublin Castle, n.d. (ibid. 620/18/14).

[88] Information of Thomas Corbett, 1796 (ibid. 620/27/1).

[89] Higgins to Dublin Castle, 30 Sept. 1796 (ibid. 620/18/14).

in partys [*sic*] of three or four—one from a party is seen to go to another party, and in this way they communicate their sentiments.'[90] Generally, radicals met at private houses. If large assemblies were desired, however, the radicals could meet under the cover of wrestling matches, race meetings, football matches, or other seemingly innocuous recreational gatherings, where large crowds would not raise suspicions among the authorities.[91] Under such circumstances, it was difficult to impose the same kind of structure employed by republicans in the north. But in February 1797 leading radicals met to consider a proposal to reconstitute the Dublin republican clubs on the northern model, largely at the urging and with the assistance of the Belfast United Irishmen themselves.[92] Three weeks later a committee of public safety was established in the capital, and the task of bringing order and regulation to the chaos of Dublin republicanism was well under way.[93]

There were some differences between the organization in Dublin and the system adopted in Ulster. Societies in the capital were to be restricted to no more than eleven members, each of whom, barring apprentices, was to pay 6½*d*. as an entrance fee and 6½*d*. in monthly dues.[94] The restriction in size of each local society was probably imposed because of the greater need for security among the clubs in the capital, but in fact entry into the organization seems to have been a relatively easy matter. One government agent attended a local meeting only to find more than a hundred people there.[95] The real direction was provided by the 'grand committee' or committee of public safety, which, like its counterpart in Belfast, transacted the major business of the organization in the capital.[96] The committee of public safety met regularly, but not the reconstituted local United Irish clubs. The central committee was empowered to prohibit the subordinate committees from meeting if circumstances warranted.[97] It is surely more than coincidental that the very structure proposed by Neilson to the Dublin club in 1794 came to dominate the activities of the entire United Irish organization in the late 1790s.

There were thus two parallel developments in the transformation of the United Irish societies into a mass-based revolutionary movement in the mid-1790s. In the north, with its network of militant affiliated clubs enjoying some direction from a secret committee in Belfast, the United Irishmen

[90] Boyle to ——, [1797] (ibid. 620/18/3).
[91] Boyle to ——, 5 July, 9 Dec. 1796, Apr. 1797 (ibid.); —— to Dublin Castle, 1 Nov. 1796 (ibid. 620/26/3).
[92] Higgins to Dublin Castle, 16 Feb. 1797 (ibid. 620/18/14).
[93] Higgins to Dublin Castle, 9 Apr. 1797 (ibid.).
[94] Plan of organization of the United Irishmen in Dublin (ibid. 620/34/51).
[95] Edward Nicholson to Edward Cooke, 13 Apr. 1797 (ibid. 620/29/240).
[96] Higgins to Dublin Castle, 18 June 1797 (ibid. 620/18/14).
[97] Boyle to ——, 29 Aug. 1797 (ibid. 620/18/3); Camden to Portland, 8 Aug. 1797 (PROHO 100/70/93–4).

merely needed to regulate the creation of additional clubs. This was achieved by the institution of a hierarchical system based on the town or parish unit and culminating in a provincial and, finally, a national committee. The system was thus designed to enhance communication with the subordinate societies and to impose discipline and order on them. In Dublin, however, the society had to be completely overhauled. Republican and Defender clubs proliferated in the mid-1790s in Dublin, and among them were the remnant bodies of the suppressed United Irishmen. In order to impose some order and co-ordination on these various clubs, the Dublin radical leaders adapted the system established by the United Irishmen of Ulster. They did this partly because of pressure from the more advanced northerners, but mostly perhaps to contain and channel the development of artisan radicalism in the capital, which might well leave the middle-class leaders isolated and vulnerable.

Ulstermen, however, did not continue to dominate the organization that they succeeded in imposing on the capital. When the movement began to take on that national dimension essential to the United Irish strategy, the Ulster leadership found itself increasingly isolated from the central direction of the conspiracy. The ablest leaders in the north had been arrested from September 1796, and the baton of command had passed to less capable and less courageous men. As the calibre of these new northern leaders was not such as to place them in the forefront of the movement, the initiative passed easily to the Dublin republicans.

A national executive directory was appointed in November 1797 with five members, one from each of the four provinces of Ireland and one director. But it was not a northerner, but rather a relative newcomer to the republican movement, Arthur O'Connor, who represented Ulster.[98] A barrister and the nephew of a peer, O'Connor was a native of County Cork. His rather tenuous connection with the north was established when he attempted unsuccessfully to be returned for County Antrim in the 1797 general election. Thus Ulster was virtually unrepresented on the national executive which provided central direction for the United Irish movement. It was a remarkable turn of events, after the lead that the province had taken in radical politics over the last two decades.

But it was neither the calibre of the leadership nor its geographical base that alarmed the government. The arrest of the northern leaders from the autumn of 1796 had failed to throw the United Irish movement into disarray, prompting Camden to tell Portland: 'It is therefore the regularity of their system which is to be dreaded more than any individual ability.'[99] The strength of the United Irish organization thus lay in this ability to withstand frequent assaults—the arrest of the northern leaders, the dragooning

[98] Higgins to Dublin Castle, Jan. 1798 (SPOI, Rebellion papers, 620/18/14).
[99] Camden to Portland, 17 June 1797 (PROHO 100/69/397–9).

of Ulster in 1797, and even the arrest of the Leinster directory in 1798. If the aim of the United Irishmen was to establish that contradiction in terms, a mass-based conspiracy, they succeeded to a remarkable degree.

But, as James Hope had observed, oaths would not bind rogues, and the major weakness to afflict the United Irish organization was that it was far too easy to infiltrate. The most serious threats to United Irish security came not from the lower ranks, but from those holding fairly responsible positions in the organization. The government was fortunate in the erstwhile revolutionaries whom it detached from the republican movement—men such as Leonard McNally, a trusted barrister and one of the earliest members of the Dublin society as well as an active organizer in his native Cork. Frightened by his implication in the Jackson episode and pessimistic about the ultimate fortunes of the United Irishmen, McNally furnished the authorities with detailed and reliable reports concerning the activities of friends and colleagues in the organization, especially in Dublin.[100] Lord Castlereagh's old mentor, the Revd James Cleland, a County Down magistrate, secured the valuable services of Nicholas Magin. A Catholic farmer, Magin was a member of the Ulster provincial committee and a colonel in the United Irish army of Down. Magin's motives, like McNally's, may not have been entirely self-serving. When he first discovered his own distaste for the course pursued by the republican movement, Magin simply wanted to retire, but, at Cleland's urging, he remained as a government agent.[101] Perhaps Magin and McNally believed that they were serving their country and even their friends by attempting to mitigate the consequences of the revolutionary zeal of the republican movement. By keeping the government informed, they may have wished to prevent a rising, the outcome of which, in their view, could only prove disastrous.

McNally and Magin were joined by scores of other informers, including perhaps the most self-interested and most colourful scoundrel of them all, Edward Newell.[102] A miniature-painter in Belfast, Newell at one time boasted that he was the 'cause of confining 227 innocent men to either the cell of a bastille or the hold of a tender'.[103] Originally from Dublin, where he was a member of the radical Philanthropic Society, Newell arrived in Belfast early in 1796 and was quickly sworn into the Defender/United Irish organization by John Gordon, a clerk to John McCracken. Newell promptly insinuated himself into the inner circles of radical and republican

---

[100] Elliott, *Partners in revolution*, 64, 73.

[101] John Magin to Viscount Castlereagh, 30 June 1800 (PRONI, R. C. Lytton White papers, D714/5/2).

[102] For Newell's own self-serving account of his career, see John Edward Newell, *The apostacy of Newell, containing the life and the confessions of that celebrated informer* (London, 1798).

[103] Quoted in Charles Dickson, *Revolt in the north: Antrim and Down in 1798* (Dublin, 1960), 70.

Belfast and became privy to many United Irish secrets, or so he claimed. A boastful and indiscreet man, he soon called himself to the attention of the authorities, and, rather than face punishment for his seditious activities, he accepted with alacrity the government's offer of a pardon in exchange for information. In May 1797 Newell provided the secret committee of the Irish house of lords, established to examine the progress of the United Irishmen, with valuable and damaging testimony.[104] But perhaps the most serious consequence of Newell's activity on behalf of the government was the arrest of numerous United Irishmen in the upper and middle ranks of the organization in Belfast. Mary Ann McCracken informed her brother Henry Joy that twenty-one United Irishmen were arrested in one night, and 'it is supposed Newell the painter was the informer'. It became something of a rather macabre, nocturnal ritual for Newell, hooded or masked, to accompany the military about Belfast in order to identify and arrest suspected United Irishmen.[105]

The proliferation of informers and government agents in the society was not the only menace. Leaders elected by the rank and file, chosen largely for their social consequence rather than their courage or intelligence, often defected from the movement when put to the test. 'The desire for distinction was a motive that induced many to accept of appointments without seeing the responsibilities attached to them', wrote James Hope,

or the consequence to others of their delinquency, which led them to save themselves at any price, even the blood of the men who appointed them . . . I do not rank them with the common herd of traitors; they are rather men who unthinkingly staked more than was really in them—they were like paper money, current for the time, keeping business afloat without any intrinsic value.[106]

The system was also supposed to facilitate communication between the central leadership and the rank-and-file societies through the medium of delegates and representatives to a succession of superior committees. Although this was certainly an improvement over the loose network of clubs which had characterized the early years of the United Irish movement, it was still fundamentally flawed. As far as possible, the United Irishmen avoided putting anything on paper, and consequently relied on messengers. Such a mode of communication suited the smaller organization that had operated within a twenty-mile radius of Belfast, where information could be relayed speedily and efficiently. But as the organization grew, communi-

[104] See Pelham's notes on Newell's testimony before the secret committee of the Irish house of lords, 2–3 May 1797, in 'Private memoranda by T. Pelham', in Sir John T. Gilbert (ed.), *Documents relating to Ireland, 1795–1804* (Dublin, 1893), 104–8 (hereafter cited as 'Pelham memoranda').
[105] Mary Ann McCracken to Henry Joy McCracken, 13 Apr. 1797 (TCD, Madden papers, MS 873/117).
[106] Hope, 'Autobiographical memoir', 122.

cations became a real problem. During times of special government vigilance, the executive ordered subordinate committees to cease meeting, thus cutting off that particular channel of communication. Even when effective, however, county and provincial meetings only met monthly. A speedy, efficient mode of issuing orders or information to subordinate committees continued to elude an organization which tried to keep its activities as secret as possible and relied for its success on a nationwide and, consequently, dispersed network of local societies. If the leaders were frustrated in their attempts to issue direct orders to subordinate societies, the local societies themselves were often discouraged by their inability to secure reliable information from their leaders. A farm labourer in north Derry, Charles McFillin, described such a situation late in 1796: 'It was rumoured that the French had arrived, and a member rode instantly to Belfast to know the truth; on his return he expressed much surprise that the executive directory had no intelligence of the coming of the French.'[107] This, of course, was a reference to the invasion attempt at Bantry Bay in December 1796.

'They are preparing for some great event,' James Stewart warned Abercorn about the United Irishmen in Donegal.[108] Rents and debts remained unpaid as the countryside awaited the expected rising.[109] Oliver Bond, an active Dublin United Irishman with roots in Derry, distributed promissory notes to the poor, payable after the revolution, to encourage support and to create a vested interest in the outcome.[110] But despite the fears of almost every northern magistrate that a rising was imminent, from 1796 through much of 1797 the United Irish organization in the north was less formidable than it appeared to outsiders. Co-ordination and co-operation among the numerous local societies were often loose. The lower levels of the United Irish hierarchy were generally unaware of the identity of their superior leaders, but their ignorance was deliberately contrived to preserve secrecy.[111] The executive urged that meetings be held regularly, but never in the same place twice.[112] Treasonable letters were written in lemon juice, an invisible ink which could be made visible by heating the paper.[113] In May 1797 the Belfast leaders issued new orders calculated to produce even tighter security. If possible, all communications were to be verbal, and new signs and passwords were required. Secretaries were pro-

---

[107] *Rep. secret comm.* 79.

[108] Stewart to Abercorn, 3 Mar. 1797 (PRONI, Abercorn papers, T2541/IB2/2/6).

[109] See e.g. Andrew Newton to Revd Richard Bourne, 15 Aug. 1796 (SPOI, Rebellion papers, 620/24/120); Revd George Lambert to Dublin Castle, 22 May 1797 (ibid. 620/30/145).

[110] 'Left Hand' to Pelham and Cooke, [1797] (ibid. 620/30/211).

[111] Hope, 'Autobiographical memoir', 108.

[112] William Hales to Gen. Charles Vallancey, 22 May 1797 (SPOI, Rebellion papers, 620/30/190).

[113] Revd George Lambert to Edward Cooke, 22 Jan. 1797 (ibid. 620/28/167).

hibited from holding meetings in public houses or inns. No more than three committee secretaries were permitted to meet together at any one time, and then only in the most secluded spot. And secretaries were forbidden to carry official papers on their persons.[114]

Another problem in the United Irish organization was that, even when orders were speedily and secretly relayed, the republican rank and file might refuse to obey them. The system depended on the willingness of local societies to accept direction and discipline, but the organization had few means to enforce its decisions. An informer or traitor within the movement, of course, could be assassinated, but what was to be done with a society which refused to accept the executive's prohibition against arms raids? How could the leadership deal with local chiefs who refused to mobilize their followers when summoned? During the rebellion in the north, many erstwhile United Irish captains failed to marshal their men to do what they themselves now thought better of—risk their lives in a contest of arms with disciplined government troops.

But the United Irish leaders could not afford to discipline their followers, for they might lose them. The most serious flaw in the United Irish system was also the source of its greatest strength—its numbers. The more extensive the system, the more vulnerable it became to informers, lack of discipline, confusion, and the half-hearted commitment of its loosely recruited members. The movement, so the leaders assumed, could only achieve success if it could demonstrate the popular will in action, mobilized in United Irish societies throughout the country, and waiting to strike if the government persisted in its intransigent refusal to make timely concessions. Consequently, recruitment was the top priority.

United Irish organization in Ulster after 1795 reflects the tension resulting from the conflict between ideological and pragmatic impulses which combined to create that seeming contradiction in terms, a mass-based, secret society. The attempt to imbue this organizational structure with democratic and republican forms was not always successful. The requirements of secrecy often collided with the desire for widespread, informed participation. The tensions thus produced created certain structural strains which weakened the organization as an efficient revolutionary tool. And yet these tensions also produced certain strengths which were successfully tested when the Irish government launched an aggressive campaign to root out sedition in Ulster. The combined effects of mass arrests, judicial activism, martial law, and especially General Lake's dragooning of Ulster seem to have succeeded in subduing revolutionary ardour in the north, accounting, so it has been argued, for the pathetic showing of the northern United Irishmen in the rebellion in Antrim and Down in June 1798.[115] Yet while

[114] Earl Annesley to Dublin Castle, 30 May 1797 (ibid 620/30/254).
[115] 'What did *not* happen in the north is as important as what did in the south' (R. F.

these events may have had a chilling effect on many leaders and casual supporters of the United Irish movement, the organizational structure survived
intact and, in some ways, may have been strengthened by the defections of
the weakly committed.[116]

As a model for an underground revolutionary organization, the United
Irish movement was wanting in several respects. Its network was too
vulnerable to infiltration, confusion, and insubordination. The larger the
organization became, the more difficult it was to manage. But such vulnera-
bilities were the price of the ideological and propagandistic functions of the
organization. For a chief priority of the republicans was to educate the citizen, to, as Thomas Addis Emmet put it, 'make every man a politician'.[117]
This involved embracing mass participation, and instituting, as far as circumstances permitted, democratic and republican practices. The movement
lingered on after 1798 as a tiny conspiracy until Robert Emmet's insurrectionary outburst in 1803, reconstituted in such a way as to eliminate what
was regarded as its major weakness, its mass-participatory and quasi-
democratic character.[118] But never again did an underground republican
movement enjoy as massive a following or as formidable and extensive an
organization as the United Irishmen in the 1790s.

Foster, *Modern Ireland, 1600–1972* (London, 1988), 279); see also Elliott, *Partners in revolution*,
125–30, 166, who argues the partial success of Lake's campaign and the subsequent alteration
of the United Irish movement.

[116] See Ch. 10 for the persistence and strength of the United Irish organization in Ulster.

[117] Thomas Addis Emmet, 'Part of an essay towards the history of Ireland', in MacNeven,
Pieces of Irish history, 77.

[118] See Elliott, *Partners in revolution*, 244–50, 303–22.

5

Recruitment and Social Composition

RECRUITMENT was the chief activity of the United Irishmen—recruitment among the military, among Defenders, and among the popular classes in town and countryside. And recruitment was a provocative and inclusive act. The diffusion of United Irish propaganda—newspapers, pamphlets, songs, and demonstrations of republican strength and solidarity—paved the way for the legions of emissaries sent out by the central leadership in Belfast and Dublin during the second half of the 1790s. Indeed, in the early years of this revolutionary phase Belfast took the lead in extending the organization among the lower classes, not only in the Ulster countryside, but in the capital as well. Leonard McNally reported as late as February 1797 that as many as 1,400 northerners were engaged in organizing in Dublin.[1] This reflected the ascendancy that northern leaders enjoyed with the movement during the middle years of the decade. By the following June, however, the Dubliners themselves had assumed primary responsibility for organizing the province of Leinster, and sent scores of emissaries into the counties of Wicklow, Wexford, and Carlow.[2]

The leaders, whether in Dublin or Belfast, co-ordinated the activities of the United Irish agents whom they sent into the countryside. 'Every member that travels', remarked the informer John Smith, 'has a certificate from his particular society signed by some of the Belfast committee. . . . This empowers him to take tests and create new clubs in all parts of Ireland and to stimulate them to greater exertion.'[3] In Dublin Francis Higgins regretted that he had the duty 'to communicate that working tradesmen and manufacturers are set on by the committee to institute republican clubs under the name of United Irishmen'.[4] Such emissaries were liberally supplied with United Irish funds to defray their expenses and furnish the material inducements often needed to attract new recruits. The Belfast leaders, for example, sent a number of dry-goods pedlars on a recruiting mission from the north through the rest of the country and as far south as County Waterford: 'They had the command of bushels of money,' declared one informer.[5]

---

[1] 'J. W.' to Edward Cooke, 5 Feb. 1797 (SPOI, Rebellion papers, 620/36/227).
[2] Francis Higgins to Dublin Castle, 8 June 1797 (ibid. 620/18/14).
[3] Information of John Smith (alias Bird), 1795–6 (ibid. 620/27/1).
[4] Higgins to Dublin Castle, 16 Oct. 1796 (ibid. 620/18/14).
[5] —— to Thomas Knox, 11 June 1796 (ibid. 620/23/165).

Clergymen persistently demonstrated their usefulness in drawing crowds and in enlisting United Irish supporters. Probably more than two-thirds of the northern United Irishmen were Presbyterians, a circumstance easily explained by Ulster's peculiar demographic position as the bastion of dissent in Ireland.[6] The encouragement that Presbyterian ministers gave to their congregations to participate in radical and revolutionary politics was an important factor in mobilizing support throughout the Ulster countryside. 'The Presbyterian ministers', insisted Lord Downshire in November 1796, 'are unquestionably the great encouragers and promoters of sedition.'[7] With some exaggeration, Colonel James Leith of County Tyrone confirmed this observation: 'nine out of ten of the Dissenting clergy are united and active in the department of secretaries to revolutionary committees, and all the schoolmasters.'[8] The minister of the seceding community in Tyrone, the Revd John Lowry, used his pulpit to condemn enrolment in the loyalist yeomanry corps. He even refused the sacrament to one member of his congregation who had been particularly active in suppressing the United Irishmen.[9] An itinerant Presbyterian preacher named William Gibson, a Covenanter, roamed County Antrim 'to preach sedition and the word'. Lecturing in the fields, he often attracted crowds of several thousand. Unfortunately, he sometimes forgot himself and made untoward allusions to the 'whore of Babylon'. His superiors in the movement soon replaced him with another preacher of the same sect, a man named Joseph Orr. Gibson was appointed to another preaching circuit, where his anti-Catholic lapses were perhaps less offensive.[10]

Revolutionary republicanism was also disseminated in urban areas and commercial centres which attracted people from the countryside. On these visits to the towns, they were exposed to the politics of the United Irishmen and carried these new ideas back with them to their own neighbourhoods. James Hope declared: 'The influence of the union began to be felt at all public places, fairs, markets, and social meetings, extending to all the counties of Ulster, for no man of an enlightened mind had intercourse with Belfast who did not return home determined on disseminating the principles of the union among their neighbours.'[11] The fairs held in most of the provincial towns provided United Irishmen with opportunities to increase communication between town and countryside. The linen industry was still largely a domestic one, conducted in cottages throughout Ulster. Belfast

[6] Revd J. B. Woodburn, The Ulster Scot: his history and religion (London, 1915), 308.

[7] Marquess of Downshire to Dublin Castle, [?] Nov. 1796 (SPOI, Rebellion papers, 620/26/27).

[8] Col. James Leith to Thomas Pelham, 21 Mar. 1797 (ibid. 620/29/100).

[9] Thomas Forsyth to Dublin Castle, 2 Aug. 1797 (ibid. 620/32/50); see also R. M. Young, Ulster in '98: episodes and anecdotes (Belfast, 1893), 67–8.

[10] Samuel McSkimin, Annals of Ulster from 1790 to 1798, ed. E. J. McCrum (Belfast, 1906), 41.

[11] Hope, 'Autobiographical memoir', 104.

was the great market centre, but there were others, such as Lurgan, Dungannon, Coleraine, and Derry. In all these towns United Irish merchants and manufacturers were busy advancing the cause. When the United Irish organization did become rooted in the countryside, it was often in key linen-manufacturing areas.

While the central leadership, first in Belfast and then in Dublin, assumed primary responsibility for extending the revolutionary organization throughout the country, local societies were required to find their own recruits. It was, of course, in their interest to attract new members, for the safety of the republicans was enhanced when the surrounding community supported them. Furthermore, the aims of the movement would be realized more quickly with the addition of more and more recruits to their organization. Local recruiters would also be made more sensitive to the grievances and fears which gripped their neighbours, and could exploit this knowledge in their quest for new adherents.

In general, the United Irish recruiters, whether local or employed by the central leadership, based their appeals on four themes. The first, and most often used among Catholics and Defenders, was sectarian—heightening tensions and fears between Catholics and protestants in order to bring the former into the republican fold. The exploitation of confessional grievances was a double-edged sword in the hands of the United Irishmen. It accounted in part for the extensive participation of Presbyterians and their ministers in the Ulster organization. But United Irish efforts to enlist Catholics, and especially Defenders, in the republican organization underscored rather than alleviated sectarian tensions in Ireland. And whereas many Presbyterian radicals sought the abolition of any state religion in Ireland, Defenders seemed to espouse the replacement of protestant by Catholic ascendancy. The course and consequence of United Irish efforts to recruit Catholics and Defenders will be discussed in the next chapter.

The second appeal was ideological, reflected in much of the United Irish propaganda, and sought to attract recruits by painting in glowing colours the intrinsic value of popular democracy and republicanism. To a certain extent, republicanism became associated in the common mind with low rents, the abolition of tithes, and a tax burden borne by the wealthy and idle rather than by the poor and industrious. But it also conferred the privileged status of 'citizen' on the mass of the people and invited them to participate meaningfully in the government of their country. In addition, republicanism was intellectually and emotionally attractive in Ulster, especially given the affinity between Presbyterianism and political radicalism.

A third approach was based on the social and economic grievances of the Irish people—rents, tithes, and taxes—and insinuations about material benefits which would follow a successful revolution. As we shall see, recruiters not only promised the alleviation of such grievances in the republican future, but also offered various financial inducements to new members in the immediate present. The fourth mode of recruitment, usually employed when material self-interest and reason failed to move the people, relied on intimidation and terror. Not only did many republicans use direct threats, but they also assiduously encouraged the conviction that the United Irishmen, emerging as the strongest party in the state, must surely overwhelm the unpopular established regime.

'The lower order of the people and most of the middle class are determined republicans, have imbibed the French principles, and will not be contented with anything short of a revolution,' General Lake observed to Chief Secretary Pelham in March 1797.[12] The inhabitants of the neighbourhood of Carrickfergus refused to take an oath of allegiance to the established government, owing, according to a local priest, to the 'blasphemous doctrines of Thomas Paine and his pupils'.[13] Political radicalism pervaded the north, according to a Belfast correspondent: 'A republic upon the French plan is the object of all the men and women of this part of Ireland (with very few exceptions).'[14] Clearly, the *Northern Star* and other vehicles for the dissemination of republican principles had succeeded in arousing an interest in a change of government. The work of the recruiters was made easier, therefore, when such notions began to take root among the people. All that was left for them to do was to convince the politically concerned that involvement in the United Irish movement alone would secure meaningful and sweeping reforms in Ireland.

Convinced democrats might nevertheless be reluctant insurrectionists, and many United Irish recruiters hoped to sweeten the pill of dangerous and illegal paramilitary activity with the bait of material gain to be derived from involvement in the revolutionary movement. 'The luring prospects of division of property which they [the United Irishmen] hold out', reported Sir George F. Hill, far outweighed the dread of legal punishments.[15] 'Such inducements are held out', observed a clerical magistrate in County Derry, 'as scarcely ever fail to gain over those who come first only from a principle of curiosity.'[16]

What were these inducements? They ranged from the general and vague to the particular and specific. Some United Irish recruiters and the handbills that they circulated suggested that a major redistribution of land would follow a successful revolution: 'The lands were promised "to be their own and divided equally", and thus the United Irishmen are able to seduce the peas-

---

[12] Gen. Gerard Lake to Thomas Pelham, 13 Mar. 1797 (BL, Pelham papers, Add. MS 33103/224–5).

[13] Revd James McCarry to Edward Cooke, 2 Jan. 1798 (SPOI, Rebellion papers, 620/35/8).

[14] James Cuff to Thomas Pelham, 13 Apr. 1797 (ibid. 620/29/236).

[15] Sir George F. Hill to Thomas Pelham, 20 Mar. 1797 (ibid. 620/29/96).

[16] Revd Isaac Ashe to Sackville Hamilton, 27 Jan. 1796 (ibid. 620/23/14).

antry.'[17] This particular chord had to be played softly and with circumspection so as not to echo offensively in the ears of middle-class supporters of the cause. The United Irishmen did promise that church lands and those properties belonging to opponents of the new revolutionary order would be confiscated. But Tone and the other negotiators in France had already promised the Directory that these confiscated estates would be sold to repay the expenditures of the promised invasion. It is hardly likely that the republican leadership itself seriously intended to institute a major redistribution of land. Indeed, such a suggestion can only be regarded as a lure held out to the distressed lower classes to attract their participation. But in their other promises about the economic benefits to be derived from a republican government the leaders were in earnest.

The abolition of tithes and taxes was a rallying cry around which merchant and weaver, manufacturer and farmer, professional man and labourer could gather enthusiastically. General Knox observed that, initially, the northern United Irishmen attempted to use the issue of Catholic emancipation to attract the lower class: 'It failed in the effect of rousing the lower order of Roman Catholics, and the republicans were therefore obliged to throw in the bait of abolition of tithes, reduction of rents, etc. This has completely answered the purpose, and the whole mass of the Catholics of Ulster are United Irishmen.'[18] A United Irish agent in County Armagh told his recruits that the republicans would do away with tithes and taxes, and promised, for example, that shoes which now cost 7 shillings would cost only three 'when once they had liberty'.[19] A recruiter at a public house in County Down announced that the United Irish movement was 'the best thing going', and that its first act in power would be 'to pull down tythes'.[20] A United Irish circular letter associated these economic grievances with tyrannical government, thus linking republicanism to material self-interest. Rack-rents and tithes 'were the oppressive curse of the industrious and made a free people become Negroes'.[21]

Some potential recruits preferred immediate financial inducements to join the republicans rather than mere promises of what was to come. Recruitment was an expensive enterprise and a great strain on the republican war chest. Agents were obliged to entertain (often a euphemism for ply with drink) prospective members, and often pledged economic assistance of various sorts. A network of hospitality was made available whereby all

---

[17] Higgins to Dublin Castle, 13 May 1798 (ibid. 620/18/14); see also ibid. 620/2/32/1, for a United Irish handbill promising an equal division of land.

[18] Gen. John Knox to Thomas Pelham, 28 May 1797 (BL, Pelham papers, Add. MS 33104/139).

[19] William Brownlow to Thomas Pelham, 17 Dec. 1796 (SPOI, Rebellion papers, 620/26/133).

[20] Robert Waddell to Edward Cooke, 9 Aug. 1796 (ibid. 620/24/100).

[21] Higgins to Dublin Castle, 12 Feb. 1797 (ibid. 620/18/14).

members could be assured of free board and lodging from comrades throughout the nation.[22] In County Antrim weavers were induced to join the movement by an offer of 1 guinea extra for each web from United Irish linen drapers. Shopkeepers promised to forgive the small debts of those willing to join the society.[23] In the simple matter of employment, United Irish manufacturers would hire only those of similar political sympathies. In Belfast, with its high concentration of radical employers, such conditions posed a severe problem for loyalist labourers, who petitioned the government for relief in October 1796.[24] As consumers, too, the United Irishmen exerted pressure by boycotting loyalist enterprises.[25] Thus individual self-interest, and sometimes economic survival, played an important role in United Irish recruitment.

Francis Higgins claimed that the United Irish appeal was based on terror and reward.[26] When conviction, persuasion, or financial inducements failed to attract the Ulster masses to the cause of republicanism, the United Irishmen were not squeamish about employing the time-honoured methods of intimidation to increase their numbers. A threatening notice posted in May 1796 at Bushmills, Country Antrim, warned the inhabitants that now was the time to join the United Irishmen 'if you have any thoughts of self-preservation or living in freedom thereafter, for before the latter end of June you may expect to see as great a revolution in Ireland as you ever heard of being in France'.[27] Both the carrot and the stick of United Irish recruitment were found in this injunction. The threat of destruction for failure to join the republicans was incongruously linked with the promise of freedom and liberty. 'The United Irishmen are doubling their activity and are now proselytizing by terror,' Cooke reported in August 1796.[28] 'There is such a system of terror on foot in this neighbourhood', declared Nathaniel Alexander in County Tyrone, 'as ever was in France. . . . There has not been a person here that has not received the most threatening letters, even to the lowest cottages, to force them to unite.' Dire consequences awaited those who refused to patronize United Irish inns, public houses, or shops.[29] 'There is scarcely a peaceable, well-disposed person in this whole neighbourhood', observed a gentleman near Cookstown, 'who has not

[22] Thomas Whinnery to Dublin Castle, 1 Oct. 1796 (SPOI, Rebellion papers, 620/25/137); earl of Portarlington to Dublin Castle, 10 Oct. 1796 (ibid. 620/25/156).

[23] Examination of William Hart, 22 Sept. 1795 (ibid. 620/22/41).

[24] See 'Petition from distressed loyalists in Belfast', 10 Oct. 1796 (ibid. 620/25/159); George Murdoch to duke of Devonshire, 12 Oct. 1796 (ibid. 620/25/165).

[25] 'Pelham memoranda', 115.

[26] Higgins to Dublin Castle, [1798] (ibid. 620/18/14).

[27] Edward Cooke to Gen. George Nugent, 25 July 1796 (NAM, Nugent papers, 6807/174/147–8).

[28] Cooke to Nugent, 11 Aug. 1796 (PRONI, McCance papers, D272/73/161).

[29] Nathaniel Alexander to Henry Alexander, 15 Nov. 1796 (SPOI, Rebellion papers, 620/26/85).

received anonymous letters threatening him with loss of life if he did not join their societies.'[30] Captain Andrew Macnevin of Carrickfergus reported that the inhabitants of Doagh, Ballinure, and Ballyclare in south Antrim risked having their homes burned down if they did not swear to support the United Irishmen.[31]

Threatening letters prepared the way for the United Irish recruiters, who confronted potential supporters in person. Robert Carlisle near Dungannon was accosted by two United Irishmen one night. They asked him which side he was on—Defenders, Orangemen, or 'Liberty Men'. Carlisle replied boldly that he preferred none of these, but was a protestant and would support the protestant interest. This was not exactly what his interrogators wished to hear, and they forced him, on pain of death, to swear 'to fight against king and government when called upon, and that he would aid and assist the French in their landing in this kingdom'; he was also never to give king's evidence or swear information against the United Irishmen, an oath that Carlisle clearly broke.[32] An army lieutenant in Coleraine asserted that people were joining the United Irishmen in droves, not out of political commitment, but because it appeared that the crown's forces could not protect them from the republicans.[33] 'I am strongly of opinion', asserted the Revd William Richardson in County Tyrone, 'that the number of active United Irishmen is less than is supposed, but the *passive* ones, that is, those who have taken the oath of secrecy . . . are without numbers, that is the whole country.' Richardson accused United Irish recruiters of working upon the fears of women in particular, so that they might persuade 'their husbands to take this step [of swearing support for the United Irishmen] for the protection of their lives, their children, and houses'.[34] Also in Tyrone, Nathaniel Alexander maintained that United Irish recruiting practices concentrated on enlisting 'the herd boys and scum of the country, and by these means to threaten and intimidate others'.[35]

United Irish efforts at direct intimidation were enhanced by indirect intimidation as well. 'Their system of propagation by terror is growing formidable,' declared Cooke in August 1796. 'They will soon be thought the strongest, and when that idea prevails generally, all is lost.'[36] In their propaganda the United Irishmen took great pains to convey the impression that a republican victory was inevitable. Events were interpreted to confirm this impression. The failed invasion attempt at Bantry Bay in December 1796,

---

[30] Richard Vincent to Gen. William Dalrymple (ibid. 620/24/174).
[31] Andrew Macnevin to Edward Cooke, 24 July 1796 (ibid. 620/24/52).
[32] Thomas Knox to Dublin Castle, 4 Apr. 1796 (ibid. 620/23/65).
[33] Col. Lucius Barber to Edward Cooke, 24 Sept. 1796 (ibid. 620/25/104).
[34] Revd William Richardson to Dublin Castle, 8 Apr. 1797 (ibid. 620/29/200).
[35] Nathaniel Alexander to Henry Alexander, 15 Nov. 1796 (ibid. 620/26/85).
[36] Edward Cooke to Lord Auckland, 22 Aug. 1796 (BL, Auckland papers, Add. MS 34454/51–2).

for example, provided indubitable proof that the republicans had forged a powerful alliance with France. Recruitment increased rapidly in the following months. The invasion attempt had, according to one County Down informer, 'inspired them [the United Irishmen] with the hope that the French would land and that the present *system of government* might thereby be easily overturned'.[37] Indeed, any triumph of French arms on the Continent seemed to redound to the benefit of United Irish recruiters.[38]

'Nothing can be more alarming than the present state of this country,' insisted a County Down magistrate in April 1797. 'Almost all the peasantry of every religious description are United Irishmen—multitudes of [the] rich and of the middle class are avowedly of the confederacy; and many of the principal gentry are so much inclined that way that nothing seems wanting but a French invasion to induce the people to rise in mass.'[39] The great strength of the United Irish organization was certainly this ability to absorb thousands of discontented Irishmen into an underground revolutionary movement. But the United Irishmen were only moderately successful in moving out from their urban middle-class and artisanal base into the Irish countryside. The core of United Irish support, where the true republican ideologues and activists were to be found, still resided in Dublin and the towns and neighbouring environs of Ulster, among a class of men whose economic interests were predominantly commercial and industrial rather than agricultural. 'It is a Jacobin conspiracy throughout the kingdom,' Lord Castlereagh observed in June 1798.[40] As a Jacobin conspiracy, the United Irishmen found their most consistent source of support among the 'middling' classes of Irish society—the artisans and tradesmen of the countryside, the publicans and shopkeepers of the provincial towns, and the commercial and professional classes of Belfast and Dublin.

According to their official returns at least, the United Irishmen could claim to represent a mass movement. Starting from a base of about 5,000 republicans in the vicinity of Belfast in May 1795, the organization grew to monumental proportions. By February 1798 Neilson boasted that the United Irishmen had more than half a million sworn supporters, and the paper strength of the army of Lord Edward Fitzgerald in May 1798 was just under 300,000.[41] Table 5.1 indicates the phenomenal expansion of the movement in the stronghold counties of Antrim and Down.

[37] John Macarra to Gen. George Nugent, 8 Aug. 1797 (BL, Pelham papers, Add. MS 33105/14–15).
[38] See e.g. John Lees to Sackville Hamilton, 7 June 1796 (SPOI, Rebellion papers, 620/23/155).
[39] Extract of a letter from a Co. Down correspondent of Sir John Macartney, forwarded by him to Dublin Castle, 26 Apr. 1797 (ibid. 620/29/324).
[40] Viscount Castlereagh to William Wickham, 12 June 1798 (*Memoirs and correspondence of Viscount Castlereagh, second marquess of Londonderry*, ed. Charles Vane, marquess of Londonderry (4 vols., London, 1848–9), i. 219).
[41] Higgins to Dublin Castle, 21 Feb. 1798 (SPOI, Rebellion papers, 620/18/14); resolutions

TABLE 5.1. *United Irish membership in Antrim and Down, 1795–1797*

County	July 1795	Sept. 1795	Oct. 1796	Feb. 1797	May 1797
Antrim	3,000	6,400	15,000	20,940	22,716
Down	2,000	4,000	11,016	15,000	26,153
TOTAL	5,000	10,400	26,016	35,940	48,869

Source: United Irish membership returns in Kent CAO, Pratt papers, U840/0147/17; PROHO 100/62/333–4; SPOI, Rebellion papers, 620/22/41, 620/28/285, 297, 620/30/61.

The pattern displayed is one of continued growth. From the original base of 5,000 in these two counties, the United Irishmen more than doubled their membership within only a few months. Little more than a year later, another 15,000 had joined. Then came Bantry Bay in December 1796, affirming the promised French alliance and consequently contributing to the impression, which the United Irishmen sought to create, that their triumph was inevitable. Another 10,000 joined the movement within only a few months. On the eve of Lake's Draconian disarming policy in Ulster in May 1797, Antrim and Down had probably reached their peak strength of nearly 50,000. In the entire province of Ulster at this time the United Irishmen counted 117,917 supporters.[42]

These figures are a useful indication of the rapid growth of the United Irish movement between 1795 and 1798, but they certainly exaggerate actual participation in the movement. The numerical returns that the United Irishmen made were deliberately inflated for propagandist purposes. The secret committee of the Irish house of lords reported in 1797 that 'the returns of the several counties are considerably overrated; for it has been stated . . . in evidence that every artifice is used to keep up [the United Irishmen's] spirits by exaggerated reports of their strength.'[43] Camden assured Portland in August 1796 that 'the leaders in their conversations naturally magnify them [i.e. the United Irish returns of membership] with a view to inspire confidence on one part and terror on the other'.[44] Furthermore, even if these returns were an accurate reflection of sworn members of the movement, they would still exaggerate the real strength of the committed United Irishmen, for they included all those who had sworn an oath of secrecy, whether freely or under duress.

and returns of the national committee (of the United Irishmen), 26 Feb. 1798 (PROHO 100/75/132–5).

[42] Edward Boyle to Edward Cooke, 12 May 1797 (SPOI, Rebellion papers, 620/30/61).
[43] *Rep. secret comm.* 71.
[44] Earl Camden to duke of Portland, 6 Aug. 1796 (PROHO 100/64/168–72).

There were, in fact, two kinds of United Irishmen, claimed a clerical magistrate in County Armagh, the Revd William Richardson: 'deep, intriguing politicians and loosely connected recruits'. The latter he considered relatively insignificant. Though sworn into the organization, they would surely 'wait for events before they risked everything' in a rising staged by their superiors. The 'deep, intriguing politicians', however, posed a grave threat to order and stability. They were the 'shopkeepers, petty merchants, and innholders in the country towns—a set of men more out of reach of grievance and oppression than any other description I know of'. Prospering through the 'increased demand for commodities in our improving country', these members of the petty bourgeoisie were encouraged in political activism by the 'great democrats in Belfast and Newry, who furnish them with goods for the country and topics for sedition'.[45] Although the United Irishmen infiltrated all classes of Irish society, most of their recruits were passive supporters, eager enough to march with the republicans in time of victory, but ready to shirk their obligations if defeat proved imminent. 'The class most formidable and permanent in their exertions', observed a Derry magistrate, Henry Alexander, 'are all those whom the expectation of power leads to a continually varying but unremitting activity.'[46]

Who were these unrelenting republicans who formed the activist core of the United Irish movement? Having collected the names of thousands of United Irishmen either directly implicated in the rebellion or actively involved in its preparation in Dublin and Ulster between 1795 and 1798, I have identified the occupations of 1,731 (see Appendix). The sample presented here should prove a valuable indicator of the social composition of those United Irishmen who were most active in, and therefore most committed to, the republican cause. Table 5.2 presents the number and percentage of participants from specific occupational groups in Dublin and Ulster, and also gives the combined total. Thus, for example, the category of merchants, manufacturers, and shopkeepers accounts for 18.7 per cent of the total of 1,731, for 20.6 per cent of the committed republicans identified in Dublin, and for 17.2 per cent of those in Ulster.

What is most striking about this data is the proportional significance of the professional, manufacturing, and commercial sectors in the United Irish movement, and the low representation of the agricultural sector. To determine the extent to which these general occupational areas were over- or underrepresented in the United Irish movement, we can turn to the census figures of 1821 and 1841. Problematical as these enumerations are, they can still offer a general idea of the relative size of each occupational sector, and so provide a basis of comparison with United Irish participation. Thus, it is

---

[45] Dr William Richardson to marquess of Abercorn, 22 Feb. 1797 (PRONI, Abercorn papers, T2541/IB3/6/5).

[46] Henry Alexander to Dublin Castle, 1 Aug. 1796 (SPOI, Rebellion papers, 620/24/76a).

TABLE 5.2. *Occupational breakdown of United Irish membership, 1795–1798*

Occupation	Dublin		Ulster		Total	
	No.	%	No.	%	No.	%
The professions						
Officers	4	0.6	8	0.8	12	0.7
Barristers	13	1.8	3	0.3	16	0.9
Solicitors	17	2.3	12	1.2	29	1.7
Physicians, surgeons, and apothecaries	25	3.4	37	3.7	62	3.6
TOTAL	59	8.1	60	6.0	119	6.9
The church and education						
Presbyterian ministers	0	0.0	71	7.0	71	4.1
Schoolmasters	9	1.3	31	3.1	40	2.3
Protestant clergy	1	0.2	6	0.6	7	0.4
RC priests	33	4.5	12	1.2	45	2.6
TOTAL	43	6.0	120	11.9	163	9.4
Commerce/manufacturing						
Textiles	42	5.8	77	7.7	119	6.9
Spirits	21	2.9	11	1.0	32	1.9
Hardware/iron	10	1.4	7	0.7	17	1.0
Grocers	41	5.6	22	2.2	63	3.6
Miscellaneous	36	4.9	56	5.6	92	5.3
TOTAL	150	20.6	173	17.2	323	18.7
Agriculture						
Gentlemen	10[*]	1.4	15	1.5	25	1.4
Farmers	13[*]	1.8	133	13.2	146	8.4
Labourers	0	0.0	62	6.2	63	3.6
TOTAL	23	3.2	210	20.9	233	13.4
Service industries/trade						
Luxury/cloth	118	16.2	78	7.7	196	11.3
Weavers	21	2.9	84	8.4	105	6.1
Butchers/bakers	14	1.9	10	1.0	24	1.4
Printers	27	3.7	17	1.7	44	2.5
Building trades	49	6.7	45	4.5	94	5.4
Smiths	29	4.0	40	4.0	69	4.0
Miscellaneous	1	0.2	11	1.1	12	0.7
Publicans and innkeepers	64	8.8	110	11.0	174	10.1
TOTAL	323	44.4	395	39.4	718	41.5
Miscellaneous						
Clerks	46	6.3	20	2.0	66	3.8
Others	83[**]	11.4	26	2.6	109	6.3
TOTAL	129	17.7	46	4.6	175	10.1
TOTAL	727	100.0	1,004	100.0	1,731	100.0

[*]Includes gentlemen and farmers active in the neighbourhood of Dublin.
[**]Includes 59 Dublin labourers not included in agriculture.

Source: see Appendix.

possible to claim, in the light of the figures presented in Table 5.3, which contains a breakdown of United Irish participation by occupational sector, together with comparable figures provided by the 1821 and 1841 censuses, that the agricultural sector was strikingly underrepresented within the United Irish movement, while the professional, commercial, and manufacturing sectors were overrepresented. Only 13.2 per cent of United Irish activists in Ulster were found to be farmers, and farmers comprised a mere 8.4 per cent of the total number of United Irishmen included in the sample, while in 1821 the agricultural sector accommodated 40 per cent of the workforce. Such a disparity requires some explanation.

TABLE 5.3. *Occupational breakdown (%) within United Irish membership (UIM) and the 1821 and 1841 censuses*

Sector	Total UIM	Ulster UIM	1821	1841
Agriculture	13.4	20.9	40.1	51.3
Commerce and industry	60.2	56.6	41.3	33.6
Professional	16.3	17.9	n.d.	1.6
Other	10.1	4.6	18.6	13.5

Note: n.d. = no data.

Source: Table 5.2; for the 1821 census figures, see John Powell (ed.), *Statistical illustrations of the territorial extent and population, rental, taxation, finances, commerce, consumption, insolvency, pauperism, and crime of the British empire* (London, 1827), 35; for the 1841 census, see Mary E. Daly, *Social and economic history of Ireland since 1800* (Dublin, 1981), 104.

Part of the problem may lie in the nature of the sample itself. Over half (937 out of 1,731, or 54.1 per cent) of the total number of United Irishmen for whom I found occupations resided in Belfast or Dublin. Thus, this survey of United Irish social composition is strongly biased towards urban participants. If we separate these activists, we get a clearer idea of the occupational composition of United Irish support in the countryside. Table 5.4 compares such a breakdown of United Irish membership in Dublin and the stronghold counties of Antrim and Down with a similar analysis derived from the 1821 census. Here the seeming underrepresentation of the agricultural sector in the United Irish movement is less dramatic. A complicating factor, though, is the structure of the Ulster rural economy, which was very much a mixed economy. Many of the participants included not only in the commercial/industrial category but in the professional sector as well may also have engaged in farming. The most notable and frequent example of this in Ulster is the case of weavers, many of whom occupied small farms. Nevertheless, it is probably fair to assume, on the basis of the

TABLE 5.4. *Occupational breakdown (%) of United Irish membership (UIM) in town and country*

Sector	Dublin		Antrim		Down	
	UIM	1821	UIM	1821	UIM	1821
Agriculture	3.2	0.5	19.8	26.6	30.1	27.7
Commerce and industry	65.0	54.6	63.7	57.2	47.3	57.0
Other	31.8	44.9	16.5	16.2	22.6	15.3

Source: Table 5.2; for the 1821 census figures, see John Powell (ed.), *Statistical illustrations of the territorial extent and population, rental, taxation, finances, commerce, consumption, insolvency, pauperism, and crime of the British empire* (London, 1827), 35.

evidence collected, that the agricultural sector was somewhat underrepresented in the United Irish movement.

While one should not discount the many grievances that vexed agriculturalists, this did not seem to be a compelling reason to engage in insurrectionary activity. The United Irishmen offered very few specific remedies for agrarian ills, except the generalized demands for the abolition of tithes and for the reduction of rents and taxes, issues which found support well beyond the agricultural community. Indeed, the success of the United Irish appeal was based on its ability to transcend specific class or sectoral interests and to divert existing social and economic discontent against the establishment in Ireland—the church of Ireland, the Anglo-Irish landed ascendancy, and the government's subservience to Pitt's tory party. Magistrates' reports abound with references to the success with which the United Irishmen courted a broad-based popular following by addressing these widespread grievances. A clerical magistrate in Omagh, County Tyrone, reported: 'No tythe, half rent, and a French constitution is the favourite toast of the day and the bait held out to allure the populace, who catch at it greedily.'[47] Another loyalist correspondent recognized the potency of such appeals, particularly with regard to the salt tax: 'The poor family . . . never set [sic] down to a meal of potatoes that this tax is not aggravating, while the great men carries [sic] off the wealth of the country and does [sic] not assist in the expenses of the kingdom where his property is protected.'[48]

By targeting the burden of taxation on the poor, and its relative lightness on the rich, the United Irishmen were able to discredit the whole establishment in Ireland. 'There is diffused through the middle and lower orders of

[47] Revd James —— to bishop of Clogher, 9 May 1797 (SPOI, Rebellion papers, 620/30/40).
[48] Edward Moore to John Lees, 30 Mar. 1797 (ibid. 620/29/142).

the people', wrote an English traveller through Ulster, 'a general discontent to [*sic*] the . . . mode of government in this country.'[49] The prospect of a change in this situation raised popular expectations that their economic circumstances would be improved. James Buchanan summed up the United Irish appeal to the people as the 'cry of emancipation, being represented in parliament, removal of rackrents and middle landlords, removal of tythes, and a reform which they know nothing of, but from the noise made about it some great immediate good is expected'.[50] By harping on the fiscal insensitivity of an alien and unresponsive government, the United Irishmen were able to convince many among the rural as well as urban classes that the source of their economic deprivation was an evil administration. The republicans thereby sought to channel general economic discontent in a specific political direction.

The social composition of the United Irish activists does display a strong bias towards trade, commerce, and industry, though the range in social status may have been very wide indeed. Class antagonisms were no doubt a potent factor in the origin and development of the United Irish movement. But one of the clearest manifestations of these antagonisms was the conflict between a rising and self-conscious middle class and a hereditary landed class with a monopoly of political power. 'The struggle at that period', the disillusioned social revolutionary James Hope recalled, 'was merely between commercial and aristocratic interests to determine which should have the people as its property or its prey, each contending for the greatest share. When an appeal was made to the mass, the mercantile interest had the support of opinion; but the aristocracy, which carried with it the landed interest and the court, had the absolute sway.'[51] The Derry magistrate Henry Alexander analysed the conflict in the 1790s in similar terms. He described the greatest republican activists as those men of fortune 'who, elated by sudden acquisition of wealth, and . . . with strong but underrated minds, perpetually brood over the artificial distinctions birth and rank create in society [and conclude] that landed property supplies the means of oppression'.[52]

The United Irishmen enjoyed significant support from the merchants, manufacturers, and artisans involved in the textile industry in Ireland, primarily in the linen trade. Table 5.5 isolates this occupational category, distinguishing between those involved in the textile trade and those involved in other industries. In the diversified economy of the capital, textile merchants and manufacturers accounted for over one-quarter of the United

---

[49] A. Lecky to W. Madgett, [Sept.] 1796, forwarded to Dublin Castle, 1 Oct. 1796 (SPOI, Rebellion papers, 620/25/140).
[50] James Buchanan to Thomas Pelham, 14 Apr. 1797 (ibid. 620/29/254).
[51] Hope, 'Autobiographical memoir', 104.
[52] Henry Alexander to Dublin Castle, 1 Aug. 1796 (SPOI, Rebellion papers, 620/24/76*a*).

TABLE 5.5. *Commercial focus of United Irish merchants, manufacturers, and shopkeepers*

	Dublin		Belfast		Ulster		Total UIM	
	No.	%	No.	%	No.	%	No.	%
Textile trade	42	28.0	30	49.2	47	42.0	119	36.8
Other	108	72.0	31	50.8	65	58.0	204	63.2
TOTAL	150	100.0	61	100.0	112	100.0	323	100.0

Source: Table 5.2.

Irish presence in this occupational category. As we move to the north, however, the proportion becomes larger. In Belfast the split between textile entrepreneurs and other businessmen was about even, and in provincial Ulster, excluding Belfast, textile merchants and manufacturers accounted for 42 per cent of these commercial activists. The total involvement of textile merchants and manufacturers falls to 36.8 per cent when the entire sample is considered. It is not surprising that those associated with the textile industry should have participated in the United Irish movement with greater frequency in the north, and especially in Belfast, than elsewhere, for the industrial economy of Ulster was based on the manufacture and sale of linen. What is significant is that proportionately larger numbers of those involved in the northern linen trade felt compelled to engage in insurrectionary activity. The reasons can be adduced from a brief overview of the industry during the last decades of the eighteenth century.

The linen industry in Ireland underwent a rapid expansion between 1783 and 1795, followed by a period of stagnation for the next twenty years.[53] During the years of prosperity, many fortunes were made, and, as we have seen, some loyalists blamed the rapid enrichment of this group for the political dissatisfaction and resentment which they articulated in the 1790s. Ireland's entry into the war against France, coinciding with the severe credit shortage of 1793 and contributing to an initial trade slump, provided one check to the advance of the linen industry. The bad harvest of 1795 exacerbated the situation.[54] All of this may have recalled the depression in the industry during the late 1770s, when, as in the 1790s, economically vexed merchants blamed a war fought against liberal principles for their financial woes. The industry maintained itself during this twenty-year stagnation by keeping prices low. This was done at the expense of the weavers, whose wages rose scarcely at all and certainly not in proportion to the general

[53] Conrad Gill, *The rise of the Irish linen industry* (1st edn., 1925; Oxford, 1964), 221–2.
[54] John F. Burke, *Outlines of the industrial history of Ireland* (Dublin, 1920), 163–4.

increase in war-inflated rents and food prices.[55] Technological advances also contributed to the relative immiseration of the northern weavers.[56] The combination of poor linen markets and high food prices created a climate in which rural unrest thrived.

Can the rise of the United Irishmen in the north be closely related to adverse conditions in the linen trade? Andrew Newton of County Tyrone complained that he and his neighbours were unable to sell their linen.[57] One loyalist observed: 'I have learned that one great cause of the present commotion [in the north] . . . is that they can find no sale for the great staple of that part of the kingdom, their *linen cloth*.'[58] General Knox in Dungannon confirmed this concern that the depression in the linen industry was encouraging a rise in sedition.[59] 'All the linen merchants', declared an alarmed County Armagh magistrate, 'are already, or about to being, *up*' (sworn into the United Irish movement).[60] But while this depression in the linen industry may well have exacerbated commercial and industrial hostility against the landed interest, it hardly caused it. Clearly, the merchants and manufacturers who were so prominent in the foundation of the United Irish movement had been sufficiently provoked prior to the downturn in the industry. Their prosperity had only underscored the contrast between their economic power and their political exclusion. The depression in the linen trade, following on the heels of such prosperity, could only confirm the merchants' and manufacturers' determination to take charge of the running of the country. Illiberal and unresponsive government, according to them, was responsible for the economic slump. The only remedy was to establish a new government responsive to the needs of the people, and thus the depression added further compulsion towards radical activity.

The case of the weavers in the industry is more problematic. Textile workers accounted for 16.1 per cent of the total United Irish participation in Ulster (see Table 5.2), a figure that was only slightly higher than their presence in the workforce in 1821.[61] It was this group which bore the brunt of the depression in the linen industry, enduring high food prices, low wages, and a loss of independence as the industry became more proletarianized. Under such circumstances, one would expect sharp tensions between capital and labour in the industry. But this did not occur. Rather, such

[55] Gill, *Linen industry*, 225.

[56] W. H. Crawford, *Domestic industry in Ireland: the experience of the linen industry* (Dublin, 1972), 41–2.

[57] Andrew Newton to Revd Isaac Ashe, 2 Dec. 1796 (SPOI, Rebellion papers, 620/26/93).

[58] Joseph McCormick to Charles Greville, 3 June 1797 (ibid. 620/31/85).

[59] Knox to Pelham, 14 Mar. 1797 (ibid. 620/29/67).

[60] C. M. Warburton to Richard Archdall, 17 Apr. 1797 (ibid. 620/29/242).

[61] See Liam Kennedy, 'The rural economy, 1820–1914', in Liam Kennedy and Philip Ollerenshaw (eds.), *An economic history of Ulster, 1820–1940* (Manchester, 1985), 12. Kennedy provides figures based on the 1821 census in which textile workers account for 13% of the workforce in Co. Antrim and 16% of the workforce in Co. Down.

conflicts became subordinated to ideological concerns. Representatives from all ranks of the linen industry participated in the United Irish movement, a movement which included comfortable farmers who resented the increase in rent associated with the extension of linen manufacture. United Irish employers, in recruiting their dependents for the republican cause, frequently offered weavers higher market prices for their webs, thus diverting industrial discontent away from the bosses and towards the state.[62] But the rhetoric of the United Irish propagandists contained no reference to measures designed specifically to help weavers, other than the non-controversial desire to improve Irish trade. They constituted no special interest group within the organization, though no doubt they warmly advocated the abolition of tithes, hearth money, excise taxes, and other measures intended to relieve rural distress in general. In this sense, their dissatisfaction was, in part, economically motivated. But to discuss the United Irish appeal mainly in terms of trade fluctuations is to overlook the ideological and religious underpinnings of the radical movement.

Certain occupational groups were actively courted by the movement for the unique services that they could provide. Printers and booksellers produced and distributed United Irish and radical publications. Lawyers were given ample opportunity to exercise their talents on behalf of the society throughout the country. Gunsmiths and blacksmiths were of key importance as the organization began to arm itself. Former army officers and deserters had the frustrating responsibility of imposing military discipline on the rebel forces. Among those included in the residual category in Table 5.2 were several smugglers, whose special skills proved invaluable as the United Irishmen began smuggling arms into northern Ireland from France and America.

Publicans and innkeepers, accounting for one out of every ten United Irishmen identified in my sample, offered valuable services to the underground revolutionary movement. Public houses and inns provided recruiting grounds for the United Irishmen. It was at the Sign of the Swan in Antrim town that two soldiers were approached by its proprietor, John Hyndman, and a neighbouring farmer, William Orr, the celebrated martyr, about joining the republican movement.[63] Public houses and inns also furnished convenient and inconspicuous places for United Irish committees to meet and transact business.[64] Not surprisingly, publicans and innkeepers often assumed positions of leadership on baronial committees and served as secretaries to local societies. And, of course, publicans, especially in the countryside, provided important links between the local community and a wider, cosmopolitan world. Taverns and public houses supplied reading

[62] Examination of William Hart, 22 Sept. 1795 (SPOI, Rebellion papers, 620/22/41).
[63] Thomas Pelham to Earl Camden, 1 Apr. 1797 (ibid. 620/29/255).
[64] *Rep. secret comm.* 135.

material for their customers, acquainting them with national and international affairs. Travellers from other parts of the country regaled the innkeeper with information about affairs in the rest of the land and made him a pivotal figure for the integration of his community in the wide, imagined nation of the radicals.

But the involvement of clergymen and schoolmasters is especially noteworthy, both in terms of the services that they rendered to the republican movement and the insight that such activity provides into the appeal of the United Irish movement. According to Table 5.2, Presbyterian ministers, probationers, and other protestant clergymen formed over 10 per cent of the United Irish participants to be found in Ulster. One should be cautious, however, about asserting that one out of every ten United Irishmen was a Presbyterian minister. The other occupational categories include only a fraction of the total number of United Irishmen. But the figure for dissenting clergymen, seventy-one, probably represents their maximum participation. Nevertheless, the strong participation of Presbyterian clergymen is certainly noteworthy. David Miller has estimated that there were about 250 Presbyterian congregations in Ulster.[65] One loyalist complained that 'there is not one in twenty' Presbyterian ministers who was loyal—an exaggeration, to be sure, but not a gross one.[66] In fact, the United Irishmen claimed support from nearly a third of all the Presbyterian ministers in Ulster.

Presbyterian ministers were also highly placed in the revolutionary organization. The Revd Arthur McMahon of Hollywood, County Down, was treasurer to the Ulster provincial committee of the United Irishmen, besides being Sam Neilson's most trusted agent in the north.[67] Dr William Steele Dickson served as adjutant-general for County Down until his arrest just prior to the northern rising.[68] And when the United Irishmen elected members for the new parliament that would assemble after a successful rebellion, Presbyterian ministers figured prominently. Of the seven delegates mentioned by the informer Nicholas Magin, three were Dissenting clergymen.[69] Catholic priests and schoolmasters were also in a position to offer spiritual and intellectual sanctions for rebellion. As with Presbyterian ministers, their standing in the community made them useful local United Irish leaders.

Religion was clearly one of the most important factors in shaping participation in the republican movement. Catholics and Presbyterians found a common meeting-ground on the great issue of tithes. No other grievance

---

[65] David W. Miller, 'Presbyterianism and "modernization" in Ulster', *Past and Present*, 80 (Aug. 1978), 79 n.

[66] Anon. to Thomas Pelham, 27 May 1797 (SPOI, Rebellion papers, 620/30/208).

[67] Marquess of Downshire to Edward Cooke, 20 Feb. 1797 (ibid. 620/28/288); report of Nicholas Magin, n.d. (PRONI, R. C. Lytton White papers, D714/2/3).

[68] Ibid. D714/2/16.

[69] 'Black Book of the rebellion, 1798' (ibid. McCance papers, D272/1).

was voiced with greater frequency in the countryside. United Irishmen in Tyrone took an oath to abolish tithes and 'destroy the clergy of the established church'.[70] John Beresford noted that opposition to the payment of tithes 'animates the minds of the lower order of people, both papists and Dissenters'.[71] A travelling United Irish agitator in County Armagh promised that the revolution would put down Anglican bishops and parsons, abolish tithes, and provide for the renting of church lands to the poor at half a crown per acre.[72] In County Derry the Revd Isaac Ashe believed that the grievance over tithes was merely a pretext for rural unrest. Tithe rates in his parish were low, lower than they had been during the previous decade, in fact.[73] But Ashe clearly misunderstood the motive behind the grievance. Unlike previous rural insurgents who attacked the established clergy, the United Irishmen were not interested in merely regulating tithe rates. At issue now was the right of the established church to tax a population which rejected its spiritual domination and pastoral care.[74] Following the example of the American and French revolutions, the United Irishmen repudiated outright the notion of a state church. The established church in Ireland, of course, was closely identified with the hegemony of the Anglo-Irish ascendancy and was therefore associated in the minds of the rural lower classes and the urban commercial classes with economic and political oppression by the landed élite. Thus, in their assault on the tithe, Catholics and Presbyterians allied in the United Irish movement were attacking one potent symbol of ascendancy rule. Tithe was therefore both an economic hardship and a symbolic grievance.

One should beware of making sweeping claims, however, for the role of religion in shaping United Irish participation. Not all Presbyterians joined the republicans, and many Ulster Catholics stayed aloof from the disturbances. When Catholics participated, it was usually because they were on the defensive against the Orange Order and militant protestant loyalism. For the Defenders, an alliance with the United Irishmen in Ulster was almost a practical necessity. Religion, however, supplied a community of interest which could be exploited for either revolutionary or reactionary ends. Catholics were not alone in the siege mentality that they presented in their Defender associations; protestants, too, responded to growing Catholic militancy by joining Orange lodges. Much depended on the efforts made to

[70] William James Armstrong to Dublin Castle, 6 Dec. 1796 (SPOI, Rebellion papers, 620/26/117).

[71] John Beresford to Lord Auckland, 24 Oct. 1797 (*The correspondence of the right hon. John Beresford*, ed. William Beresford (2 vols., London, 1854), ii. 146).

[72] C. M. Warburton to Edward Cooke, 29 Jan. 1798 (SPOI, Rebellion papers, 620/35/74).

[73] Revd Isaac Ashe to Dublin Castle, 19 Sept. 1796 (ibid. 620/25/84).

[74] See e.g. the *Northern Star* publication, *The oppression of tithe exemplified, or a review of a late contest between conscientious scruple and ecclesiastical exaction, as exhibited in a number of publications in the 'Northern Star', which are now collected into a pamphlet at the desire of many respectable persons who are not subscribers to the paper* (Belfast, 1797).

mould a fellowship based on confessional affiliation into a political movement, whether this was Orange and loyalist or United Irish and republican.

How did the composition of the revolutionary United Irish movement
compare with that of the early reformist phase? Speaking in the Irish house
of commons, Sergeant Barrington referred to the United Irishmen of the
first half of the decade as 'doctors without practice, barristers without
briefs, bullies without spirit, foolish gentlemen, mad printers, malcontent
politicians, and idle tradesmen'.[75] If the pejorative qualifications of this
assertion are ignored, one is left with a fairly accurate statement of United
Irish social composition between 1791 and 1794. The early United Irishmen
were an overwhelmingly middle-class body. Thanks to the meticulous
research of R. B. McDowell, who drew upon the reports of the informer
Thomas Collins, a great deal is known about the membership of the Dublin
Society of United Irishmen.[76] McDowell determined that, between the society's foundation in November 1791 and its suppression in May 1794, some
400–25 persons were admitted. Of these, 200 were active members, defined
as those who attended meetings with some regularity. Most members
resided in Dublin, but nearly fifty came from other parts of Ireland, and
many of them were active in local politics or were delegates to the Catholic
convention. The society was evenly divided in religious affiliation between
Catholics and protestants.

McDowell identified 363 of these early United Irishmen by occupation.
Table 5.6 presents the occupational breakdown of these participants, using
some of the categories that I applied to my own sample and comparing the
figures with those for the post-1794 Dublin organization and for the total
number of republicans identified by occupation during the revolutionary
phase. It is abundantly clear, though not surprising, that the transformation
of the Dublin United Irishmen from a reform club into a revolutionary
organization was accompanied by a marked extension of the social bases of
United Irish participation. Clerks, labourers, apprentices, and servants were
totally unrepresented in the reform club. One lonely publican attended the
relatively open meetings in Tailors' Hall in Dublin in the early 1790s, while
at least sixty-four were active participants in the insurrectionary movement.
The clergy, Catholic and protestant, held notably aloof from the organization. Gentlemen, army officers, and lawyers accounted for over one-quarter
of the Dublin United Irish reformers and were thus a highly overrepresented occupational category. Merchants, manufacturers, and shopkeepers
also participated with greater frequency in the reform movement. Even the
category of artisans, weavers, and tradesmen reflects a strong middle-class,
propertied bias in the social composition of the early United Irishmen. The

---

[75] *FJ*, 6 Mar. 1794.
[76] R. B. McDowell, 'The personnel of the Dublin Society of United Irishmen, 1791–4', *Irish Historical Studies*, 2/5 (Mar. 1940), 12–53.

eighty-one members whom McDowell placed in this occupational group were not mean mechanics, but rather master craftsmen and relatively prosperous tradesmen. The Dublin United Irishmen of the early 1790s were men who had much to gain by a reform of parliament, and also much to lose if they resorted to a risky insurrection. The two-thirds of the early United Irishmen who belonged to the commercial and industrial sector can thus be described as overwhelmingly middle class. After 1795, however, with the influx of the lower orders into the organization, the 75 per cent or so of the revolutionary Dublin United Irishmen who belonged to this sector represented a potent, and perhaps contradictory, mixture of petty-bourgeois and plebeian elements.

TABLE 5.6. *United Irish participation in Dublin, 1791–1798, by occupation*

Occupation	1791–4		1795–8		Total UIM	
	No.	%	No.	%	No.	%
Gentlemen	92	25.4	44	6.1	82	4.7
Ministers	3	0.8	10	1.5	118	6.8
Priests	0	0.0	33	4.5	45	2.6
Merchants	160	44.1	150	20.6	323	18.7
Farmers	0	0.0	13	1.8	146	8.4
Doctors	24	6.6	25	3.4	62	3.6
Publicans	1	0.3	64	8.8	174	10.1
Artisans	81	22.3	259	35.6	544	31.4
Clerks	0	0.0	46	6.3	66	3.8
Labourers	0	0.0	59	8.1	121	7.0
Miscellaneous	2	0.5	24	3.3	50	2.9
TOTAL	363	100.0	727	100.0	1731	100.0

Source: R. B. McDowell, 'The personnel of the Dublin Society of United Irishmen, 1791–4', *Irish Historical Studies*, 2/5 (Mar. 1940),

The lower social status of the revolutionary United Irishmen becomes increasingly clear through an examination of the professional sector. Professionals accounted for more than one in every four United Irishmen who attended the meetings of the reform club in Dublin. Between 1795 and 1798, however, they accounted for only 14 per cent of republicans in the capital, less than the level of professional participation elsewhere in the late 1790s. Professionals accounted for over 22 per cent of the United Irishmen outside Belfast and for 17.7 per cent of the total number of republicans included in my sample.

Not only did professional participation in Dublin decline proportionately

after 1794, but the social status of these professionals also underwent a
transformation. Table 5.7 offers a breakdown of the involvement of the
professional sector in Dublin before and after 1794. Lawyers accounted for
61.9 per cent of the professional participation in the early United Irishmen
and for only 29.5 per cent after 1794. Furthermore, their actual number
declined, from fifty-six to thirty, no doubt as a result of the United
Irishmen's rejection of constitutionalism and their adoption of an insurrectionary strategy. The number of doctors remained constant, twenty-four
before 1794 and twenty-five in the late 1790s, but the proportion of physicians to surgeons and apothecaries altered dramatically. The higher ranks
of the medical profession outnumbered the lower by two to one before
1794 and were clearly an overrepresented occupational group. After 1795,
however, this ratio was reversed.

TABLE 5.7. *United Irish participation by the professional sector in Dublin, 1791–1798*

Occupation	1791–4		1795–8	
	No.	%	No.	%
Solicitors	30	33.3	17	16.7
Barristers	26	28.6	13	12.8
Officers	6	6.6	4	3.9
Physicians	16	17.5	8	7.8
Surgeons/apothecaries	8	8.8	17	16.7
Schoolmasters	3	3.3	9	8.8
Priests	0	0.0	33	32.3
Other	2	2.2	1	1.0
TOTAL	91	100.0	102	100.0

Source: R. B. McDowell, 'The personnel of the Dublin
Society of United Irishmen, 1791–4', *Irish Historical
Studies*, 2/5 (Mar. 1940), 12–53; Table 5.2.

Surgeons and apothecaries accounted for one of only three occupational
groups within the professional sector which increased their participation,
numerically and proportionately, after the United Irishmen opted for revolution. The number of schoolmasters tripled, and Catholic priests, totally
unrepresented in the early movement, accounted for nearly one-third of
professional participation in the late 1790s. Three conclusions can be drawn
from these developments. First, as the United Irishmen turned towards mass
insurrection, representation among the more socially exalted occupational
groups, like barristers, gentlemen, and professional soldiers, decreased, per-

haps reflecting a reluctance among the upper ranks to risk their considerable status and fortunes in uncertain revolutionary mobilization. Secondly, and maybe both a cause and a consequence of the previous occurrence, the social composition of the United Irishmen increasingly came to be characterized by a lower petty-bourgeois element. And, thirdly, the dramatic involvement of Catholic priests in the organization in Dublin after 1794 suggests the desecularization of the revolutionary movement, which, in order to extend its base of support among the urban and rural masses of Ireland, resorted to the exploitation of religious tensions within the country. Not only did Catholic clergymen participate with greater frequency in the mass-based revolutionary United Irish organization, but Dissenting ministers and probationers accounted for a significant proportion of the professional sector of United Irish activists in the province of Ulster.

Data for the pre-revolutionary northern United Irishmen are woefully lacking, and conclusions about the participation of various occupational groups can be drawn only from the most impressionistic of evidence. The Ulster radicals were, of course, overwhelmingly Presbyterian, and throughout the 1790s the United Irishmen counted a number of Dissenting ministers among the most active adherents to the cause. As in Dublin, the commercial sector was strongly represented. In refuting the allegation that the United Irishmen were composed of unstable social and economic elements, the, admittedly partisan, *Northern Star* insisted that they were the 'first merchants in two of the most commercial cities of Ireland, Dublin and Belfast'.[77] Perhaps because of the prevailing democratic, Presbyterian spirit of the north-east, United Irish societies there rested on a broader socio-economic base than they did elsewhere. Northern gentlemen such as Gawin Hamilton and Dissenting ministers such as Thomas Ledlie Birch of Saintfield, County Down, organized United Irish societies in their neighbourhoods. But clerks, small tradesmen, and artisans participated with more frequency in Belfast than in Dublin.[78]

The whole question of social status as determined by occupation is complicated in the late eighteenth century. The chandler Rowley Osborne, chairman of the apparently plebeian Irish Jacobins in 1792, was described as a 'radical mechanick' by Martha McTier.[79] Yet her own husband, Samuel McTier, was a chandler and soap-boiler whose business went bankrupt in the 1780s.[80] Her disdainful comments on Osborne's obscure social status might suggest that he was either a journeyman or an apprentice in the trade. A warrant for his arrest in September 1796, however, described Rowley Osborne as a gentleman; in addition to his business in Belfast, he

[77] *NS*, 28 Apr. 1792.
[78] Ibid. 6 Feb. 1793; McSkimin, *Annals*, 5.
[79] Martha McTier to William Drennan, 28 Oct. 1792 (PRONI, Drennan letters, T765/345).
[80] Anon. letter from Belfast, 1 Nov. 1792 (PRO, Chatham papers, 30/8/331/88–9).

had a small estate in the neighbouring countryside.[81] Thus, to represent Osborne as a mere chandler obscures the financial and social position that he seems to have acquired. Similarly, David Shaw of Saintfield, County Down, was described simply as a shopkeeper in a government list of state prisoners, but Thomas Ledlie Birch, the local Presbyterian minister, reported that Shaw was a grocer, spirits dealer, leather merchant, woollen draper, and cotton manufacturer—in short, an active and aggressive capitalist entrepreneur.[82] Likewise, Henry Munro, leader of the Down insurgents in 1798, was sparingly described by the authorities as a Lisburn shopkeeper, when in fact he was a wealthy woollen draper involved in a variety of commercial enterprises.[83] Mobility up and down the range of commercial occupations was probably very fluid.

The commercial and manufacturing orientation of the town of Belfast certainly shaped United Irish participation. Table 5.8 offers a comparison between the occupational composition of the organizations in Dublin and

TABLE 5.8. *United Irish participation in Belfast and Dublin, 1795-1798, by occupation*

Occupation	Belfast		Dublin		Total UIM	
	No.	%	No.	%	No.	%
Gentlemen	7	3.3	44	6.1	82	4.7
Ministers	2	1.0	10	1.5	118	6.8
Priests	0	0.0	33	4.5	45	2.6
Merchants	61	29.0	150	20.6	323	18.7
Farmers	0	0.0	13	1.8	146	8.4
Doctors	10	4.8	25	3.4	62	3.6
Publicans	35	16.7	64	8.8	174	10.1
Artisans	68	32.4	259	35.6	544	31.4
Clerks	15	7.1	46	6.3	66	3.8
Labourers	8	3.8	59	8.1	121	7.0
Miscellaneous	4	1.9	24	3.3	50	2.9
TOTAL	210	100.0	727	100.0	1731	100.0

Source: Appendix.

[81] *BNL*, 14 Oct. 1796; *NS*, 11 Nov. 1796; arrest warrants, 14 Sept. 1796 (SPOI, Rebellion papers, 620/25/60).

[82] List of prisoners, 24 Aug. 1798 (SPOI, Rebellion papers, 620/39/203); Revd Thomas Ledlie Birch, *Letter from an Irish emigrant to his friend in the United States* (New York, 1798), 12.

[83] *BNL*, 18 June 1798; W. T. Latimer, *Ulster biographies relating chiefly to the rebellion of 1798* (Belfast, 1897), 21.

Belfast. Nearly 90 per cent of active United Irishmen in Belfast belonged to the commercial and manufacturing sector, almost a third of them being merchants. Whether these merchants were over- or underrepresented in the Belfast United Irish organization is difficult to determine, but it is possible to draw certain conclusions regarding artisanal participation.

What is interesting about the sample of active Belfast United Irishmen who can be identified by occupation is the extent to which the group comprising artisans and tradesmen corresponds to the actual profile of this group for the town as a whole. Table 5.9 compares the number and percentage of artisans in Belfast in 1791 with the number and percentage of United Irishmen in this occupational category within the town. In 1791 the *Belfast News-Letter* estimated the total population at 18,320, a figure which included 8,932 males. Thus artisans accounted for about one-quarter of the male population.[84] Of the 210 United Irishmen in Belfast for whom occupations have been established, there were fifty-five artisans (printers are excluded here), accounting for slightly more than one-quarter of the republicans included in my sample. Thus the percentage of artisans in the United Irish organization corresponded closely to the percentage of artisans in the town as a whole. When we break this category down, however, some differences between the structure of the Belfast artisan group and the tradesmen and craftsmen within the movement appear. The luxury and clothing trades were overrepresented in the republican movement, weavers participated in similar proportions, and the building trades were grossly underrepresented among the United Irishmen.

This is not really surprising, however, if we note the high level of participation by merchants and manufacturers in the United Irish movement. In Belfast this group accounted for 29 per cent of total United Irish participation. Weavers and artisans from the luxury and cloth markets were deeply

TABLE 5.9. *Belfast artisans and United Irish participation, 1791*

Occupation	No. in Belfast	% of male population	% Belfast UIM
Luxury goods/cloth	673	7.5	12.4
Weavers	673	7.5	7.1
Butchers/bakers	106	1.2	0.5
Building trades	533	6.0	3.8
Smiths	69	0.8	1.4
Miscellaneous	220	2.5	1.0
TOTAL	2,274	25.5	26.2

Source: BNL, 28 Oct. 1791; Table 5.2.

[84] *BNL*, 28 Oct. 1791.

involved in the trading and commercial networks of the town, many of them dependent on the commercial élite for commissions and employment. Any latent antagonism between the élite and the lower levels of the commercial and manufacturing sector was temporarily set aside as these groups joined together against oligarchic ascendancy control. Radical wholesalers influenced and reinforced the radicalism of the smaller retailers to whom they supplied goods. Continual contact between farmers and merchants, between linen weavers and drapers, between tradesmen and shopkeepers promoted the spread of United Irish principles. Such contacts helped to shape the social composition of the United Irishmen. 'If all the merchants of that [town of Belfast] and four other towns were hanged,' declared a Tyrone magistrate, 'it would be for the benefit of this country.'[85] Even as early as 1792 Chief Secretary Hobart observed that 'the source of all the mischief is the town of Belfast. The principal merchants of that town are the persons principally at the bottom of it.'[86]

The dominance of the commercial and professional middle class in the United Irish movement is apparent in the occupational structure of the leadership. Here the historian's task is made considerably easier by the existence of a document, the 'Black Book' of the rebellion in Ulster, compiled by crown servants from the detailed reports of Nicholas Magin. Magin had risen through the ranks of the United Irish leadership, from the baronial structure up through the provincial committee. In his reports to his patron, the Revd John Cleland, Magin identified 188 persons present at these county and provincial committee meetings.[87] Of these individuals, I have been able to establish occupations for 121, and the results appear in Table 5.10. A comparison is thus available between the social composition of United Irish activists in Ulster and that of the northern leadership. Again, what is abundantly clear is the predominance of the middle classes in the United Irish leadership. With the first seven categories used to represent upper- and middle-class participation, the results indicate that, whereas these groups account for only 54.9 per cent of total United Irish participation and 60.8 per cent of Ulster participation, they account for an impressive 83.4 per cent of those listed in the Ulster 'Black Book'. The only two of these seven categories to show a decrease in participation at the level of leadership are priests (only two of whom are listed in the 'Black Book') and publicans and innkeepers, whose participation is more than halved in the upper committees of the organization. It is not surprising that the involvement of gentlemen, lawyers, Presbyterian ministers, merchants, manufacturers, and shopkeepers should increase within the higher ranks of the organization, nor that the presence of artisans, weavers, and tradesmen

[85] A. Cole Hamilton to Dublin Castle, 21 Sept. 1796 (SPOI, Rebellion papers, 620/25/88).
[86] Robert Hobart to Evan Nepean, 29 Dec. 1792 (PROHO 100/42/9–12).
[87] 'Black Book' (PRONI, McCance papers, D272/1).

should decline. Yet the commercial and manufacturing element, while still considerable, has declined from over two-thirds of total United Irish participation to just under half of the Ulster leadership. This may reflect the fact that this sector had been purged of its lower elements. The involvement of artisans, weavers, and tradesmen also decreases, from 28.4 per cent of all Ulster activists to only 11.6 per cent of the leadership. And the professional sector is grossly overrepresented in the leadership, owing especially to the strong participation of Presbyterian ministers in the upper ranks.

TABLE 5.10. *Occupational breakdown of the Ulster 'Black Book'*

Occupation	Black Book		Ulster		Total UIM	
	No.	%	No.	%	No.	%
Gentlemen	11	9.1	38	3.8	82	4.7
Ministers	15	12.4	108	10.7	118	6.8
Priests	2	1.6	12	1.2	45	2.6
Merchants	35	29.0	173	17.2	323	18.7
Farmers	27	22.3	133	13.2	146	8.4
Doctors	5	4.1	37	3.7	62	3.6
Publicans	6	4.9	110	11.0	174	10.1
Artisans	14	11.6	285	28.4	544	31.4
Clerks	3	2.5	20	2.0	66	3.8
Labourers	3	2.5	62	6.2	121	7.0
Miscellaneous	0	0.0	26	2.6	50	2.9
TOTAL	121	100.0	1004	100.0	1731	100.0

Source: 'Black Book of the rebellion, 1798' (PRONI, McCance papers, D272/1); Appendix.

Thomas Bartlett has suggested that the social turbulence in Ireland in the 1790s can be partly explained by the collapse of the 'moral economy'.[88] Denied the paternalist regard of a protestant gentry made paranoid by the advance of republican ideas and Catholic relief, and seemingly abandoned by the Catholic upper and middle classes, who pursued their own political agenda, the lower orders reciprocated by withholding their deference and obedience. The implicit social contract that bound rich and poor in a community of mutual benefit had been broken. Consequently, the traditional methods of containing popular fury collapsed, evidenced not only by the unprecedented scale of violence which accompanied the militia riots of 1793, but also by the sanguinary confrontations of the later 1790s.

[88] Thomas Bartlett, 'An end to moral economy: the Irish militia disturbances of 1793', *Past and Present*, 99 (May 1983), 41–64.

The collapse of the traditional paternalist nexus, however, may not have been as dramatic as Bartlett suggests. L. M. Cullen, for example, explains the insurgency in Wexford within the context of intense political and social rivalry between the ranks of the gentry.[89] More significantly, however, those occupational groups most strongly represented in my sample of United Irish activists were the least susceptible to traditional notions of a moral economy. This is not to say that the republicans did not appeal to popular themes of a fair rent and a just wage to attract supporters. Nor do I wish to discount the deferential and paternalist bonds that may have existed in certain industries: we have already seen how linen merchants encouraged their dependents to join the United Irish movement. More important, however, in enticing these activists into dangerous insurrectionary behaviour may have been an ideology which placed value on industry, the entrepreneurial spirit, and the rights of the individual. The merchants and shopkeepers among the United Irish activists were the beneficiaries of that market economy which was encroaching on traditional society. The petty-bourgeois activists who were the core of the United Irish movement opposed the landed élite not so much because the gentry had shirked its social obligations, but because that class possessed a political monopoly which obstructed the advance of good government and consequent economic prosperity. Consequently, like that of nineteenth-century republican movements, the social composition of the United Irishmen displayed a strong bias towards trade, commerce, and industry.[90]

[89] L. M. Cullen, 'The 1798 rebellion in its eighteenth-century context', in Patrick J. Corish (ed.), *Radicals, rebels, and establishments* (Belfast, 1985), 91–113; id., 'The 1798 rebellion in Wexford: United Irishman organisation, membership, leadership', in Kevin Whelan and William Nolan (eds.), *Wexford: history and society* (Dublin, 1987), 248–95.

[90] See e.g. Samuel Clark's analysis of the occupational structure of suspected Fenians, 1866–71, in Samuel Clark, *Social origins of the Irish land war* (Princeton, NJ, 1979), 203. Clark's data suggest that 21.2% of the Fenians belonged to the agricultural sector, while 66% were employed in commerce or manufacturing.

6

Defenders and Militiamen

WHILE the middle-class United Irishmen were waging their campaign for reform and emancipation in the early 1790s, artisans and labourers in Belfast and Dublin were mobilizing in their own political organizations. In Belfast, agitation for reform was hardly confined to the merchant élite. Henry Joy McCracken, a cotton manufacturer and a leading advocate of the principles of the United Irishmen, promoted the establishment of a circulating library in Belfast for the benefit of the working classes.[1] His close friend and political ally Thomas Russell was appointed librarian of this Belfast Society for Promoting Knowledge in January 1794.[2] This group and a similar organization called the Belfast Reading Society appear to have been dominated by radical artisans, who used the clubs for political ends as well as self-improvement. Early in 1792 the Belfast Reading Society published a set of resolutions in the *Northern Star* calling for immediate parliamentary reform and Catholic emancipation. The language of these resolutions recalls Paine: 'Civil and religious liberty is the birthright of every human being. . . . Governments were formed to secure them in the possession of this right. . . . Doctrines of faith and modes of worship can neither give nor take away the rights of man.'[3] Such an organization, with its decidedly political orientation, could prove a useful tool in the further dissemination of United Irish principles among Belfast's lower classes.

Another club established by working men in Belfast drew even more inspiration from radical ideology. This was the Irish Jacobins. Though their inaugural address of December 1792 adopted resolutions closely resembling those of the United Irishmen (the necessity for radical parliamentary reform, Catholic emancipation, and a union of all Irishmen to achieve these aims), the Irish Jacobins went further. These unabashed republicans (their name alone provoked the government) denied the very existence of a constitution and called for a national convention, to include delegates from England and Scotland, at which a truly popular constitution could be established.[4] Hobart noted with some distaste the 'obscure' social composition of the new club, but warned that though 'these proceedings give disgust to

---

[1] W. T. Latimer, *Ulster biographies relating chiefly to the rebellion of 1798* (Belfast, 1897), 2.
[2] R. R. Madden, *The United Irishmen, their lives and times*, 3rd ser. (7 vols., London, 1842–5), ii. 156.
[3] *NS*, 28 Jan. 1792.   [4] *NS*, 15 Dec. 1792.

men of property and detach them from such assemblies . . . I fear they attract the ignorant and thoughtless'.[5]

At first glance, the Irish Jacobins seem to represent an autonomous flowering of artisanal radicalism, somewhat distanced politically from the more circumspect, middle-class United Irishmen. But a closer look reveals links between the bourgeois and the plebeian organizations. The chandler Rowley Osborne, the chairman of the Irish Jacobins, was the brother of William Osborne, chairman of the Second Society of United Irishmen of Belfast.[6] This circumstance suggests a measure of co-operation, and perhaps some affiliation, between the two movements. Furthermore, the secretary and co-founder of the Irish Jacobins, Samuel Kennedy, was the chief compositor of Sam Neilson's United Irish newspaper, the *Northern Star*.[7] It would seem that the Irish Jacobins were not a plebeian breakaway group from the mainstream of Belfast radicalism represented by the United Irishmen; rather, they were an auxiliary force, perhaps encouraged to take a more radical stand to test the waters of public opinion while the United Irishmen cultivated their image of responsible, respectable reformers.[8]

The involvement of McCracken and Russell in the Belfast reading clubs and the participation of some members of the mercantile and professional élite in the Irish Jacobins might suggest that the town's artisans and labourers were merely directed and exploited by the middle-class United Irishmen.[9] But inter-class co-operation in Belfast was hardly unusual. The rich, the comfortable, and the poor lived alongside one another, without class distinctions in residence.[10] Perhaps because of the relative placidity of class relationships, Belfast radicals were fervent democrats who welcomed the participation of the lower orders in politics. Encouraging and even instigating artisanal radical activity, the middle-class radicals nevertheless recognized that the popular classes had minds of their own, at a time when, as Martha McTier put it, 'every mechanik [*sic*] is roused into public spirit and dares avow it'.[11]

This affinity between the working and middle classes which characterized Belfast, however, was not present in Dublin, where co-operation between

[5] Robert Hobart to Evan Nepean, 20 Dec. 1792 (PROHO 100/38/180–1).

[6] *BNL*, 10 Oct. 1792.

[7] Notes by John Smith on United Irish leaders, *c*.1796 (PROI, Frazer papers, IA/40 111*a*/40); arrest warrants, 14 Sept. 1796 (SPOI, Rebellion papers, 620/25/60); information of John Smith (alias Bird), 1795–6 (ibid. 620/27/1).

[8] For more on the Irish Jacobins, see Nancy J. Curtin, 'The transformation of the Society of United Irishmen into a mass-based revolutionary organisation, 1794–6', *Irish Historical Studies*, 24/96 (Nov. 1985), 471–3.

[9] For élite participation in the Irish Jacobins, see list of Jacobin club members and principal republicans in Belfast, [June 1795] (Kent CAO, Pratt papers, U840/0147/4/2).

[10] John J. Monaghan, 'A social and economic history of Belfast, 1790–1800', MA thesis, (Belfast, 1936), 18.

[11] Martha McTier to William Drennan, 28 Oct. 1792 (PRONI, Drennan letters, T765/345).

the classes was much slower to materialize, and then did so largely as a result of intervention on the part of the northern democratic republicans. As in Belfast, there was a progressive middle class which pressed radical demands for the reform of parliament. Newspapers were readily available to artisans and labourers who interested themselves in the progress of revolution in France and of reform in Ireland. It is not surprising, therefore, that the working classes in Dublin, inspired by the publicity given to these events, should form their own political organizations. The more proletarianized workers in Dublin, however, also enjoyed a vibrant tradition of collective action in the form of trade unions. C. R. Dobson has identified at least twenty-seven labour disputes in Dublin between 1717 and 1800.[12] Five of these conflicts occurred between 1790 and 1792, creating not only an immediate precedent for artisanal organizations, but also a sharpening of class divisions. The absence of further industrial disputes during the rest of the decade suggests two things. First, with the combination laws of 1780 still in effect and with the government ever vigilant to suppress any perceived radical activity, Dublin workers may have cautiously refrained from industrial activism. Secondly, the projection of political change and reform as a panacea for a variety of social and economic ills by the United Irishmen probably served to divert these workers from economic to political action. The result was a blossoming of working-class republican clubs in Dublin in the early and mid-1790s, operating autonomously from the middle-class reform movement.

In November 1792 *Freeman's Journal* denounced one unnamed club recently established in the capital whose charter toast was 'May mankind trample upon royalty.'[13] Another club composed of lower-class members and espousing republican principles was set up in the winter of 1792–3; it was called the Originals.[14] At the same time, *Faulkner's Dublin Journal* reported the existence of a 'six-penny Jacobin club'.[15] In December 1792 James Alexander McDowall informed the government that working-class Catholics in Dublin had founded a new society 'upon the principles of republicanism, who call themselves "the Sons of Freedom" and whose object is to effect a revolution in Ireland'.[16]

A more significant organization was the Philanthropic Society, founded in 1794 by John Daly Burk, who had been expelled from Trinity College for his deistical beliefs.[17] Containing both petty-bourgeois and plebeian ele-

[12] C. R. Dobson, *Masters and journeymen: a prehistory of industrial relations, 1717–1800* (London, 1980), 154–70.
[13] *FJ*, 8 Nov. 1792.   [14] *FJ*, 1 Dec. 1792.   [15] *FDJ*, 6 Dec. 1792.
[16] James Alexander McDowall to ——, 4 Dec. 1792 (PROHO 100/34/75–6).
[17] See Joseph I. Shulim, 'John Daly Burk: Irish revolutionist and American patriot', *Transactions of the American Philosophical Society*, NS 54/6 (Oct. 1964), 7–9; John Burk, *The trial of John Burk of Trinity College for heresy and blasphemy before the board of senior fellows, to which is added his defence, containing a vindication of his opinions, and a refutation of those*

ments, the Philanthropic Society was ostensibly founded for the purposes of education and self-improvement. But in fact Burk was organizing a revolutionary network in Dublin which had some connections with the Defenders. Each member was required to enlist his own revolutionary cell of ten men. Among their plots were schemes to rescue some imprisoned colleagues, to assassinate Cockayne, the crown's witness against the French agent Revd William Jackson, and, more ambitiously, to storm Dublin Castle with one hundred members dressed as British soldiers.[18] In April 1795 the society circulated a handbill in County Sligo, then the scene of an intensive Defender mobilization, calling for vengeance 'against the oppressors of the poor; against *monopolists* and *those who put the people down* by supporting illegally their diabolical system of abuses and peculation', and demanding a return to the 'primitive purity' of the constitution.[19] The capture of numerous Defenders in the city and county of Dublin in that year revealed that some of them had been members of the Philanthropic Society.[20] Such organizations (and they were numerous in the capital in the mid-1790s) not only served to keep republicanism growing in Dublin while the United Irish movement there was in disarray, but they also provided crucial entry points for northern emissaries into the Defender movement.[21] When the Ulster agents sought to impose the United Irish system on all the republican clubs in the capital, they also courted the Defender societies. By March 1797 these Defenders had been incorporated into the United Irish network.[22]

   When the original United Irishmen resolved to expand their membership in 1792, they turned to such existing organizations as the Volunteers and the masonic lodges. Similarly, in 1795 the reconstituted and revolutionary Society of United Irishmen sought allies in potentially the nation's most revolutionary body—the Defenders.[23] Lower-class protestants felt threatened

inquisitorial charges, in which he shews that his opinions are perfectly consonant to the spirit of the gospel (Dublin, 1794).

[18] Thomas McNevin, *The leading state trials in Ireland from the year 1794 to 1803, with an introduction, notes, etc.* (Dublin, 1844), 352–75.

[19] Handbill circulated in Co. Sligo, Apr. 1795 (Kent CAO, Pratt papers, U840/0145/1/2).

[20] *FJ*, 1 Mar. 1796.

[21] For republican clubs such as the Druid's Lodge, the Spread Club, the Telegraph Club, and many more, see the reports of Thomas Boyle (SPOI, Rebellion papers, 620/18/3) and Francis Higgins (ibid. 620/18/14); for their connections with the Defenders, see the confession of William Kennedy (ibid. 620/23/60).

[22] P. Stewart to Edward Cooke, 4 Mar. 1797 (ibid. 620/29/22*a*).

[23] For the Defenders, see Thomas Bartlett, 'Select documents, xxxviii: Defenders and Defenderism in 1795', *Irish Historical Studies*, 24/95 (May 1985), 373–94; L. M. Cullen, 'The political structures of the Defenders', in Hugh Gough and David Dickson (eds.), *Ireland and the French revolution* (Dublin, 1990), 117–38; Curtin, 'Transformation'; Marianne Elliott, 'The origins and transformation of early Irish republicanism', *International Review of Social History*, 23/3 (1978), 405–28; Tom Garvin, 'Defenders, Ribbonmen, and others', *Past and Present*, 96 (Aug. 1982), 133–55; David W. Miller, 'The Armagh troubles, 1784–95', in Samuel Clark and James S. Donnelly, jun. (eds.), *Irish peasants: violence and political unrest,*

by the Catholic relief measures of 1778 and 1782, which permitted Catholics to compete on a more or less equal basis with protestants in the buying and leasing of land. This resentment was particularly acute in County Armagh, which possessed not only a land-hungry peasantry of weavers and small farmers, but also a nearly equal division of population into Anglican, Presbyterian, and Catholic camps.[24] Catholics, accustomed to a lower standard of living, were willing to pay exorbitant rents, antagonizing prospective protestant tenants, who were outbid.[25] Furthermore, during these declining years of the Volunteers, Catholics were admitted to the corps. The sight of Catholics parading in arms was galling to lower-class protestants, who jealously guarded their exclusive right to bear arms not only as a badge of citizenship, but as an important attribute of their superior status. Nevertheless, sectarian hostility did not animate the initial outbreaks of violence among the northern lower classes. An observer of the conflict asserted that Peep o' Day Boys and Defenders emerged in 1784 after a routine faction fight at Markethill. The losers organized themselves and their friends into the Nappach Fleet to wreak vengeance on their opponents, who subsequently formed themselves into the Hamilton's Bawn Fleet.[26] At first, Catholics participated in both factions, but in 1785 the sectarianism which was to realign the antagonists into Peep o' Day Boys and Defenders became noticeable. Attacks on Catholics began as part of an attempt by the Nappach Fleet to arm itself. After they had plundered most of the arms in their own neighbourhood, their leader reportedly directed them to pursue the quest for weapons in other areas.[27]

At the spring assizes of 1785 some members of the Nappach Fleet, mostly linen weavers, were tried and found guilty, but, through the intercession of a local gentleman, they escaped punishment.[28] This only encouraged further activity on the part of the Nappach Fleet, which by now had assumed the name of 'Peep o' Day Boys'.[29] It was not long before their Catholic victims began to organize themselves into defence associations. The Defenders first appeared at Bunkershill, a village near the town of Armagh, but sectarianism could not as yet have been well defined, since they chose a Presbyterian, a former Steelboy, as their captain. In 1786, however, the disturbances in Armagh ceased to be drunken brawls and faction fights and

---

1780–1914 (Madison, Wis., 1983), 155–91; James Smyth, 'Popular politicisation, Defenderism and the Catholic question', in Gough and Dickson (eds.), *Ireland and the French revolution*, 109–16.

[24] Miller, 'Armagh troubles', 157–61.

[25] Dr William Richardson to marquess of Abercorn, 14 Feb. 1797 (PRONI, Abercorn letters, T2541/IB3/6/4).

[26] [J. Byrne], *An impartial account of the late disturbances in the county of Armagh* (Dublin, 1792), 7.

[27] Ibid. 9.   [28] Ibid. 11.

[29] They were also called Break o' Day Men. The name derived from the fact that their raids often occurred at dawn ([Arthur O'Connor], *A view of the present state of Ireland* (London, 1797, 5).

became a religious war. This escalation of the conflict was largely due to the exercise of biased justice on the part of many Armagh magistrates who were sympathetic to the protestant Peep o' Day Boys.[30] Thus, what began as mere faction fighting in County Armagh soon developed into full-scale sectarian warfare characterized by ritualized acts of intimidation, intrusion into disputed territory, and nightly raids to disarm opponents.

The subsequent history of Defenderism, at least until the rebellion of 1798, can be divided into five phases. First, there was the spread of the movement into north Leinster in the early 1790s, largely as a result of contagion. The second phase, which resulted in the further extension of the movement, coincided with the embodiment of the Irish militia in 1793. During the third phase, occurring in 1795, Defenderism began to assume revolutionary proportions, particularly in Connacht, where extraordinary and illegal measures were undertaken by the Irish commander-in-chief, Lord Carhampton, to suppress the movement. The fourth phase saw the resurgence of sectarian warfare in Ulster, the birth of the Orange Order to counter the Defenders, and the polarizing effects of the so-called 'Armagh outrages'. Finally, largely as a consequence of previous events, the rural, Catholic Defenders formed an alliance with the urban middle-class republicans associated in the United Irish movement.[31]

By the summer of 1792 Defenderism had become particularly rampant in north Leinster. In Louth in December 1792, Defenders raided the houses of nearly forty protestants in a quest for arms. *Faulkner's Dublin Journal* reported that the rebels 'infested the road from Drogheda to Dunleer, stopping passengers for arms'.[32] When 700 Defenders paraded with arms near Dunleer, *Freeman's Journal* claimed that they 'consisted of the lowest peasantry of the country'.[33] Their numbers gave them the boldness to attack even military barracks in their search for weapons.[34] But the disturbances were not confined to Louth alone. 'The counties of Meath, Cavan, Louth, and Monaghan continue in a very disturbed state,' Hobart reported to the home office. 'The Defenders, as they style themselves, are all Catholics; they have disarmed almost every protestant in those counties.'[35]

Three related reasons apparently account for this spread of Defenderism outside County Armagh. First, Catholics expelled by Peep o' Day Boys in the north fled into the border counties with tales of the attacks perpetrated against them by ruthless protestant bands. These tales, naturally, incensed and alarmed the Catholics of the neighbouring counties. Hobart, for example, attributed the institutionalization of Defenderism in Louth to the fact

---

[30] Miller, 'Armagh troubles', 170–8.

[31] One might add a sixth phase—the survival of the Defenders into the 19th century, forming the basis for the emergence of Ribbonism: see Garvin, 'Defenders, Ribbonmen, and others'.

[32] *FDJ*, 1 Jan. 1793.   [33] *FJ*, 3 Jan. 1793.   [34] *FJ*, 5 Jan. 1793.

[35] Hobart to Nepean, 9 Feb. 1793 (PROHO 100/42/268–9).

that northern protestants frequented the fairs in that county 'to purchase wool and such other commodities as their own part of the country does not sufficiently supply them with'. The appearance of these northerners provoked rioting among the Catholic inhabitants, who were inflamed by reports about the fate of their co-religionists in Armagh. Eventually, during one such fair, 'a numerous body of Defenders (Roman Catholics) marched through the place, overturned and broke the cars of the northern people, who had made their purchase[s], tore open their sacks, and scattered the wool about and destroyed it, beating the owners unmercifully, one of whom was killed by the strokes of a loaded whip.'[36] A Catholic gentleman explained the intrusion of Defenderism into his county exclusively in terms of this contagion effect. 'The evil came full formed from the county of Louth to the county of Meath.'[37]

Clearly, however, other factors facilitated the institutionalization of the Defenders in any given county. A second major reason was that Defenderism thrived on a fear of protestant persecution, and, as Robert Kee has noted, it became almost an ideology based on the assumption that 'the whole Catholic peasant identity in Ireland required defence on principle, and that the best form of defence was attack'.[38] Meath, for example, possessed a protestant gentry violently opposed to Catholic relief. 'This beneficent and patriotic act', observed a Catholic gentleman in Meath of the 1793 law, 'seems to have fretted and disturbed the minds of prejudiced men more than all the enormities of the Defenders. Disappointment and revenge began to operate.'[39] The speaker of the Irish house of commons, John Foster, a fervent opponent of the relaxation of the penal laws, was the dominant landed and political figure in County Louth. Lower-class Catholics, aware of such illiberal attitudes on the part of the natural rulers of the county, no doubt associated them with the marauding bands of protestant partisans in the north. Thus the Catholics formed themselves into pre-emptive Defender associations. This in turn led to the circulation of wild rumours concerning a 'popish conspiracy' to massacre all protestants. This sanguinary plot allegedly included all Catholics, 'from peer to peasant, and the Catholic clergy were said to be at the bottom of all'.[40] These fears served to polarize both religious communities, confirming them in the necessity of mobilization, legitimizing their paranoid expectations, and leading to irrational sectarian warfare.

But sectarianism alone did not entirely account for the disturbances. The further the Defenders were separated from Armagh, the more they lost their

---

[36] Robert Hobart to ——, 8 Oct. 1792 (ibid. 100/38/11).
[37] *A candid and impartial account of the disturbances in the county of Meath in the years 1792, 1793, and 1794, by a County Meath freeholder* (Dublin, 1794), 1.
[38] Robert Kee, *The green flag: a history of Irish nationalism* (London, 1972), 44.
[39] *A candid account*, 8.   [40] Ibid. 6–7.

sectarian character and assumed the aims and tactics of traditional, oath-bound, agrarian secret societies. The conservative *Freeman's Journal* offered a third and economic reason for this latest outburst of agrarian rebellion: 'Rack rents, fines, and interfering middlemen have produced more troubles in Ireland for the last 30 years than in some of its former wars. Besides being the curse of the peasantry, such [factors] have uniformly prevented a beneficial yeomanry.'[41] The usual peasant grievances concerning tithes, rents, wages, and taxes provided a permanent backdrop to protest in rural Ireland throughout the last half of the eighteenth century. Clearly, these perennial grievances alone could not trigger an outburst of agrarian rebellion. Two factors in potent combination explain both the timing of these disturbances in the early and mid-1790s and the distinctive blend of old and new forms of collective mobilization peculiar to the Defender movement. The first factor was, again, the demonstration effect. The mobilization of Defenders in Armagh, even though it was a response to sectarian harassment, nevertheless revived the possibility that the traditional agrarian secret society could serve the purposes of the peasantry in alleviating their economic distress. Thus Westmorland reported to Pitt that the 'general plan [of the Defenders] is too swear the whole country to be true to the Irish nation and to resist all payments of rents, taxes, etc., to resist all law but their own laws called parish law', that is, the traditional economic code of the secret societies.[42] A second factor was the impact of the French revolution and its associated egalitarianism, popularized by Paine and propagated by the United Irishmen. Irish peasants were encouraged to believe that radical political change would relieve them of their vexatious economic burdens. As Hobart observed, the lower classes in the counties infected with Defenderism 'are universally impressed with ideas (however vague) of considerable advantages to be gained to them by some convulsion in the state'.[43] What made Defenderism a new and alarming departure from the tradition of Irish agrarian protest was this conjunction of Whiteboyism and radical political ideas, associated with a revolutionary and belligerent power. 'Amongst other considerations,' reported Hobart on the motives of the insurgents, 'a release from tithes, rents, and taxes forms no small part of the inducements held out to them, and they are taught to expect the assistance of the French.'[44]

The vigorous exertions of the local magistracy, backed by government troops, and the effective use of the courts to try and execute disturbers of the king's peace led to a temporary restoration of tranquillity in north

---

[41] *FJ*, 14 Aug. 1792.
[42] Earl of Westmorland to William Pitt, 7 Jan. 1793 (PRO, Chatham papers, 30/8/331/105–10).
[43] Hobart to Nepean, 29 Dec. 1792 (PROHO 100/42/13).
[44] Hobart to Nepean, 17 June 1793 (ibid. 100/44/147–50).

Leinster early in 1793.[45] But within months the government was faced with even more widespread popular agitation when it began enrolling recruits for the newly authorized Irish militia.[46] The militia act directed that the new corps be reserved for service in Ireland, but it was widely rumoured that such troops would be sent into service abroad. Throughout the spring and summer of 1793, and in well over half the counties of Ireland, suspicious peasants rioted in protest against the act and its procedure of balloting local inhabitants into county regiments. The most formidable demonstrations occurred in the Athboy district of recently pacified Meath, where for several days nearly a thousand people robbed houses of arms and swore the inhabitants 'not to be inimical to them'. The outburst was soon put down, with some severity, and peace was restored.[47]

The significance of these anti-militia riots for the development of Defenderism is not the disturbances themselves, formidable as they may have been. The embodiment of a largely Catholic militia meant that many Defenders were balloted into the new regiments. Since these regiments were expected to be more effective and controllable if they served outside their home counties, they often carried the contagion of Defenderism into previously uninfected areas of the country.[48] Even more significant, the presence of Defender militiamen in such republican areas as Dublin and Belfast assisted the efforts of the United Irishmen to forge an alliance with the Catholic insurgents, an achievement which will be discussed more fully below.

One effect of Defender mobilization in general and of the anti-militia riots in particular was the contribution that both made to the development of what Thomas Bartlett calls an 'anti-state attitude' on the part of the Irish peasantry and to a further erosion of the deference, whether instrumental or sincere, which they accorded to their social superiors.[49] Any remaining respect on the part of the peasantry for the laws of the land was undermined by the Draconian repression of Defenderism in the west by Carhampton in 1795. As early as August 1794 Cooke reported that the lower classes were mobilizing in Defender associations in the counties of Cavan, Leitrim, and Roscommon.[50] The local authorities failed to contain

---

[45] At the spring assizes of 1793 in Trim, Co. Meath, 8 Defenders were convicted of capital offences and 40 more were remanded in custody (*FJ*, 9 Mar. 1793). In Dundalk, Co. Louth, over a dozen Defenders were hanged following their conviction at the spring assizes (*FJ*, 30 July 1793).

[46] For the anti-militia riots, see Thomas Bartlett, 'An end to moral economy: the Irish militia disturbances of 1795', *Past and Present*, 99 (May 1983), 41–64; Sir Henry McAnally, *The Irish militia, 1793–1816: a social and military history* (London, 1949), 31–7.

[47] *A candid account*, 11–13; W. E. H. Lecky, *A history of Ireland in the eighteenth century* (5 vols., London, 1898), iii. 216–17.

[48] Bartlett, 'Defenders and Defenderism', 375.

[49] Ibid. 374; id., 'An end to moral economy'.

[50] Edward Cooke to Thomas Broderick, 16 Aug. 1794 (PROHO 100/46/184).

the disturbances, leading the newly arrived viceroy, Earl Fitzwilliam, to lament in January 1795: 'I am sorry to say that not a day has passed since my arrival without intelligence received of violences committed in Westmeath, Meath, Longford, and Cavan. Defenderism is there in its greatest force, and it must be crushed or it will become dangerous.'[51] By the spring of 1795 Defenderism had infected much of northern Connacht.[52] Although Defender oaths and catechisms in this area were redolent with republicanism and expectations of French assistance, the motivation for the insurgents' mobilization seems to have been largely economic. The local magistracy was unwilling to confront the insurgents; indeed, many compounded their cowardice with bad judgement when they conceded the Defenders' demands, agreeing 'to give them larger wages and to let them land at a cheaper rent'.[53] Such success only encouraged the Defenders in other areas, who redoubled their efforts. Unable to rouse the local authorities to vigorous action, Camden dispatched Lord Carhampton to Connacht with unlimited authority 'not only to *check* but if possible to extinguish this spirit of rapine and of cruelty'.[54] Under the general's direction, magistrates and officers arrested those suspected of Defenderism and, without bringing them to trial, sent them to serve in the fleet.[55] More than a thousand of these unfortunate agricultural labourers and small farmers were dispatched to the tenders. By July Camden could report that Carhampton's extraordinary measures had restored tranquillity to the area.[56] But this flagrant violation of the law created intense and widespread hostility towards the government. Emmet remarked:

Indeed, the objects of this summary measure were frequently seen tied down on carts in the bitterest agonies, crying out incessantly for trial but crying in vain. This conduct marked his lordship's attachment to government too closely not to have its imitators. Magistrates, therefore, without military commissions but within the influence of his example, assumed to themselves also the authority of transporting without trial.[57]

---

[51] Earl Fitzwilliam to duke of Portland, 10 Jan. 1795 (PROHO 100/46/259).

[52] —— to Thomas Pelham, 30 Apr. 1795 (Kent CAO, Pratt papers, U840/0145/4).

[53] Earl Camden to duke of Portland, 30 Apr. 1795 (PROHO 100/57/225–6); for the timidity of the local magistracy, see e.g. William Newenham to Ross Mahon, 30 Apr. 1795 (Kent CAO, Pratt papers, U840/0145/6/2): 'I have made the best preparations in my power to defend myself and am determined to do so, tho' abandoned by all the gentlemen in the neighbourhood [of Galway], who have either left the country or have refused to act with me.'

[54] Camden to Portland, 5 May 1795 (PROHO 100/57/257–9); for Portland's approval of Camden's 'perfectly just, manly, and liberal' intentions, see duke of Portland to Earl Camden, 11 May 1795 (ibid. 100/57/265–6).

[55] Lecky, *History of Ireland*, iii. 420.

[56] Camden to Portland, 15 July 1795 (PROHO 100/58/135–7).

[57] William James MacNeven, *Pieces of Irish history illustrative of the condition of the Catholics of Ireland* (New York, 1807), 112.

In 1796 the government passed an indemnity act legalizing these transgres-
sions retroactively, and then proceeded to codify them in the form of the
notorious insurrection act.[58]

While Carhampton was indiscriminately transporting suspected
Defenders to the fleet, vigilante groups of Armagh protestants were forming
to suppress Defender activity in the north-east. Since the Catholic relief act
of 1793, lower-class protestants had felt particularly vulnerable. The extension of the vote to Catholics made these protestants less valuable to their
landlords. Moreover, the Volunteers, a largely protestant defence force, had
been dissolved and replaced by a militia of armed Catholics. Lower-class
protestants came to believe that the administration had abandoned them to
the emboldened and better-organized Defenders. Out of these fears grew
the infamous Orange Order.[59] In 1794 James Wilson, a substantial
Presbyterian farmer and freemason in County Tyrone, organized a small
band of protestants who adopted the name 'Orange Boys'. Similar bands
were formed later, and though their numbers may not have approached
those of the Defenders, their members were armed and determined to suppress the Catholic militants. Initially, these bands were indistinguishable
from the Peep o' Day Boys. For a while the Orange factions contented
themselves with parading and other relatively harmless acts of bravado.

Then, in June 1795, the Defenders and Orange Boys engaged in a battle
near Loughgall, County Armagh. The military arrived to restore order,
under the leadership of two magistrates named Turner and McCann.
Turner encountered a group of feudists only to discharge them when he
discovered that they were protestants. McCann, on the other hand, captured fifty-eight armed Catholics and sent them to Armagh gaol.[60] Once
again, the failure of the Armagh magistracy to mete out equal justice to
Catholic and protestant alike led to an escalation of the conflict. Though
they were subsequently released, the Defenders naturally felt that they were
the injured party. They returned to Loughgall in the following September
determined on one great effort to establish themselves as the dominant
power in that part of the county. The Catholics were superior in numbers,
but their opponents were better armed, and many of them had been
Volunteers.

The battle of the Diamond, as it became known, began in the usual
desultory fashion, with the antagonists taking ground on opposing hills and
firing, out of range, at one another. A truce was then arranged by three
Catholic priests and two magistrates. Meanwhile, however, Defender reinforcements had arrived at the Diamond. Unaware of, or ignoring, a truce to

---

[58] Lecky, *History of Ireland*, iii. 420.
[59] Hereward Senior, *Orangeism in Ireland and Britain, 1795–1836* (London, 1966), 13–14.
[60] Thomas Lane to marquess of Downshire, 20 June 1795 (PRONI, Downshire papers,
D607/C/103).

which they had not been a party, they attacked Dan Winter's inn, the site of an earlier Peep o' Day Boy–Defender brawl and now a shelter for a small but well-armed party of protestants. Orange Boys, returning home after the truce, heard the shots and regrouped. Although the protestants were outnumbered by an estimated 400 Defenders, their superior arms and training led them to victory. According to William Richardson, forty-three Catholics were left dead on the field.[61]

Immediately after this brief engagement, the victors assembled in Loughgall at the inn of James Sloan, whose signboard displayed an image of William of Orange crossing the Boyne. In this congenial bastion of protestantism, the first lodge of the Orange Order was established, adopting the paraphernalia of secrecy used by the Defenders and originating with the freemasons. The members of the lodge were initially weavers and small farmers.[62] The Orange Order spread rapidly through Armagh and neighbouring Tyrone and soon gained the support of some members of the protestant gentry, who were impressed by the Orangemen's oath to support and defend the protestant ascendancy in Ireland. But as matters stood at the end of 1795, Orangeism was still essentially a lower-class protestant reaction to Defenderism.

In the first flush of victory after the battle of the Diamond, a victory which they regarded as having given them divine sanction to pursue their association, the Armagh Orangemen perpetrated a series of vicious attacks on the Catholic peasantry which came to be known as the Armagh outrages.[63] Orangemen banded together for nightly raids to drive the Catholics from their lands, directing them to go to 'to hell or Connacht'. They burned several Catholic chapels, and the persecutions spread to Tyrone, Down, Antrim, and Derry. It was estimated that up to 7,000 Catholics were driven out of Armagh alone.[64] Lord Altamont, who received many of these refugees on his estate around Westport, County Mayo, informed Camden: 'An idea has gone abroad that the persecutions in the north have been fomented by government, and however diabolical and absurd such a measure could be for any purpose of politics, it has gained belief and has disaffected a great body of Catholics of every rank throughout the kingdom.'[65] General Dalrymple in Armagh was equally concerned. The rumour that the government was covertly encouraging the Orangemen, he believed, would

[61] Richardson also noted that many more bodies were found afterwards, when the potatoes were harvested (Richardson to Abercorn, 22 Feb. 1797 (PRONI, Abercorn papers, T2541/IB3/6/4)); for another account of the battle, see James Dawson to ——, 19 Sept. 1795 (SPOI, State of the country papers, carton 154/32).

[62] R. M. Sibbett, *Orangeism in Ireland and throughout the empire* (2 vols., Belfast, 1914–15), i. 233–4.

[63] See Patrick Tohall, 'The Diamond fight of 1795 and the resultant expulsions', *Seanchas Ardmhacha (Armagh Diocesan Historical Society)*, 4 (1957), 19–50.

[64] Lecky, *History of Ireland*, ii. 432–5.

[65] Lord Altamont to Earl Camden, 27 July 1796 (SPOI, Rebellion papers, 620/24/62).

undermine the Catholics' faith in the law and the disposition of the state to protect them, thus making them likely candidates for Defender recruitment. Describing a series of outrages in his neighbourhood, Dalrymple lamented: 'The Catholics conceive the fault to be mine, that I am partial and attached to their enemies . . . and when I advise them to apply to the magistrates, their answer is constantly [that] their own case is hopeless. . . . The evil will surely increase and [will] very soon be followed by acts of outrage.'[66]

Orangeism contributed powerfully to the alliance between Defenders and United Irishmen. Thomas Addis Emmet later testified that 'we always found [that] whenever it was attempted to establish a lodge [of the Orange Order], the United Irishmen increased very much.'[67] By the end of 1795 the Defenders were confronted with a government ruthlessly bending the law to deal with agrarian outrages and with a newly organized band of vigilante loyalists, proclaiming their support for the protestant ascendancy and receiving sympathetic, if covert, assistance from some members of the gentry and magistracy. The Armagh outrages confirmed the Defenders' vulnerability to this twin assault. It is no small wonder that the Catholic militants began to look for allies in their struggle, and the one group ready to receive them with open arms was the United Irishmen.

The urban, middle-class republicans, however, were slow to court the active support of the militant Catholic peasants, and it was not until 1795 that the reconstituted and revolutionary Society of United Irishmen decided that the advantages of mobilizing these angry peasants were well worth the risk of turning them loose on the protestants and property of the country. Not surprisingly, conservatives had frequently blamed the rural disturbances of the early 1790s on the United Irishmen.[68] *Freeman's Journal* claimed that such events were actuated by a 'wild and incoherent disposition to riot, insurrection, and resistance to the laws, originating in a confused notion of Mr Paine's villainous pamphlets, so industriously dispersed throughout the country last summer by those dangerous nests of conspirators—the United Irishmen'.[69]

But aside from the circulation of seditious literature, there were very few instances of United Irish–Defender co-operation in the first few years of the decade, and in those few cases they were either trying to quell embarrassing sectarian hostilities or to direct the energies of the agrarian rebels into political channels. In July 1792 three gentlemen of the Catholic Committee in Dublin journeyed to County Down at the request of the Belfast United Irishmen to investigate the Defender–Peep o' Day Boy

[66] Gen. William Dalrymple to Thomas Pelham, 9 Aug. [1796] (BL, Pelham papers, Add. MS 33101/142–3).

[67] MacNeven, *Pieces of Irish history*, 116–17.

[68] See e.g. John Fitzgibbon to John Beresford, 14 May 1793 (*The correspondence of the right hon. John Beresford*, ed. William Beresford (2 vols., London, 1854), ii. 14).

[69] *FJ*, 18 July 1793.

disturbances in the barony of Rathfryland. Finding that the Catholics were usually the victims rather than the perpetrators of the outrages in that neighbourhood, the Catholic representatives and the United Irishmen distributed a circular letter promising the support and protection of the Catholic Committee and the Volunteers to any victim of sectarian hostility.[70] At the same time, Neilson, Tone, and Alexander Lowry, a County Down linen draper, travelled to Rathfryland in order to mediate between the warring factions. Neilson subsequently visited County Armagh with similar intent.[71]

Perhaps the future mobilization of the lower classes was in Neilson's mind, but his immediate purpose was to quell disturbances which were giving the lie to the radicals' proclaimed union of Catholic and protestant. A similar mission was independently undertaken by a Catholic priest, Father James Coigley. Coigley had escaped from France in 1789 only to return to Armagh, where he found the county plagued by brawls between Peep o' Day Boys and Defenders: 'I immediately attempted to reconcile the parties but was much discouraged by several leading gentlemen of that country.' Undeterred, he persisted in his role as mediator, and dampened sectarian animosities between 1791 and 1793 in the districts of Randalstown, Maghera, Dungiven, and Magilligan. 'My success would have been trifling,' he recalled, 'had it not been for the spirited exertions of that truly respectable, virtuous, and enlightened body, the Dissenters of Antrim, but chiefly and particularly those of Belfast.'[72]

These attempts at conciliation should have been beyond the reproach of the most loyal supporters of the government, but the effort of James Napper Tandy to infiltrate the Defenders was not. In March 1793 a warrant was issued against Tandy for distributing seditious literature in County Louth, then the scene of intense Defender disturbances.[73] Tandy's real mission was to acquaint himself with the objectives of the Catholic insurgents. Emmet reported that Tandy 'contrived to communicate this wish to some of the Defenders; and as his character was long known to them', they agreed to provide him with information on condition that he bind himself to secrecy. He consented to this, and met a party of them at Castlebellingham, where he took the Defender oath. When informed of the warrant for his arrest, Tandy, in justified panic, fled the country.[74] Nothing would have pleased the government more than to prove that one of the leaders of the Dublin United Irishmen was also a sworn Defender. Of course, even the case of Tandy offers no real evidence that the United Irishmen were covertly fomenting agrarian rebellion. Far more plausible is

---

[70] MacNeven, *Pieces of Irish history*, 52–3.   [71] Latimer, *Ulster biographies*, 40–1.
[72] Revd James Coigley, *The life of Revd James Coigley, an address to the people of Ireland, as written by himself during his confinement in Maidstone gaol* (London, 1798), 1–13.
[73] *FDJ*, 16 Mar. 1793.   [74] MacNeven, *Pieces of Irish history*, 48.

the explanation that the United Irishmen helped to create a climate in which radical political ideas were infused into Defenderism, providing it with a dimension lacking in previous secret societies.

The viceroy, Lord Westmorland, attributed the spread of Defenderism to the 'levelling principles of the French revolution' propagated by the republicans of Belfast and Dublin.[75] A secret committee was appointed in February 1793 to investigate any links between Defenders, the Catholic Committee, the United Irishmen, and the French. The committee described the Defenders as

of the Roman Catholic persuasion; in general poor, ignorant labouring men, sworn to secrecy and impressed with an opinion that they are assisting the Catholic cause; in other respects they do not appear to have any distinct, particular object in view, but they talk of being relieved from hearth money, tithes, county cesses, and of lowering their rents. . . . Their measures appear to have been concerted and conducted with the utmost secrecy and a degree of regularity and system not usual in people of such mean condition, and as if directed by men of superior rank.[76]

The committee was unable to prove what its report tried to imply—that the insurgent peasants were led by Catholic Committeemen and United Irishmen. All it could say was that the Catholic leader, John Sweetman, had enquired into the activities of Defenders awaiting trial at Dundalk, and that seditious literature emanating from Belfast and Dublin had 'encouraged the Defenders in their proceedings'.[77]

What transformed these initial, tentative overtures into an earnestly sought alliance between the United Irishmen and the Defenders was the changing circumstances of radical mobilization after 1794. Coercive legislation, judicial harassment, and, finally, the suppression of the Dublin Society of United Irishmen in 1794 isolated and frustrated the middle-class radicals, making them receptive to the idea of forging links with the less respectable lower classes. But in many ways it was an incongruous,—indeed, unnatural—alliance which bound the United Irishmen to the Defenders. Robert Kee has cautiously described the Defenders as an 'organisation on the brink of a crude political attitude, primitive and ill-coordinated, and yet expressing incoherently the everyday grievances and resentments of over a century'.[78] Though the Defenders advocated a rather vulgar democratic republicanism, they were much more concerned with the alleviation of economic complaints and sought 'equality of property, a raising of the price of

---

[75] Quoted in Lecky, *History of Ireland*, iii. 219.　　　　　[76] *Rep. secret comm.* 37.

[77] Ibid. 38–9. For Catholic refutations of these charges, see *Defence of the subcommittee of the Catholics of Ireland from the imputations attempted to be thrown on that body, particularly from the charge of supporting the Defenders, published by order of the subcommittee* (Dublin, 1793); John Sweetman, *A refutation of the charges attempted to be made against the secretary to the sub-committee of the Catholics of Ireland, particularly that of abetting the Defenders* (Dublin, 1793).

[78] Kee, *Green flag*, 44.

labour, and a lowering of the price of land and provisions'.[79] Politics were secondary to these concerns, and, unfortunately, religious differences were closely tied to economic grievances, giving Defenderism much of its sectarian character. The seditious aspect of Defenderism arose from its vague support for a French invasion which would assist Irish rebels to procure the redistribution of protestant estates. In investigating the origins of Irish republicanism in the 1790s, Marianne Elliott wisely noted that it would be foolish to dismiss the sense of dispossession still felt by Catholic peasants long after the confiscations of the sixteenth and seventeenth centuries.[80] Echoing the fears of the Anglo-Irish ascendancy, the earl of Westmorland observed: 'The lower orders or old Irish consider themselves as plundered and kept out of their property by the English settlers and on every occasion are ready for riot and revenge.'[81] And Thomas Bartlett has reminded us of the vibrant millenarianism of Defender catechisms, which had its roots in early seventeenth-century Gaelic poetry. 'When the French revolution burst upon a startled world,' Bartlett maintains, 'the Gaelic mind, essentially the outlook of the lower orders, found no difficulty in assimilating French developments into the by now time-honoured themes of deliverance from abroad, besting the Saxon and destroying the Protestants.'[82]

The crude Catholic nationalism of the Defenders, their emphasis on social and economic change, and this aspiration to despoil the protestants hardly recommended the rural insurgents to the United Irishmen, who sought to erase sectarian tensions, emphasized political change as a panacea for all grievances, and exalted the right to property. The United Irishmen mobilized with the model of the Volunteers in mind—the nation in arms asserting its will. The Defenders, however, employed the time-honoured devices of the agrarian secret society, the proven techniques of violence and intimidation. But as an urban, largely middle-class revolutionary movement, the United Irishmen could expect little success without the formidable assistance of Ireland's rural lower classes.

By 1795 the Defenders were clearly a much more imposing revolutionary body than the United Irishmen, though they hardly formed a single, coherent movement. As we have seen, Defenderism in the north tended to represent an assertion of the Catholic peasant identity, while as it moved southwards it took on more of the character of the traditional secret society. Similarly, the degree to which the Defenders absorbed pro-French political notions varied from place to place. Any association of agrarian rebels was likely to be labelled as supporting Defenderism and hostile to the political establishment by the besieged ascendancy. There was, nevertheless, a highly co-ordinated system of Defenderism which was particularly pro-

---

[79] Madden, *United Irishmen*, i. 60.   [80] Elliott, 'Origins and transformation', 413.
[81] Earl of Westmorland to Henry Dundas, 24 May 1793 (PRO HO 100/43/319–20).
[82] Bartlett, 'Defenders and Defenderism', 378.

nounced in Ulster and north Leinster. Camden reported in May 1795 that the Defenders were organized into a system of affiliated lodges, the principal lodge being at the house of an Armagh publican named Robert Campbell.[83] It was Campbell who signed the 'tickets for changing the secret signs and passwords'.[84] The County Roscommon magistrate J. W. Fleming claimed that the 'Defenders all over Ireland are formed into lodges' under this publican's leadership. In fact, it was Campbell 'who issues out the different orders which are dispersed by agents under him'. Fleming secured this information from a Defender agent calling himself an 'inspector general' in the organization, who was sent to oversee the movement in the west.[85] But a Catholic priest, engaged by the government to infiltrate the Defender movement, claimed that Campbell was merely the assistant of the 'real head of the Defenders', John Magennis, a 'respectable tenant under Lord Downshire'.[86]

The Defenders met at night, generally for the purpose of military drilling (accompanied by fife and drum), administering unlawful oaths, and committing 'outrages' against the property and, very often, the persons of unpopular landlords and magistrates, clergymen, and farmers. Camden observed that 'in the counties where Defenderism prevailed, almost all the lower orders have been sworn. They meet in bodies of several hundreds, and on some occasions 3,000 or 4,000 have assembled.'[87] As one observer noted: 'By their extreme ferocity, of which there are many horrid instances, they have established such an ascendancy over the lower orders of people that government has never been able to obtain an entire scheme of intelligence.' Defenders set wage rates and rents; petty juries could not be trusted to try them; and in some neighbourhoods protestants were totally disarmed.[88]

Until 1795 the Defenders had little in common with the United Irishmen.

---

[83] Camden to Portland, 25 July 1795 (SPOI, Rebellion papers, 620/22/19). For further information on Campbell, see the file of letters from Thomas Boyle (ibid. 620/18/3) and Francis Higgins (ibid. 620/18/14); examinations of Michael Phillips, 29 Oct. 1795 (ibid. 620/22/47) and Thomas Kennedy, Mar. 1795 (ibid. 620/23/60); examination of Thomas Mulheran, 27 July 1795 (PROI, Frazer papers, IA 40/111a/1). A northern magistrate also affirmed that the Defenders were 'directed by committees . . . which are linked together throughout the kingdom' (William Smyth to Dublin Castle, 15 Nov. 1795 (SPOI, Rebellion papers, 620/22/54)).

[84] —— Knott to James Fleming, 7 July 1795 (Kent CAO, Pratt papers, U840/0149/4/2); see also Henry Major to Thomas Pelham, 29 July 1795 (ibid. U840/0149/16/1). Major discovered a number of these Defender tickets, 'from which you will see that these wretches, the Defenders, are every day forming themselves into companies. With the tickets, I discovered a stamping-iron marked R*C, the initial letter of Robert Campbell.'

[85] J. W. Fleming to Thomas Pelham, 27 June 1795 (ibid. U840/0147/14/1).

[86] Edward Cooke to Thomas Pelham, 4 Dec. 1795 (BL, Pelham papers, Add. MS 33101/358–9). Campbell left the country sometime in 1795, after his secretary in the organization was arrested and 3 soldiers in the Armagh militia swore an affidavit against him (Cooke to Pelham, 29 Oct. 1795 (ibid. 33101/327–8)).

[87] Camden to Portland, 25 July 1795 (SPOI, Rebellion papers, 620/22/19).

[88] Lecky, *History of Ireland*, iii. 389.

But the radicals' untiring efforts to propagate the cause of the French and of democratic republicanism imbued both organizations with a shared commitment to the ideals of the French revolution, even though they may have disagreed in their understanding of these ideals. The Defenders were clearly impressed with the revolution in France. Marianne Elliott has suggested that they were in contact with French agents as early as 1792.[89] Perhaps in tribute to the French, the Defenders incorporated committees of public safety into their lodges, and one informer claimed, with wild exaggeration, that the entire organization was divided into departments and communes.[90]

Another powerful motive for the Catholics and republicans to band together was their common antipathy to the ascendancy. The dreadful Defender threats to Irish protestants certainly alarmed many middle-class radicals, but they were blithely dismissed. The republicans interpreted these threats in two reassuring ways. First, Defender sectarianism was a function of the influence of their priests, which could be overcome eventually, the radicals thought.[91] More reassuring was the belief that Defender hostility was directed not towards protestants in general, but against protestant landlords and rulers in particular. As Tone wrote from America: 'I have the greatest compassion for them [the Defenders]. . . . I look on the culprits as fellow sufferers.'[92] Even General Abercromby, the briefly tenured commander-in-chief, expressed a grudging sympathy for the Defenders' grievances: 'I believe the lower ranks heartily hate the gentlemen because they oppress them, and the gentlemen hate the peasants because they deserve to be hated.'[93]

The Belfast radicals, with their dreams of a union of all Irishmen based on a complete separation of church and state in an enlightened democratic republic, had some misgivings about an alliance with the militant Catholicism represented by the Defenders. Beguiled by overconfidence, the republicans counted on their ability to channel Defenderism into their own version of the national cause and underestimated the endurance of sectarian hostility. Neilson regarded the Defenders as 'nothing more than an undisciplined rabble'. 'Their number', he said, 'makes them formidable, their wrongs make them desperate, and though they would probably render no good by themselves, yet with proper rulers they might be made of very

[89] Elliott, 'Origins and transformation', 420–1.

[90] Séamus Ó Loinsigh, 'The rebellion of 1798 in Meath', *Riocht na Midhe: Records of the Meath Archaeological and Historical Society*, 4/2 (1968), 36; information of Friar Philips, 4 Feb. 1795 (Kent CAO, Pratt papers, U840/0150/3).

[91] Information of John Smith (alias Bird), 1795–6 (SPOI, Rebellion papers, 620/27/1).

[92] 'William Penn' [T. W. Tone] to Thomas Russell, 25 Oct. 1795 (TCD, Russell correspondence, MS 868/2[N.4.3]/13–15).

[93] Sir Ralph Abercromby to William Pitt, 28 Jan. 1798 (NLI, Lord-Lieutenants' correspondence, MS 886/197–8). Abercromby had his own reasons to hate the gentlemen of Ireland as well, for they were lustily demanding his dismissal. See below, Ch. 10.

great service to the game.'[94] Robert Simms informed Tone of the progress of the United Irish integration with the Defenders: 'It will require great exertions to keep this organization [the Defenders] from producing feuds among the different sects, for the Presbyterians in general, knowing nothing of their views and plans, look on them with great jealousy.'[95]

Reactionary protestantism, most brutally represented in the emergence of the Orange Order in Armagh, was certainly one of the most important engines in driving the Defenders into an alliance with the United Irishmen. The County Down magistrate Robert Waddell complained to the government that the Orangemen 'have driven some hundreds to join the United Irishmen'.[96] Wherever possible, the United Irishmen attempted to conciliate the warring sectaries and to bring them both over to the republican cause, but more often they took the side of the Catholic victims, tried to bring Orangemen to justice, and sought to expose partial magistrates. Emmet observed: 'Prosecutions were therefore commenced and carried out by the executive at the desire of the provincial committee of the United Irishmen against some of the most notorious offenders and some of the most guilty magistrates; but that measure appeared only to redouble their efforts.'[97] Even Camden blamed these Armagh magistrates who, 'having imbibed the prejudices which belong to it, and having been swayed by those predilections in the discharge of their duty,' encouraged the Orangemen and contributed to the persistence of sectarian warfare in the county.[98] The failure of attempts to secure legal redress convinced the Defenders and the victimized Catholic peasantry that 'effectual relief was thus indeed, for the most part, withheld from the oppressed; but they learned to look upon the United Irishmen as their only friends, to confide in the sincerity of those protestants who had joined the nation, and no longer to look with hope or affection towards the existing law or its remedies.'[99] The United Irishmen provided such eminent barristers as William Sampson and Thomas Addis Emmet, as counsel for arrested Defenders. By employing their own members in this capacity, the republicans were thus able to establish vital links between the two organizations.[100] In addition, Belfast republicans formed

[94] Information of John Smith (alias Bird), 1795–6 (SPOI, Rebellion papers, 620/27/1).

[95] R[obert] S[imms] to Theobald Wolfe Tone, 18 Sept. 1795 (Tone, *Life*, i. 284).

[96] Robert Waddell to Robert Ross, 29 July 1796 (SPOI, Rebellion papers, 620/24/65).

[97] MacNeven, *Pieces of Irish history*, 116.

[98] Camden to Portland, 22 Jan. 1796 (PROHO 100/62/15–20). General Dalrymple of Armagh also lamented that the magistrates 'seem inclined to give this contest an appellation that ought in prudence ever to be avoided, a religious dispute'. The general then quoted, for the purpose of illustration, a magistrate's report of a battle 'between the Catholics and protestants' in which 22 of the former were left dead on the field, but 'providentially no protestant blood was spilt' (Dalrymple to Pelham, 25 Sept. 1795 (BL, Pelham papers, Add. MS 33101/284–7)).

[99] MacNeven, *Pieces of Irish history*, 117.

[100] *BNL*, 4 Sept. 1795; letters of Thomas Boyle and Francis Higgins (SPOI, Rebellion

committees to prosecute biased magistrates who encouraged or condoned protestant attacks on Catholics. Prominent in this enterprise were two Presbyterians, Henry Joy McCracken and the Belfast tailor Joseph Cuthbert, and three Catholics, the solicitors James McGucken and Daniel Shanaghan of Belfast and Bernard Coyle, a prosperous linen merchant from Lurgan, County Armagh.[101]

Not only did the United Irishmen place their professional expertise and their treasury at the service of victims of the Armagh outrages, but they also offered more immediate relief. Catholic families who had been expelled from their homes by Orangemen were invited to Belfast by Presbyterian United Irishmen, and from there they were sent to farmers in Down and Antrim, where 'they were secured from danger, provided with employment, [and] treated with affectionate hospitality'.[102] This policy of active support served to remove some of the traditional suspicion in which Presbyterians were held by Catholics, and the United Irish system became known throughout the north for these charitable deeds. Exploiting the goodwill they had established among the Catholic peasantry, the United Irishmen began to enrol in Defender bodies. They were able to convince the Defenders that, as Emmet noted:

the *something* which the Defenders vaguely conceived *ought to be done for Ireland* was by separating it from England to establish its real as well as nominal independence; and they urged the necessity of combining into one body all who were actu-·ated with the same view. At last their exertions were favoured with entire success. The Defenders, by specific votes in their own societies, agreed to be sworn United Irishmen and incorporated into the nation.[103]

Among the most prominent United Irishmen involved in this effort were Sam Neilson, who had cultivated contacts with John Magennis, the supposed leader of the northern Defenders, and Henry Joy McCracken, who was dispatched throughout the northern counties in order to unite the Defenders with the United Irishmen.[104] At a meeting of the County Antrim United Irishmen in the autumn of 1795, William Halliday, a Presbyterian farmer near Kells, 'promised to use his influence with the Defenders of Armagh to enlist them as United Irishmen'.[105] About a hundred protestant

papers, 620/18/3, 14); William Sampson, *Memoirs of William Sampson, an Irish exile, written by himself* (London, 1832), pp. xxii–xxiii.

[101] Examination of James McGucken, Aug. 1798 (SPOI, Rebellion papers, 620/3/32/13); Edmund Boyle to Edward Cooke, 9 Aug. 1796 (ibid. 620/24/93*a*); Gen. William Fawcett to Dublin Castle, 30 Nov. 1796 (ibid. 620/26/109); information from John Smith, 1796 (ibid. 620/27/1); fragment of information on *King v. McCann* (PROI, Frazer papers, IA 40/111*a*/13); Madden, *United Irishmen*, ii. 401–3.

[102] MacNeven, *Pieces of Irish history*, 117.
[103] Ibid. 119.
[104] Cooke to Pelham, 4 Dec. 1795 (BL, Pelham papers, Add. MS 33101/358–9); R. R. Madden, *Antrim and Down in '98* (Glasgow, n.d.), 13–14.
[105] Examination of William Hart, 22 Sept. 1795 (SPOI, Rebellion papers, 620/22/41).

tenants of the marquess of Downshire, demonstrating their commitment to the cause of union in Ireland, enrolled in a Defender association.[106] The republicans also sent their Catholic brethren to work among the Defenders. Here the most active figure was Charles Teeling, the son of Luke Teeling, a Lisburn linen manufacturer, who, at the tender age of 17, was said to have assumed chief command over the Down, Antrim, and Armagh Defenders.[107]

Exactly when the formal alliance between the Defenders and the United Irishmen occurred is unclear. Camden claimed that a national meeting of delegates from the United Irishmen and the Defenders was planned for August 1796 in Dublin.[108] A Roscommon magistrate reported in April 1797 that the commander-in-chief of all the Defenders resided in Belfast, and that a meeting of leaders from all over the country was to occur there later that month.[109] Emboldened by this alliance with the radical protestants, and thriving on the perception that the local authorities sided with the Orangemen, Defenderism once again spread throughout the northern counties. But it was an even more dangerous movement now, asserted Camden in January 1796: 'Infinite pains are taken to swear all descriptions of persons, not only to be true to each other according to the former tenor of their oaths, but to unite and to correspond with the Society of United Irishmen.'[110] Furthermore, the exodus from the north of so many Catholic victims with their tales of Orange persecution served to extend the Defender system, and thus that of the United Irishmen, beyond Ulster. 'I fear', reported the viceroy, that they 'have excited a spirit of revenge among their Catholic brethren'.[111]

The republicans hoped to exploit this 'spirit of revenge' by seducing Catholic soldiers from their loyalty to the king. The advantages of participation by soldiers and militiamen were well worth the risks taken in recruiting them. First, in the event of an insurrection, the United Irishmen within a regiment could influence their fellow soldiers to abandon the government and join the rebels. Secondly, they could assist in acquiring arms and ammunition. And, thirdly, soldiers could be induced to desert and then be used to train and drill the civilian republican army. During this period there were three military organizations in Ireland: regular British troops, the Irish militia, and the yeomanry. By 1798 there were well over 80,000 troops available to Dublin Castle, including 35,000 yeomanry, 25,000

---

[106] Dalrymple to Pelham, 25 Sept. 1795 (BL, Pelham papers, Add. MS 33101/284–7).
[107] Madden, *Antrim and Down*, 13.
[108] Camden to Portland, 6 Aug. 1796 (SPOI, Rebellion papers, 620/18/11/1).
[109] J. W. Newenham to Thomas Pelham, 10 Apr. 1797 (ibid. 620/29/215).
[110] Camden to Portland, 22 Jan. 1796 (PROHO 100/62/15–20).
[111] Camden to Portland, 6 Aug. 1796 (SPOI, Rebellion papers, 620/18/11/1); see also the report of a Kerry magistrate, who complained of Co. Derry refugees inciting the inhabitants of Tralee to sedition (Sutton Frizell to Thomas Pelham, 4 Dec. 1796 (ibid. 620/26/98)).

militia, and more than 20,000 men in regular divisions or English and Scottish fencible units.[112]

The cornerstone of United Irish strategy was to mobilize an armed force to overawe the Irish government into reforming itself. This was the lesson that the radicals derived from the Volunteer success in 1782 as well as from the role that the National Guard had played in France in preserving the revolution from the forces of reaction. In the early 1790s the United Irishmen attempted to marshal the Volunteers, old and new, for this purpose. In classical republican ideology, entrusting national defence to a volunteer citizen army represented the very hallmark of good and virtuous government. A paid force subject to central control, however, was more likely to suppress popular liberty than to defend it. Nevertheless, the suppression of the Volunteers eventually directed the republicans' attention to their replacements, the militia regiments. Whereas the Volunteers were largely composed of protestants of the middle classes (merchants, farmers, shopkeepers, and tradesmen), the militia consisted mostly of Catholics of the urban and rural lower classes. Pelham reported to the duke of York that 'the peasants could seldom be persuaded under any circumstances to quit their families and place of nativity. I know that rather than quit a farm or even a cabin the tenant would give a sum that no Englishman under similar circumstances could afford.' Consequently, roughly two-thirds to three-quarters of every Irish militia regiment were 'manufacturers and mechanics'.[113] The chief secretary, however, based his analysis on the County Dublin regiment, and thus his claim that artisans were highly over-represented in the militia can be questioned. But it was precisely this social group that found the democratic republicanism of Tom Paine so attractive, making its members likely converts to the United Irish cause.

The reformist United Irishmen were slow to regard the militia as suitable allies in their campaign to effect radical political change. Nevertheless, as early as April 1793, at least one Belfast United Irishman was engaged upon an attempt to undermine the loyalty of his majesty's forces in Ireland. Joseph Cuthbert was found guilty and sentenced to a year in prison for 'attempting to seduce the soldiers from their allegiance and distributing among them the most seditious and treasonable handbills'. General Whyte arranged for Cuthbert to be publicly pilloried for the edification of his troops, whom he paraded before the unfortunate offender in order to inspire their contempt for such meddlers.[114] But such direct tampering with soldiers' loyalty was rare for the United Irishmen in the early 1790s. It was

---

[112] Thomas Bartlett, 'Indiscipline and disaffection in the armed forces in Ireland in the 1790s', in Patrick J. Corish (ed.), *Radicals, rebels, and establishments* (Belfast, 1985), 115–16.

[113] Thomas Pelham to duke of York, 14 Nov. 1796 (BL, Pelham letter-book, Add. MS 33113/66–9).

[114] Gen. Richard Whyte to Evan Nepean, 8 Apr. 1793 (PROHO 100/46/59).

not until they adopted an insurrectionary strategy that they reached out to the soldiers, and especially to the militia.

Loyalists distrusted the militia from the start. As one of them remarked in February 1794: 'I know that Ireland is at this moment marshalled by a militia, but I know it is in a *most dangerous situation*, so much so that the very arms put into their hands are in danger of being turned against us.'[115] This fear was justified. Indeed, the Defenders boasted as early as February 1795 that they enjoyed the allegiance of two-thirds of the militiamen of Ireland.[116] Once an alliance was effected between the United Irishmen and the Defenders, these soldiers joined the revolutionary movement. In fact, it was this connection between Defenderism and the militia that made the United Irishmen regard their association with the Catholic insurgents as necessary and, therefore, palatable. To mobilize the militia behind the cause of an independent Irish republic was almost to assure victory. As Emmet commented: 'The union thus spread among them very extensively, and the militia regiments were often vehicles by which both systems were carried to remote districts.'[117]

Many militia regiments were particularly vulnerable to United Irish appeals endorsing political democracy and to Defender calls for radical social and economic change.[118] United Irishmen distributed handbills among the soldiers, urging them to let Ireland's call 'awaken every noble and generous sentiment in your breasts, [and] never to turn your arms against your fellow men, whose crimes are hatred to tyranny and oppression and a love of liberty'.[119] Other handbills emphasized the dangers to which the families of soldiers were exposed by a venal and tyrannical government: 'Irish blood freezes at the scenes of persecution carried on against our countrymen, against your families and friends.'[120] Aside from these appeals to the soldiers' sense of moral outrage, the United Irishmen also provided material inducements. The informer Edward Newell testified that he knew of several soldiers, including some Englishmen, who were promised commissions or farms if they joined the revolutionary movement.[121] As a United Irishman or Defender, a soldier could enjoy the hospitality of his political brothers throughout the country and receive gifts of money as well.[122] In addition, soldiers were led to believe, as one loyalist

---

[115] [T.] De la Mayne to Henry Dundas, 4 Feb. 1794 (ibid. 100/46/128–9).
[116] Information of Friar Philips, 4 Feb. 1795 (Kent CAO, Pratt papers, U840/0150/3).
[117] MacNeven, *Pieces of Irish history*, 120–1.
[118] Not all militia regiments, however, were potential hothouses of disaffection and sedition. Lord Kingsborough, commander of the North Cork militia, actively recruited protestants to his corps by offering the first 244 candidates the chance to occupy farms at reasonable rents on long leases in Munster. Perhaps as a consequence, the North Cork militia was aggressively loyal throughout the decade and distinguished for its ferocity against the rebels in Leinster: see McAnally, *Irish militia*, 48, 111.
[119] *Rep. secret comm.* 301.   [120] Ibid. 302.   [121] 'Pelham memoranda', 107.
[122] *BNL*, 22 Sept. 1797.

maintained, that *'the forfeited lands of Ireland shall be restored to their right[ful] owners, friends, and relations.* Perhaps there is not an Irishman, however poor and abject, but [who] under that expectation would feel himself entitled to a good estate.'[123]

Latent disaffection in the militia was compounded by the lack of discipline stemming from a rather amateurish and lackadaisical officer corps. Since the militia units were embodied on a county basis, the commanding officers tended to be the magnates of the area, whether resident or not. Considerations of political patronage rather than military qualifications frequently determined the appointment of subordinate officers. And since many of these officers were often members of parliament, justices of the peace, grand jurors, or landlords, they often found it necessary to take extended leaves of absence to attend to their public or private duties.[124] An English gentleman touring Ireland noted with astonishment that the Tipperary militia, then stationed in Derry, had 'no field officer with it. *The Lt. Colonel is, I think, upon his travels abroad, and there are only three captains with it.* The loyalty of the men is very doubtful indeed.'[125]

But perhaps the major reason why the militia as well as some of the regular troops were so vulnerable to seduction by republicans and Defenders was the manner in which they were deployed. The original militia act was based on the English model. The corps was to be embodied on a county basis, summoned for training and manœuvres for a few weeks out of every year, and held in reserve to repel an invasion. Quickly, however, the militia was established on a permanent basis, employed throughout the year, and then often in the capacity of a police force. Consequently, militiamen were dispersed in small parties over the county they were policing, often forming attachments with the surrounding inhabitants, many of whom were Defenders and United Irishmen. One commander in County Tyrone complained that, even though his men were currently loyal, they were scattered in billets among the inhabitants of the area, 'who are *completely organized* to overthrow the government of the country and whose assiduity to seduce the men from their allegiance is beyond what those who are unacquainted with the detail could almost believe'.[126] The Irish general staff protested that such deployment threatened to undermine the loyalty, discipline, and effectiveness of the regiments and to render nugatory their usefulness in the event of invasion. In 1795 the government established camps at Loughlinstown near Dublin, Blaris near Belfast, Clonmel, and Naul to 'render the militia of Ireland as it ought to be, completely efficient for actual

---

[123] De la Mayne to Dundas, 4 Feb. 1794 (PROHO 100/46/128–9).
[124] McAnally, *Irish militia*, 88–91.
[125] Lord Wycombe to Lady Frances Londonderry, 23 Aug. 1797 (Kent CAO, U840/C563/2).
[126] Col. James Leith to Thomas Pelham, 7 Feb. 1797 (SPOI, Rebellion papers, 620/28/228).

service, by discipline and inuring them to the field'.[127] But the desperate pleas of local magistrates for troops could not be ignored. The disturbed state of the country precluded an exclusively military function for the militia, and only when the yeomanry was embodied late in 1796 were the county regiments relieved of many of these policing duties.

Dissatisfaction with pay (usually not the level itself, but rather its irregularity), the circumstances of their deployment, fears about being sent abroad, and the standard complaints of soldiers—all contributed to the potential disaffection of militiamen. In addition, since the officer corps was almost exclusively protestant, and the rank and file overwhelmingly Catholic, sectarian tensions sometimes exacerbated discontent within the service. As early as 1793 Major George Matthews of the Downshire militia felt compelled to complain about the overtly anti-Catholic prejudices of the regiment's commanding colonel, Lord Annesley:

He is very much displeased about some of the men having gone to mass last Sunday. I don't know what to make of him. He talks of resigning and of staying at home to defend his property against the papists. . . . No men can behave better if properly treated, but if religious distinctions are kept among them, I am certain it will be attended with bad consequences.[128]

Matthews's dire predictions were confirmed a few years later, when Orangemen secured a foothold in the County Down militia. The ringleaders in the regiment insinuated that the Orange lodges enjoyed the approval of Lord Downshire himself. Matthews asked Downshire to join his troops and put a stop to it: 'There is nothing surer than that Orangemen, if it [*sic*] goes on, will be the means of making United men.'[129] If Orangemen within a regiment could contribute to disaffection among its Catholic members, so, too, could the pervasive sectarian atmosphere of some of the northern districts in which militiamen were stationed. A party of the Queen's County militia, stationed in north Armagh, were so provoked by the sight of Orangemen parading to the Diamond on 12 July that 'they broke away from their officers and began taking out the Orange cockades'.[130]

Local magistrates persistently complained about Catholic militia troops, whom they regarded as scarcely indistinguishable from the United Irishmen and Defenders disturbing their districts.[131] 'The leaders of the rebels are now busied in sending emissaries all over the country to debauch the soldiery,' Lord Clare complained in April 1797, 'and I fear they have

---

[127] *FJ*, 23 June 1795.

[128] Maj. George Matthews to marquess of Downshire, 29 June 1794 (PRONI, Downshire papers, D607/C/42).

[129] Matthews to Downshire, 5 Dec. 1796 (ibid. D607/D/372).

[130] Cooke to Pelham, 14 July 1796 (BL, Pelham papers, Add. MS 33102/68–71).

[131] See e.g. Waddell to Ross, 22 Aug. 1796 (SPOI, Rebellion papers, 620/24/144).

succeeded in a very alarming degree.'[132] Even members of the Irish general staff placed no confidence in the troops under their command. General Knox threatened resignation in Armagh in May 1797 because Carhampton, then commander-in-chief, based his deployment of forces on the assumption that the militia, with rare exceptions, constituted a dependable force. 'It is wise to hold that language to the world, but we ought not to deceive ourselves. The present is a contest of the poor against the rich—and of the Irishman against the British government. . . . The loyalty of every Irishman who is unconnected with property is artificial.'[133]

In spite of such pessimism, United Irish success among the militia was superficial and all too ephemeral.[134] The failure of the republicans to attach soldiers firmly to the popular cause was not due to lack of effort. Henry Joy McCracken and a number of other Antrim republicans, who were already active in recruiting Defenders in Armagh, also worked among the Queen's County militia stationed there. They succeeded in inducing a few to desert and become United Irish emissaries.[135] This particular regiment consequently became well known for its disaffected troops.[136] Another tainted regiment was the Tipperary militia, stationed in County Derry in the late 1790s. In December 1796 Colonel John Bagwell of this regiment complained that 'the first rank of shopkeepers' in the city of Derry were attempting to undermine the loyalty of his troops. Their task was made all the easier because the 400 men quartered there were billeted throughout the town and its suburbs, 'and consequently liable to every opportunity of seduction'.[137] United Irish agents would often befriend soldiers on guard duty, invite them to a public house, and introduce them to the republican system.[138] But by June 1797 Bagwell could report that disaffection had been weeded out of his regiment. Over fifty of his men had sworn the United Irish oath, many of them lured into the movement by young women, to whom the soldiers were particularly vulnerable, but, of these fifty, only about three or four soldiers confessed to having attended a United Irish meeting.[139]

---

[132] Lord Clare to Lord Mornington, 20 Apr. 1797 (PRONI, Fitzgibbon papers, T3287/5/1).

[133] Gen. John Knox to Thomas Pelham, 14 May 1797 (BL, Pelham papers, Add. MS 33104/59).

[134] See McAnally, *Irish militia*, chs. 7–9; Bartlett, 'Indiscipline and disaffection'. Both agree that disaffection among the troops was greatly exaggerated by contemporaries.

[135] See examination of Denis Delaney, private, Queen's Co. militia, 1 Oct. 1796 (PROI, Frazer papers, IA 40/111a/7); William Lambart to Edward Cooke, 18 Sept. 1796 (SPOI, Rebellion papers, 620/25/81); Thomas Whinnery to Dublin Castle, 1 Oct. 1796 (ibid. 620/25/137); Lord Portarlington to Dublin Castle, 10 Oct. 1796 (ibid. 620/25/156).

[136] Matthews to Downshire, 5 Dec. 1796 (PRONI, Downshire papers, D607/D/372).

[137] Col. John Bagwell to Thomas Pelham, 7 Dec. 1796 (SPOI, Rebellion papers, 620/26/104).

[138] Examinations of Patrick Baldwin and George Hennessy, privates of the Tipperary militia, Dec. 1796 (ibid. 620/26/107).

[139] Col. John Bagwell to Dublin Castle, 28 June 1797 (ibid. 620/31/167).

Not surprisingly, the scene of the most intensive United Irish efforts to recruit soldiers was Blaris camp, near the centre of the republican movement, Belfast. The camp housed about 7,000 troops.[140] The confinement of the soldiers under conditions of strict military discipline certainly made them more susceptible to the opportunities for recreation and entertainment on offer from the surrounding inhabitants. Thomas Lane, Lord Downshire's agent in Hillsborough, had his suspicions aroused in May 1796, when he encountered near the camp a body of about 150 men 'assembled to see a protestant and a papist chieftain fight. The latter had prevailed on about 50 of the city of Limerick militia to come to the ground to *see fair play*.'[141] Belfast republicans took great pains to display their goodwill and largesse to the troops. 'Lately on a Sunday, Shannon [Daniel Shanaghan, a Catholic solicitor] and Cuthbert, with their wives, came from Belfast to Blaris camp in a coach and four,' distributing money among the troops, according to Cooke in July 1796. The under-secretary at the castle also reported that 650 soldiers in the camp were '*up* and *up*', or sworn as both Defenders and United Irishmen, and that another 1,600 had pledged their allegiance to the republicans alone. Their boast was that 'the whole camp was at the disposal of Belfast'.[142]

In addition to entertaining the troops, republicans also tried to sow discontent within the ranks by spreading the ever-explosive rumour that the militia regiments would soon see service abroad.[143] The Limerick city militia was singled out by General Nugent as unreliable owing to this kind of republican infiltration. The leader was apparently Corporal Burke, who was 'well treated and well paid' by the Belfast radicals.[144] In August 1796 Nugent unsuccessfully urged the removal of the Limerick regiment from Blaris, the militiamen having 'been so long at Lisburn and intimately connected with the people there'.[145] Finally, in September, Pelham urged Nugent to set up an investigation at the camp to weed out sedition: 'The suspicion of the militia has become so general, and it is necessary to try some means of restoring confidence in them.'[146] Nugent rejected the idea of a public inquiry as injurious to military morale, but he did order

---

[140] McAnally, *Irish militia*, 80.

[141] Lane to Downshire, 24 May 1796 (PRONI, Downshire papers, D607/D/62).

[142] Edward Cooke to Gen. George Nugent, 25 July 1796 (NAM, Nugent papers, 6807/174/147–8).

[143] Gen. George Nugent to Edward Cooke, 30 July 1796 (SPOI, Rebellion papers, 620/24/66).

[144] Cooke to Nugent, 1 Aug. 1796 (NAM, Nugent papers, 6807/174/151–4).

[145] Nugent to Cooke, 20 Aug. 1796 (SPOI, Rebellion papers, 620/24/132); for Camden's refusal, see duke of Portland to Thomas Pelham, 28 Aug. 1796 (BL, Pelham papers, Add. MS 33102/113–14).

[146] Thomas Pelham to Gen. George Nugent, 26 Sept. 1796 (BL, Pelham papers, Add. MS 33102/192–4); the idea for such an inquest was originally Castlereagh's (Viscount Castlereagh to Pelham, 23 Sept. 1796 (ibid. Add. MS 33102/182–3)).

the colonels to conduct informal investigations within their respective regiments.[147] They appear to have been successful in using their personal influence to recall their men to a sense of duty and loyalty. Colonel Charles Leslie of the Monaghan militia was perhaps less effective than the rest, for his investigations, though successful in identifying malcontents within his corps, resulted in widespread publicity being given to disaffection within the military.

Nevertheless, the government took full advantage of this opportunity to expose republican ineffectuality in protecting seditious soldiers. Dreadful examples were made of the consequences of disloyalty. In April 1797 Colonel Leslie apprehended a corporal named Reed, the apparent leader of the United Irishmen within the Monaghan militia. In return for a pardon, Reed agreed to identify the leaders of the disaffected in each of the companies of the regiment.[148] Leslie arrested about ten offenders and then summoned the whole regiment, impressing upon his troops the 'atrocity of the crime' of disloyalty and warning them that mercy would not be granted unless they confessed their involvement in the conspiracy. The colonel's threat worked, and seventy men came forward to repent their involvement with the United Irishmen. Leslie insisted that four particularly active conspirators be tried by general court martial and, if condemned, executed as an example to future wayward soldiers.[149] Pelham had already decided that exemplary executions were in order. A military execution would 'do more good than fifty civil prosecutions'.[150] And so the four Monaghan militiamen, despite their pleas for mercy and offers to make whatever amends were required of them, met their death, only to be apotheosized as republican martyrs.[151] But the executions, as Bartlett has claimed, represented a 'carefully managed exercise in official terror'. Thousands of soldiers were summoned to witness the executions and then marched past the bullet-riddled bodies of their unfortunate comrades.[152] Here was a dreadful lesson in the consequences of disaffection.

The experiment succeeded. Henceforth the Monaghan militia were to be fierce in the assertion of their newly recovered loyalty. They wreaked vengeance on their former republican brethren in Belfast and were instrumental in silencing the *Northern Star*.[153] 'The decided aversion the Monaghan have taken to the United Irishmen is beyond all conception,' a

---

[147] Gen. George Nugent to Thomas Pelham, 30 Sept. 1796 (BL, Pelham papers, Add. MS 33102/209–11).

[148] Col. Charles Leslie to Gen. Gerard Lake, 25 Apr. 1797 (ibid. Add. MS 33103/397).

[149] Gen. Gerard Lake to Thomas Pelham, 1 May 1797 (ibid. Add. MS 33104/3–4).

[150] Thomas Pelham to Gen. Gerard Lake, 27 Apr. 1797 (ibid. Add. MS 33103/401–2).

[151] For requests for pardon, see Pelham to Lake, 14 May 1797 (ibid. Add. MS 33104/53).

[152] Bartlett, 'Indiscipline and disaffection', 127.

[153] See Ch. 8 for the suppression of the *Northern Star*.

delighted General Lake reported in June 1797, 'and I am convinced if ever they are ordered to act against them, the carnage will be dreadful. They have this town [Belfast] in complete order and are most useful and much to be depended upon.'[154]

The execution of the four Monaghan militiamen was a turning-point in the fortunes of the United Irishmen. The fact that the executions took place in the republican heartland and that the United Irishmen were impotent to prevent them seriously damaged the radicals' credibility with the troops. This was most apparent in the subsequent ultra-loyalist behaviour of the Monaghan regiment. It was almost as if these soldiers were revenging themselves on the republicans for plunging the troops into so much trouble with their officers and then doing so little to get them out of it. The success with which the officers regained the obedience of their troops augured ill for the United Irish strategy of turning the militia against the government in the event of an insurrection. But what should have been most disturbing to the republicans was the ease with which these soldiers recanted their brief infatuation with radical ideas. When put to the test, they turned against the United Irish movement which they had solemnly sworn to uphold. Admittedly, militiamen, away from home, chaffing under unaccustomed military discipline, and sensitive to stories about protestant persecution, were particularly vulnerable to friendly overtures from neighbouring republicans. It is not surprising that, under these circumstances, soldiers often returned such kindnesses as drink and good company by enlisting in the republican movement. But in most cases the militiaman's commitment was based primarily on a desire to please his hosts and represented only the most tenuous adherence to the republican cause. The oft-repeated boast that the militia would side with the people against the government in the event of a contest was shown to be, as best, dubious.

The United Irish alliance with the military thus proved superficial. The perception that such an association existed, however, was a useful propaganda tool for the republicans. Belief that the militia supported the popular cause would induce further recruits to flock to the United Irish standard. Loyalists, unable to depend on this force for their defence, might concede United Irish demands in order to avert a conflagration. But confidence in the militia was somewhat restored by Nugent's exertions at Blaris and by the subsequent display of aggressive loyalty by the Monaghan regiment. The militia acquitted itself beyond all government expectations during the rebellion of 1798.[155]

---

[154] Lake to Pelham, 4 June 1797 (BL, Pelham papers, Add. MS 33104/175).
[155] McAnally, *Irish militia*, 128–30.

7

Literary Mischief

'THE Society of United Irishmen', as a loyalist observed in April 1794, 'use every ingenious device to promote discord and sedition. Addresses, odes, songs—in short, every species of literary mischief is resorted to and circulated at an extraordinary expense to every part of the kingdom and amongst all the lower orders of the people.'[1] The literary productions of the republicans reflected the gradual democratization of political culture during the last third of the eighteenth century in the British Isles. John Brewer has argued that the Wilkite agitation of the 1760s initiated the 'commercialization of politics', by which he means not only an expansion of the print industry, and especially that sector within it devoted to political subjects, but also a new attitude towards popular political mobilization based on a market analogy. The aim of the Wilkite radicals was to attract popular support for their challenge to oligarchic rule. To do this, they exploited the press, newspapers, pamphlets, broadsheets, and caricatures to create a climate of public opinion sympathetic to their champion, John Wilkes. Directing their appeal out of doors, away from the oligarchs in parliament whom they were attacking and towards the people at large, the radicals, through the medium of the press, hoped to establish a national political culture, uniting the Londoner and the provincial, the merchant and the farmer, in defence of the liberties of the subject and in favour of some measure of parliamentary reform. In a sense, they sought to create a demand for political information analogous to the merchant's efforts to create a demand for his wares, with the result that, as Brewer puts it, 'politics, so long regarded as a luxury good, was beginning to transform itself into yet another mass marketable commodity.'[2]

The achievement of Wilkes was something of a breakthrough in political methods, employing almost commercial and marketing means for political ends. The Wilkite example served as the starting-point for subsequent political movements in Ireland as well as in Britain, though in Dublin in the middle decades of the eighteenth century the city and parliamentary politician Charles Lucas was already anticipating the radical assault on oligarchy.[3] At

---

[1] A. Charles Murphy to Dublin Castle, 10 Apr. 1794 (PROHO 100/46/150–1).

[2] John Brewer, *Party ideology and popular politics at the accession of George III* (Cambridge, 1981), 160.

[3] See e.g. R. B. McDowell, *Ireland in the age of imperialism and revolution* (Oxford, 1979), 211–12; Sean Murphy, 'Charles Lucas and the Dublin election of 1748–9', *Parliamentary History*, 2 (1983), 93–111; id., 'The Dublin anti-union riot of 3 December 1759', in Gerard O'Brien (ed.), *Parliament, politics and people* (Dublin, 1989), 49–68.

the root of such campaigns was a very radical principle for the eighteenth century—that all citizens possessed an equal interest in the governing of the nation. To disseminate political information among the masses was, in effect, to confer upon them the rights and duties of 'citizens', a term defined narrowly by the oligarchy. The radicals were creating a national political culture by arguing for the existence of an extensive political nation. Thus the late eighteenth century witnessed a conflict between two political nations: the narrowly defined one countenanced by the ruling oligarchy, and the extensive one imagined by the radical challengers.

The radicals' political nation could include either everyone within the nation's boundaries or merely economically independent adult males, depending on the radicals' definition of citizenship. Their polity could be realized in a network of political clubs enjoying the participation of the socially diverse citizens of the nation. But the most important vehicle in extending consciousness about this imagined community of citizens was the printed word, directed to the citizens themselves. Newspapers, pamphlets, and handbills addressed to all members of the community thus conferred upon those members their national unity and political status. Appeals in the press, made accessible to weavers, farmers, and artisans, invited these groups to participate in political affairs, to claim their rights and to assume their duties as citizens. The evolution of the demand for civil equality and political democracy had to be accompanied by the democratization of political culture, by a break in the monopoly of the élite on political discourse in order to make, as Thomas Addis Emmet said, 'every man a politician'.[4]

The process of disseminating political information to a mass public by means of the printed word was not a smooth one over the course of the eighteenth century. The pattern seemed to be two steps forward during times of heightened political discourse, and one step back during the succeeding lull. Thus the proliferation of political literature accompanying the Wilkite agitation in the 1760s was followed by a period of relative quiet in the early 1770s. Still, the infrastructure for the dissemination of political literature had been established along with an expanded market, only to be revived and increased during the agitation accompanying the American revolution. The 1780s saw another relatively quiet period, only to be followed by the contentious decade of the 1790s. Each new spurt of propagandist activity built upon the preceding agitation, thus continually expanding the demand for political material.[5]

In Ireland the pattern was similar. Prior to the Volunteer movement in the late 1770s and early 1780s, the Irish press only occasionally indulged in

[4] William James MacNeven, *Pieces of Irish history illustrative of the condition of the Catholics of Ireland* (New York, 1807), 77.
[5] See Richard Altick, *The English common reader: a social history of the mass reading public, 1800–1900* (Chicago, 1957); Brewer, *Party ideology*, 139–62, 219–39.

domestic political debate. Irish newspapers filled their columns with material reprinted from the London papers and catered largely to a commercial public. The American revolution and the accompanying Volunteer movement heightened political interest among a self-defining and expanding political nation, a phenomenon reflected in the proliferation of pamphlets and the establishment of many more newspapers in Ireland. Belfast, for example, acquired, in addition to the long-established *Belfast News-Letter*, a more radical paper, the short-lived *Belfast Mercury*.[6] During normal times the north could scarcely support an additional newspaper, but, as with the *Mercury* in the early 1780s and the *Northern Star* in the 1790s, heightened political interests created, and in part were created by, more aggressive, militant propaganda. In the capital the *Dublin Evening Post*, established in 1778 to support the cause of the Volunteers, enjoyed the highest circulation of all Irish papers at the time. With about ten newspapers appearing in the capital during this period, the *Dublin Evening Post* had a circulation of nearly 4,000.[7] Such a figure may appear insignificant, but when compared to the circulation of established British papers, it is clear that the Irish were as interested in political matters as their neighbours across the water. In London the *Public Advertiser* sold fewer than 3,000 copies per issue, climbing to about 3,400 between 1769 and 1771, when the paper published the famous letters of 'Junius', but reverting to about 3,000 thereafter. By 1800 the circulation of *The Times* had climbed to about 4,800, while in the mid-1790s the *Northern Star*, a provincial Irish paper albeit a popular radical organ, enjoyed a circulation of about 5,000.[8] Available statistics on the number as well as the circulation of Irish newspapers compare favourably with those in Britain, considering the difference in population and economic development. It is estimated that there were perhaps as many as fifty provincial newspapers in Britain by 1780. In Ireland during the 1790s there were at least twenty-six provincial newspapers as well as eleven in Dublin.[9]

Thanks to the foundations laid down by the Volunteers, which in turn may have been inspired by the Wilkite and American agitations, the United Irishmen were able to build an impressive apparatus of political dissemination. Publishers and authors estimated that each newspaper or pamphlet purchased was read by at least twenty and perhaps by as many as fifty people.[10] Circulating libraries, reading societies, and coffee-houses and tav-

[6] R. R. Madden, *The history of Irish periodical literature* (2 vols., London, 1867), ii. 224–5.

[7] Ibid. 297. The *Dublin Evening Post* was originally published in 1732 and revived in 1756. Both times its appearance was short-lived, until 1778, when it was revived by L. H. Powell; in 1788 it was bought by John Magee.

[8] Altick, *English common reader*, 48.

[9] For British estimates, see Brewer, *Party ideology*, 143; Irish estimates are based on the number of newspapers mentioned by Brian Inglis, *The freedom of the press in Ireland, 1784–1841* (London, 1954), and Madden, *Irish periodical literature*.

[10] Brewer, *Party ideology*, 148.

erns provided an interested public with easy and free access to newspapers and the latest political pamphlets. 'In the coffee houses of Dublin', reported one concerned loyalist, 'there is that kind of conversation which in London would produce serious consequences.'[11] In other words, it would produce arrests and prosecutions, so seditious were the interchanges in these places of political enlightenment. Bookshops themselves became venues for the informal congregation of radicals, who would meet there to examine and discuss the new material just off the presses.[12]

Two reading societies in Belfast, one headed by the United Irishman Thomas Russell, catered to the growing political appetite of the town's journeymen, mechanics, and small tradesmen.[13] Reading clubs in the countryside brought weavers and farmers into the imagined political nation of the radicals.[14] In 1790 one pamphleteer satirized these rustic book clubs, claiming that they were merely excuses for drinking and usually ended in brawls:

> Thus meeting to dispute, to fight, to plead,
> To smoke, to drink—do anything but read—
> The club—with staggering steps, yet light of heart,
> Their taste for learning shewn, and *punch*—depart.[15]

But Martha McTier regarded these reading clubs, at least in Belfast, as positive vehicles for the political education of the lower classes. 'Our best writers, speakers, and actors', she informed her brother in 1792, 'are now those whom *nobody* knows. Of this number are two reading societies who for three years past have been collecting a number of the most valuable books, not merely to *look* at; among these are the *Encyclopaedia* the parliamentary statutes, etc.'[16] Illiteracy was no barrier to familiarizing oneself with the polemics of a Paine or a Tone.[17] Oral readings were a commonplace, noted for their recreational as well as their instructional features. One magistrate complained of two men who appeared after Sunday mass to read republican newspapers to the assembled crowds.[18] Another United Irish agent

---

[11] Murphy to Dublin Castle, 10 Apr. 1794 (PROHO 100/46/150–1).

[12] See e.g. Tone, *Life*, i. 126; 'Evidence of Captain Armstrong in the trial of Henry and John Sheares' (*Rep. secret comm.* 189–92).

[13] W. T. Latimer, *Ulster biographies relating chiefly to the rebellion of 1798* (Belfast, 1897), 2; R. R. Madden, *The United Irishmen, their lives and times*, 3rd ser. (7 vols., London, 1842–5), ii. 156; *NS*, 28 Jan. 1792.

[14] For country reading clubs, see F. J. Bigger, 'Rural libraries in Antrim', in the *Irish Book Lover*, 13 (Nov. 1921), 47–52; see also John Hewitt, *The rhyming weavers and other poets of Antrim and Down* (Belfast, 1974).

[15] *The country book club: a poem* (Dublin, 1790), 32.

[16] Martha McTier to William Drennan, 28 Oct. 1792 (*The Drennan letters*, ed. D. A. Chart (Belfast, 1931), 92).

[17] For a discussion of literacy and popular literary culture in Ulster, see J. R. R. Adams, *The printed word and the common man: popular culture in Ulster, 1700–1900* (Belfast, 1987).

[18] Maurice Tracy to Thomas Pelham, 26 May 1797 (SPOI, Rebellion papers, 620/30/198).

travelled about County Galway with the sole purpose of providing rural dwellers with oral readings of the radical press.[19]

Newspapers undoubtedly provided the most efficient medium for reaching a mass audience, but the political content of Irish newspapers was restricted both by the need to fill columns with advertisements to keep the enterprise solvent and by constraints placed upon the opposition press by the government. From the contentious days of the Volunteers, the government became alarmed at the heightened popular interest in politics promoted by the papers and sought to boost the price beyond the reach of the masses by raising the tax on printed material. Furthermore, the Irish administration had few qualms about bringing publishers to trial for printing seditious libel against the government. Even though jurors frequently acquitted these publishers, the expenses incurred in their defence could induce a degree of self-censorship.[20] As vehicles for radical propaganda disseminated by the United Irishmen, therefore newspapers were of only limited utility. They could go only so far, as the eventual suppression of the United Irish newspapers, the *Northern Star* and the *Press*, demonstrated, before the government would officially or unofficially silence them.[21]

The dissemination of political pamphlets was one way in which to evade government interference with printed propaganda. As Drennan observed in his *Letter to Earl Fitzwilliam* in 1795: 'Whoever ventures to talk with the populace is looked upon as holding correspondence with the enemy.'[22] Such was the government's attitude to the United Irish efforts to democratize political culture, and in too many cases the authorities sanctioned their disgust with such endeavours by prosecuting United Irish authors and publishers for seditious libel.[23] If the subject-matter was so politically explosive that it might provoke government action, a pamphlet could be written and published anonymously. But political pamphlets, even those addressed to a mass audience, could be prohibitive in price. The first edition of the first part of Paine's *Rights of man*, for example, sold for 3s., far beyond the

[19] William Birmingham to Dublin Castle, 24 Dec. 1796 (SPOI, Rebellion papers, 620/26/153).

[20] See Inglis, *Freedom of the press*, 19–51.   [21] See Ch. 8.

[22] William Drennan, *A letter to his excellency Earl Fitzwilliam* (Dublin, 1795), 5.

[23] See W. P. Carey, *An appeal to the people of Ireland by W. P. Carey, late proprietor of the 'National Evening Star' and intended proprietor of the 'New Evening Star'* (Dublin, 1794); *A full report of the trial at bar in the court of king's bench, in which the right hon. Arthur Wolfe, his majesty's attorney general, prosecuted, and A. H. Rowan, Esq., was defendant, on an information filed ex-officio against the defendant for having published a seditious libel* (Dublin, 1794); *A full report of the trial at bar in the court of king's bench, of William Drennan, MD, upon an indictment charging him with having written and published a seditious libel* (Dublin, 1794); William Ridgeway, *A report of the trial of Peter Finnerty, upon an indictment for a libel* (Dublin, 1798); William Sampson, *A faithful report of the second trial of the proprietors of the 'Northern Star' at the bar of the court of king's bench on the 17th of November, 1794, on an information filed ex-officio by the attorney general . . .* (Belfast, 1795); id., *A faithful report of the trial of the proprietors of the 'Northern Star' at the bar of the court of king's bench on the twenty-eight of May, 1794 . . .* (Belfast, 1794).

means of the humble classes it championed. But those radicals more interested in propaganda than profit could reprint cheap editions of important
and suitable political pamphlets.

No publication of the early 1790s was more industriously promoted by
Irish radicals than Paine's *Rights of man*. The first part was distributed so
extensively in Ireland that 'people were hired to read it to those who could
not read themselves'.[24] The devotion of Belfast radicals to part I of Paine's
work has already been noted. Part II, published in February 1792, was an
even more radical document. By this time the United Irishmen had an organization to ensure even wider dissemination of Paine's republican principles.
United Irish bookseller John Hughes was the first to make the *Rights of
man*, part II, available to Belfast readers.[25] Not long afterwards other
Belfast booksellers were featuring Paine's work prominently in their newspaper advertisements.[26] The first edition to be published in Dublin appears
to have been the work of another United Irishman and member of the
Catholic Committee, Patrick Byrne, in March 1792.[27] Since the usual selling
price of 3s. for both parts of the *Rights of man* was too high for propagandist purposes, the Dublin Society of United Irishmen entered into a subscription to publish a 1d. edition.[28] *Freeman's Journal* reported in the
spring of 1792 that 2d. editions were circulating in Dublin as well as in the
north, and in Cork copies were distributed free.[29] Paine's work was given
additional prominence in the public eye when he was tried by the British
government for seditious libel in December 1792. Even conservative papers,
in their accounts of the trial, printed those statements for which Paine was
found guilty, thus giving his ideas even wider circulation.[30] Though Paine's
work was officially suppressed, the popular taste had been thoroughly
whetted. *Faulkner's Dublin Journal* reported in August 1793 that nightly
book auctions were held in Dublin at which copies of the *Rights of man*
were covertly purchased.[31] And the *Northern Star* claimed in January 1794
that the popularity of Paine's book was greater than ever: 'Had Tom Paine
and his books never been prosecuted, he would now be forgotten; but the
fact is, the numbers published clandestinely since his conviction (such is the
curiosity of man) has [sic] increased considerably above the number sold
before his trial.'[32]

Sales of the *Rights of man* in the British Isles were indeed spectacular.
Within the first few weeks of publication, part I sold 50,000 copies; by
1793 parts I and II combined sold 200,000 copies.[33] There is no way of

[24] Robert Kee, *The green flag: a history of Irish nationalism* (London, 1972), 44.
[25] NS, 29 Feb. 1792.
[26] BNL, 1 May 1792. The *Rights of man* was advertised in this issue by 3 booksellers—
William Magee, William Mitchell, and Henry Warren.
[27] FJ, 17 Mar. 1792.   [28] FJ, 5 Jan. 1793.   [29] FJ, 2 June 1792, 5 Jan. 1793.
[30] FJ, 27 Dec. 1792.   [31] FDJ, 22 Aug. 1793.   [32] NS, 13 Jan. 1794.
[33] Altick, *English common reader*, 70.

determining how many people actually read the book, but it was circulated informally as well as through libraries and reading societies. In addition, multitudes became familiar with Paine's principles through accounts or extracts printed in newspapers and handbills. Popular enthusiasm for the *Rights of man* seemed so widespread in Ireland that the conservative *Freeman's Journal* felt provoked to remark: 'Public *taste*, like unfortunate *females*, like those *best* who *debauch them most*.'[34] If conservatives in Ireland found the public's acceptance of Painite principles highly unpalatable, the United Irishmen were heartened. Paine played a great role in inspiring the Irish radicals who founded the Society of United Irishmen, but he played an even greater role in preparing a large segment of the public for the acceptance of radical United Irish principles. 'His works are in every one's hands and in every one's mouth,' Leonard McNally reported to the government. 'They have got into the schools and are the constant subjects of conversation with the youth.'[35]

The phenomenal experience of the *Rights of man* confirmed what the United Irishmen had already learned from the Volunteer agitation of the previous decade—that the battle for public opinion could be fought effectively with the weapon of the political pamphlet. The standard edition of the average publication was 500 copies; more successful productions could sell between 1,500 and 3,000 copies, and a spectacular success might produce sales of as many as 5,000 copies, modest figures indeed when compared with those of Burke's *Reflections on the revolution in France* or the *Rights of man*.[36] With a standard selling price of more than 1s., such pamphlets catered to a middle-class reading public, exactly the audience from which the United Irishmen sought a hearing in their reformist phase. But through their dissemination of cheap editions of radical pamphlets, the radicals also provided the lower classes with a republican political education. In a sense, the medium of the pamphlet was poised as the rival to parliament in creating a forum in which the political questions of the day could be debated and the popular will of the nation could be expressed. Furthermore, the anonymously written and published pamphlet provided the means to evade government suppression of United Irish literature, or at least the harassment of its authors. This became especially important during the second half of the decade, when the United Irishmen adopted insurrectionary tactics and a more inflammatory rhetoric. Recourse to the political pamphlet was a feature of United Irish propaganda activity during both its reformist and its revolutionary phases.

Controversy was the lifeblood of a thriving and expanding print industry in Ireland, which realized its power and potential during the free-trade and

[34] *FJ*, 21 June 1792.
[35] 'J. W.' to ——, [Apr.] 1795 (Kent CAO, Pratt papers, U840/0144/10).
[36] Brewer, *Party ideology*, 146.

constitutional agitations of the late 1770s and early 1780s.[37] The 1790s provided even more contentious subjects worthy of public debate through the medium of the pamphlet. The French revolution, the Catholic question, and the desirability of parliamentary reform were among the topics which exercised the talents of a plethora of pamphleteers. The result was hundreds of political pamphlets, an extensive sample of which can be found in the Haliday collection of the Royal Irish Academy.

The success of Paine's *Rights of man* merely confirmed the role of the pamphlet as a tool of political education. More immediate evidence was provided by Tone's *An argument on behalf of the Catholics of Ireland*, which proved highly significant in directing radicals in Belfast to launch their new political initiative of an alliance between Catholic and protestant in the cause of reform and emancipation. To a certain extent, the United Irishmen owed their formation to the persuasive polemics of Tone. Not surprisingly, one of the first acts of the newly formed Belfast Society of United Irishmen was to produce a 3*d.* edition of Tone's pamphlet; 10,000 copies were printed for distribution.[38] Immediately after their formation, the Dublin United Irishmen established a publications committee to supervise the society's literary productions.[39] While president of the society in Dublin, Simon Butler published a *Digest of the popery laws*, of which 10,000 copies were printed and made available to other societies upon request.[40] In October 1793 the Dublin club decided to publish all the addresses and publications of the society under one cover. In March 1794 William Stockdale printed 1,000 copies, which were sold to members at a rate of sixteen for half a guinea under the assumption that they would distribute them widely.[41]

The *Northern Star* also promoted the circulation of radical political pamphlets. The serialization of such works as William Sampson's *Trial of Hurdy Gurdy*, Sampson and Thomas Russell's *Review of the lion of old England*, and the Revd James Porter's *Billy Bluff and the squire* in the columns of this United Irish newspaper contributed greatly to its popularity. Each of these works was also made available by the *Northern Star* in pamphlet form, as were several other items with a wide public appeal.

William Sampson wrote his *Trial of Hurdy Gurdy* as a satirical indictment against the proliferation in 1793 and 1794 of prosecutions against reformers, and especially the *Northern Star* itself, for seditious libel. What was his crime? The indictment maintained that '*Hurdy Gurdy*, alias *Barrel Organ*, alias *Grinder*, alias *Seditious Organ*', had played the popular French

[37] See R. B. McDowell, *Irish public opinion, 1750–1800* (London, 1944), 39–73.

[38] *BNL*, 11 Nov. 1791; MacNeven, *Pieces of Irish history*, 16.

[39] R. B. McDowell, 'The proceedings of the Dublin Society of United Irishmen', *Analecta Hibernia*, 17 (1949), 8.

[40] Ibid. 19–20.   [41] Ibid. 87, 121.

revolutionary song, 'Ça ira',[42] The triviality of the offence was one source of grim amusement and yet concern, for Sampson was drawing parallels with the vulnerability of reformers and their publications to government harassment. But he also wished to make the point that such trials were unfairly conducted under the current corrupt and self-interested administration in Ireland. Sampson therefore drew up a list of jurors to try the seditious 'Barrel Organ'. Among them was Tyrant Caliban of Fleeced-island, a reference to the unenlightened, barely civilized Squire Westerns among the Irish gentry, and Croucher Toryman, obviously representing the devious and elusive political opportunists who attached themselves to the party of William Pitt. And to make the point that the only political party to represent the people was the United Irishmen, Sampson introduced another juror, called Whig Tallyho Turncoat of Glorious Memory, a reminder that the whigs had betrayed the principles of representative and responsible government. Here, then, was the formidable coalition ranged against reform— whigs, tories, and a self-interested propertied class.[43]

The *Review of the lion of old England*, which appeared in the *Northern Star* in 1794, was a free-ranging, satirical castigation of the sacred British constitution, Pitt's war policy, the subversion of English law to weed out perceived sedition, and the current political leadership of the nation. Written in epic form, the *Review* was dedicated 'to the Empress Catherine II of Russia, a natural patroness and protector of the lion of old England, who is exalted above all other rulers and kings of the earth by her virtue and deportment.'[44] Thus the lion, Great Britain itself, was implicated with the most despotic of European autocrats. Sampson and Russell, like the other United Irishmen, regarded the war with France as a contest between despotism and liberty, and so they sympathized with republican France. In addition to this ideological concern, they pointed to the dire economic consequences of protracted European warfare. But to these objections the lion closed his ears: 'Scorn the vile traders, who to peace incline, | War, raging war, is glorious and divine.'[45] Reform upon liberal principles was something abhorrent to the lion's acolytes. Pitt and his home secretary, Dundas, considered the matter. 'There is a fatal tendency', Dundas observed,

---

[42] William Sampson, *A faithful report of the trial of Hurdy Gurdy at the bar of the court of king's bench, Westminster, on the 28th day of May 1794, on an examination filed ex-officio by the attorney general* (Belfast, 1794), 2–3. The date on which this fictional trial began is the same as that on which the proprietors of the *Northern Star* first appeared before the bench on a charge of seditious libel for publishing the address of the Irish Jacobins. See Sampson, *Faithful report of the trial of the proprietors of the 'Northern Star'*.

[43] Sampson, *Hurdy Gurdy*, 1.

[44] Thomas Russell and William Sampson, *Review of the lion of old England, or the democracy confounded, as it appeared from time to time in a periodical print* (Belfast, 1794), preface.

[45] Ibid. 6.

To that same something, which they freedom call;
This must be checked, 'twill make men good and brave,
And then in vain would we our country save.

And Pitt, the reformer in his youth, agreed:

I know it well, there is a certain cant,
In which who better than myself did rant,
E'er I became a minister of state,
And hung upon my nod, the nation's fate.[46]

The *Review* then offered a short survey of English history, singling out
Henry VIII and Elizabeth I for scornful irony, until the authors arrived at
that watershed in British history, the Glorious Revolution of 1688. Irish
radicals since 1791 had rightly discarded much of the myth of 1688 as a rallying symbol for the campaign for good government. The glorious memory
of William III provided a source of division rather than unity among
Irishmen. Because of this, and given the record of such religiously based
hostility in the Irish past, the United Irishmen frequently rejected arguments
from history in legitimizing the claims of the present generation.[47] Sampson
and Russell therefore felt free to describe the Glorious Revolution as it
really was to them—an exercise in aristocratic domination. It was a revolution 'which, under Providence, preserved us from wooden shoes and left us
free to go barefoot'.[48]

The authors directed their most impressive satirical outburst at Edmund
Burke, reviled by radicals for his condemnation of the cause of liberty in
his classic *Reflections on the revolution in France*. The centrepiece of the
Review of the lion of old England took place in a temple erected to the lion,
Great Britain, with his prophet and chief priest, Edmund Burke, in attendance. 'I believe in the mysteries of this glorious temple [English history],
as expounded to me by the prophet Edmund. I believe in God Almighty as
by law established,' an allusion to the presumption of parliament to decree
the content and form of religious worship.

I believe that the subjects of this realm are inheritable in no other manner or form
than that pointed out at the Glorious Revolution, and explained in the books of the
prophet Edmund—and that he who thinks otherwise is an atheist and guilty of a
libel, with force and arms, against the Glorious Revolution. I believe that kings are
the fountain of all honours, justice, wisdom, and mercy; and that lords are *by birth*
judges, legislators, and counsellors. I believe that in the fictions of the law is contained all the equity of the law.[49]

What Sampson and Russell did here was to turn Burke's own words
around and direct them against himself. Burke maintained that human

---

[46] Ibid.   [47] See Ch. 1 for the United Irish view of history.
[48] Russell and Sampson, *Review*, 47.   [49] Ibid. 47–8.

reason was an inadequate and uncertain basis upon which to build and maintain a society, 'because we suspect that this stock [of reason] in each man is small, and that individuals would do better to avail themselves of the general bank and capital of nations and ages'.[50] Tradition formed the rightful basis of civil society, and the Glorious Revolution had laid down the principles which ought to be followed by all succeeding generations. The revolution had occurred to 'preserve that ancient constitution which is our only security for law and liberty'.[51] When Sampson and Russell attributed to the Prophet Edmund the belief that the subjects of the realm were inheritable, suggesting that, in fact, they were the chattels of England's rulers, they were really alluding to the following assertion of Burke: from Magna Carta to the Bill of Rights 'it has been the uniform policy of our constitution to claim and assert our liberties as an entailed inheritance received to us from our forefathers, and to be transmitted to our posterity—as an estate specially belonging to the people of this kingdom, without reference whatever to any other more general or prior right.'[52] It was an unfortunate, if elegant, metaphor, likening the rights and liberties of the subject to an aristocratic estate to be willed from one generation to another, and a metaphor easily exploited when attacking Burke. Paine took the opportunity to denounce such claims by asserting that 'government [from] beyond the grave is the most ridiculous and insolent of all tyrannies. . . . I am contending for the rights of the *living*, and against their being willed away and controlled and contracted for by the manuscript-assumed authority of the dead; and Mr Burke is contending for the authority of the dead over the rights and freedom of the living.'[53] So, too, Sampson and Russell implied that Burke's intention was to suggest that the people were willed to succeeding generations as part of the property of the aristocracy.

The purpose of the *Review of the lion of old England*, therefore, was not only to discredit specific government policies regarding the war with France and the campaign against seditious libellers, but also to undermine the very premisses of the glorious constitution of Great Britain. Like Paine, the authors agreed that the mumbo-jumbo of precedents was no substitute for a clearly codified written constitution. With Paine, they maintained that the record of history had nothing to contribute to the civil and political requirements of the present age. Tradition was merely a trap for the people set by a rapacious aristocracy whose privileges were rooted in superstition and ignorance and not in reason, the only determinant of what was just and good. By presenting Burke as the high priest worshipping in paganistic

---

[50] Edmund Burke, *Reflections on the revolution in France*, ed. Thomas H. D. Mahoney (Indianapolis and New York, 1955), 99.

[51] Burke, *Reflections*, 35.   [52] Ibid. 37.

[53] Thomas Paine, *Rights of man*, ed. and introd. Henry Collins (Harmondsworth, Middlesex, 1976), 64.

fashion at the shrine of the Glorious Revolution, Russell and Sampson were making another point particularly relevant to Ireland. Priests and prelates—and the religious bigotry that they fostered—contributed to the fatal disunity of the Irish people, which prevented them from asserting not merely their nationhood, but also their natural rights. The British system of government, considered as inviolable as any Christian doctrine, was merely another form of religion designed to keep the people superstitious and ignorant. But once reason shed its light on the artifices of priestcraft and statecraft, hereditary government and religious hostility must surely shrink away into the shadows of history. The conclusion to be drawn, then, from Sampson's and Russell's lampoon was that the lion of old England was just another fraud designed to delude the people into submission. Reject tradition, for the past is only the record of discord and enslavement, and look to a bright new future in which reason and liberty march forward together.

The Revd James Porter of Grey Abbey also turned his obvious talents for satire against a regime which sought to halt the march of progress. In one of the most popularly oriented literary productions of the United Irishmen, he endeavoured to expose the system of espionage instituted by the government and the unchristian role played by clerical magistrates in suppressing the popular will. From May to December 1796 Porter contributed a number of columns to the *Northern Star* which were later collected in pamphlet form under the title *Billy Bluff and the squire, or a sample of the times.*[54] The Dublin United Irishmen printed 3,000 copies for free distribution among the peasantry.[55] So popular was this pamphlet that it was reprinted even as late as 1840, becoming something of a classic.[56]

Billy Bluff was a farmer, a neighbour of R——, a Presbyterian minister, representing Porter himself. R—— kept the readers of the *Northern Star* amused by recounting the antics of his unenlightened neighbour, a protégé of Squire Firebrand, who in turn took his orders from Lord Mountmumble. These last two characters were modelled respectively on the Revd John Cleland, a clerical magistrate and former tutor to Lord Castlereagh, and his lordship's father, the earl of Londonderry. Squire Firebrand had sent Billy Bluff to spy on the United Irishmen in general and on his neighbour, the Presbyterian minister, in particular. 'He's at the old cur,' the dutiful Billy reported, 'railing against the war, against the tithes, and against game laws; and he's still reading at the newspapers.' Worse yet, Billy caught the minister having a cordial drink with the local Catholic priest: 'They shaked hands, so they did, drank toasts, and sung songs.' The horrified Squire

---

[54] Revd James Porter, *Billy Bluff and Squire Firebrand, or a sample of the times, as it appeared in five letters, with a selection of songs from 'Paddy's resource'* (1st edn., 1796; Belfast, 1812).

[55] Patrick Kennedy to bishop of Ossory, 9 Oct. 1796 (SPOI, Rebellion papers, 620/25/157).

[56] R. R. Madden, *Antrim and Down in '98* (Glasgow, n.d.), 217.

enquired into the nature of these toasts, one of which wished 'union and peace to the people of Ireland'. This was too much for Squire Firebrand. 'He who wishes union wishes ruin to the country,' he explained to Billy, '. . . and as to peace, 'tis flying in the face of government to speak of it.'[57]

Indeed, Billy received quite a political education at the hands of Squire Firebrand, an education which clearly showed Porter's readers the unacceptable face of ascendancy dominance and misrule:

D——m thinking, Billy, 'tis putting the world mad. O, what a happy country we had before men turned their thoughts to thinking! Catholics thought nothing but just getting leave to live, and working for their meat; Presbyterians thought of nothing but wrangling about religion and grumbling about tithes; and protestants thought of nothing but doing and saying what their betters bid them; and the gentlemen thought of nothing but drinking, hunting, and the game laws. O! how times are changed, and all for the worse. Your Catholic college—your Catholic schools—your Catholic emancipation—your Sunday schools—your charter schools—your book societies, your pamphlets and your books, and your one h——l or another are all turning the people's head and setting them a thinking about this, that, and t'other.[58]

It was just this increased level of thinking among the people which threatened the system of government, as the Squire dreaded and Porter hoped. But worse than the thinking and the reading, according to Squire Firebrand, was the singing, an apparently innocuous popular pleasure which must now fall victim to the government's wrath:

'Tis songs that is most to be dreaded of all things. Singing, Billy, is a d——d bad custom; it infects a whole country and makes them half-mad; because they rejoice and forget their cares, and forget their duty, and forget their betters. By H——ns, I'll put an end to singing in this part of the country in a short time. And there's whistling is near as bad: do you hear much whistling nowadays?[59]

While *Billy Bluff and the squire* was a delightful lampoon on the irrationality of the old regime, it also contained the reasoned voice of the future. The Squire, astounded that a Presbyterian minister and a Catholic priest should hold a friendly meeting with one another, accused R—— of fostering an unexpected and 'unnatural' friendship. 'It is not so new, sir,' the minister replied,

It has existed for several years; but it is not long since it began to frighten our enemies. . . . It shows, Mr Firebrand, that we are wiser than our ancestors; that we are convinced that a man may live in this world and the world to come without having imbrued his hands in his neighbour's blood about religion; and it shows that we think peace on earth and goodwill to all men, the foundation of all religion and it

---

[57] Quoted in Madden, *Antrim and Down*, 219.
[58] *NS*, 18 July 1796.   [59] *NS*, 2 Sept. 1796.

proves that our absurd dissensions were the cause of our national poverty, ignorance, degradation, and slavery.[60]

With the sensibilities of a later age, the historian R. R. Madden regarded the language of Porter's 'impudent publication' as of a 'character very ill suited to the pursuits of the author', a Presbyterian minister. 'The application of scriptural expressions to a subject of this kind, and the use of names which one is accustomed to hear pronounced with reverence, in connection with such topics, are much to be regretted.'[61] But this was exactly the point that Porter wished to make. It was not R——, the enlightened United Irish Presbyterian minister, who interspersed his speech with oaths and curses, but the Revd John Cleland, represented by Squire Firebrand. What was undignified, unchristian, and certainly inappropriate was this use of the men of God as the tools of a corrupt state to suppress the righteous indignation of an aggrieved people. 'There is nothing like making clergymen magistrates,' the Squire explained to Billy Bluff, for 'it adds a double edge to the sword; shows the world the necessity of uniting church and state; makes the dove bite like the serpent, and converts the lamb into the lion, all for the good of mankind and the happiness of souls.'[62] Porter sought to expose the hypocrisy of tyranny masquerading as religion. He did not attack religion itself, at least in so far as it was founded on Christian charity and tolerance. The government had established a religion, the religion of a Firebrand, which proved inconsistent with the conscience of the mass of the Irish people. This religion, as practised by a Firebrand, was merely a tool to delude and prevent them from claiming their due rights.

But there was another reason for the colourful and colloquial language of Porter's productions besides that of discrediting the government's use of Anglican clergymen to buttress its tyrannical rule. Porter's letters to the *Northern Star* were intended to amuse his readers as a prelude to enlightening them. The dignified homilies of R——, the rational United Irishman, were by then a familiar staple of the *Northern Star*'s columns, but the lively interchanges between the Squire and his crony were designed to create a shock of recognition among readers. Billy Bluff could be their neighbour, Squire Firebrand their magistrate, Lord Mountmumble their landlord. Porter ripped the veil of benignity from the face of the people's so-called betters, exposing a visage scarred by lies, crass manipulation, greed, and self-interest. That the people owed a degree of deference to such as these went against all reason. The government, which claimed to attend to the needs of all the people, was actually using a Bluff or a Firebrand to undermine popular interests. Porter exposed such hypocrisy with humour and a touch of realism in the language and manners that he attributed to his characters.

[60] *NS*, 2 Dec. 1796.   [61] Madden, *Antrim and Down*, 218.   [62] *NS*, 2 Sept. 1796.

While the radicals may have been somewhat deficient in military and political expertise, they enjoyed an abundance of literary talent. Tone, Drennan, Russell, Sampson, and Porter were among the leading writers of the movement, but scores of other members and fellow-travellers lent their pens to the service of the cause of reform and emancipation in Ireland. Many of these productions, such as Tone's *An argument on behalf of the Catholics of Ireland* or Thomas Russell's *Appeal to the people of Ireland*, were straightforward appeals to the reason and civic virtue of the reader.[63] Some others, like those of Porter and Sampson, sought to entertain as well as to edify the public and represented exemplary political satires. A few pamphleteers employed catechetical methods or dialogues in which positions and arguments were simplified, obviously with a lower-class readership in mind.[64] And some United Irishmen and their sympathizers adapted conventional literary forms for propagandist political purposes. In 1797, for example, the *Northern Star* office published *Hibernia: a poem* by the respected Ulster poet William Hamilton Drummond, dedicated to the 'true friends of Ireland' and urging them to liberate their country from tyranny:

> Oh wretched Erin! for thy sons unblest,
> Oft' with big sorrow heaves my troubled breast.
> Still art thou doom'd to feel oppression's rod?
> Still hang obsequious at the despot's nod?
>
> Still art thou doom'd to fatten thy gore,
> The bloody precincts of a distant shore?
> And see thy lifeblood tinge th'empurpled wave,
> Weak to redress, and impotent to save?[65]

Later that year Drummond published *The man of age: a poem*, in which he detailed in poetic form the social and economic afflictions endured by Ulster folk over the last quarter of a century, culminating in the brutal repression by Lake's troops, when 'law bound justice in her legal chain'.[66]

Religious literature was also promoted by northern radicals. The Revd James Glendy, the United Irish minister of the Presbyterian congregation of Maghera, published a sermon in December 1792 in which he claimed that the French revolutionaries had benefited from divine intervention.[67] Dr

---

[63] Thomas Russell, *A letter to the people of Ireland on the present situation of the country* (Belfast, 1796); see also [William Sampson], *Advice to the rich by an independent country gentleman, pointing out the road to security and peace* (Dublin, 1796).

[64] See e.g. 'The union doctrine, or the poor man's catechism' (SPOI, Rebellion papers, 620/43/6); 'The children's catechism' (Belfast, Linenhall Library, Joy papers, 8/15/3).

[65] William Hamilton Drummond, *Hibernia: a poem, part the first* (Belfast, 1797), 8.

[66] Id., *The man of age: a poem* (Belfast, 1797), 17. United Irishmen actively subsidized such literary efforts. The volume of poems by Newry's John Corry contains a list of subscribers which constitutes a veritable who's who of radical republicans. See John Corry, *Odes and elegies, descriptive and sentimental, with 'The patriot', a poem* (Newry, 1797).

[67] *NS*, 12 Dec. 1792.

William Steele Dickson, a Presbyterian minister, explained the virtues of Catholic emancipation and pointed out that it was justified by revealed religion.[68] Early in 1794 the Revd Thomas Ledlie Birch's *The obligations upon true Christians* appeared, a millenarian tract with political overtones, based on a sermon delivered before the Synod of Ulster in June 1793.[69]

As the subject of Birch's tract suggests, the United Irishmen were concerned not only that God was on their side, but that the course of divinely ordained history assured victory to the opponents of the administration as well. Rumours concerning an imminent massacre of either protestants or Catholics were rife, and the popular mind, anticipating cataclysmic events, became particularly susceptible to the apocalyptic literature circulated by the United Irishmen. 'They have a vast number of emissaries', complained a bitter John Beresford in 1796, 'constantly going through the country to seduce every person they can and swear them; they have songs and prophecies just written, stating all late events in order to persuade the people that as a great part of them had already come to pass, so the remainder will certainly happen.'[70] In 1795 the *Northern Star* office reprinted an edition of Robert Fleming's famous sermon of 1701 under the title, *A discourse on the rise and fall of Antichrist, wherein the revolution in France and the downfall of monarchy in that kingdom are distinctly pointed out.*[71]

The magistrate Arthur Cole Hamilton secured a mildly millenarian tract from a pedlar at Gortin fair in County Tyrone which he subsequently forwarded to the government in March 1797 because of his alarm over the 'levelling principles' contained in it.[72] The prophecies of a seventeenth-century Scottish Covenanter, Alexander Peden, circulated in parts of Antrim and Derry, where they were construed to foretell the deliverance of Ireland by the French.[73] Another rehashing of an even older prophecy was one attributed to a thirteenth-century poet and seer, Thomas the Rhymer. A United Irish committee in the Rasharkin district of County Antrim was so impressed with these two sets of prophecies that it resolved to send agents among the people to read and explain their contents, that is, 'the French news'.[74]

No prophecies, however, enjoyed greater vogue than those ascribed to

[68] *NS*, 26 Feb. 1793; William Steele Dickson, *Three sermons on the subject of scripture politics* (Belfast, 1793).

[69] *NS*, 16 Feb. 1794; David W. Miller, 'Presbyterianism and "modernization" in Ulster', *Past and Present*, 80 (Aug. 1978), 80.

[70] John Beresford to Lord Auckland, 4 Sept. 1796 (*The correspondence of the right hon. John Beresford*, ed. William Beresford (2 vols., London, 1854), ii. 128).

[71] Miller, 'Presbyterianism', 81; see also James S. Donnelly, jun., 'Propagating the cause of the United Irishmen', *Studies*, 69/273 (Spring 1980), 15–20.

[72] A. Cole Hamilton to Dublin Castle, 2 Mar. 1797 (SPOI, Rebellion papers, 620/29/8).

[73] Miller, 'Presbyterianism', 81.

[74] Samuel McSkimin, *Annals of Ulster from 1790 to 1798*, ed. E. J. McCrum (Belfast, 1906), 32.

Colum Cille. In some popular versions, they carried strong sectarian overtones as well as the, by then, conventional allusions to the liberation of
Ireland through foreign invasion.[75] De Latocnaye, a French traveller,
became acquainted with a form of these predictions during his journey
through County Armagh. There, in the winter of 1796–7, the Orangemen
'circulated adroitly among the peasants an old prophecy of St Columba'
which proclaimed that a time of war and famine would destroy that part of
the kingdom, but that the faithful 'beyond the Shannon' would prosper.[76]
Thus, in the loyalist protestants' exploitation of the prophecy, 'faithful'
Catholics were urged to depart for the west of Ireland, a less traumatic reason for exodus than the infamous Armagh outrages. In the west the
prophecy was a source of great comfort, for the civil war about to convulse
Ulster would leave the Catholics of Connacht untouched.[77] Northern
United Irishmen, however, could also find encouragement in the supposed
writings of Colum Cille, for he was said to have predicted great events in
Ulster which would bring about a national revolution.[78]

Keith Thomas has accounted for the general appeal of prophecies in two
ways. First, as a simple propaganda device, prophecies clothed an enterprise
in certitude; the success of the venture was guaranteed, so why not march
with the future? Secondly, prophecies provided a 'validating charter', sanctioning innovative measures by reference to ancient authorities.[79] This latter
aspect was particularly important to Catholics, for whom revolution, as so
recently demonstrated in France, was anathema to their church. David
Miller has argued that prophecies, though sometimes interpreted differently
by Catholic and Dissenter, served to bring members of the two religious
communities together in revolutionary action. In the millennium one religion would reign, and either Catholics or Dissenters would thus be relieved
of their heretical ways.[80] Millenarian literature thus served to legitimate
revolt—and, indeed, sanctioned it as inevitable. Clearly, the United
Irishmen calculated that this would prove to be the case as they promoted
particular prophecies among particular communities. The informer John
Smith, alias Bird, recounting a dinner that he shared with Sam Neilson,
reported that during the course of the meal the *Northern Star*'s editor
received a letter from a correspondent. It 'contained a foolish old prophecy
which he [Neilson] said he must insert to please his country readers'.[81]

[75] Prophecy of Colum Cille (SPOI, Rebellion papers, 620/48/46).
[76] De Latocnaye, *A Frenchman's walk through Ireland, 1796–7*, trans. John Stevenson
(Belfast, 1917), 263.
[77] Sir Richard Musgrave, *Memoires of the different rebellions in Ireland from the arrival of
the English* (2 vols., Dublin, 1802), i. 81.
[78] McSkimin, *Annals*, 32.
[79] Keith Thomas, *Religion and the decline of magic* (New York, 1971), 422–32.
[80] Miller, 'Presbyterianism', 84–5.
[81] Information of John Smith (alias Bird), 1795–6 (SPOI, Rebellion papers, 620/27/1).

Yet, leaving such manipulative exploitation aside, there were also some United Irish leaders, Birch and Thomas Russell among them, who possessed a sincere intellectual curiosity and belief in millenarian ideas.[82] Nor should we underestimate the sanctioning powers of religious literature in general in mobilizing the people for or against the United Irishmen. Even that demigod of the radical cause, Tom Paine, was compromised among many Presbyterian radicals for espousing what were thought to be irreligious notions. His *Age of reason*, published in 1795, was circulated by many free-thinking or deistical United Irishmen concerned to break the people's attach-ment—or enslavement, as they would have it—to their priests and ministers. The Revd William McClure complained that a great number of copies of the *Age of reason* had been thrown into the houses of his congregation at Carnmoney, County Antrim. And, according to Mary Ann McCracken, 'at the [rebel] camp at Ballynahinch, a great number of pious Covenanters left the camp in consequence of the irreligious expressions and profanations of the Sabbath day, saying it could not have the blessing of God.'[83]

The democratization of political culture did not depend on the use of pamphlets alone. The handbill also proved to be a mighty weapon in the United Irish propaganda arsenal. The Dublin Society of United Irishmen printed 5,000 copies of a circular letter announcing their foundation and aims early in 1792.[84] Sympathetic addresses from English, Scottish, and domestic organizations and assemblies were reprinted for distribution.[85] Generally, handbills were placed in various parts of the assembly hall in Dublin before each United Irish meeting, and members were expected to help themselves before the proceedings commenced. In this way, those responsible for any publication might retain anonymity.[86] Distribution was usually left to individual members, 'particularly', according to the informer Collins, to 'professional men going on circuit, as there are the strongest rea-sons to believe that those papers have been hitherto suppressed in the post office'.[87] Archibald Hamilton Rowan possessed his own printing-press at his home at Rathcoffey near Dublin on which he churned out United Irish handbills.[88] But access to a printing-press posed no particular problem to the United Irishmen. Radicals in Cork and Belfast as well as in other provincial towns had the means to print statements of their position on events within hours of their occurrence.[89] For example, 20,000 copies of

[82] For Russell's interest in prophecies, see TCD, Russell correspondence, MS 868/1 [N.4.2]/1–2, 26.

[83] Mary Ann McCracken to R. R. Madden, 13 Nov. 1857 (TCD, Madden papers, MS 873/70).

[84] *Rep. secret comm.* 94.

[85] McDowell, 'Proceedings', 19–20.

[86] Ibid. 95.

[87] Ibid. 16.

[88] Edward Cooke to Evan Nepean, 29 May 1793 (PROHO 100/44/15–17).

[89] Marquess of Downshire to William Pitt, [?] Mar. 1795 (PRO, Chatham papers, 30/8/327/296–7).

Grattan's 'inflammatory address' to his Dublin electors in 1795 on the questions of reform and emancipation were distributed 'by a number of decent persons' throughout the streets of Dublin within hours of its deliverance. Thousands more were sent all over the rest of the country.[90]

If the actual production of these handbills posed no real problem for the United Irishmen, neither did their distribution, though the government was ever alert to the dissemination of such seditious literature. Handbills and broadsheets were posted on chapel doors, on prominent buildings, and even on the houses of parliament.[91] United Irish carmen and pedlars were designated to carry bundles of such handbills for distribution throughout the countryside, slipping such productions under the doors of cabins, houses, shops, public houses, and barracks.[92] Market-days and fairs provided excellent opportunities for the radicals to reach a wide audience with their abbreviated literary productions. Colonel Lucius Barber complained that market-day in Belfast in February 1797 witnessed the United Irishmen taking 'uncommon pains' to circulate news of the French victory in Italy by distributing copies of a handbill to that effect 'to every person quitting town'.[93]

Such activity, characteristic of both the reformist and the revolutionary phases of the United Irishmen, did not escape the notice of the authorities and their conservative allies. As early as 1792 the loyalist press expressed its alarm at the success of the United Irishmen in disseminating their many publications: 'Scraps of sedition are circulated throughout every part of the country, more particularly [in] the north and the capital.'[94] The government was equally alert to the danger posed by the United Irishmen in arousing public indignation against the abuses of the existing administration. Unable in most cases to identify the authors of such inflammatory handbills, the authorities contented themselves with arresting the distributors.[95]

Handbills provided an excellent means by which the radicals as well as their enemies could target specific grievances and then direct them to those sectors of the population most concerned. Thus the United Irishmen aimed their protests about the calamitous economic effects of the war with France at the increasingly unemployed manufacturers of the capital.[96] Jurors and

---

[90] 'A loyalist' to William Pitt, 17 Mar. 1795 (PRO, Chatham papers, 30/8/328/284).

[91] Threatening notice posted on Parliament House (SPOI, Rebellion papers, 620/19/63); Sir William Godfrey to Dublin Castle, 22 Jan. 1797 (ibid. 620/28/129); report of Constables Marsden and Fitzpatrick on the posting of United Irish broadsheets in Dublin (SPOI, State of the country papers, carton 154/171).

[92] —— to Dublin Castle, n.d. (SPOI, Rebellion papers, 620/53/25).

[93] Col. Lucius Barber to Edward Cooke, 10 Feb. 1797 (ibid. 620/28/248).

[94] *FJ*, 11 Dec. 1792.

[95] See e.g. William Wenman Seward, *Collectanea politica* (3 vols., Dublin, 1801–4), ii, 100; *FJ*, 30 July 1793; *FDJ*, 22 Aug. 1793.

[96] 'Address to the manufacturers of Dublin', [1793] (SPOI, Rebellion papers, 620/20/12); see ibid. 620/20/19–20, for other anti-war handbills.

county electors could be instructed on specific issues through the handbill.[97] The men of landed property could be educated on the dangers of resistance to the popular will.[98] The lower classes in the countryside could be induced to support the United Irishmen in handbills that urged them to withhold their rents until the republican revolution was effected.[99] The Orange Order and the yeomanry were exposed as vicious Turks lusting after Catholic blood and Irish women.[100] Government harassment of United Irish leaders could be exposed, and the martyrs to the cause of liberty could be used to arouse popular indignation against the established order and sympathy for the republicans.[101] Irish soldiers were urged to protect and defend their countrymen and -women from a rapacious government by lending their support to the radical cause.[102] The handbill and broadsheet provided the United Irishmen with one of their most effective literary means of disseminating radical principles throughout the countryside and among the masses.

Also important was the radicals' calculated exploitation of a vibrant oral cultural tradition. 'They set ballad singers in the streets,' the earl of Westmorland complained late in 1792, and thus 'this levelling spirit has gained much ground here.'[103] Societies of United Irishmen in Belfast, Dublin, and Cork issued broadsheets containing political songs and ballads and scattered them along the roads or left them at the doors of cottages. Merchants were known to have wrapped their goods in them.[104] Initially, such songs appeared as adjuncts to United Irish meetings and demonstrations. The 1792 commemoration of Bastille day in Belfast inspired the publication of a booklet entitled *Songs on the French revolution that took place at Paris, 14th July 1789, sung at the celebration thereof at Belfast on Saturday, 14th July 1792.*[105] Not surprisingly, at a time when the United Irishmen sought to create a sympathetic hearing for the French revolution, their

[97] See e.g. 'To those gentlemen who generally compose the petit juries', 17 Mar. 1797 (ibid. 620/29/86).
[98] See e.g. 'To the men of landed property in the county of Down, by a United Irishman' (ibid. 620/33/139); 'Address to the more wealthy classes of United Irishmen' (SPOI, State of the country papers, carton 154/172).
[99] See e.g. United Irish handbills in *Rep. secret comm.* 279–80.
[100] 'Fabricated rules and regulations of the Orangemen' (ibid. 252); Nathaniel Alexander to Henry Alexander, 8 Nov. 1796 (SPOI, Rebellion papers, 620/28/249).
[101] See e.g. 'Sacred to the memory of William Orr' (ibid. 620/52/36).
[102] 'Soldiers' (ibid. 620/43/5); United Irish handbills distributed among soldiers (*Rep. secret comm.* 301–5); for an example of the soldiers themselves generating such literature, see 'An address from the 105th and 113th regiments to the public and their brothers in arms' (NAM, Nugent papers, 6807/370/42).
[103] Earl of Westmorland to William Pitt, 10 Dec. 1792 (NLI, Lord-Lieutenants' correspondence, MS 886/61–7).
[104] Georges-Denis Zimmermann, *Songs of Irish rebellion: political ballads and rebel songs, 1780–1900* (Hatboro, Pa., 1967), 37.
[105] Ibid. 37 n.

songs included English translations of 'Ça ira', the 'Marseillaise', and the 'Carmagnole'.[106]

Original Irish songs in praise of the revolution in France cited the lessons to be drawn from the French experience. The revolution marked the dawn of a new age of liberty and reason, and this sentiment was expressed in song as much as it was discussed in sympathetic newspapers and pamphlets. A ballad entitled 'The standard of freedom' announced:

> Too long had oppression and terror entwin'd
> These fancy form'd chains that enslave the free mind;
> Whilst dark superstition with nature at strife
> Had lock'd up for ages the fountain of life.
>
> And the demons fled, the delusion is past,
> And reason and virtue are conquered at last;
> Seize the glad moment, and hail the decree
> That bids millions rejoice, and a nation be free.[107]

The universal implications of the French revolution were also expressed in 'The jovial friend':

> May French exertions never cease
> Till Europe shall reformed be,
> And union, liberty, and peace
> Succeed oppression's fell decree.
> Then every freeman's toast will be
> Union, peace, and liberty.[108]

'Union, peace, and liberty'—these sentiments sum up the content of a great many United Irish songs, especially in the early reformist days. The necessity for unity was expounded in such lyrics as 'See your country righted', containing the chorus:

> Boldly with heart and hand
> Here we meet united,
> And by each other firmly stand,
> To see our country righted.[109]

In another song articulating the theme of non-sectarianism, Peter, Martin, and John, representing the three religious communities in Ireland, join together against the forces of bigotry:

> In darkest days of yore, we all three were made foes,
> By priestcraft and statecraft were led by the nose,

---

[106] NS, 7 Apr. 1792; *Paddy's resource, being a select collection of original and modern patriotic songs, toasts, and sentiments compiled for the use of all firm patriots* (Philadelphia, 1796), 25.

[107] *Paddy's resource*, 5.   [108] Ibid. 18.   [109] Ibid. 15.

> The great and the clergy too well did succeed,
> Disunion and prejudice make us all bleed.[110]

The war with France added grist to the songster's mill. The United Irishmen based their opposition to the war not only on the ideological similarities between Irish reformers and French revolutionaries, but also on the grounds that conflict was bound to produce economic hardship in Ireland. One of the liveliest United Irish ballads, adapted from an English piece, underscored both these objections. Entitled 'Billy's undone by the war', the song castigated the conflict as a 'foul bit of work the damn'd tory's [William Pitt] conniving at!' One verse discouraged Irishmen from serving in the British armed forces:

> A wise figure we make, to be starv'd to help slavery,
> Fighting for others with profitless bravery;
> O! get out! you'll undo a good nation with knavery,
> Billy's undone by the war.

Another verse played upon the domestic hardships caused by the war:

> For the poor out of bread, what a fine consolation too,
> Winter at hand, and all trade in stagnation too;
> Nothing to swallow, but lumps of taxation too,
> Billy's undone by the war.[111]

In both style and content, most of these songs tended to fall into two groups. The more lyrical and fulsome musical poems celebrated brave Hibernia and the lofty sentiments of reason, patriotic virtue, and national unity. Other songs, composed in a more popular style, dealt with specific social, political, and, especially, economic grievances. Anti-tithe verses appeared in many of these ballads. One song, 'Church and state, or the rector's creed', was a satirical address from an avaricious and corrupt clergyman of the established church.

> Ye men of my parish I pray you take heed,
> Till I give you a sketch of my time-serving creed—
> My creed it is cash, and my stipend salvation,
> For which I'll destroy all the swine in the nation,
> With my black coat and my cravat so white.[112]

Another song written to court popular support for the radical cause hinted at a redistribution of economic resources:

> No longer the agents of power
> Will by our hard labour be fed;
> And the labouring poor of the nation
> Will then find plenty of bread.[113]

---

[110] Ibid. 55.   [111] Ibid. 29–30.   [112] Ibid. 16.   [113] Ibid. 31–2.

The themes of these songs reflect United Irish efforts to expose the government to the people as a self-serving, exploitative regime.

The range in style and content of these productions serves to highlight the propagandist skill of the United Irishmen. As Charles Teeling observed: 'The popular songs of the day, suited to the temper of the times, were admirably calculated to rouse the national spirit and elevate the mind to a contempt of danger and the most enthusiastic feelings which love of liberty and of country could inspire.'[114] Music forms a vital part of any culture, but in eighteenth-century Ireland, with its vibrant oral traditions, songs could be used to great effect in diffusing the sentiments and principles of a committed corps of republican propagandists. In 1795 the Belfast United Irishmen collected many of these songs together in a booklet entitled *Paddy's resource*. Several new and revised editions soon appeared from the presses in Belfast, Dublin, and even America.[115] 'Its [*sic*] sung by the Irish sans-culottes with great eclat,' one United Irishman boasted to his friend in America.[116] To Sir George F. Hill it was 'as filthy and stinking as equality could wish it to be'.[117] The didactic purposes of the songs included in *Paddy's resource* are evident from their content. Anti-monarchical allusions helped to prepare the public mind for extreme republicanism, as did celebrations of the victories of the French revolutionaries. By invoking the virtues of patriotism and the rights of man, the United Irishmen sought to appeal to merchants, tradesmen, and artisans who hoped to gain the political rights so long denied them. In calling attention to peasant grievances, the radicals were telling Ireland's restive rural masses that a solution to their problems was within their grasp. But these songs were written not only with the idea of educating the popular mind in the principles of the United Irishmen; they were also intended to be sung at popular gatherings, especially those in public houses, where political discussion was a commonplace. The radicals were quick to exploit the drinking-song, as, for example, 'The hearty fellow's delight':

> The mighty Thomas Paine,
> Who freedom did maintain
> With energy and reason and sense,
> Was stupid as an ass
> Till first he took a glass
> Then truth sprang from his *cruskeen lan*.[118]

When the Revd James Porter's creation, Squire Firebrand, told his agent Billy Bluff that ''tis songs that is to be dreaded of all things', he may well

---

[114] Charles Hamilton Teeling, *The history of the Irish rebellion of 1798* (1st edn., 1876; Shannon, 1972), 11.

[115] Zimmermann, *Songs of Irish rebellion*, 38.

[116] Thomas Potts to James Lemon, 17 Nov. 1795 (PRONI, T1012).

[117] Sir George F. Hill to Edward Cooke, 27 Dec. 1796 (SPOI, Rebellion papers, 620/26/165).

[118] *Paddy's resource*, 23.

have captured the government's point of view. Newspapers and pamphlets may have espoused seditious and treasonable sentiments, but they paled beside the content of the songs themselves, especially those circulated during the revolutionary phase of the United Irish movement, which exhorted people to rebellion:

> Then let us calmly wait the time
> And strike the final blow,
> To punish traitors for their crimes
> And lay the tyrant low.
> Hail then Hibernia's isle
> The gloomy night is near on,
> The day begins to smile.

The magistrate who forwarded this seditious ballad to the government was considerably alarmed: 'Just think, then, what our state must be when in almost every village house is a night assembly of deluded wretches maddening themselves with these infernal inventions.' Another song enclosed in the magistrate's report announced:

> The trying period is at hand
> Which must decide the cause,
> Whether we'll free our native land
> Or yield to tyrants' law.[119]

These songs clearly called for the downfall of monarchy and its associated tyranny in Ireland. In a parody of 'God save the king', the radicals credited George III with an unlimited capacity to consume the wealth of his subjects in the form of taxes:

> Long live our gracious king,
> To him our treasure bring,
> Generous and free!
> His feelings are so tough
> You ne'er can bring enough;
> Why keep you back the stuff,
> Rebels you be.[120]

But the charge of excessive taxation, associated as it was with the lack of representation that marked a tyrannical government, was a less compelling reason for rebellion than the actual violence perpetrated by the king's servants on the people of Ireland. Many of the ballads of the late 1790s detailed vividly the sufferings of a people living under a state of savage military repression. The following verses evoked the plight of rural patriots:

---

[119] Alexander Knox to Peter Burrowes, 3 Mar. 1797 (SPOI, Rebellion papers, 620/29/30).
[120] 'Collection of '98 songs compiled by Edmund R. Willis' (NLI, Bourke collection, MS 9870/21–2).

> The mother bereft of her son,
> The cottage too robbed of its sire,
> The widow and orphans undone,
> While the husband and father expire.
>
> The fair face of Nature complains
> Of oppression, the cause of her grief,
> The oppressor unfeeling remains,
> Can reason point out no relief.
>
> O Liberty! Justice! arise;
> Let thy aid to the wretched be given,
> May the tyrant that's deaf to these cries,
> From his blood-reeking throne soon be driven.[121]

In 'The victim of tyranny' a man called Pat offers the sad tale of his own experience under military rule and landlord rapacity. Forced to flee Ireland, to leave his wife and family, lamenting that all his friends are in dungeons, he proclaims that his only crime was a love of his country, a sentiment abhorred by his landlord, who, in the context of the ballad, could also represent the king himself.

> I had a tyrant landlord,—base,
> Who knew my heart to Erin yearned,
> Even with the ground, my cot did raze,
> And fired my substance dearly earned;
> Unmoved—remorseless now he sees
> My cottage falling, as it burns,
> My wife for mercy, on her knees,
> From him with ruthless frown he spurns.[122]

Another song, composed by an imprisoned United Irishman, expressed the hope that:

> May we but live to see the day
> The crown from George's head shall fall,
> The people's voice will then bear sway
> We'll humble tyrants one and all.[123]

Not only did these later songs openly espouse rebellion, but they gloried in the prospect of a French invasion to help Irish patriots liberate their country. The most famous of these songs was the 'Shan van vocht', which invoked the allegorical figure of Ireland as a long-suffering, crippled old woman, the Catholic peasant's counterpart to the middle-class intellectual's graceful Hibernia:

---

[121] 'Collection of '98 songs compiled by Edmund R. Willis' (NLI, Bourke collection, MS 9870/15–16).

[122] Ibid. 53–4.   [123] State prisoners' papers (SPOI, Rebellion papers, 620/41/112).

> Oh, the French are in the bay,
> They'll be here without delay,
> And the Orange will decay,
> Says the shan van vocht.[124]

This reference to the coming destruction of the Orange Order scarcely stood alone. As another rebel ballad phrased it: 'Sure you might know how Irish freemen | Soon would put your Orange down.'[125] Abuse was also heaped upon the pernicious informers who betrayed the cause. One song had for its subject the notorious Edward Newell:

> Allied to friends and foes, but false to all,
> He gained their confidence to work their fall,
> He sold his land and spent the gold in vice,
> Renewed his means, for blood still had its price.[126]

Just as the ballads excoriated yeomen, Orangemen, informers, and a tyrannical government, so too they celebrated the virtues of martyrs to the cause of liberty in Ireland. Particularly remarkable was the virtual apotheosis of William Orr, the first man to be hanged under the infamous insurrection act for administering an illegal oath. The *Belfast News-Letter* described the Presbyterian Orr as a 'respectable farmer and man of property in the neighbourhood of Antrim', about 30 years of age, 'remarkably good-looking', a devoted husband, and the father of six young children.[127] This eminently suitable hero seemed to embody the ideal of the sober and industrious farmer, the broad-minded Christian, the loving husband and father—the backbone of rural society. Through Orr's career and untimely death, these rustic virtues came into direct opposition to a corrupt, bigoted, foreign-dominated government. His famous elegy, circulated in the *Press*, was written by Drennan:

> Oh William, how pale was thy cheek
> Where beauty so lately did dwell;
> When thy true love hung faint on thy neck,
> And thy breast heaved to her—the farewell.
>
> .   .   .   .
>
> O wither the pitiless hand
> Could execute such a decree,
> And the heart that could give the command,
> A stranger to peace let it be.[128]

---

[124] Turlough Faolain, *Blood on the harp: Irish rebel history in ballad (the heritage)* (Troy, NY, 1983), 278.

[125] T. Crofton Croker, *Popular songs illustrative of the French invasions of Ireland* (London, 1845), 68.

[126] R. R. Madden, *Literary remains of the United Irishmen of 1798* (Dublin, 1887), 72.

[127] *BNL*, 22 Sept. 1797.   [128] Madden, *Literary remains*, 43–4.

The numerous encomiums to Orr's manly beauty and heroic virtues in song and poetry recall the ancient legend of Cincinnatus, the great republican hero—a simple rustic who saved Rome and then returned virtuously to his plough, rejecting power and glory. Cincinnatus, sacrificing his private interest to the public good, had been the ideal, incorruptible citizen of the Roman republic, just as Orr came to symbolize the ideal citizen of an Irish republic. Orr's association with ancient virtues and sturdy rural values, however romanticized, made his death a rallying cry against the government: 'Vengeance, Irishmen, vengeance on your oppressors. Remember what thousands of your dearest friends have perished by their merciless orders. Remember their burnings, their rackings, their torturings, their military massacres, and their legal murders. Remember Orr!'[129] A northern schoolmaster declared: 'Orr is the password to liberty.'[130]

The court martial and execution of four young soldiers of the Monaghan militia at Blaris camp near Lisburn in May 1797 rivalled Orr's death in its propagandist exploitation by the United Irishmen. Again, the theme of noble and virtuous youth pitted against the ruthless oppression of the state was employed. 'Like lambs led to slaughter, bleeding for liberty', they gallantly and defiantly met their executioners, at least according to the ballad 'Blaris Moor':

> Altho' we are young and tender, to you we will not surrender,
> And Hibernia's bold defenders we will always constant prove;
> We own we are united, and by death we'll not be affrighted,
> But in hopes to be requited by him who rules above.[131]

If the literature surrounding Orr's death recalls the civic virtues of the Roman republic, 'Blaris Moor' suggests the martyrdom of the early Christians. Religious martyrs crowded the hagiographical landscape of Presbyterians as well as Catholics, and the tradition was skilfully exploited by the United Irishmen in their handling of the deaths of these four unfortunate soldiers.[132]

These rebel songs may well have been the most effective means of spreading United Irish principles among the rural lower classes. At least they were useful in arousing discontent and indignation against the policies of the government and its loyal supporters. The message of the ballads was simple. Ireland was ruled by tyrants. Only a union of Catholic and protes-

---

[129] John Sheares's proclamation of the provisional Irish government, May 1798 (*Rep. secret comm.* 208).

[130] Intercepted United Irish letter, 28 Jan. 1798 (SPOI, Rebellion papers, 620/35/71); see also Tone's epitaph on Orr, 'Let Orr be the watchword of liberty' (TCD, Madden papers, MS 873/33).

[131] Zimmermann, *Songs of Irish rebellion*, 131.

[132] See also the poetic account of the death of a Defender, *The martyr of liberty: a poem on the heroic death of Lawrence O'Connor, executed at Naas in Ireland on a charge of high treason, September 7th, 1796* (Dublin, 1798).

tant could overthrow these oppressors. The record of government travesties against the people was vividly exposed. The French were allies in the cause of Irish liberty and would offer timely assistance to Irish patriots. The choice was between freedom and slavery. Vague promises of profound economic and social change were offered. How effective these songs were in educating United Irish followers in sound republican principles is less certain. But the United Irishmen themselves regarded them as sufficient explanations of their policies. One emissary presented a ballad to a potential recruit, telling him that it would explain what the United Irishmen were all about.[133]

Such a propaganda strategy had its advantages as well as its disadvantages. Songs and ballads certainly promoted interest in the United Irish cause and served to channel economic, social, and political discontent into a general opposition to ascendancy rule. As a form of political education, however, these songs were of obviously limited utility. Rather than producing a disciplined revolutionary republican movement, they may well have been partly responsible for the insurrection which afflicted Wexford in 1798—a popular rising that fed on well-founded fears of government terror. United Irish leaders tended to disown the rising in Wexford, especially its most overtly sectarian aspects. The government, they maintained, had precipitated the rebellion once the disciplined influence of the republican leadership had been neutralized by mass arrests.[134] But whether or not the leadership would have been successful in channelling peasant fury into an organized, disciplined, national, and consequently less bloody, insurrection is a moot point. What can safely be said, however, is that the United Irishmen themselves were largely responsible, through their emotional propaganda, for turning peasant fears into vengeful paranoia, for exacerbating sectarian tensions, and for raising peasant expectations about the fundamental social and economic transformations that would follow a successful rebellion. Popular fury, so carefully cultivated by the republican leaders, was certainly triggered by the government's counter-terror campaign in the countryside, but it was the United Irishmen who actually provided the ammunition.

[133] Sir George F. Hill to Edward Cooke, 8 Dec. 1796 (SPOI, Rebellion papers, 620/26/107).
[134] See Thomas Addis Emmet, Arthur O'Connor, and William James MacNeven, *Memoire or detailed statement of the origin and progress of the Irish union* (Dublin, 1798), 12–13, 20–1, 65, 74.

8

The Republican Press

'I HAVE often heard of the electrical effect of this first newspaper,' recalled John Caldwell of the establishment of the *Belfast News-Letter* in 1737:

It raised the curiosity of the people, set them reading and from reading to thinking, and from thinking to acting and exerting their energies and their rights in sending from the counties men of their choice well qualified to represent them in parliament. This was the first fruits of newspaper knowledge disseminated amongst a people, naturally a well-informed race, who needed only such a stimulus to urge them forward and show them to the world such as they really were, a thinking and well-meaning community.[1]

This absolute faith in the power of the press as a tool of political education led United Irish radicals in Belfast to found their own newspaper, the *Northern Star*, early in 1792. Indeed, even before the formal inauguration of the Society of United Irishmen on 19 October 1791, Belfast radicals had turned their attention towards establishing a newspaper which would take Irish political education beyond the mainstream whiggism provided by Henry Joy's *Belfast News-Letter*.

On 19 September 1791 as many as 136 of Belfast's most respectable citizens, men who were likely to take out advertisements in newspapers, pledged to give their support and their custom to a second paper in the town.[2] Thus encouraged, in October 1791 Belfast radicals, under the leadership of Samuel Neilson, sent prominent reformers throughout the towns and villages of the northern counties a prospectus outlining the liberal and enlightened principles upon which the new paper would be founded. Would they, Neilson's committee enquired, subscribe to a rival paper to the already popular and influential *Belfast News-Letter* and do what they could to secure additional subscriptions in their neighbourhoods? The response was overwhelmingly favourable. Of the fifty-three who answered Neilson's queries, forty-two offered to help launch the new paper and eleven declined, but half of these did so reluctantly.[3] George Dickson of Portadown reflected the sentiments of several of these less enthusiastic correspondents when he claimed that he feared that such a paper would 'tend

---

[1] Autobiographical account of John Caldwell, jun. (PRONI, Caldwell papers, T3541/5/3).
[2] Signatures of those prepared to subscribe to a second newspaper (the *Northern Star*) in Belfast (SPOI, Rebellion papers, 620/19/25).
[3] Letters promising or refusing support for a second newspaper in Belfast (ibid. 620/19/42).

to promote anarchy and discord'.[4] Other correspondents applauded the principles of the proposed paper, but cordially declined to support it for fear of alienating the *Belfast News-Letter*'s editor and publisher, Henry Joy, who was well within the reformers' fold. A future United Irishman, the Presbyterian minister Thomas Ledlie Birch, pleaded that, while the ideas and sentiments behind the project enjoyed his hearty approbation, he was on 'the most friendly footing with Mr Joy' and was convinced that the *Belfast News-Letter*'s publisher 'wishes well to the cause of liberty'. Furthermore, Joy had assured Birch that the *Belfast News-Letter*'s columns were always open to the observations of the radical minister.[5] Another future United Irishman, Alexander Crawford of Lisburn, also reluctantly withheld his support from Neilson's proposal: 'I think that whatever tends to cultivate knowledge of the rights of man—to diffuse political information and to promote unanimity and concord amongst Irishmen has a strong claim in the countenance and protection of every good Irishman.' Nevertheless, the newspaper-buying public could not sustain two Belfast papers, and there was no reason to overthrow the *Belfast News-Letter*.[6]

But while Neilson could take some encouragement from such cordial refusals to lend support to the proposed paper, he could not afford to be too optimistic on the basis of the forty-two letters which offered assistance. Most of their authors qualified their support by observing that, although they themselves stood firmly behind the effort, they could guarantee few subscribers in their neighbourhoods. Robert Bell of Newry informed Neilson that 'as all here are quiet, cool, and seemingly satisfied with their several rights, privileges, and conditions, wherefore I humbly presume you have to look for little from this quarter.'[7] Thomas Stott of Dromore lamented the political apathy of his neighbourhood, which would impose an obstacle to the progress of the proposed newspaper: 'Since my return from Dublin I have applied, but without success, to several persons here to subscribe. Some startle at the mentioning [of] *Rights of men* and political *information* and immediately conclude it will be filled with inflammatory matter tending to excite a spirit of discontent and licentiousness in the people.'[8] Of course, it was just this lethargy and suspicion about the radical cause that had convinced Neilson and his committee that a second Belfast paper was essential.

The political education of the northern people had to be addressed, and this was why many provincial reformers offered their support to Neilson's project. A second and more radical Belfast newspaper 'may have a tendency

[4] George Dickson to Samuel Neilson, 10 Oct. 1791 (ibid.).
[5] Revd Thomas Ledlie Birch to Samuel Neilson, 14 Oct. 1791 (ibid.).
[6] Alexander Crawford to Samuel Neilson, 11 Oct. 1791 (ibid.).
[7] Robert Bell to Samuel Neilson, 28 Oct. 1791 (ibid.).
[8] Thomas Stott to Samuel Neilson, 19 Oct. 1791 (ibid.).

more effectively to draw forth the strength of the *publick mind*', William
Sinclaire of Newtownards observed.[9] Alexander Patton of Tanderagee
noted that the 'field' of radical consciousness was 'truly barren' and that
the proposed paper was greatly needed.[10]

   With right and reason on their side, Irish reformers wanted only the
means to mobilize public opinion. This could be accomplished through the
political education provided in the columns of Neilson's paper—no 'milk
and water' whiggism, but rather a celebration of the principles of the rights
of man and the French revolution. Finding their sentiments adequately
reflected in the northern countryside, at least among the more influential
members of the provincial community, Neilson and his committee set about
bringing their proposed project to fruition. The proprietors of the new
Northern Star, launched in January 1792, consisted of twelve Belfast
Presbyterian radicals. Neilson, the principal shareholder, was its first editor,
and John Rabb served as printer and publisher. The chief contributors
included Thomas Russell, the barrister William Sampson, and three
Presbyterian ministers—James Porter of Grey Abbey, Sinclair Kelburne of
Belfast, and William Steele Dickson of Portaferry. The circulation of the
newspaper eventually reached 4,000–5,000, and its influence was still greater
than this figure suggests.[11]

   In the first issue of the *Northern Star*, in January 1792, the proprietors
made no attempt to veil their aims: they had come together to secure the
reform of parliament:

To this great object the efforts of the *Northern Star* will continue to be exerted
until the venal borough trade shall terminate, until corruption shall no longer be at
least publicly avowed, and until the commons house of parliament shall become the
real organ of the public will; then and only then shall the labours of the *Northern
Star* in this great national business cease.[12]

To promote the union of all Irishmen was the second motive of the proprietors in founding the *Northern Star*. 'The public will our guide—the public
good our end': this was the motto, devised by Drennan at Neilson's
request, which appeared on the masthead of every issue.[13] In addition, the
proprietors promised extensive coverage of commercial news and events in
France and America. The annual price for subscribers was between 16s.
and 19s.[14]

   [9] William Sinclaire to Samuel Neilson, 15 Oct. 1791 (SPOI, Rebellion papers, 620/19/42).
   [10] Alexander Patton to Samuel Neilson, 14 Oct. 1791 (ibid.).
   [11] R. R. Madden, *The United Irishmen, their lives and times*, 3rd ser. (7 vols., London
1842–5), i. 102; W. T. Latimer, *Ulster biographies, relating chiefly to the rebellion of 1798*
(Belfast, 1897), 39; John Hall Stewart, 'The Irish press and the French revolution', *Journalism
Quarterly*, 39 (1962), 516–17.
   [12] *NS*, 4 Jan. 1792.
   [13] William Drennan to Samuel McTier, [Nov. 1791] (*The Drennan letters*, ed. D. A. Chart
(Belfast, 1931), 63).   [14] *NS*, 4 Jan. 1792.

The *Belfast News-Letter* provided northern readers with an alternative to the unabashedly partisan *Northern Star*. Reformers could find sympathetic encouragement in *Belfast News-Letter* editorials during the proprietorship of Henry Joy in the early 1790s. Joy himself was an advocate of moderate parliamentary reform, but he espoused gradual rather than immediate Catholic relief. While he shared some of the United Irishmen's aims, he believed that they pursued them too aggressively. Along with other former leaders of the reform movement like Grattan and Charlemont, Joy found his moderation increasingly out of place in the new political climate of Belfast.[15] When the whig reformism of the *Belfast News-Letter* was placed in direct competition with the radicalism of the *Northern Star*, the circulation of the former suffered, reflecting the polarization of public opinion in Ireland under the impetus of the radical challenge from the United Irishmen.[16] Newspaper circulation generally increased in this period, mainly because of the heightened interest in public affairs stimulated by the French revolution. The *Belfast News-Letter* enjoyed extensive sales by eighteenth-century standards. In 1792 its circulation stood at 2,400, rising to 2,900 two years later. But as the paper became more conservative under the new ownership of George Gordon in 1795, this figure declined to about 2,200.[17] With circulation and advertising revenues dipping dangerously low, Gordon found himself in desperate straits and requested government assistance. In November 1796 he applied to the Castle under-secretary, Edward Cooke, for aid, lamenting to the administrator that the greater part of Belfast's citizens had withdrawn their subscriptions and their advertisements from the paper. Gordon reminded Cooke that a loyalist newspaper was urgently needed in the seditious north, and pointed out astutely that a great victory would be achieved by the republicans if they could silence a pro-government propaganda organ.[18]

If subscription figures and Gordon's pleas for assistance are any indication, the *Northern Star* clearly won the propaganda war between the two Belfast newspapers. And, of course, circulation figures alone do not reveal the extent of the influence of this radical newspaper in the north. The newspaper was a central medium through which the political radicalization of the Ulster countryside was accomplished. Indeed, the *Northern Star* directed its appeal throughout Ireland. A magistrate as far south as Waterford complained to the government that the *Northern Star* was being distributed free of charge in his neighbourhood.[19] It was 'hawked about' at barracks and in coffee-houses in Dublin.[20] 'At every cabin around us,'

[15] Henry Joy, *Belfast politics* (Belfast, 1794), introd.
[16] Stewart, 'Irish press', 515.
[17] Arthur Aspinall, *Politics and the press*, c.1780–1850 (London, 1949), 111.
[18] George Gordon to Edward Cooke, 25 Nov. 1796 (SPOI, Rebellion papers, 620/26/78).
[19] Isaac Heron to Dublin Castle, 2 Jan. 1797 (ibid. 620/28/16).
[20] Francis Higgins to ——, 19 May 1797 (ibid. 620/18/14).

reported George Dallas while touring in Ulster, 'you will see them [the lower classes] reading the *Northern Star*.' Indeed, Dallas often met 'labourers walking to their work and reading this paper as they went along'.[21] Martha McTier, writing to her brother William Drennan in January 1795, acknowledged that such newspapers were responsible for her own political education, and observed further that they were 'so ardently . . . sought for and enjoyed by the lower orders'.[22] 'If it were not for newspapers,' James Stewart of Killymoon observed, 'we should not know that Napper Tandy or Thomas Paine were in existence.'[23] More than one loyalist attributed the unsettled state of the Irish countryside in the mid- and late 1790s to United Irish exploitation of the press. Alexander Knox, for example, remarked that the public mind had been inflamed by various publications of the United Irishmen and 'through the medium of such newspapers as were willing to increase their circulation by courting depravity and sacrificing truth'.[24]

The *Northern Star*'s impact as a propaganda organ, designed both to recruit and rally supporters to the radical cause while discrediting the system of government, cannot be overstated. The paper would not have assumed such dominance among the newspaper-reading public of Ireland if its columns had not been fashioned to suit popular tastes in style and content. From the beginning, northern radicals sought to attract supporters from all levels of Ulster society, and their newspaper contributed to this effort by offering something for almost everyone in its columns. Basically, the content and style of the *Northern Star* can be classified under the following heads: first, there was extensive and favourable coverage of the fortunes of republicanism in Europe and America; secondly, the reporting of current affairs in Ireland was highlighted and slanted to expose the tyrannical tendencies of the government and the unjust treatment accorded to its critics; thirdly, advertisements from various reform-minded societies and institutions throughout the province proclaimed the swelling opposition to the establishment; fourthly, lengthy and learned articles on the appropriateness of radical solutions to Ireland's problems filled its pages; fifthly, there were brief but memorable epigrams from radical or whig authorities as well as from the editor and contributors themselves; and, lastly, the *Northern Star* printed original works which later appeared as pamphlets designed to enlighten and amuse the popular classes.

The sympathetic coverage of the cause of radicalism in Europe, America, and, of course, Ireland was addressed to all the *Northern Star*'s readers.

---

[21] [George Dallas] to William Huskisson, 10 July 1797 (BL, Huskisson papers, Add. MS 38759/36–54).

[22] Martha McTier to William Drennan, 25 Jan. 1795 (PRONI, Drennan letters, T765/540).

[23] James Stewart to earl of Charlemont, 7 July 1792 (RIA, Charlemont papers, MS 12 R 17/27).

[24] Alexander Knox, *Essays on the political circumstances of Ireland written during the administration of Earl Camden* (Dublin, 1799), 56.

The advertisements proclaiming support for the process of reform not only added to the *Northern Star*'s finances, but also served a propagandist function in attesting to the popularity of the cause. The long articles expanding on reform principles and strategies served as a forum in which United Irish political discourse could be clarified, and appealed largely to an educated middle-class audience. But all this could be found, more or less, in the pages of the *Belfast News-Letter* or in the opposition papers in Dublin. What distinguished the *Northern Star* from other newspapers at this time was its appeal to the popular classes. And this was enhanced by its liberal use of pithy political epigrams as well as by the entertaining and artful productions of contributors like James Porter, Thomas Russell, and William Sampson.

The epigrams that interspersed the columns of the *Northern Star* were taken from whig authorities such as Locke or from radical popularizers such as Tom Paine. One of Neilson's objects in selecting these extracts was to make an ironic comment about growing government tyranny. For example, on 14 July 1792, three years after the storming of the Bastille, the *Northern Star* printed a few quotations from a renowned whig theorist under the title 'Seditious extracts from John Locke's *Essay on the human understanding*'. Neilson selected those passages from Locke which might serve as justification not only for the French revolution, but for the radical activity of the United Irishmen as well. Did not Locke maintain 'that *all* men are by nature *equal*', just as the French revolutionaries proclaimed in their 'Declaration of the rights of man and the citizen'? And the United Irishmen, of course, based their whole campaign for Catholic emancipation and parliamentary reform upon this bedrock. The *Northern Star* also quoted Locke to discredit hereditary government: 'That no man can, by any compact whatsoever, bind his children or posterity,' a principle that Paine was famous for popularizing. Needless to say, Locke's assertion that the consent of the governed affords the real legitimacy to government could not go unnoticed by radical propagandists.[25] The point to be drawn from this exercise was that the narrow, landed, protestant oligarchy in Ireland did not govern in the tradition of whig principles so firmly established by the Glorious Revolution of 1688, the foundation of the much-lauded British constitution.

The epigrams in the *Northern Star* were also designed to provide its readers with the memorable watchwords of the radical vocabulary. When it came to popularizing radical principles and communicating them in trenchant and direct prose, Tom Paine entertained no rivals. And so the *Northern Star* borrowed heavily from Paine's *Rights of man*. In March

[25] NS, 14 July 1792.

1792, for example, Neilson highlighted Paine's famous passage concerning the absurdity of monarchy:

Hereditary succession is a burlesque upon monarchy. It puts it in the most ridiculous light by presenting it as an office which any child or idiot may fill. It requires some talents to be a common mechanic; but to be a king requires only the animal figure of a man—a sort of breathing automation. This sort of superstition may last a few years more, but it cannot long resist the awakened reason and interest of man.[26]

It can easily be imagined with what amusement and appreciation such an observation was greeted when it was read in coffee-houses, public houses, reading societies, or even on the street corner to interested hearers.

The editor of the *Northern Star* also included his own epigrams in the paper's columns, drawing his readers' attention to the cause of liberty in France and Ireland. 'The complete overthrow and abolition of the nobility of France', the *Northern Star* observed in February 1792,

should be a warning to *titled men* in every country not to sport with the feelings of the public or prove themselves *careless of character*. If the lower orders of society should once think themselves insulted by the vices as well as arrogance of those who are called *noble* and the *great*, the political superstition which has hitherto been their security may suddenly fade away to their certain humiliation, if not to their destruction.[27]

There were two objects behind this particular message. First, the Anglo-Irish ascendancy was being warned to expect popular violence if they did not make timely concessions. And, secondly, the lower orders themselves were asked to draw attention to the profligacy and arrogance of a parasitic, hereditary ruling class. This theme, that the days of aristocratic tyranny were numbered, was frequently highlighted in the columns of the *Northern Star*: 'Despotism has been the downfall of the greatest empires in the world. The promoters of it, therefore, in all countries ought to be the objects of public vengeance.'[28]

This epigrammatic programme of political education for the masses was very effective. While the complexities and intricacies of radical Enlightenment thought were sacrificed in these oversimplified, brief, and occasionally clever messages, the basic principles of the Irish radicals were none the less clearly conveyed. Reason and the natural rights of all mankind dictated a reform of the political system which would give due weight and influence to the people. Aristocratic and hereditary government was an irrational, absurd violation of these principles. Critics of this system could be heartened in knowing that the progress of human liberty was inevitable, and yet reformers should not sit by idly and wait for events to overtake them.

---

[26] *NS*, 7 Mar. 1792.   [27] *NS*, 25 Feb. 1792.   [28] *NS*, 3 Mar. 1792.

Rather, they must form ranks in the vanguard of human progress and hasten the dawn of liberty in Ireland.

Perhaps one of the most inspired techniques for arousing the interest of the mass public, literate and illiterate, was the serialization in the pages of the *Northern Star* of popular, entertaining, but fundamentally didactic literature such as *A faithful report of the trial of Hurdy Gurdy, Review of the lion of old England, or democracy confounded*, both of which appeared in 1794, and Porter's *Billy Bluff and the squire*, which diverted the *Northern Star*'s readers from May to December 1796. The liveliness of these productions helps to explain the popularity of the paper and its effectiveness as a propaganda organ.

More convincing evidence of the *Northern Star*'s influence and its radical content is provided by the government's repeated attempts to suppress it as the voice of radical opposition in Ireland. As one Belfast loyalist observed to Dublin Castle: 'That the proprietors of the *Northern Star*, with the lower orders of the people at their backs, have done much harm to their country is a fact [which] cannot be denied.'[29] General Lake strongly urged the Castle administration to allow him to silence the paper. 'Surely,' he insisted in April 1797, 'the *Northern Star* should be stopped. The mischief that it does is beyond imagination.'[30] Twice the government called the proprietors of the *Northern Star* before the bar to answer charges of seditious libel, the first time in January 1793 for publication of the radical address of the Irish Jacobins, and the second time in November 1794 for printing the inflammatory 'Address to the Volunteers of Ireland'.[31] In both cases the proprietors were acquitted, but such harassment took its toll in onerous legal expenses. Neilson was forced to take over sole proprietorship of the paper, which was designed to produce propaganda, not a profit. Fortunately for the United Irishmen, Neilson possessed a modest fortune which he selflessly placed at the disposal of the radical cause.

Having failed to silence the *Northern Star* by using the proper legal channels, the government turned next, in September 1796, to arresting its editor and proprietor. As the clear leader of the radical movement in Belfast, Neilson was, of course, an obvious candidate for detention when the government, with material supplied by an informer, attempted to destroy the republican conspiracy by cutting off its head. Neilson was arrested not solely because he was the *Northern Star*'s proprietor, therefore, though the coincidence was not regretted by the authorities. But the radical conspiracy

[29] —— to Dublin Castle, [1796] (SPOI, Rebellion papers, 620/54/29).

[30] Gen. Gerard Lake to Thomas Pelham, 16 Apr. 1797 (BL, Pelham papers, Add. MS 33103/361–2).

[31] See William Sampson, *A faithful report of the second trial of the proprietors of the 'Northern Star' at the bar of the court of king's bench on the 17th of November, 1794* (Belfast, 1795); id., *A faithful report of the trial of the proprietors of the 'Northern Star' at the bar of the court of king's bench on the twenty-eight of May 1794* (Belfast, 1794).

in the north proved to be a Hydra-headed monster, for no sooner had the government arrested the first cadre of leaders than another stepped in to take its place. And so, too, with the *Northern Star*, for after Neilson's arrest, the management of the paper passed into the hands of the brothers William and Robert Simms.

By then, of course, the *Northern Star* was taking on the character of more than an opposition newspaper and, in the government's eyes, was becoming a forum for outright treasonable declamations. The last straw was Arthur O'Connor's address to the electors of County Antrim. O'Connor, a recent but avid recruit to the cause of republicanism in Ireland, chose to contest a parliamentary seat in County Antrim in the 1797 general election. He published his address in the *Northern Star* in January 1797, registering unequivocally his opposition to the war with France: 'Never will I seek your confidence by supporting a war that has been undertaken for the destruction of liberty abroad and for the preservation of a system of corruption at home.' More inflammatory was his open espousal of republican principles: 'If to promote the UNION of IRISHMEN be treason, and if to place the liberties of my country on its TRUE REPUBLICAN BASIS be treason, then I do glory in being a traitor—it is a treason I will seal with my blood, and that I hope to have engraved on my tomb.'[32] So indiscreet was this utterance that Martha McTier suspected that O'Connor was actually trying to provoke the government into arresting him. 'It is not a rash paper that is written in a hurry,' she remarked to Drennan. 'It has been the result both of thought and consultation, and I think the *present* effect must either be a king's messenger or the avowed cowardice of government.'[33] Certainly, O'Connor had no interest in continuing his parliamentary career. Like his friend Lord Edward Fitzgerald, he had joined the republican movement out of conviction that the Irish parliament would never reform itself. Clearly, his decision to stand for County Antrim in the election was based on his desire to find an appropriate platform from which to disseminate republican propaganda and, perhaps more importantly, to provoke a government response which would expose the tyrannical nature of the present system.[34] Perhaps O'Connor did wish to bring about his own arrest, thus setting in motion an agitation that might surpass that which had greeted the British ministry when it attempted to thwart the wishes of the electorate in the case of John Wilkes. And the government played into O'Connor's hands. In February 1797 he was arrested in Dublin, and

[32] Arthur O'Connor's 'Address to the electors of the county of Antrim' (SPOI, Rebellion papers, 620/26/123).
[33] Martha McTier to Drennan, 30 Jan. 1797 (*Drennan letters*, 249).
[34] Frank MacDermot, 'Arthur O'Connor', *Irish Historical Studies*, 16/57 (Mar. 1966), 54–5.

Colonel Lucius Barber in Belfast was ordered to raid the offices of the *Northern Star* and to arrest the Simms brothers.[35]

This was the second government raid on the *Northern Star's* office; the first had occurred when Neilson was arrested in September 1796. But it was not to be the last. The paper was revived once again, this time under the management of Thomas Corbett. The County Derry magistrate Sir George F. Hill deplored the missed opportunity to shut down the *Northern Star's* presses forever. Drennan, O'Connor, and all the men involved in the *Northern Star* should be sent 'to Botany Bay without any other trial than an act of parliament'.[36] But having already arrested a candidate for parliamentary office and closed down, at least temporarily, a popular newspaper, the government was, as yet, unprepared to risk its reputation for maintaining the liberties of the subject by resorting to such extraordinary means. Nevertheless, the days of the *Northern Star* were obviously numbered. In March 1797 Martha McTier told her brother that 'the *Star* office, I suspect, will be a third time stormed.'[37]

Now the government found new allies in its campaign against the radical press in Belfast—the Monaghan militiamen, many of whom had barely escaped the fate of their comrades who were executed at Blaris camp in May 1797. With the zeal of the newly converted, these repentant loyalists staged a riot in Belfast, attacking the homes of known or suspected republicans and, of course, the offices of the *Northern Star* itself.[38] The paper was never to recover from this last assault. And while public opinion expressed outrage at this attack on the freedom of the press in Ireland, and while Castle officials publicly deplored the overzealous actions of the militiamen, privately, loyalists were highly pleased. 'I have extreme satisfaction', declared General Lake in reporting the incident to Dublin Castle.[39] The authorities, of course, did not initiate the attack, but they could hardly disapprove of its results. The lusty voice of radical opposition in the north of Ireland had been silenced after five and a half years. Sir George F. Hill of Derry communicated to Cooke his relief that the *Northern Star* had finally been suppressed, and his observations provide a fitting obituary for the demise of this influential radical paper: 'If the *Northern Star* had continued, you never would have broken thro' the ranks of the rebels; they have nothing now to cheer them, and if it again is suffered to appear, on your heads be the consequences.'[40]

---

[35] Col. Lucius Barber to Edward Cooke, 3 Feb. 1797 (SPOI, Rebellion papers, 620/28/199, 200).

[36] Sir George F. Hill to Edward Cooke, 9 Feb. 1797 (ibid. 620/28/241).

[37] Martha McTier to Drennan, 17 Mar. [1797] (*Drennan letters*, 253).

[38] Martha McTier to Drennan, [19 May 1797] (ibid. 256); Thomas Lane to marquess of Downshire, 25 May 1797 (PRONI, Downshire papers, D607/E/266).

[39] Quoted in Brian Inglis, *The freedom of the press in Ireland, 1784–1841* (London, 1954), 97.

[40] Hill to Cooke, [?] June 1797 (SPOI, Rebellion papers, 620/31/182).

Perhaps it was appropriate that, at around the same time as the leadership of the United Irish movement was passing from Belfast to Dublin, so too, because of the *Northern Star*'s demise, did the United Irish press. The *Northern Star* was silenced, but the need for a radical newspaper was as great as ever, and Dublin republicans turned their attention to launching its successor, the *Press*, which made its début in September 1797. For a long time the United Irishmen were unable to exploit the press in Dublin as successfully as they had done in Belfast. Two newspapers in the capital were staunch supporters of the administration—*Faulkner's Dublin Journal*, edited by the government agent John Giffard, and *Freeman's Journal*, controlled by the infamous 'sham squire', Francis Higgins.[41] The circulation of these papers was not impressive, but they enjoyed considerable financial support from the government. Opposition papers included Peter Cooney's *Morning Post*, Thomas McDonnel's *Hibernian Journal*, and John Magee's *Evening Post*. While remaining independent of specific political organizations, these men sympathized with the cause of reform. Eventually, their displays of solidarity resulted in government prosecutions for seditious libel.[42] Nevertheless, the need for a uniquely United Irish newspaper was keenly felt by Dublin radicals.

Between 1791 and 1793 the *Rights of Irishmen, or National Evening Star* advanced the cause of the United Irishmen in Dublin, but government harassment of its founder, William Paulet Carey, and its subsequent proprietor, Randall McAllister, contributed to the paper's demise. Early in May 1793 the *Northern Star* announced that the *National Evening Star*, unable to withstand these assaults by the administration, had ceased publication.[43]

The Catholic Committee sitting in Dublin also attempted to establish an official newspaper to promote their cause in the early 1790s. In collaboration with the more pro-Catholic of the United Irishmen, they succeeded in launching a newspaper called the *National Journal*, which appeared from February to June 1792.[44] The sponsors apparently failed to find a suitable editor. Both Russell and Tone had been approached, but they declined. Indeed, the large number of proprietors—twenty, who had each put up £50 for the enterprise—precluded any consensus on the editorial content or management of the paper.[45] The newspaper, when it did appear, was woefully deficient, at least according to that doyen of the politically radical literati, Drennan. He dismissed the effort as 'bad and the printing often inaccurate'.[46]

[41] W. J. Fitzpatrick, '*The sham squire' and the informers of 1798, with jottings about Ireland a century ago* (3rd ed., Dublin, n.d.).
[42] Stewart, 'Irish press', 511–15; Inglis, *Freedom of the press*, 86–7.
[43] NS, 4 Jan. 1793; Inglis, *Freedom of the press*, 64–5.
[44] Drennan to McTier, [June or July] 1792 (*Drennan letters*, 89).
[45] Inglis, *Freedom of the press*, 99.
[46] Drennan to McTier, [Feb.] 1792 (*Drennan letters*, 83).

It was not until 1797 that the United Irishmen in Dublin could claim a significant newspaper of their own. The suppression of the *Northern Star* in May 1797 spurred the Dublin radicals into launching a successor. Under the nominal proprietorship of Peter Finnerty, but sponsored by such republican luminaries as Arthur O'Connor, Thomas Addis Emmet, and Lord Edward Fitzgerald, the *Press* made its début in Dublin on 28 September 1797 and enjoyed considerable influence until it, too, was silenced in March 1798.[47] This, of course, was inevitable if the *Press* was to fulfil its role as the voice of radical Ireland. The fastidious Drennan was quite impressed with the new paper, but warned that, in fact, it was too good: 'It will be put down, and perhaps this is the great reason for putting it up, to exhibit the impracticability of writing freely at present in public print. And rich men will throw away some guineas to show this, tho' I think it was plain enough before.'[48]

Perhaps this truth was plain enough to the radicals themselves, but in the war for public opinion it could not be overstated. The purpose of the new paper was avowedly 'to extinguish party animosities, and introduce a cordial UNION of ALL the PEOPLE on a basis of toleration and equal government'. This, of course, was the proclaimed aim of all United Irish publications and activities. But perhaps the real purpose of the *Press* was to get itself put down by the government, as Drennan maintained, to put the British constitution's ever-lauded liberty of the press to the test in Ireland. In the last few years, only one newspaper in Ireland had dared to take a strong line independent of the administration, and this paper, the *Northern Star*, was 'put down by military interposition', thus proving to the radicals' satisfaction that liberty of the press was a sham in their country. 'No maxim is more true than this, "that no liberty can survive the liberty of the press",' the *Press* declared in its first issue:

But it must be acknowledged that by some fatality of late, the press in this harassed country has been either negligent or apostate. . . . So many and so sad have been the apostacies which have taken place in this respect, that a skepticism humiliating and derogatory to the Irish character has obtained, and the best disposed men, with great reason, have been led to doubt the existence of a pure patriotism, unalloyed by a mixture of the selfish passions; they have seen the press introduced to them in all the charms of a virtuous virgin, shortly degenerate and receive the private embraces of the minister behind the curtain—or act the bolder part of a public prostitute.[49]

But did Irishmen need to be convinced that their press was shackled by a corrupt administration? Certainly, the harassment and eventual destruction of the people's tribune, the *Northern Star*, had proved that this was so. To

---

[47] Inglis, *Freedom of the press*, 98–104.
[48] William Drennan to Martha McTier, 29 Oct. 1797 (PRONI, Drennan papers, T765/677).
[49] *Press*, 28 Sept. 1797.

whom, then, was the *Press* addressing its remarks? The Irish people, or at least those likely to sympathize with the radical cause, were well aware that the freedom of the press was a dead letter. The administration could not be moved by such protests. In fact, these lamentations about the loss of liberty in Ireland were directed across the Irish Sea to the opposition whigs in England.

Both O'Connor and Fitzgerald were intimates of the opposition politicians in England and were particularly related, by ties of blood and affection, to the Holland House circle led by Charles James Fox, which was almost alone in its opposition to Pitt's foreign and domestic policies.[50] The names of these two eminent and well-connected Irishmen lent considerable respectability to the Irish radical cause in the eyes of opposition politicians at Westminster. And O'Connor attempted to exploit this aura of respectability in launching his newspaper. The *Press* would present the acceptable face of Irish radicalism in contest with the unacceptable face of Castle tyranny. In courting the English whigs, O'Connor and his colleagues recognized that the alternative United Irish strategies were losing ground. The administration's ruthless endeavours to suppress radicalism in Ireland, its reign of terror in the north, capped by the suppression of the *Northern Star*, made it patently clear that concessions would never be granted by the Irish government. Irish radicals still aggressively pursued a French alliance, but they were increasingly frustrated, especially in that year of lost opportunity, 1797.[51] France's failure to exploit the Nore and Spithead mutinies of the British fleet in the summer of 1797 was a discouraging blow for their Irish partisans. Thus, one of the tactics pursued by the radicals in their reformist phase reappeared in the disappointing year of 1797: apply pressure on Pitt to alter the basis upon which Ireland was governed. Pitt would not be moved by Irish public opinion, as his recall of the popular Fitzwilliam had demonstrated. But perhaps he could be swayed by English public opinion marshalled behind the cause of reform in Ireland.

The great attention that was paid to the literary quality of the *Press* suggests that it was designed to appeal to a more refined public in Ireland and Great Britain. The *Northern Star* had emphasized plain talk for plain people, while the *Press* filled its columns with countless literary allusions and a florid prose style intended to impress the most cultivated sensibility. Moreover, the first issue of the *Press* set out to appeal to the sympathies of the British public by juxtaposing the virtues of English government with the vices of the Irish administration. Irishmen were not intent on establishing a Jacobinical tyranny hostile to British interests, or so the *Press* implied in its

---

[50] Arthur O'Connor to Charles James Fox, 24 Dec. 1796 (SPOI, Rebellion papers, 620/15/3/7).

[51] See Marianne Elliott, *Partners in revolution: the United Irishmen and France* (New Haven, Conn., and London, 1982), 124–62.

prospectus. Rather, they sought to secure for themselves the same rights and freedoms as those enjoyed by British citizens. If imitation is the highest form of flattery, the proprietors of the *Press* hoped to flatter English politicians into reforming Ireland. The first issue of the *Press* sharply contrasted the condition of Ireland with that of England:

In England the great body of the people have some interest in the soil; there are few so wretchedly poor as not to have something worth defending. The national religion is that professed and established by government. Landed property is held by the tenure of family successions. The chief magistrate is a native; the ministers who compose his council are natives; they have no interest to prefer to that of the country which they govern. They have a common cause with the people and a great security in the complete cooperation of almost all the more wealthy and exalted persons.

Thus, in this idealized and flattering account of English society, the *Press* appealed to the whig principle that a society's natural rulers (i.e. the aristocracy) were the true guarantors of liberty, property, and good government.

In Ireland, on the contrary, the great body of the people have no interest whatever in the soil; there are not many so far above absolute poverty as to have anything worth defending. The religion professed by government and established by law is not that of the majority of the people. Much landed property is held by the tenure of forfeitures and confiscations. The chief magistrate is not a native; the ministers who compose his councils are not natives. They have an interest to take care of separate from, and possibly incompatible with that of the country which they govern and which they may prefer. They can of course have no common cause with the people and have not a shadow of security in their affections, since it is clear that they are only kept in obedience at the point of a bayonet.

What might be the result of these glaring inequities between the sister kingdoms? England would lose Ireland to France. Injustice in Ireland made her vulnerable to a foreign invasion. If England should lose Ireland, she 'would lose her right arm'. If only for their own security, Englishmen should put pressure on Pitt to institute good government in Ireland:

Common sense suggests that if invasion is likely to take place or be attempted, nothing will be so likely to flatter the hopes of the enemy as information that administration, instead of uniting the people of all persuasions—chooses to pass by some millions of Dissenters and Catholics—and to risque the event with mercenary forces and a few troops of *chosen* religion.[52]

Thus, as the Americans had done before them, the Irish radicals who sponsored the *Press* sought to present the righteousness of their cause to Englishmen in terms that their audience could not, in good conscience,

[52] *Press*, 28 Sept. 1797.

reject. What else did they want, after all, but to enjoy those liberties of the citizen enshrined in the glorious British constitution? O'Connor and the other writers in the *Press* therefore sought to show how these freedoms had been eroded in Ireland. It was illiberal government and not French-inspired conspiracies that created discontent in Ireland and thus threatened British security interests. The *Press* detailed the loss of those liberties taken for granted by British citizens but denied to Irishmen by the self-interested administration—trial by jury, the rights of petitioning and assembling, the right to bear arms. And if the record of their sins thus paraded for public scrutiny provoked the administration into silencing its opposition, the *Press* and its proprietors would effectively prove to English sympathizers that freedom of the press was held in low regard by the narrow interest which governed Ireland. The Castle press and the authorities would falsely accuse Irish patriots of treason and sedition when, in fact, their only crime was to seek for themselves the same rights as those enjoyed by Englishmen.

Thus, in this first issue of the *Press*, the Irish radicals attempted to confirm what opposition whigs in England were already too happy to believe—that the Irish agitation was fundamentally inspired by a desire to reform the system, that Jacobin agitators in its ranks were the rare exception, and that such crimes of terror and sedition which could be laid at their door were actually provoked by the government's insensitive and Draconian rule. For the British opposition, the crisis in Ireland was more than an internal struggle within the sister kingdom. If Irish civil liberties could so easily be trampled underfoot by the executive power, would Britons themselves long enjoy the protection of their own glorious constitution? The persistence of illiberal government in Ireland would soon tear to shreds the fabric of British constitutional liberty. That moderate, respectable, and propertied men led and controlled the Irish reform movement was confirmed by the presence of O'Connor and Fitzgerald at the forefront of the campaign. Furthermore, in May 1797 the Irish whigs themselves, led by Grattan, Ponsonby, and Curran, announced their determination to withdraw from parliament in protest against ruthless misgovernment. 'Having no hopes left to persuade or dissuade,' Grattan proclaimed, 'and having discharged our duties, we shall trouble you no more; and after this day shall not attend the house of commons.'[53]

The opposition whigs at Westminster were delighted to have a further charge to lay at the feet of the apparently impregnable prime minister. Since the beginning of the French revolution, whig supporters had been rallying to the new tory party led by Pitt, the most grievous blow being the adhesion of the Portland whigs to the ministry in the summer of 1794.

---

[53] Quoted in W. E. H. Lecky, *A history of Ireland in the eighteenth century* (5 vols., London, 1898), iv. 73.

Their enforced years in the political wilderness might be shortened, however, if the opposition whigs could attack the prime minister for an illiberal
Irish policy which, by implication, threatened English political and civil liberties. Late in 1797 the liberal Lord Moira called for an investigation into
the deepening crisis in Ireland, laying before the British and Irish houses of
lords a catalogue of outrages committed against the people by the government and its loyal supporters.[54] The British government refused to countenance such an inquiry. Nevertheless, Moira's accusations proved acutely
embarrassing not only to Pitt, but to the Irish administration as well. They
weathered the storm, however, and the debates in College Green and at
Westminster ended with overwhelming support for the measures of coercion in Ireland.

Although the assault on Pitt's government failed, it revealed the willingness of the British whigs and Irish radicals to co-operate with one another
if it suited their respective purposes. Clearly, the whigs were willing to
overlook the obvious republican and Jacobin-inspired tendencies of the
Irish agitators. Indeed, the ammunition for Moira's attack on Pitt's Irish
policy came from the United Irishmen themselves. The radical barrister
William Sampson supplied the information about government outrages to
the noble earl himself, and had established his Society for Obtaining
Authentic Information of Outrages Committed on the People in part for
this purpose. Associated in this effort were such eminent Irish whigs as
Grattan, the Ponsonbys, and Curran, thus representing that broad alliance
of English and Irish whigs and respectable United Irishmen which provided
the acceptable façade of Irish radicalism. Moira would take the issue to the
British and Irish parliaments, while Sampson would use the information in
the *Press*. United Irish propaganda had succeeded in convincing the whigs
that the persistence of a coercive and ruthless government policy against the
people would soon goad them into rebellion. Since the parliamentary opposition in both countries was, by itself, incapable of curbing these tyrannical
and destructive tendencies of the administration, an alternative strategy to
restrain the government had to be found. This alternative was to publicize
the findings of Sampson's investigatory society in the *Press* and, 'by the dis-
closure of these enormities, to restrain the perpetrators of them and to render it impossible for the government, which had hitherto connived at these
proceedings, to plead ignorance of them'.[55] In a letter to Lord Moira,
Sampson reiterated the point, implicating the earl himself in the strategy
adopted: 'The use of the *Press* was to publish those facts, of which you
were desirous also to be the publisher—the suppression and subsequent

---

[54] See *The debate in the Irish house of peers on a motion made by the earl of Moira, Monday,
February 19, 1798* (Dublin, 1798).
[55] Madden, *United Irishmen* (12 vols., New York, 1916), iv. 36.

impunity of which you seemed to foresee, as well as I did, would lead to rebellion.'[56]

The problem with this broadly aligned whiggish assault on Pitt and his Irish policy was that it proved ineffective. The British whigs persisted in painting Irish radicals in reformist colours, despite the great pains that the administrations of both countries took to disabuse them of such misguided notions. The report of the secret committee of the Irish house of lords in 1797 attempted to show clear links between Irish radicalism and French republicanism, yet the alarm fell on deaf ears. Even O'Connor's arrest at Margate early in 1798 and evidence that he was, in fact, on his way to negotiate an invasion with the French Directory did not turn the Foxite whigs against the Irish radicals.[57] Rather, they rallied around O'Connor at his trial in the following May, desperate to acquire some political capital with which to outbid Pitt for the support of parliamentary backbenchers.

Of course, the United Irishmen quickly realized that the game was over soon after it had begun. They already had sufficient evidence that Pitt would be moved by neither the Irish people nor his parliamentary opposition into imposing unwanted reforms on the ascendancy. Nor would he threaten English control over the sister kingdom by establishing a popular government in Ireland. Yet the radicals would not spurn the misguided and ineffectual sympathy from British opposition politicians. Such support, however incapable of bringing about desired policy changes, nevertheless added respectability to a movement which the administration was trying to paint as subversive of both government and property. Furthermore, the whigs might succeed in restraining the forces of coercion in Ireland which were sapping republican strength. So, while the columns of the *Press* offered ammunition to English whigs in their campaign to embarrass the prime minister, the United Irishmen realized that insurrection alone—quick and bloodless, it was hoped—would secure their objectives. And to bring this day of reckoning closer, the *Press* played its part.

The *Press* was concerned with establishing a reputation for literary excellence which would add to the intellectual and social status of the United Irish movement, but it also had to serve as an organ for the political education of Irishmen in general, especially after the abrupt demise of the *Northern Star*. The principal aim of this political education was to persuade Irishmen that insurrection was their only form of redress. Thus the *Press* became increasingly intemperate and vigorous in its attacks on the govern-

---

[56] William Sampson, *Memoirs of William Sampson, an Irish exile, written by himself* (London, 1832), 16–17.

[57] See MacDermot, 'Arthur O'Connor', 58–60; James Gurney, *The trial of James O'Coigly, otherwise called James Quigley, otherwise called James John Fivey, Arthur O'Connor, Esq., John Binns, John Allen, and Jeremiah Leary for high treason under a special commission at Maidstone in Kent on Monday the twenty-first and Tuesday the twenty-second days of May 1798* (London, 1798). O'Connor was acquitted.

ment. This in turn reflected the heightened urgency with which the United Irishmen were preparing for rebellion, both in their negotiations with the French and in their efforts to mobilize the south into a revolutionary organization. The executive directory of the United Irishmen, centred in Dublin, controlled the editorial content of the *Press*, and though the directory was divided over the question of whether to wait for the French or to rise without them, there were some fundamental themes which they agreed to highlight in the newspaper.

As in all their propaganda, the United Irishmen exploited those fears which had been engendered in the population by the ruthlessness of the government's counter-insurgency policy. The catalogue of outrages collected by Sampson, many of them only too true, even if others were fabricated, received prominence in the columns of the *Press*, impressing upon its readers the real physical dangers that they faced if illiberal government continued in Ireland. Those who had witnessed the excesses of Orangemen, magistrates, and soldiers were invited to send their accounts to the office of the *Press*, which then printed the reports of such incidents in its columns. For example, on 3 March 1798 the *Press* reported a 'roasting' at Castleward, County Down, where a father and son had their heads roasted on an open fire to extort a confession regarding concealed arms. There followed the distressful tale of one Ruddy, a 'wealthy man' in Dungannon. The Orangemen had gone on a rampage, burning down two Catholic chapels before they attacked the house of Ruddy. 'In attempting to save his daughter from their brutal lust, [Ruddy] was killed by the blow of a hatchet. They afterwards set fire to his house and that of his son's [*sic*] and consumed the whole of their property.'[58] In this brief description the *Press* was able to convey a vivid image of government terror and to expose the authorities as violators of the fundamental liberties of all Irishmen. The fact that Ruddy was a wealthy and respectable man showed the Orangemen's disdain for the rights of property. Their burning of chapels displayed their bigotry and their fundamentally irreligious tendencies. And, of course, the rape of Ruddy's daughter was a further testimony to the inhumanity and brutality of the loyalists as well as a reminder of the fate which might await all fair Irish maidens if government licentiousness was allowed to go unchecked by strong republican resistance. With such accounts, the *Press* eagerly played the Orange card in order to attract frightened Catholics to the cause and to taint the government further by exposing its barbarous champions. On 12 October 1797 its editors fabricated and printed the oath of the allegedly government-sponsored Orange Order: 'I, A. B., do hereby swear that I will be true to king and government, and that I will *exterminate as far as I am able the Catholics of*

---

[58] *Press*, 30 Jan., 3 Mar. 1798.

Ireland.[59] This deliberate and calculated attempt to drive alarmed Catholics into the republican movement in search of protection contributed greatly to the bloody sectarian nature of the rebellion of 1798, and it called into question the lofty non-sectarianism of the United Irish movement. To claim that the protestant Orangemen, in league with the protestant government, were bent on a genocidal policy against Catholics inflamed confessional fears and hostilities. It was an easy step to see all protestants as Orangemen, and, consequently, as malevolent in their intentions towards Catholics. Such fears, planted in the popular mind, would then go a long way in justifying the massacres of protestants at Scullabogue and Wexford Bridge, massacres which disgusted the very authors of these paranoid fantasies.

The *Press* sought to strike the chord of fear among militiamen as well, in an effort to bring them into the United Irish fold. On 5 December 1797 it announced that Pitt's government intended to release the Irish militia for foreign service, a clear violation of the militia act and a great concern which had fed the anti-militia riots which greeted the act in 1793. But 'without an act of parliament they dare not attempt it, as they know well that the Irish militia, in so just a cause, would resist force by force and be supported in such resistance by every honest man in the nation.'[60]

While the *Press* thus sought to instil fear of the government among potential supporters of the republican movement, it also hoped to alarm the government itself about the consequences of its ruthless policies. An oft-repeated theme in the *Press* was that insurrection was inevitable, and that those responsible for its imminent arrival were not the people's tribunes, the United Irishmen, but the government itself. Of course, this was also the message to be sent to whig sympathizers as well, but even they must have been alarmed at the sanguinary threats which appeared in the columns of the *Press*. On that day when Erin's oppressed sons would take the field, 'Tyrants' blood in streams shall flow, | Prostrate fall the haughty foe.'[61] The people had been so severely oppressed by their rulers that such a reign of terror was to be expected following a successful revolution in Ireland. The *Press*, however, sought to soften the hearts of a rightfully vengeful people: 'They may, perhaps, soon have an opportunity of shewing, by acts of mercy and forgiveness more sublime than fortune has yet put into their power to exercise, that virtue which it shall be our province to cultivate and foster.'[62] In modifying its predictions of the popular fury to be unleashed against Ireland's governors by calling for the exercise of 'the delightful prerogative of tempering justice with mercy', the *Press* called its readers' attention to three points.[63] First, insurrection was inevitable. Secondly, it was justified by repeated and systematic government tyranny.

[59] *Press*, 12 Oct. 1797.   [60] *Press*, 5 Dec. 1797.   [61] *Press*, 30 Nov. 1797.
[62] *Press*, 16 Jan. 1798.   [63] *Press*, 26 Dec. 1797.

And, thirdly, and this was implied, the insurrection would lead to a reign of terror unless tempered by the reasoned and moderate leadership of the middle-class United Irishmen. The revolution was inevitable, but it could prove to be as bloodless as the glorious one of 1688 if the government would cease its campaign of violence against the people and join the United Irish leaders in carrying through peacefully a restructuring of the system of government in Ireland on a popular basis.

The assertion that revolution was inevitable was designed not only to alarm the government and its supporters, but also to encourage United Irish sympathizers with the notion that success was a certainty. The dire warnings of what might befall Ireland's deposed rulers were always accompanied with the calm assurance that fallen they would be:

Above all, do not despond of the republic. Believe me, it shall not be lost. The present silence of the people is not the silence of fear and despondence but of discretion—the public cause is not abandoned, notwithstanding the terrors of military execution, etc., but the day must come when the people shall firmly rally round the constitution and range themselves boldly under the standard of freedom.[64]

The *Press* took great pains to assert that nearly all the people had already rallied to the United Irish cause. The United Irishmen, the paper maintained, 'steadily kept their ground; they have been, like the early Christians, persecuted, put to death and torture—they have still persevered. . . . We believe they are now, with the exception of a few thousands, commensurate with the population of the nation.'[65]

The forces arrayed against tyranny in Ireland were truly formidable:

The Catholics and Presbyterians are united in indissoluble ties, dying like martyrs in a common cause, priding themselves in mutual good offices, and forever adjuring the barbarous fanaticism that made them hate each other. From the protestants of the establishment every man of worth, of talent, or of honour has ranged himself by their side, and nothing remains now against *Irish union* but 25,000, as near as may be, of bigots, hirelings, and dependents—just enough to furnish the lord lieutenant with addresses.[66]

This deliberate exaggeration of the strength of the United Irish movement was calculated to obscure the real state of affairs—that the movement was in turmoil as a result of internal dissensions, the failure of the French to appear, and the success of the government in subduing the conspiracy in the north. The decision to rise in 1798 was particularly urgent because of this rapid waning of United Irish fortunes. If they waited much longer, the United Irishmen would see their support further eroded. The organization, such as it was, might not last until the promised French invasion arrived. But the columns of the *Press* revealed none of this uncertainty. In fact, they

[64] *Press*, 21 Nov. 1797.   [65] *Press*, 16 Jan. 1798.   [66] *Press*, 19 Dec. 1797.

contradicted government claims that its campaign against the seditious was
succeeding, and assured readers that the United Irish movement was going
from strength to strength:

The cant of the day with our faithful rulers and their parasites is that *the north* is
now quiet and has resumed its industry. The fact is, the north had no disturbances,
save those carried on by the Orangemen and General L[ake]. . . . But the idea
intended to be conveyed to the south by this cant is that the northerners have withdrawn from the public cause.[67]

Clearly, the government could not continue to tolerate a newspaper
which repeatedly legitimized and encouraged rebellion in Ireland. The *Press*
declared: 'What a people can do, the people of North America have done;
what a people ought to do, the people of Ireland are considering.'[68] The
fact that the *Press* was so influential added urgency to the government's
desire to suppress it. And the paper itself was fully aware that its days were
numbered: 'The *Press* will continue to its last hour to despise its adversaries, and be it silenced when it may, it will live in the remembrance of
Irishmen, whose union is now complete, who know their duties and will
perform them.'[69] In taking a bold and vigorous stand against the coercive
policy of the Irish administration, the *Press* might hope to temper government harassment of the republican movement. This was only a faint hope,
but it suited the propagandist purposes of the newspaper to highlight this
aim. Realistically, however, the best that it could do was to provoke the
administration into further reaction, thus exposing its tyrannical tendencies,
which in turn would lend legitimacy to the insurrectionary movement. It
was as if the proprietors of the newspaper were handing the government
the hammer with which to pound the final nail into the coffin of freedom
of the press in Ireland.

No sooner, then, had the government breathed a sigh of relief at the suppression of the obnoxious *Northern Star* than an even more troublesome
paper appeared in the capital. The Castle quickly determined on its destruction, at first by petty harassment and finally by outright suppression. The
administration secured the imprisonment of the editor of the *Press*, Charles
Brennan, for debt, hoping to persuade him to betray the proprietors.
Brennan attempted to blackmail O'Connor into relieving him of his financial difficulties, and when O'Connor refused, Brennan carried out his threat
and provided the government with information about the newspaper.
Contributors were spied upon, carriers were assaulted, and information of
a clearly libellous nature was planted so as to give the government cause to
prosecute the *Press*.[70] A little more than a month after the appearance of

[67] *Press*, 6 Mar. 1798.   [68] *Press*, 22 Feb. 1798.
[69] *Press*, 22 Feb. 1798.   [70] Inglis, *Freedom of the press*, 100–1.

the first issue, Peter Finnerty, the nominal proprietor, was arrested on the charge of exciting sedition.

Finnerty's offence was to question the justice of the execution of the celebrated United Irish martyr William Orr, who had been found guilty of administering the republican oath, a capital offence under the insurrection act. Following his report that Orr's jurors had been plied with spirits to produce a guilty verdict, Finnerty was successfully prosecuted by the attorney-general and sentenced to two years in prison. During the trial the *Press* missed one issue, and it looked as if the government might succeed in silencing this organ of sedition. Arthur O'Connor, however, stepped into the breach in December 1797 to assume the nominal as well as the real proprietorship of the paper. Immediately, the circulation figures of the *Press* climbed from an impressive 3,000 to an astonishing 6,000, a testament to O'Connor's reputation.[71]

Having survived this first major assault, the *Press*, reflecting O'Connor's own growing militancy, became even more intemperate in its bold attacks on the Castle. In February 1798, while O'Connor was in England, William Stockdale took charge of the paper and duly appeared in the dock for printing aspersions against a supporter of the administration. He was found guilty and was sentenced to an excessive six months' imprisonment for what would normally have been regarded as a modest offence. Again, the *Press* ceased publication temporarily, but reappeared in early March, much to the government's frustration. The paper was now carried on by William Dowdall, a former secretary to Henry Grattan. O'Connor's arrest in England in late February had provided Camden and his associates with the excuse that they needed to silence this troublesome and seditious organ once and for all. A warrant was issued to this effect, and in mid-March 1798 the military was dispatched to the *Press* office to seize copies of the paper and destroy the presses. Although the attack was planned anyway, the nominal pretext was the inflammatory nature of the last issue, 68, which contained an address to the 'author of coercion', presumed to be the lord chancellor, Lord Clare, and which had been penned by the incarcerated Thomas Russell:[72]

I know, my lord, you plume yourself on the imaginary safety of your situation. But pride not yourself any longer on that circumstance; deceive yourself no more; I tell you, you are in danger: think not to screen yourself behind the shield of parliamentary support; repose not on your delusive promises of military protection; they will avail you nothing in the dread moment of national retribution, and amid the

---

[71] Madden, *United Irishmen* (1916 edn.), iv. 31.

[72] Camden had decided to close down the *Press* when O'Connor was arrested. His decision was confirmed by the inclusion in the paper of the 'most shocking exhortation to assassinate the chancellor, and which there is reason to believe from the manuscripts seized, was composed by Captain Russell, who has long been confined in Newgate under a charge of high treason' (Earl Camden to duke of Portland, 7 Mar. 1798 (PROHO 100/75/183–4)).

confusion of revolutionary vengeance. . . . There will be no necessity for suborned testimony or intoxicated jurymen to procure your condemnation. Ireland can afford the clearest evidence of your crimes; the unanimous voice of its inhabitants will pronounce you guilty; on such an occasion our disgust against the duty of the executioner will be suspended, and men will contend for the honour of terminating so destructive an existence.[73]

It would be difficult not to interpret this, as the government did, as a call for the assassination of the lord chancellor.

Ironically, it was just this violently provocative tone which the *Press* had attempted to counter when it first appeared in the autumn of 1797. Although the *Press* was principally established to carry on where the *Northern Star* had left off and to serve as the voice of the United Irish leadership, now centred in Dublin, there was another consideration in its founding as well. In the summer of 1797 a newspaper of sorts began to appear intermittently in the capital—the *Union Star*. It was not really a newspaper in the conventional sense; its undated issues were printed on one side of a page as handbills or broadsheets to be posted for public view. In essence, the *Union Star* purported to identify the enemies of the people in the hope that they would become targets for assassination. Each issue carried the following injunction:

As the *Union Star* is an official paper, the managers promise the public that no characters shall be hazarded through its medium but such as are denounced by authority as being the partners and creatures of Pitt and his sanguinary journeyman, Luttrell [the earl of Carhampton]. The *Star* will be published occasionally, as new and notorious characters appear, which the committee may think proper to guard the Society of United Irishmen against. The *Star* offers to public justice the following detestable traitors, spies, and perjured informers. 'Perhaps some arm more lucky than the rest may reach his heart and free the world from bondage.'[74]

There then followed one or two dozen names and descriptions of these so-called traitors to the people.

Union Star handbills carried only the list of those deemed suitable for assassination, but the broadsheets contained editorials on government policy and sang the praises of violent insurrection.

Insurrection and revenge, however decried or discountenanced by the abettors of tyranny, should always be respected by a people, as they have operated powerfully towards the preservation of liberty and the distribution of justice. . . . History ornaments her page with the bold struggles as honourable, edifying, and worthy of imitation by suffering humanity.[75]

The Irish people were ground down by a tyrannical government, and the *Union Star* highlighted the social and economic consequences of this

___

[73] *Rep. secret comm.* 274.   [74] PROHO 100/70/235.   [75] Ibid.

tyranny, addressing its remarks not to the middle-class United Irish leadership, but to the lower classes, and especially to dispossessed rural Catholics. In one issue, it condemned the confiscations of the seventeenth century and insinuated that an insurrection would return these estates to their former owners: 'The *Star* does not *unjustly* advise a thought that would injure the proprietor of an estate acquired by mercantile or mechanic industry. The *Star* [aims] only at those properties wrested from our murdered ancestors by English perfidy.'[76] Ireland was on the brink of liberation if only Irishmen would persevere: 'No more will the lazy lord enjoy the fruits of your labour and starve you into the ranks to please his ambition or extend his power.'[77]

The United Irish leaders could hardly countenance such a paper, especially since their names were directly associated with its editorial content and purpose. If the *Press* was designed to show the respectable face of Irish radicalism, the *Union Star* displayed a visage that was not only repellent to whig sympathizers with the republican cause, but the wild rantings of which were equally shocking to the United Irishmen themselves. The Irish republican leaders formally condemned the *Union Star*, decisively dissociating themselves from any connection with its unsavoury rage and its calls for widespread assassination. The United Irishmen even suggested that the *Union Star* was actually sponsored by the Castle to discredit the cause of virtuous republicanism.[78] As a propaganda weapon, the *Union Star* clearly contained ammunition that could be directed against the radicals. The government justified its Draconian measures in Ireland on the grounds that it was facing a violent and socially levelling conspiracy. The United Irishmen and the *Press* were claiming the contrary, that they sought to preserve the constitution, purified, of course, and that the government was actually goading a legitimately aggrieved people into open rebellion. The *Union Star* seemed to lend credence to the administration's claims.

Was it possible that Dublin Castle itself was manufacturing such damning material about the United Irishmen? There is no clear evidence that the government backed the newspaper. On the contrary, when it appeared in the summer of 1797, the government unleashed its kennel of informers into the capital to determine the identity of this would-be Irish Marat, the publisher of the *Union Star*, but no one was able to return with anything but unsubstantiated rumours. Finally, in December 1797, Under-secretary Cooke could report to Pelham that the *Union Star* had been suppressed. A man named Walter Cox, a gunsmith who was known to have distributed the paper, offered to disclose its author in return for a blanket pardon. Cooke agreed to Cox's terms, and was then astonished to learn that the

---

[76] SPOI, Rebellion papers, 620/54/50.   [77] PROHO 100/70/235.
[78] Edward Sproule to ——, [May 1798] (SPOI, Rebellion papers, 620/53/36); *Press*, 30 Jan. 1798.

informer himself was the sole author, printer, and publisher of the *Union Star.*[79]

Who was this Walter Cox who proved so troublesome to the authorities and republicans alike? Typical in some ways of the artisanal radical attracted to the republican movement, but never fully absorbed into the United Irish organization, Cox was first brought to the Castle's attention as a member of the Huguenots, 'a new penny club' with advanced political principles, in 1795. The Huguenots was just one of a number of working-class republican clubs in Dublin in the mid-1790s.[80] In the following year Cox was described as a member of a seditious masonic lodge, a member of the radical Telegraph Club, and a man who possessed a private press.[81] Cox's father, a bricklayer, was imprisoned by Lord Carhampton, a fact which may have accounted for the journalist's particular vendetta against the general in the pages of the *Union Star*.[82] If and when he actually joined the United Irishmen is unclear, though Cox later boasted that he had drawn up the plans for defending Dublin streets during the insurrection which were found on Lord Edward Fitzgerald when he was arrested.[83] Since many of these radical artisan clubs were either incorporated in, or at least associated with, the United Irish movement, Cox can fairly be considered a member, but it is unlikely that he ever advanced to significant office in the organization. He clearly launched the *Union Star* on his own initiative.

Francis Higgins forwarded a profile of the agitator to his patrons in Dublin Castle. Higgins had determined that Cox was a distributor of the *Union Star*, and described him as having a 'mean and despicable appearance', but also noted that he was an 'astonishing autodidact' who taught Euclid to working-class scholars.[84] A talented, if frenzied, journalist, Cox continued to pursue his new-found profession into the nineteenth century.[85] He explained to Cooke his reasons for publishing the *Union Star*. It was allegedly more 'from vanity than mischief', though Cox suggested that he had come to believe that the republican movement would ultimately fail, and by some twisted logic, or so he conveyed to the Castle official, he hoped that the violent tone of the *Union Star* would somehow serve to pre-empt an insurrection. This, of course, was a standard excuse of informers,

---

[79] Edward Cooke to Thomas Pelham, 14 Dec. 1797 (BL, Pelham papers, Add. MS 33105/262).

[80] See the collection of papers on the alleged plot of these radical clubs to seize the magazine at Phoenix Park, forwarded to Dublin Castle by Alderman James, Mar. 1796 (SPOI, Rebellion papers, 620/23/60); Cox was named as a member of the Huguenots, a so-called 'penny club' for radical artisans, established in 1795.

[81] Higgins to ——, [?] Aug. 1796 (ibid. 620/18/14).   [82] Fitzpatrick, *'Sham squire'*, 259.

[83] [Francis Higgins] to William Wickham, 10 Mar. 1798 (SPOI, Rebellion papers, 620/3/32/28).

[84] Francis Higgins to Dublin Castle, 29 Nov. 1797 (ibid. 620/36/226).

[85] Fitzpatrick, *'Sham squire'*, 258–63.

who justified their betrayal on the grounds not of forsaking reform principles, but of preventing the calamity to which those principles might lead. The self-important Cox may also have resented his exclusion from the upper ranks of the United Irish leadership in Dublin. 'He says', reported Cooke, 'they [the United Irish leaders] keep themselves behind the curtain and urge the lower classes to their destruction; and only mean to take the lead and come forward if insurrection should be successful.' Cox urged the government to publish all its damning information on the United Irishmen in the hope of forestalling their planned rebellion.[86] After receiving his pardon, Cox did offer to write anti-United Irish tracts for the government, but his offer was refused.[87] The United Irishmen suspected him of being a government agent, and in the end both sides refused to trust the disreputable, rather unbalanced, but certainly clever activist and journalist.

The involvement of the plebeian Cox in the dissemination of republican propaganda demonstrates the culmination of the process of the democratization of political culture which the United Irishmen pursued so vigorously after their foundation in 1791. When the middle-class radicals were firmly in control of the content of this programme in political education, they gloried in the rights of a free press. But when the upstart Cox entered the scene, Dublin United Irish leaders looked forward to the *Union Star*'s demise as eagerly as any Castle bureaucrat. Here was one of the dangers to the republican movement of mass involvement—the masses might well take a line independent of their leaders.

Still, some of the most impressive propaganda victories of the Irish radicals were associated with public displays of their mass support. Words alone would not intimidate the administration, nor were they sufficient to inspire confidence in ultimate success among radical followers who were asked to risk their private interests in the service of the public cause. Deeds and demonstrations of patriotic action also played a prominent role in the theatre of United Irish civic culture.

[86] Cooke to Pelham, 14 Dec. 1797 (BL, Pelham papers, Add. MS 33105/262).
[87] Walter Cox to Dublin Castle, n.d. (SPOI, Rebellion papers, 620/53/133).

9

Propaganda by Deed

THE United Irish message was not conveyed by literary productions alone. The radicals were also skilful manipulators of a sort of propaganda by deed. During their reformist phase the United Irishmen avidly exploited planned, orderly demonstrations, often celebrating the progress of the cause of liberty in revolutionary France. It did not suit the propagandist purposes of the United Irishmen and their allies in the Volunteer and the Catholic movements to be labelled as rabble-rousers. The radicals were primarily concerned to project the image of a socially respectable, disciplined, and responsible campaign for civil and political liberty. Any disorderly or riotous outbursts by the crowd would have shown that they were unable to control the popular classes, that they were dangerously tampering with a sleeping giant and encouraging a levelling spirit as well. It would serve radical purposes better if the government could witness the widespread mobilization of a disciplined and orderly urban crowd, who knew well, as the *Northern Star* observed, the difference between 'liberty and licentiousness', and who deferred to their middle-class leaders in the reform and emancipation movements.[1] The latent threat of force would be used to greatest effect here, for the radicals would be signalling to the government that they controlled the 'mob', that they had the mass of the population on their side, and that the government had better deal seriously with the middle-class reformers, or popular violence might well be unleashed.

In a sense, the Society of United Irishmen emerged from the Volunteer demonstration in Belfast on 14 July 1791 in support of the French revolution.[2] Even though this Bastille day celebration failed to provide the establishment of the new political club so desired by Irish radicals, it was nevertheless a significant propaganda event and became a model for successive demonstrations.[3] Here can be found the many tools that the United Irishmen employed in constructing an edifice of popular support. An impressive procession of Volunteers and Northern Whigs in full uniform parading through the streets of Belfast not only bound the participants together in purposive patriotic action, but also displayed the socially

---

[1] For United Irish reform demonstrations, see *NS*, 17, 24 Mar., 21, 24 July, 26 Sept., 19, 31 Oct., 2 Nov. 1792.

[2] *BNL*, 16 July 1791.

[3] See Nancy J. Curtin, 'Symbols and rituals of United Irish mobilisation', in Hugh Gough and David Dickson (eds.), *Ireland and the French revolution* (Dublin, 1990), 69–71.

respectable basis of the reform movement. A democratically run public assembly adopted resolutions and addresses elucidating their principles. That moderate reformer, Henry Joy, provided favourable press coverage in the *Belfast News-Letter*. Newspaper advertisements as well as handbills announced the forthcoming celebration. And symbols of their mobilization were to be found in every aspect of the radicals' demonstration. The participants were dressed in uniform, a reminder that they formed a patriotic citizen militia dedicated to Ireland's best interests. They marched behind Volunteer flags and banners celebrating revolutionary heroes in America and France. Green cockades, the symbol of Irish nationality, adorned the hats of participants and observers alike. The ritual of concluding such assemblies with public toasts was adapted to celebrate the cause of reform in Ireland and revolution in America and France. All these techniques were designed to bring favourable attention to the cause of reform, but, equally important, their exploitation was also a means of binding the participants even more firmly together in the endeavour. Lastly, such demonstrations were good fun. Parading in uniform before an admiring populace which would likely include one's family or sweetheart, assembling at a public dinner, and concluding the evening in respectable intoxication were activities prized by the participants and envied by the observers.[4]

The Bastille day celebration of 1792 afforded the newly formed United Irishmen another opportunity to discharge their arsenal of propaganda weapons in their campaign to capture Irish public opinion. Indeed, more impressive and more carefully orchestrated than the event of the previous year, this demonstration was especially significant, as it came at a time when Irish support for the French revolution was waning considerably.[5]

The role of the press in this particular propaganda exercise was crucial. The *Belfast News-Letter* reported that attendance at the meeting at the Linen Hall was 1,500, an impressive number, to be sure, in a town of under 20,000 inhabitants.[6] But the partisan *Northern Star* claimed a figure of some 5,000 participants.[7] Of course, it suited the radicals, with their emphasis on numbers, to portray the Bastille day celebrations as a mass demonstration of the popular will. And the popular will in Belfast would be more credible if it was seen to be unanimous. The two Belfast newspapers downplayed considerably the extent to which inflammatory addresses to the French National Assembly and the Irish people had been debated. Government intelligence, however, had a different story to tell. Chief Secretary Hobart,

---

[4] For recreational aspects of later republican movements, see R. V. Comerford, 'Patriotism as pastime: the appeal of Fenianism in the mid-1860s', *Irish Historical Studies*, 22/87 (Mar. 1981), 239–50.

[5] Henry Joy, *Belfast politics* (Belfast, 1794), 371–81; John Lawless, *The Belfast politics enlarged, being a compendium of the political history of Ireland for the last forty years* (Belfast, 1818), 329–43.

[6] *BNL*, 16 July 1792.   [7] *NS*, 14 July 1792.

informing the home office of the proceedings, maintained that 'the account [of the celebration] is much exaggerated [in the newspapers] and is calculated to convey to the public the idea that the sentiments contained in the two addresses are the real sentiments of a great majority of the Volunteers, where the contrary is the truth.' Indeed, a number of Volunteer corps withdrew from the assembly in protest, 'and many of the principal people of the town highly disapproved the address[es], particularly of that to the people of Ireland'.[8]

However contrived the impression that they created, the Bastille day celebrations of 1792 served their purpose in portraying solid support in the Presbyterian north for the causes of parliamentary reform, Catholic emancipation, and the revolution in France. Readers of the *Northern Star* could not help but marvel as they perused its columns at the demonstrations staged throughout the north, not only in Belfast, but in Ballymoney, Newtownlimavady, and Derry.[9] Such impressive, spirited, and respectable demonstrations for fundamental reform of the Irish system of government could not go unnoticed and greatly boosted the political capital of the United Irishmen and their Volunteer allies as leaders of the popular interest in Irish politics.

This same year, 1792, witnessed the second and last of the carefully orchestrated commemorations in Ireland of the storming of the Bastille. Once Britain and Ireland entered the war against France, radicals could hardly display their partisanship for the cause of the enemy in so public a manner. But 14 July was not the only sacred day in the radical calendar. St Patrick's day provided another annual occasion for the display of patriotic spirit, and in 1792 particularly, the year when the radicals most exploited the public demonstration as a propaganda device, 17 March was a day for concerted activity. Volunteer companies throughout the north of Ireland paraded through their towns and dined together, indulging again in the intoxicating ritual of emptying their glasses in salute to the cause of reform. Indeed, the Donaghadee Volunteer company boasted of drinking at least ten such toasts, including one expressing the hope that 'the spirit of liberty realized [may] extend from nation to nation till it covers the utmost corners of the earth'.[10]

Colonel William Sharman, addressing an assembly of Volunteers at Dromore in September 1792, recalled that he had two motives for attending the French revolution celebration in Belfast in July:

One was to rejoice at it—as a dissolution of one of the greatest tyrannies of the world. The other was to rejoice at it—as a memento [*sic*] to the several govern-

---

[8] Robert Hobart to ——, 19 July 1792 (PROHO 100/37/179).   [9] *NS*, 21, 24 July 1792.
[10] *NS*, 17, 24 Mar. 1792. Such celebrations were not the sole preserve of the radicals; see Jacqueline Hill, 'National festivals, the state, and "protestant ascendancy" in Ireland, 1790–1829', *Irish Historical Studies*, 24/93 (May 1984), 30–51.

ments of the earth to make a timely reform of abuses—for discontents among the people may be compared to geometrical progression—in the beginning of the climax it has the appearance of a pigmy [*sic*]—as it advances it becomes a giant: and where the end of it will be, it is beyond the power of human calculation to determine. . . . It is a maxim in politics that no indictment can lie against the will of the whole people, because when they come forward as one man, they come forward with both the right and the power on their side.[11]

Sharman thus alluded to the main purpose of these public demonstrations—to represent the national will of Ireland. Such demonstrations were dictated by the fundamental strategy pioneered by the Volunteers and inherited by the United Irishmen, and were intended to overawe the government by the potential force of the mobilized masses. Sharman was, in fact, threatening the government, insinuating that, if the reform movement were allowed to thrive by feeding on the abuses and corruption of government, it would grow to uncontrollable proportions and perhaps emerge as a monster of vengeance against Ireland's present governors. Thus the radicals took every opportunity to display their discipline and strength of numbers.

The expulsion of invaders from their borders by the French in October 1792 greatly heartened Irish radicals and afforded them the happy opportunity to make their joy a public event. The *Northern Star* called upon all the Volunteers in Belfast to celebrate the occasion. The committees of the different Volunteer companies in the town gathered at the Donegall Arms to plan the demonstration, and on the day appointed, 30 October, the Volunteers of Belfast 'turned out very numerously to testify their joy at the success of the *French Republic*'. They gathered at the White Linen Hall, where they fired three '*feu de joies* amidst the heartfelt exclamations of the people'. That evening, citizens and Volunteers assembled at the Donegall Arms to consider a suitable declaration for the occasion. They decided, however, that a declaration issuing from a tavern would be both unseemly and liable to the charge that it did not represent the universal opinion of the town. Even so, the Donegall Arms was a most appropriate place for the closing scene common to all these demonstrations—the drinking of toasts. The *Northern Star* reported that no less than twenty-three toasts were drunk on this occasion, saluting the usual causes. But even in their toasts the radicals sought to intimidate the government with the threat of revolution if the reform movement continued to be frustrated. They ominously lifted their glasses in approbation of the thought 'May a timely reform prevent the necessity of a tumultuous revolution and equally disappoint faction and tyranny.'[12]

While the leading radicals of the town were convened in the Donegall Arms, drinking in the cause of reform, the rest of the citizens staged a far

[11] *NS*, 26 Sept. 1792.   [12] *NS*, 19, 31 Oct. 1792.

more impressive show of support for the cause of French arms. Even the moderate *Belfast News-Letter* attested to the scope of the celebration:

The town was almost universally illuminated. Everyone demonstrated sincere pleasure in the disgrace of two tyrannical courts [Prussian and Austrian] that attempted to dragoon an united nation into that deplorable state of spiritual as well as political bondage from which it was just recovering; and that dared to tell twenty-five millions of men—*ye shall not be free.*[13]

The *Northern Star* observed that 'there was not a street in the town but presented a blaze of approbation, and many of the houses and shops were decorated with transparencies, labels, etc.' which honoured the rights of man, success to the French army, and, of course, the need for a union of all Irishmen.[14]

Equally disciplined demonstrations celebrating the French victory occurred in other northern towns, including Lisburn, Ballynure, and Randalstown.[15] The *Northern Star* also maintained that a general illumination in support of the French cause occurred in Dublin as well.[16] Dublin radicals certainly paid a great deal of attention to publicizing the proposed celebration. Notices were placed in the newspapers calling for an illumination of the capital as a demonstration of joy at the defeat of the duke of Brunswick's armies, and handbills were distributed throughout the city. 'This was supposed to be done with the intention of trying the pulse of the people upon that subject,' the Castle official Sackville Hamilton informed Evan Nepean of the home office, 'and it was expected that a mob would be collected to break the windows of those who would refuse to illuminate.' The city magistrates issued a proclamation against any tumultuous assembly and called on the garrison to patrol the city and enforce the prohibition. As a consequence, or so Hamilton maintained, the evening passed off peacefully.[17]

Until war was declared on France in February 1793, such illuminations were the preserve of the United Irishmen and their allies. But loyalists were quick to imitate such devices in order to discredit the radical Francophiles and to display their own firm attachment to king and constitution. In April 1793 the town of Carrickfergus was illuminated in honour of an allied victory over France.[18] A similar demonstration was attempted by loyalist elements in Belfast, but was thwarted when the '*sans-culottes* assembled in force' to resist it.[19] Early in December 1793 the common council in Derry ordered the illumination of the town to celebrate a British naval victory. The council declared 'that if the *Nappers* did not illuminate their windows,

[13] *BNL*, 2 Nov. 1792.   [14] *NS*, 31 Oct. 1792.   [15] *NS*, 14 Nov. 1792.
[16] *NS*, 31 Oct. 1792.
[17] Sackville Hamilton to Evan Nepean, 20 Oct. 1792 (PROHO 100/38/59).
[18] *BNL*, 19 Apr. 1793.   [19] *FDJ*, 20 Apr. 1793.

they should be every one broken'. The town remained darkened, and there were no reports of any broken windows.[20]

Thus the war for public opinion was reduced to a matter of whether one should or should not leave a burning candle in one's window. Innocuous as that may seem, the matter soon became an issue to be contested in the streets. In April 1794 an illumination was ordered in Dublin to celebrate a British naval victory in the West Indies. Nevertheless, *Freeman's Journal* reported that a 'hired mob afterwards went through several parts of the town huzzaing for Marat, Robespierre, the guillotine, etc., and broke the windows of the houses that were illuminated'.[21] Clearly, the government and loyalists were unable to exploit the crowd as fully as British conservatives were able to do in the 'church and king' riots in London and Birmingham during this period. And when a loyalist crowd was mobilized against the reformers, it served as a propaganda victory of sorts for the radicals themselves. On the same evening as the Dublin crowd roamed the streets attacking the illuminated houses of loyalists, a different kind of disturbance broke out in Strabane. The provost of the town ordered an illumination with which all but a man named William Ross complied. Ross protested that the 'destruction of his fellow creatures' was not a 'proper subject of triumph', a point apparently overlooked by his fellow reformers when Brunswick's army was turned back in 1792. The Wicklow militia, currently stationed in the town and enthusiastic participants in the celebration of British naval power, became 'heated with liquor' and attacked Ross's darkened house, breaking the windows and shouting threats at the poor man, while their officers stood by passively, 'apparently exulting spectators of the act'. Two days later a town meeting was convened, attended by those who had obeyed the provost's orders, to condemn the militia and praise Ross's exercise of his conscience.[22]

The inability of the government to exploit such illuminations without incident suggests that the United Irishmen and their radical allies did indeed have some hold over public sympathies. It also reveals a new trend in United Irish propaganda: to condone, or perhaps encourage, crowd violence in an effort to discredit the authorities. By 1794 the opportunities for a peaceful and orderly display of public opinion through the medium of the mass demonstration had been seriously curtailed for the radicals. The repressive legislation of 1793 had revealed the government's determination to resist the radicals' pretensions to represent the national will. The United Irishmen therefore sought to highlight what they saw as the increasingly tyrannical proclivities of the administration, exacerbated as these were by the waging of a war against liberal principles. Under the new circumstances, the spontaneous outbursts of an aggrieved people were to be

---

[20] *NS*, 12 Dec. 1793.   [21] *FJ*, 26 Apr. 1794.   [22] *Londonderry Journal*, 6 May 1794.

regretted, but not condemned. Indeed, such incidents of crowd violence merely confirmed what the radicals had maintained all along—that only a timely reform of government could prevent a violent conflagration between the authorities and the people in Ireland.

It is uncertain to what extent the United Irishmen actually co-ordinated or instigated such riots. Certainly, in Belfast, where the United Irishmen enjoyed the allegiance of a broad social base, such disturbances were rare, occurring only in response to military provocation.[23] In Dublin, however, as *Freeman's Journal* insinuated, the radicals were accused of unleashing a 'hired mob' to harass loyalists. If such riots were not spontaneous, and there is no evidence that they were planned in 1793 and 1794, it may not have been the United Irishmen who were the instigators. By this time there were a number of artisan political clubs in the capital—the Philanthropic Society, the Telegraph Club, and a group of urban Defenders.[24] It may well have been the lower orders themselves who provided the impetus and leadership for these disturbances—if, indeed, they were planned. But again there is no evidence to confirm this, aside from the accusations of the conservative press and the suspicions of the administration.

If the United Irishmen were innocent of fomenting the illumination riots of 1793–4, they certainly can be held responsible for the disturbances surrounding the departure of the popular viceroy, Earl Fitzwilliam, and the arrival of his successor, Earl Camden, in the spring of 1795. Here the riot as a propaganda vehicle came of age in the United Irish repertoire. The public disturbance, of course, had accompanied the popular demonstration from the beginning of the revived reform campaign. As early as July 1791 riots marred the Bastille day celebration in Dublin, an occurrence deplored by the radicals and ironically hailed by the conservative press. 'The promise of any exhibition which can give a pretext for idleness, will never fail to strike in with the passions of the rabble,' observed *Freeman's Journal*. In response to advertisements in the press and in widely distributed handbills, 'a mob did assemble . . . ignorant people flocking to enjoy the fight without giving one thought to its cause.' The clearly biased reporter proceeded to paint the demonstration in even more damning colours as he described a 'handful' of Volunteers leading the parade of this 'train of rioters, vagabonds, and felons, with which all great cities abound, to the terror and annoyance of peaceable citizens. If they wished to degrade the illustrious character of the Irish Volunteers, they could not take a more effectual method.' A lantern decorated with a transparency heralding the 'rights of man' was the standard for the procession as it moved through the streets of Dublin. 'Wherever the magic lantern appeared, the inhabitants were obliged

---

[23] See e.g. *BNL*, 9 Mar. 1793.

[24] See the series of letters from government agents Thomas Boyle and Francis Higgins (SPOI, Rebellion papers, 620/18/3, 14).

to illuminate their windows, on pain of instant demolition, by the rabble that followed in its train.' Well supplied with stones, the crowd reputedly broke the windows of houses darkened in protest against the proceedings, and even attacked a few illuminated houses as well, such was the ignorance and lack of discipline of the 'mob'. *Freeman's Journal* castigated those Volunteers who sponsored the event for unleashing this 'mob of butcher-boys, chandler boys, glazers' apprentices, and their vagabond assistants, who, it is notorious, have been hired on such occasions to destroy the property of their fellow citizens'. Furthermore, the criminal element seized the opportunity to assault citizens and pick pockets, 'all in *honour* of the revolution in a country ever distinguished as our enemy'. Eventually, the city magistrates were obliged to call in the army to restore order in the streets.[25]

It was this sort of bad press which confirmed the radicals in their intention to discourage bonfires, illuminations, and any nocturnal assembly of the people which might lead to another public disturbance in Dublin. But if the United Irishmen attempted to avoid such violent displays of popular discontent, they were hardly able to suppress them entirely. Spontaneous disturbances became a commonplace as popular political consciousness and expectations were raised by United Irish propaganda. Radical partisans rioted in Dublin theatres to object to the singing of 'God save the king'. A respectable meeting of Catholics in Carrick unintentionally provoked their lower-class co-religionists to run through the streets of the town offering 'a penny for a protestant'.[26]

Such displays did not advance the cause of reform in the early 1790s. But by 1795 that cause had been redefined as a result of the frustration which accompanied the brief lord-lieutenancy of Earl Fitzwilliam. The earlier United Irish strategy had been to show the Irish government that parliamentary reform and Catholic emancipation were essential policies to preserve the country from the contagion of continental revolution. But, realizing that the Anglo-Irish ascendancy would not reform itself out of existence, the radicals' main objective became to convince the British prime minister, William Pitt, that Ireland could no longer be secured by a narrow governing oligarchy, and that the maintenance of its constitutional link with Great Britain depended on a restructuring of the Irish system of government on a more popular and representative basis. Hopes were raised of the fulfilment of this objective when Pitt appointed Fitzwilliam to the viceregal office in Ireland. High as those expectations rose, the more cruelly were they dashed when Pitt recalled the popular viceroy, signalling clearly by his refusal to countenance the dismissal of such Anglo-Irish stalwarts as

[25] *FJ*, 16 July 1791; *FDJ*, 19 July 1791.
[26] Earl of Westmorland to William Pitt, 10 Dec. 1792, 18 Jan. 1793 (NLI, Lord-Lieutenants' correspondence, MS 886/61–7, 125–36).

John Beresford that Britain would stand or fall with the ascendancy, at least while war was being waged on the Continent. Frustrated in their strategies for constitutional reform, the radicals explored insurrectionary solutions to Irish misgovernment, but they never lost hope that the British prime minister would come to his senses and recognize that the political expedient of Ireland's loyalty and contentment could be happily wedded to principles of political justice. It might still be possible to frighten Pitt into reforming the government of Ireland and ousting the hated Anglo-Irish ascendancy from its political monopoly. It is in this context that the riots in Dublin in 1795 should be seen.

Catholic leaders were especially frustrated by Fitzwilliam's recall. Less concerned with the so-called protestant cause, parliamentary reform, they were sorry to see the issue of Catholic emancipation so cruelly rejected by the British ministry. Up to this point, they had allied only cautiously with the Presbyterian radicals of the north, fearing to compromise their campaign for the final abolition of the penal laws by associating directly with the levelling and republican spirit ascribed to the United Irishmen. But with Fitzwilliam's recall, all avenues to the goal of Catholic emancipation had been barred except the one which led, if not to revolution, at least to the threat of it. Consequently, according to the reliable informer Leonard McNally, an intimate of many of their leaders, the Catholics began openly to declare 'that they will never again apply to government or any branch of it for redress, but [rather they will] join their influence, their interest, and their strength with the people at large'.[27] Thus the Catholics confirmed the strategy adopted by the northern United Irishmen and discarded their old tactic, suitable for a constitutional campaign, of mobilizing the respectable, middle-class opinion of the country. They would now direct their activities into marshalling the lower classes into an irresistible popular movement which would either make a revolution or force the government into adopting the reforms necessary to prevent one. A display of popular fury would add credibility to that threat. Thus the Dublin radicals, protestant and Catholic alike, set out to make the arrival in Dublin of Fitzwilliam's successor, Earl Camden, a showcase for violent popular resentment in Ireland.

On 31 March 1795 Lord Camden arrived in an Ireland that was sullen about Fitzwilliam's recall and approaching a state of smouldering insurrection. Reports from Castle informers throughout the city of Dublin warned that the new viceroy's entry into the capital would be greeted by a hostile, and possibly a violent, crowd. At the last moment, therefore, the route of Camden's procession was changed, and he arrived at Dublin Castle without incident. Not so fortunate, however, were those who had escorted the new lord-lieutenant to his Dublin residence. A disappointed crowd, thwarted by

---

[27] 'J. W.' to marquess of Downshire, [Apr.] 1795 (PRO, Chatham papers, 30/8/327/308–9).

the change of venue, regrouped outside Dublin Castle on Dame Street in time to find the hated chancellor, Lord Clare, the archbishop of Armagh, and the lords justices preparing to depart after their attendance on the new viceroy. 'Not a numerous but a well-regulated mob' began to insult this illustrious delegation as it passed through the Castle gate. The chancellor, thinking that his ostentatious coach and six would surely outdistance the other coaches and the pursuing crowd, ordered his coachman to drive away quickly. This served only to isolate Lord Clare, for the crowd was not interested in the other dignitaries when they held the deeply resented lord chancellor within their grasp. They followed Clare's carriage down Dame Street, hurling dirt and abuse at the chancellor and his servants, until they arrived in Grafton Street, where they began throwing stones. One of these, hurled by a servant named O'Brien, grazed the chancellor on the temple. The crowd then pursued the carriage to Clare's residence and proceeded to break the windows of his house. Having made the chancellor painfully aware of their sentiments, the crowd then attacked the residences of John Foster, speaker of the Irish house of commons, and Alderman Warren on their way to the Custom House, where they hoped to confront another pillar of the Anglo-Irish ascendancy, John Beresford. They broke the windows of Beresford's apartments and provoked the commissioner of the revenue's son, John Claudius Beresford, to fire upon the assembly. One man died and several others were injured. At this point the magistrates arrived with troops and fired upon the crowd, wounding many and successfully dispersing the rioters.[28]

Government informers were convinced that the United Irishmen and their radical Catholic allies were behind this carefully orchestrated riot. 'The persons who attacked the primate and chancellor', declared Chief Secretary Thomas Pelham, 'appeared to be above the common class and could not be ignorant of the offence they were offering to order and authority, and their expressions were as inflammatory as their actions were rebellious.'[29] Leonard McNally claimed that the attack on Clare was premeditated and not the result of the spontaneous resentment of an aggrieved people. He maintained that the radical leaders had set up a decoy in King Street, where a large crowd assembled in a threatening mood, in order to draw the magistrates and troops away from the main action at the Castle. The agents of Francis Higgins, editor of the pro-government *Freeman's Journal*, provided interesting information on exactly how this hostile crowd had been assembled. Radical agents had been sent throughout the liberties and the neighbourhood of Dublin Castle to announce the planned riot. Those who

---

[28] John Lees to Viscount Townshend, 1 Apr. 1795 (NLI, Townshend letters, 394/18); 'J. W.' to Downshire, [Mar.–Apr. 1795] (PRO, Chatham papers, 30/8/327/308–9); Thomas Pelham to John King, 1 Apr. 1795 (PROHO 100/57/45).
[29] Pelham to King, 1 Apr. 1795 (PROHO 100/57/45).

wished to participate were told to go to Henry Jackson's foundry, where they would be given a card entitling them to free porter and spirits from local publicans. For a few, the lure of free liquor was insufficient to induce them to break the king's peace, and small sums of money were offered instead. But most of the crowd was sufficiently emboldened by drink to make their concerted assault on the chancellor. Indeed, the brother of O'Brien, the man who was arrested for throwing the stone that found its mark on Clare's temple, was a publican in Essex Street who kept his house open all day for the benefit of the rioters.[30]

Rioting continued throughout April as Grattan prepared to bring in, for the last time in the Irish house of commons, a bill for the emancipation of the Catholics. With Fitzwilliam's recall, the bill had no chance of being passed, and therefore no crucial votes would be lost by violent street demonstrations. Such riots would rather confirm the United Irish contention that the continuance of illiberal government in Ireland would lead to chaos and anarchy. A meeting of radicals was held at the house of Richard McCormick, a Catholic Committeeman, where it was resolved to send agents to the various journeymen's and tradesmen's clubs in the capital to persuade them to take to the streets on the day that Grattan was to introduce his Catholic bill. Higgins described the crowd as 'an infatuated number of low working artisans, restless, drunken, and riotous, capable of any mischief, and to keep down whom strong steps will be necessary to be timely taken'. But he also remarked that they were 'something above the common rabble', for the avid reading of radical newspapers and their familiarity with Paine's writings and ideas were 'making them truly desperate'.[31] It was not always necessary either to hire a mob or to create one through the liberal supply of spirits.

At the other end of the social scale, the students at that bastion of the ascendancy, Trinity College, also contributed to the riotous days of April. With the poet Thomas Moore acting as secretary, an assembly of students presented an address to Grattan favouring Catholic emancipation. They also declared that 'they were ready to join *in any act* with the Catholics, damning the present administration, and calling out *Fitzwilliam and Grattan forever*'. Later that evening a party of students took to the streets of Dublin, reinforcing these sentiments more volubly.[32]

Radical attempts at crowd mobilization were not always successful, and it seems that, by the summer of 1795, the lower classes were becoming immune to the usual seductions. In June an attempt was made to stage a street demonstration for the viceroy's edification: 'The incendiaries . . .

[30] Francis Higgins to Sackville Hamilton, 10 Apr. 1795 (Kent CAO, Pratt papers, U840/0143/2).
[31] Higgins to Hamilton, 13 Apr. 1795 (ibid. U840/0143/3).
[32] Higgins to Hamilton, 10 Apr. 1795 (ibid. U840/0143/2).

went to different parts of the city and Liberty to procure a mob to hiss and insult his excellency returning from the house of peers.' But this time the people were reluctant to riot, and even the usual lures of money and drink failed to rouse them. A committee of radicals went from one public house to another trying to bring the denizens into the streets, but they failed in the attempt. Worse yet, the silk weavers of the capital, dependent on the patronage of the wealthy, took the opportunity to show their affection and respect for the viceroy by offering to draw his coach through the streets.[33]

Thus ended the United Irishmen's brief flirtation with the urban riot as a propaganda device. The middle-class Dublin radicals ceased to exploit such crowd disturbances for two reasons. First, the crowd itself began to prove reluctant to supply the shock troops for use in such street engagements. Lives had been lost and nothing had been achieved. Indeed, such tampering with the mob had confirmed the government in their perception of the United Irishmen as levelling Jacobins who would regard any concessions as merely the first stage in the eventual establishment of a democratic republic in Ireland. Rioting in Dublin may well have influenced a procrastinating Lord North to concede Irish free-trade demands in 1779, or so the radicals assumed, and perhaps a similar fracas in the capital in 1795 might induce another prime minister to purchase order in Ireland through timely concessions. But the strategy failed, and it was pointless for the radicals to risk their credit with the Dublin crowd by pursuing a patently bankrupt policy.

Moreover, this realization that Pitt and his allies could not be moved by minor skirmishes in the streets of Dublin dictated a different course of action, one which had already been embarked upon, however tentatively, by the northern radicals in 1792. The basic aim of using the threat of force to scare the government into reforms remained the same, but rather than apply the pressure through the occasional riot, the northern United Irishmen pursued their objective by mobilizing an underground citizen army. Discretion and circumspection were essential here. As far as possible, United Irish efforts to organize the lower classes had to be unhindered by government harassment. Violent outbursts would only draw government repression. Following the suppression of the Society of United Irishmen in the capital in May 1794, the radical leadership in Dublin had drifted somewhat aimlessly until the transformed northern organization had extended its influence to the south. This was accomplished throughout 1795 and early 1796. Thus the planned riot was only a temporary tool of the United Irishmen, employed by an uncertain executive in Dublin, and appropriate only to the special circumstances of the spring of 1795. The second reason, then, for the demise of the riot as a propaganda weapon was the restoration of central direction and organization to the radical movement in the

---

[33] Higgins to Hamilton, 6 June 1795 (ibid. U840/0143/5).

capital. Once the Dublin leaders adopted the model of mass revolutionary organization fashioned by the northerners, the radical middle class found a better use for the lower classes than wasting them in fruitless engagements in the streets.

The public demonstration was by no means exhausted as a vehicle for the United Irishmen. Indeed, the radicals pioneered creative methods for mobilizing large gatherings with a view to attracting new supporters and alarming the government at the same time. Apparently innocuous occasions, such as funerals, race meetings, and, in the north, potato diggings, were used by the radicals as a cloak for their assembly. Such gatherings fulfilled a variety of functions for the underground republican army. Not only did they have a propagandist value in signalling messages to the administration and potential supporters among the people at large, but they also afforded opportunities for the United Irishmen to assess their strength in a given area, to test the speed with which their adherents could be assembled, and to gather for military drill in the daytime and under the very noses of a helpless magistracy. Thus these demonstrations served at once to discipline United Irish recruits and to demonstrate their control and strength of numbers to the authorities and to potential adherents.

The use of such cloaking devices for public assemblies was equally prolific in Dublin and the north. In the capital the radicals relied mostly on funeral processions to mobilize their followers in drills and exercises in intimidation, while in the area around Belfast potato diggings served the same purpose. Funerals, real or mock, were better suited to the metropolis, where street battles would characterize a rising of the United Irishmen. The radicals were therefore concerned to train their followers to assemble at designated checkpoints in the city at short notice. The funeral of a radical martyr named Dunn in April 1797 provided the perfect occasion to practise this procedure. The Dublin leadership notified the various republican clubs to attend in strength and, unwilling to let a propaganda opportunity be lost, to sport the colour green. On that occasion, 1,500 people attended the body of their fallen comrade.[34] Similarly, William Kane, a barber executed by the government for seditious activity, was respectfully attended to his grave by a mourning society of several hundred, headed by such radical leaders as Thomas Addis Emmet, William Sampson, and Lord Edward Fitzgerald, in February 1798.[35] These mourning clubs, funeral societies, and lottery clubs, of course, were merely covers for United Irish gatherings. *Freeman's Journal* commented facetiously on the proliferation of such assemblies in Dublin in the spring of 1797 by observing: 'We understand that henceforth the death of a United Irishman is to be used as a means of

---

[34] Thomas Boyle to ——, 5 Apr. 1797 (SPOI, Rebellion papers, 620/18/3); Francis Higgins to ——, 2, 9 Apr. 1797 (ibid. 620/18/14).

[35] Higgins to ——, 26 Feb. 1798 (ibid. 620/16/14).

convention by the body at large—if so, we care not to what extent these funeral pretexts are multiplied.'[36] But the United Irishmen themselves soon saw no necessity for an actual corpse to be honoured by the ranks. Indeed, mock funerals were held with some regularity throughout 1797, with orderly processions of men (women and children were curiously absent from these supposed burial ceremonies) parading through the streets of the capital. Instead of a corpse, the coffin often contained a store of arms and ammunition. The numbers attending these mock funerals ranged from several hundred to 2,000, the participants marching 'by companies as regularly as soldiers'.[37] Such events were most commonly, but not exclusively, found in Dublin. Dean Annesley of Castlewellan, County Down, reported in May 1797 that thousands were expected to attend a funeral in his neighbourhood, though the coffin would surely be empty.[38]

A more effective opportunity for northerners to mobilize their followers at short notice, however, was the potato digging. It was not unusual for the peasantry to assemble in order to harvest the crops of a person whom they admired or respected.[39] The United Irishmen gave this traditional practice new significance when, from September 1796, numerous of their northern leaders were arrested. Over the next few months the newspapers and magistrates reported massive gatherings of country people to harvest the prisoners' crops. 'Upwards of 3,000 people', the *Belfast News-Letter* declared in October, 'assembled to raise Mr Francis Dinsmore's potatoes who is now a prisoner in Carrickfergus, which they did in six minutes.'[40] Magistrates found these displays particularly offensive. Pharis Martin, junior, described one such crowd of harvesters marching 'through the streets of [Ballynahinch] with their fifes playing and carrying their ensigns of rebellion. This was the first instant [*sic*] of those gentry having the boldness to publicly march through a town where the military is quartered.'[41] The respectable leadership of these assemblies was noted with concern by government correspondents. Donal Norwood, 'a man of extreme respectability', led a band of over 300 persons to raise the crop of a distressed cottier near Maghera.[42] In another incident the crowd was led by two Presbyterian ministers.[43] The French traveller De Latocnaye witnessed one of these impressive events in County Antrim: 'A man with nothing special to

[36] *FJ*, 8 Apr. 1797.
[37] 'Pelham memoranda', 106; see also the reports of Boyle and Higgins (SPOI, Rebellion papers, 620/19/3, 14).
[38] Dean Richard Annesley to Viscount Castlereagh, 18 May 1797 (ibid. 620/30/104).
[39] De Latocnaye, *A Frenchman's walk through Ireland, 1796–7*, trans. John Stevenson (Belfast, 1917), 202–10.
[40] *BNL*, 21 Oct. 1796.
[41] Pharis Martin, jun., to R. M. H. McNeill, 11 Nov. 1796 (SPOI, Rebellion papers, 620/26/40).
[42] Pharis Martin to ——, 16 Nov. 1796 (ibid. 620/26/55).
[43] Richard Babington to Revd James Jones, 2 Nov. 1796 (ibid. 620/26/8).

distinguish him exacted obedience and directed affairs with the hand or certain calls.' Alcohol was prohibited, 'and this certainly requires a great effort in this part of the country. . . . For the occasion the peasantry had put on their best clothes; this air of gaiety and good humour . . . would have made any spectator believe he had arrived on a fete day.'[44]

Military drill may have been the primary function of these mock funerals and potato diggings, but their propaganda value was considerable as well. The recreational aspects of such assemblies made them the more prized by the participants—and perhaps the more envied by wavering observers. One reason why the lower ranks may have joined the United Irishmen was for the sociability afforded by these assemblies. Throughout the previous two decades the popular classes had witnessed the proclaimed flower of Irish manhood and respectability parading in their expensive Volunteer uniforms. At these mock funerals and potato diggings, where all marched together in regimental discipline, the lower ranks could feel part of that glorious Volunteer past, as well as emboldened by the solidarity of their comrades in the great struggle for justice and freedom in Ireland. It was exactly the sort of public parade of strength which made the United Irish movement attractive to some of its members.

But there was a more important propaganda function involved in these public assemblies. The United Irish strategy was pinned to the conviction that, should they once appear to constitute the strongest party in the country, more recruits would flock to their standard, and either the Irish parliament or the British ministry would offer timely concessions to avert the threatened revolution. These mock funerals and potato diggings, where thousands of United Irishmen paraded in military fashion, were meant to intimidate the government as well as to assure the people at large that the republican movement was well able to defend the popular interest. The intent of these assemblies was at once to frighten and discredit the authorities.

The tactic worked, according to that most active Derry magistrate, Sir George F. Hill. Hill learned in November 1796 that many thousands planned to gather for a potato digging near Maghera. United Irish corps from Derry, Antrim, Down, and Tyrone were to converge on the site appointed, a plan that gave republican leaders the opportunity to test the gathering of their troops on command. Hill himself confronted about 2,000 men from Antrim after they had forded the Bann on their way to Maghera. He ordered them to stop and read the proclamation recently issued by the lord-lieutenant prohibiting such large assemblies.

They remonstrated with all imaginable cunning, profession[s] of peace, and humility. Would we impede them in the charitable purpose of digging a forlorn woman's

[44] De Latocnaye, *Frenchman's walk*, 209–10.

potatoes whose husband was in gaol; but if we persisted to order, they would disperse; at the same time [they] begged to be informed if they were at liberty to dig their own potatoes in their respective farms.

Feeling ridiculous, as the leaders of the crowd intended, Hill persisted in his order to disperse, which appeared to be obeyed. Hill then withdrew with his troops, only to discover that the people had regrouped, their numbers now trebled. Hill then returned with his soldiers and gave the crowd ten minutes to scatter. Not wishing to engage the cavalry while armed only with spades, the people finally complied. 'What alarmed me most compleatly [*sic*]', declared the magistrate, 'was to perceive the calmness observed by the people assembled in such multitudes from such various quarters and yet acting with one common system, most evidently by previous arrangement and under the control of an invisible guidance.'

If the stalwart Hill was intimidated by this display, he was also made to look foolish. He had been forced to disperse a well-dressed and orderly crowd protesting that it had assembled for a charitable purpose. Hill had asked the potato diggers if they would also assemble to repel a French invasion. To this the innocents replied:

We have no arms, they have been taken out of our hands by government, no ammunition, the Volunteers were put down, we must not talk politics, government have taken all upon themselves, we are resigned, and must be satisfied. We therefore comfort ourselves in living with our neighbours and all mankind in faith and friendship, we will make no disturbance, but we cannot resist the French.

Hill urged them to join the newly established yeomanry corps, to which the crowd responded that 'they would not be soldiers to protect what they did not care for and were perfectly, as Christians should be, resigned to their fate'. Thus, as Hill blustered, the crowd responded with pacific protestations, but the threat was duly noted by the vigilant magistrate:

This potato digging is not in my mind so much for the purpose of holding seditious meetings as to enable the leaders, whoever they may be, of ascertaining the numbers that have been sworn and to try if they will act by their directions and be controlled by them. Every man almost held his spade like a musket and seemed, notwithstanding their humble cant, to shew you by the manner [in which] he balanced it, and their erect gait, that he could manage the other as well. . . . I do believe that more than two-thirds of the country has been sworn.[45]

Even though Hill succeeded in dispersing this crowd, arresting only one man for his impertinence to a magistrate, the occasion could be regarded as a victory for the United Irishmen. They had proved to themselves and, more importantly, to the authorities that they could assemble and control a formidable republican army. They had also exposed the ineffectuality of the

[45] Sir George F. Hill to Edward Cooke, [Nov. 1796] (PROHO 100/62/342–5).

magistracy and troops in dealing with the situation, for, despite Hill's prohibition, a crowd of some 200 later raised the incarcerated United
Irishman's potatoes. Above all, they had given the crowd the opportunity
to laugh at their governors. Any chink that they made in the armour of
government authority was a significant victory for the United Irishmen.

In a sense, these covert United Irish assemblies constituted propaganda
by deed, designed to discipline and encourage followers as well as to
frighten and intimidate opponents. More direct methods of intimidation
also served the propagandist purposes of the United Irishmen; they frequently resorted to threats and terror in the hope of displaying themselves
to the government and the people at large as the strongest party in the
state. If United Irish chances for success in their struggle against the ascendancy were deemed a certainty, thousands more would flock to the republican standard, just as self-interested oligarchs would flee like rats from the
sinking ship of state. Furthermore, in the effort to discredit the government,
they had to prove that the official machinery of justice was ineffective. The
United Irishmen therefore took pains to intimidate jurors and witnesses, not
only because they wanted to secure acquittals for their own supporters, but
also to show the country at large that they could protect their own and
were immune from judicial harassment. Terror also had to be applied to
traitors to the movement. Since United Irish strategy dictated both secrecy
and mass mobilization, the opportunity for informers to infiltrate the organization at all levels was greatly enhanced. The United Irishmen had to
make terrible examples of such individuals in order to prevent their proliferation.

Much of republican violence was directed at certain key targets whose
harassment or demise also offered propaganda benefits. The United
Irishmen attacked yeomen in order to discourage further enrolment in the
loyalist corps. They threatened active magistrates and, in many cases, assassinated them as enemies of the people. Clerical magistrates in particular
were singled out as appropriate candidates for popular vengeance. The
Anglican parson—as magistrate, as landlord, and as a parasite who lived
off the hated tithe—was a symbol of all that the United Irishmen were trying to overthrow.

Even when the United Irishmen did not perpetrate the terror themselves,
they exploited it none the less. While espousing a brotherly union of affection among all Irishmen, they were not averse to playing the Orange card
to induce Catholics to rally to the republicans as the only force able to protect them from the dreaded yeomanry and Orangemen. In many places, of
course, the Orange threat actually existed; where it did not, the United
Irishmen chose to invent it. A Belfast correspondent informed the government in September 1796 that the radicals were actively recruiting in the
glens of Antrim, spreading tales that the lord-lieutenant had armed the

Orangemen, who were allegedly preparing to massacre the predominantly Catholic inhabitants of the area: 'After keeping the poor creatures in a state of distraction for some days, they were advised to unite as the only chance of safety. After this, they were informed that the Orangemen, finding them united, did not dare attack them.'[46]

Unfortunately, this threat of a terror to come did not always need to be fabricated. The activities of the Orangemen in Armagh gave credence to United Irish claims that loyalists everywhere were bent on massacre. Moreover, the counter-revolutionary campaign of the government served initially to alienate the people from the authorities. Government repression produced martyrs and heroes to the republican cause, most notably, perhaps, the sturdy, handsome young farmer William Orr of County Antrim, whose execution became a *cause célèbre* in the United Irish propaganda battle. The problem with exploiting loyalist successes in routing the United Irishmen, however ghastly the means used, was that it contradicted the republicans' claim that they were, in fact, the stronger party in the state. Furthermore, the attempt to celebrate United Irish martyrs may have attracted new members outraged by the injustice perpetrated by the ascendancy, but at the same time it resulted in the defection of those who were loath to meet a similar fate. The fact that the United Irishmen could boast of so many victims sacrificed upon the altar of Irish liberty only confirmed that the authorities were succeeding in their war against the republican movement.

The public demonstrations of the United Irish reformist phase, the mock funerals and potato diggings of 1796 and 1797, and even the intimidation and violence perpetrated by the republicans against the agents of the state had all been propaganda victories, for they fulfilled the related functions of discrediting the government while displaying United Irish strength in numbers and discipline. Such victories, however, were secured at a cost, for the government felt compelled to respond to such open republican mobilization not, as the United Irishmen hoped, with concessions, but with coercion. 'It was them damned funerals', remarked one radical, 'which opened the eyes of government.'[47]

Another form of propaganda by deed consisted of symbols and rituals. When Drennan first proposed the formation of a new political club to Sam McTier in May 1791, he particularly emphasized this aspect of radical mobilization. The new society should have 'much of the secrecy and somewhat of the ceremonial of freemasonry, so much secrecy as might communicate curiosity, uncertainty, expectation to [the] minds of surrounding men, so much impressive and affecting ceremony in its internal economy as,

---

[46] Anon. letter from Belfast, 24 Sept. 1796 (SPOI, Rebellion papers, 620/25/103).
[47] Boyle to ——, n.d. (ibid. 620/18/3).

without impeding real business, might strike the soul through the senses'.[48]
Oaths, ceremony, rituals, and emblems would reinforce for members the
seriousness of their association, reminding them that they were dedicated to
an important—indeed, a momentous—cause. When the newly formed
Dublin Society of United Irishmen convened in November 1791, Drennan
proposed that there should be a declaration or test as a preliminary to
membership in the club, hoping to 'strike the soul through the senses' as a
means of reminding members of the seriousness of their engagement.
Despite the objections of many of his colleagues that the test was too
rhetorical and fundamentally unnecessary, Drennan succeeded in introduc-
ing this modest ceremony into the organization.[49] He looked to freemasonry for an appropriate model of association. There he found oaths,
passwords, symbols, rituals, and enough ceremony to strike his poet's soul.
An oath or a test, binding members to one another in a political brotherhood of affection and dedicating themselves to the cause of their country,
provided the sort of shared ceremony which separated true patriots from
the less dedicated of their countrymen. It created an exclusive club, a
special society whose members were marked by their disinterested attachment to the national cause. And since these newly formed United Irishmen
represented, at least in their own minds, a regeneration of the Irish nation,
they adopted as their seal a suitable emblem designed by Drennan—a harp
with the motto, 'I am new strung and shall be heard.'[50]

Attention to the rituals and symbols of their mobilization persisted
throughout the early days of the United Irish movement. Green cockades,
illuminations, and mottoes celebrating the cause of reform and liberty were
a constant feature of United Irish demonstrations during the reform years.
But the legal, open, constitutional society that was founded in Belfast and
Dublin in 1791 needed little of the trappings of ceremony and secrecy advocated by Drennan. When the society went underground after 1794, however, the ritual of swearing in members, and the symbols and emblems
which allowed members to be known to one another, acquired a new func-
tional significance. It was then that Drennan's ideas about a secret conspiratorial society, marked by all the ceremonial of freemasonry, really took
hold—ironically, after the doctor himself had become a rather passive fel-
low-traveller in the cause of national reform. The new oath after 1795
omitted the crucial words 'in parliament' which Drennan had used to
describe the limits of United Irish reform aims:

I, A. B., do voluntarily declare that I will persevere in endeavouring to form a
brotherhood of affection among Irishmen of *every* religious persuasion, and that I

---

[48] William Drennan to Samuel McTier, 21 May 1791 (*The Drennan letters*, ed. D. A. Chart
(Belfast, 1931), 54).
[49] *Rep. secret comm.* 77–8.
[50] Rosamund Jacob, *The rise of the United Irishmen, 1791–4* (London, 1937), 73.

will also persevere in my endeavours to obtain an equal, full, and adequate representation of *all* the people of Ireland. I do further declare that neither hopes, fears, rewards, or punishments shall ever induce me, directly or indirectly, to inform on or give evidence against any member or members of this or similar societies, for any act or expression of theirs, done or made collectively or individually, in or out of this society, in pursuance of the spirit of this obligation.[51]

There was considerable local variation in United Irish oaths. John Mitchell, a south Antrim weaver, informed the authorities that when he was initiated into the society, he swore to overthrow the 'present government' by force if necessary.[52] Later United Irish oaths required the contractor to 'assist the French in case of invasion'. One man testified that every United Irishman was to raise seventeen or more comrades to assist the French on their landing.[53] Specific grievances were sometimes incorporated into the oaths, such as those requiring new members 'to stand to one another, to join the French and cut down tythes and taxes, and kill the Orangemen and yeomen'.[54] Another oath aimed 'to get rid of rent and tythe and to be free as the French and Americans'.[55] But the official United Irish oath, after it was approved by a secret convention in Belfast in May 1795, was more temperate, and left the extent of radical aims undefined. As Arthur O'Connor, Thomas Addis Emmet, and William James MacNeven explained: 'The friends of liberty were gradually, but with a timid step, advancing towards republicanism . . . The test embraced both the republican and the reformer, and left to future circumstances to decide to which the common strength should be directed.'[56]

Oaths of secrecy and obedience were also required of all officers of the revolutionary society. Indeed, the tendering of oaths was a constant feature of United Irish activity. It was often the case that every man and woman in a district was eventually required to swear to some kind of test. An oath of secrecy was required as a preliminary to full membership, but it was also imposed on non-participants in the area, including women. The United Irishmen even advocated an oath of sobriety, which served the triple purpose of reducing government revenue by cutting the consumption of spirits, adding to the comfort of the Irish household, and keeping the United Irish rank and file clear-headed and ready for action when summoned.[57]

Coercion was applied in swearing some to the United Irish oath, but the aspects of exclusivity and sociability certainly attracted many more recruits.

---

[51] *Rep. secret comm.* 48.
[52] Examination of John Mitchell, *c.*1796 (PROI, Frazer papers, IA 40/11*a*/16).
[53] *BNL*, 18 Sept. 1797.   [54] *BNL*, 14 Apr. 1797.
[55] George Macartney to ——, 2, 7 July 1796 (SPOI, Rebellion papers, 620/24/131).
[56] William James MacNeven, *Pieces of Irish history illustrative of the condition of the Catholics of Ireland* (New York, 1807), 176.
[57] *Rep. secret comm.* 248.

On one level, faction fighters, freemasons, Defenders, Orangemen, and the United Irishmen themselves could capitalize on the Irishman's desire to acquire a certain status within the community. Many of the issues that mobilized people in secret societies touched on this universal need. Faction fights determined the strongest gang in the community.[58] Masonic lodges represented a brotherhood of enlightened, rational men who prided themselves on their commitment to free enquiry and tolerance, but who also maintained that they were privy to ancient secrets, and who, through the progressive discipline of masonry, were able to achieve a true knowledge denied to less fortunate men.[59] The Peep o' Day Boys mobilized in part to contest the recently granted right of Catholics to bear arms. The Defenders associated to protect this privilege, for the right to bear arms was perhaps more important than the franchise in conferring the status of citizen on men in a pre-democratic society.[60] Orangemen were the self-appointed guardians of the established order and the protestant ascendancy. Lower-class protestants, alarmed at the progressive relaxation of the penal laws which, when in force, assured them of a higher status than that of even some propertied Catholics, clung desperately to confessional determinants of status and privilege.[61] And the United Irishmen, spearheaded by a middle class denied an appropriate role in the state, eager to assume their full share in the governance of the nation, were determined to see their worth recognized with full political and civil equality. Thus, those in quest of civil, political, or social distinction could be satisfied to a limited extent with the stature that they derived from their association with a particular secret organization. As the fortunes of that organization rose, so too did one's self-esteem. And this desire to be on the dominant side explains in part the transfer of allegiance from one organization to another, however ideologically inconsistent that leap might be. Thus, especially after the Bantry Bay invasion attempt, thousands flocked to the United Irish standard, believing the republicans to be the strongest party in the state.[62] Defenders, impressed with the United Irish leadership and the apparent strength and extent of the organization, entered into a loose alliance with the republican movement. But when United Irish fortunes in Ulster began to wane late in 1797 and early in 1798, many protestant republicans fled

[58] See Patrick D. O'Donnell, *The Irish faction fighters of the 19th century* (Dublin, 1975).

[59] Mervyn Jones, 'Freemasonry', in Norman MacKenzie (ed.), *Secret societies* (New York, 1967), 128–51.

[60] David W. Miller, 'The Armagh troubles, 1784–95', in Samuel Clark and James S. Donnelly, jun (eds.), *Irish peasants: violence and political unrest, 1780–1914* (Madison, Wis., 1983), 172.

[61] See Peter Gibbon, *The origins of Ulster unionism: the formation of popular protestant politics and ideology in nineteenth-century Ireland* (Manchester, 1975); Hereward Senior, *Orangeism in Ireland and Britain, 1795–1836* (London, 1966).

[62] *Rep. secret comm.* 317.

into the arms of those upholders of protestant exclusivity and oligarchy, the Orangemen.[63]

The aura of secrecy and exclusivity that surrounded these societies was enhanced by resort to complicated and allusive catechisms, hand-signs, and passwords by which members could know one another.[64] Thus the United Irishmen adopted the following mode of recognition:

The first sign was lift the right hand and draw it down over the right side of the face—2nd, lift the left hand and draw it down over the left side of the face—3rd, shake hands by the left hands—4th, say, What do you know? I know *U*—What do you know more? I know T, or some other letters of the word unity or united.[65]

When further proofs of membership were required, the following catechism could be used: 'Are you straight? I am. How straight? As straight as a rush. Go on then? In truth, in trust, in unity, and liberty. What have you got in your hand? A green bough. Where did it first grow? In America. Where did it bud? In France. Where are you going to plant it? In the crown of Great Britain.'[66]

Oaths and rituals of recognition served to bind members of the secret society together, preserving secrecy and, at the same time, emphasizing the exclusivity of the association and its special aims and purposes. But the United Irishmen also developed a symbology which was exploited for propagandist purposes as well. They appropriated the colour green as emblematic of the national cause. Indeed, Drennan himself had christened Ireland the 'Emerald Isle'.[67] 'All Jackson's men wear green handkerchiefs,' reported one government informer in Dublin. 'Bond sells green ribbons bearing a harp without a crown and the inscription "Ireland forever" in Irish.'[68] Edward Newell in Belfast reported that green cockades were used to distinguish officers from the rank and file in United Irish military bodies. The officers sported a cockade adorned with a harp and cap of liberty (symbolic of their republican aims) and the motto 'Liberty or death'.[69] Sympathetic non-participants wore green as a badge of their support, even though such emblems often provoked the hostility of loyalists.[70] 'Every measure that could tend to expand the system or to rouse the national feeling, was called into action,' recalled Charles Teeling.

---

[63] Senior, *Orangeism*, 22–117.

[64] For masonic catechisms, see MacKenzie (ed.), *Secret societies*, app. 1.

[65] *BNL*, 28 Sept. 1797.

[66] Quoted in John Heron Lepper, *Famous secret societies* (London, n.d.), 233; see also a list of rebel passwords (SPOI, Rebellion papers, 620/22/36a).

[67] R. R. Madden, *Literary remains of the United Irishmen of 1798* (Dublin, 1887), 37.

[68] Anon. information, 6 Mar. 1798 (SPOI, Rebellion papers, 620/14/218/5).

[69] John Edward Newell to Thomas Pelham, 15 Apr. 1797 (PROHO 100/69/202–5).

[70] Thomas Pelham to [William Pitt], 1 Nov. 1797 (BL, Pelham papers, Add. MS 33105/188–91).

Green, the national colour, and as the venerable Betagh termed it, 'the fancy colour of the Deity', was almost universally worn; few appeared without this badge of national distinction. . . . A green velvet stock or a silk robe with a shamrock device were the emblems of national feeling; and the former was not unfrequently presented to the youthful patriot by the fair daughter of Erin as the pledge of a more tender regard. The enthusiasm of the females even exceeded the ardour of the men; in many of the higher circles and in all the rustic festivities, *that* youth met a cold and forbidding reception from the partner of his choice, who either from apathy or timidity had not yet subscribed to the test of the union.[71]

Also associated with the cause of Ireland were the shamrock and the harp, representing the romantic nationalism of the movement. Republican fashion embraced the short hairstyles favoured by the French revolutionaries.[72] United Irish aims could also be reduced to emblems of mobilization. For example, an anti-slavery coin was used as a token of recognition among the United Irishmen in County Derry.[73] Commemorative cards and medals celebrating martyrs like William Orr were distributed among republican partisans.[74] Symbolic gestures contributed to the propagation of the republican cause as well. In 1796 republican Defenders plotted, albeit unsuccessfully, to saw off the head of William III's statue in Stephen's Green, a gesture of defiance towards the protestant ascendancy.[75] George Holdcroft, a magistrate in County Meath, protested that the republicans, or the 'Tandys' as he called them, in his neighbourhood of Kells 'refused to take off their hats for the playing of the national anthem'.[76]

Such gestures and symbols of mobilization served two propagandist functions for the United Irishmen: first, they displayed public sympathy for the republican cause; and, secondly, they helped to remind members of the republican movement of their special mission, while also separating selfless patriots from time-serving parasites. But another purpose of propaganda by deed as well as by word was to be provocative and, indeed, threatening—to frighten the government and its supporters into submission to republican demands. Thus the United Irishmen employed certain gestures designed to intimidate their opponents, to highlight the failure of the authorities to suppress republican provocations, and to hearten their own followers by humiliating the loyalists. Camden reported to Portland in August 1796 that

[71] Charles Hamilton Teeling, *The history of the Irish rebellion of 1798* (1st edn., 1876; Shannon, 1972), 10–11.
[72] See e.g. Alexander Knox, *Essays on the political circumstances of Ireland written during the administration of Earl Camden* (Dublin, 1799), 89; Charles McNeill to [John Beresford], 2 Aug. 1796 (SPOI, Rebellion papers, 620/24/76).
[73] Revd Clotworthy Soden to Dublin Castle, 25 May 1796 (SPOI, Rebellion papers, 620/23/124).
[74] Papers found on John Halligan, 22 Apr. 1798 (ibid. 620/36/198).
[75] Memorandum regarding Lawless, Brady, and Kennedy, [1796] (PROI, Frazer papers, IA 40/111/7).
[76] George Holdcroft to Dublin Castle, 7 Apr. 1796 (SPOI, Rebellion papers, 620/23/73).

'various accounts from the county of Antrim state the planting of the tree of liberty, the celebration of French victories by bonfires, and the open audacity of stopping passengers to shout for the French'.[77]

The planting of the liberty tree had been a favourite ritualistic device of the American revolutionaries.[78] In France the liberty tree became a symbol of the revolution.[79] Not surprisingly, then, the tree of liberty was also employed by the United Irishmen as a symbol of their mobilization.[80] The nocturnal planting of the tree of liberty served the dual purpose of giving the United Irishmen the opportunity to practise assembling and drilling and offering them an occasion to frighten surrounding loyalists who would be awakened by this ominous revolutionary event. But they were not afraid to play out their revolutionary ritual in the daytime, intimidating loyalist onlookers at first hand, and even attempted to plant 'the detestable tree of liberty' in the army camp at Blaris Moor.[81]

Planting the tree of liberty and igniting bonfires could be used to remind the surrounding community of United Irish strength and influence in the area as well as to frighten nearby loyalists in general. Just as individual partisans of the government were victimized by menacing letters, so, too, were they threatened with intimidating symbols. For example, an active magistrate named Vincent in County Tyrone, who saw it as his duty to root out sedition in his district, awoke one morning to find a gallows erected in front of his door, complete with a dangling rope.[82]

Social conviviality combined with intimidating rituals to produce another vehicle for United Irish propaganda. We have already seen that many meetings and demonstrations frequently concluded in an inn or public house, where numerous toasts were drunk to celebrate the reformist or republican cause. In these toasts, the United Irishmen often expressed an extreme and provocative political radicalism which was not necessarily consistent with their reformist posture. In 1794, for example, when the United Irishmen still supposedly avowed only reformist aims, some northerners were reported to have drunk to the 'memory of Anskterman', the assassin of the king of Sweden.[83] The intemperate nature of the proceedings perhaps accounted for the immoderate tone of the toasts themselves. A gathering of United Irishmen, Catholic Committeemen, Whigs of the Capital, and

[77] Earl Camden to duke of Portland, 24 Aug. 1796 (PROHO 100/62/190–4).
[78] Peter Shaw, *American patriots and the rituals of revolution* (Cambridge, Mass., 1981), 180–4.
[79] Lynn Hunt, *Politics, culture, and class in the French revolution* (Berkeley, Calif., 1984), 59.
[80] See e.g. M. J. McMustin to T. L——d, 11 Aug. 1796 (SPOI, Rebellion papers, 620/24/107); Holdcroft to Dublin Castle, 14 May 1797 (ibid. 620/30/73); see also William McClure to John Lee, 13 June 1796 (ibid. 620/23/171); Thomas Connolly to Dublin Castle, 19 Nov. 1796 (ibid. 620/26/61).
[81] Andrew Macnevin to Edward Cooke, 18 Aug. 1796 (ibid. 620/24/128).
[82] Andrew Newton to Revd Richard Bourne, 15 Aug. 1796 (ibid. 620/24/120).
[83] 'J. W.' to Downshire, [Dec. 1794] (PRONI, Downshire papers, D607/C/56).

Aldermen of Skinner's Alley dined together in Dublin in March 1792 and drank zealously to the desire that 'the glorious revolution in France [may] be realized in Ireland and [that] all Irishmen [may] unite to exterminate an English party influence and become a free and independent people'. Friends of the people such as Henry Grattan, William Drennan, Theobald Wolfe Tone, and James Napper Tandy were lauded to the accompaniment of draining glasses. The informer who forwarded these toasts, citing them as evidence of seditious designs against the state, listed eight of them, and noted that many other toasts were drunk as well.[84]

Even such an orgy of drink was a means of binding participants closer together in their political association. The ceremony and ritual of drinking toasts in the cause of a liberated Ireland was imitated by lower-class adherents of the United Irishmen throughout the 1790s. A favourite toast of the Defenders was 'confusion to the followers of Luther and Calvin', thus ritualizing and emphasizing the movement's sectarianism.[85] Toasts could be ghastly and threatening as well. A County Tyrone magistrate related the following blood-chilling toast to his bishop, suggestive of the acute hostility that the republicans directed at the established church: 'May the guts of the rectors become strings for the bows of the United Irishmen.'[86]

As vehicles for United Irish propaganda by deed, these ceremonies, rituals, symbols, and emblems were, like demonstrations, of mixed value. At best, they reaffirmed support for the United Irish cause. The sporting of a shamrock or a green cockade, or the adoption of a short haircut, was a public mark of support for the insurrectionary movement. As such, it reinforced the bearer's sense of patriotism and civic duty. It associated him with like-minded fellow citizens. But such emblems also targeted the bearer for official harassment and possibly arrest. Toasting radical heroes and sentiments added a vital element of sociability to United Irish mobilization and contributed to the republican effort to frighten opponents, but it could also expose the toastmaster to the unwanted attention of the authorities. For example, a Carrickfergus United Irishman, Sam Hill, was arrested for the toast 'May the arms of France never rest until they conquer their enemies and especially these three kingdoms.'[87] Furthermore, using a tavern or public house as a venue for United Irish gatherings posed serious problems for maintaining the secrecy of the movement. Public houses and inns provided recruiting grounds for United Irishmen, as well as convenient and inconspicuous places for United Irish committees to transact business. But the disadvantages of meeting in a drinking environment became increasingly

---

[84] List of toasts, 13 Mar. 1792 (SPOI, Rebellion papers, 620/19/69).

[85] William Elliott to Dublin Castle, 14 May 1795 (Kent CAO, Pratt papers, U840/0164/16).

[86] Andrew Newton to Revd Dr —— O'Connor, 16 Nov. 1796 (SPOI, Rebellion papers, 620/26/57).

[87] Memorandum on the United Irishmen in Carrickfergus, [June 1795] (Kent CAO, Pratt papers, U840/0147/4/2).

apparent. When the radicals convened at the local tavern, they tended to discuss treason and sedition over a glass of ale. This inevitably led to indiscretion as tongues were loosened under the stimulus of strong drink. Alert bystanders, having overheard some particularly damning comments, frequently reported them to the authorities in return for money or other rewards. The Ulster provincial executive eventually responded to this danger by issuing an order in May 1797 prohibiting the use of public houses for United Irish gatherings.[88]

In short, United Irish propaganda by deed served a positive purpose in creating an alternative political culture which strove to secure the allegiance of thousands of Irish men and women. At their most profound level, republican demonstrations, rituals, and symbols invited universal participation in the radical cause. Those who were denied the status of citizen under the ascendancy could hope to find full scope for civic advancement within the political world of the United Irishmen. In numerous ways, the people could demonstrate their willingness to assume civic responsibility by participating in United Irish activities or merely by wearing some emblem of republican sympathies. Thus United Irish propaganda by deed reflected the civic humanist ideology adapted by Irish reformers and revolutionaries.

[88] Earl Annesley to Dublin Castle, 30 May 1797 (SPOI, Rebellion papers, 620/30/254).

10

Rebellion

As the year 1798 opened, the government could congratulate itself on the success of its Ulster policy. 'I believe no part of the king's dominions [is] more apparently quiet or more evidently flourishing than the north of Ireland,' Under-secretary Cooke cautiously assured Lord Auckland.[1] But the revolutionary spirit in Ulster had not been completely broken by the drastic military measures implemented with such zestful enthusiasm by General Lake. Admittedly, numerous leaders and many arms, the essentials for successful revolutionary mobilization, had been seized by the government, and the country people were faced with the terrors of military occupation. But despite these adverse conditions, the embers of republicanism still stirred in the north. One anonymous writer warned the administration that the

fire of sedition *apparently* extinguished has only been covered with ashes that will rise when the United Irishmen think the moment fit in a general conflagration. It was in the north that the spirit of rebellion took its birth; it is in the north that it is fostered; it is there it was brought to its maturity; it is there, in fine, where lies the hopes, the spring, the wealth, the force of the United Irishmen.[2]

But despite the confident claims of this writer, by 1798 the centre of the conspiracy had shifted from Belfast to Dublin. In November 1797 a national directory was established in the capital, the culmination of the activities of northern republican emissaries to extend the movement throughout the four provinces of Ireland. By February 1798 the United Irishmen boasted half a million members, over 280,000 of whom were apparently armed and ready for battle.[3] But the United Irishmen frequently exaggerated their numbers; every one who had ever sworn the oath, willingly or not, was counted.[4] It did seem, however, that the republicans would enjoy widespread support in the country if and when they should take the field. Ulster promised 110,990 active insurgents, while Munster

---

[1] Edward Cooke to Lord Auckland, 19 Mar. 1798 (BL, Auckland papers, Add. MS 34454/181–2).
[2] —— to Dublin Castle, 28 Mar. 1798 (SPOI, Rebellion papers, 620/36/88).
[3] Francis Higgins to Dublin Castle, 21 Feb. 1798 (ibid. 620/18/14); resolutions and returns of the national committee (of the United Irishmen), 26 Feb. 1798 (PROHO 100/75/132–5).
[4] Edward Boyle to Edward Cooke, 12 May 1797 (SPOI, Rebellion papers, 620/30/61); *Rep. secret comm.* 71.

claimed 100,634 and Leinster 68,272. No returns were available from Connacht, where the movement was enjoying only slight success.[5]

Most disturbing for the government were the reports that the revolutionary system was at its most perfect in those counties where peace and stability apparently prevailed.[6] Thus the restored quiet of Ulster, Dublin, and Meath was a mere delusion, and the renewed outbreak of agrarian disturbances in Munster and south and west Leinster was simply an expression of local discontent among the lower classes, a revival of Whiteboyism rather than an extension of Jacobinism throughout the country. If the government was to concentrate its forces on those areas in an actual state of disturbance, would it then permit those counties most riddled with republicanism to strengthen their organization and prepare for open rebellion? How, indeed, was the administration to deploy its limited forces in the face of such a dilemma?

This was the problem that faced the recently appointed commander-in-chief in Ireland, Sir Ralph Abercromby, late in 1797. One of the ablest generals in the British army and a proven and humane administrator, Abercromby did not take long to realize that the armed forces in Ireland were in desperate need of reform.[7] What concerned the general most, however, was the manner in which his forces were deployed. Abercromby saw his primary responsibility as defending Ireland against a French invasion. But the government had allowed more than half of its regular troops to be dispersed in small parties throughout the country to protect the gentry in disturbed areas. 'In their present state,' Abercromby insisted in December 1797 to General Lake, commander of the northern district, 'they are exposed to be corrupted, to be disarmed and made prisoners.'[8] This kind of police work should be left to the local yeomanry, with the regulars and militia stationed in large bodies in garrison towns, ready to move and meet any invasion attempt.[9]

Abercromby held the magistracy and gentry responsible for permitting the defence of the nation to deteriorate into such an alarming condition. If the country gentlemen would only exert themselves, assisted, as intended, by the local yeomanry, regular troops could be deployed to resist invasion. 'On the yeomanry and the exertions of the gentlemen and of the

---

[5] Resolutions and returns of the national committee (of the United Irishmen), 26 Feb. 1798 (PROHO 100/75/132–5).

[6] Earl Camden to duke of Portland, 6 Aug. 1796 (ibid. 100/64/168–72).

[7] W. E. H. Lecky, *A history of Ireland in the eighteenth century* (5 vols., London, 1898), iv. 199–200.

[8] Quoted in Thomas Pakenham, *The year of liberty: the story of the great Irish rebellion of 1798* (London, 1978), 60.

[9] Gen. Sir Ralph Abercromby to Thomas Pelham, 23 Jan. 1798 (BL, Pelham papers, Add. MS 33105/334).

Rebellion

well-disposed inhabitants of the country,' he declared, 'its internal security must principally depend.'[10]

The supineness of the local magistracy had been a constant complaint among Castle officials, who readily endorsed Abercromby's view of the matter. Yet the daily flood of letters from country gentlemen urgently requesting military protection could not be ignored. And when Abercromby issued his famous order on 26 February 1798, he called down upon himself the fury and outrage not only of the Irish gentry, but of his subordinate officers and key officials in the administration as well. After returning from a tour of the south, Abercromby sent a circular letter to all generals and commanding officers which proclaimed that the Irish army was 'in a state of licentiousness which must render it formidable to everyone but the enemy'.[11] He reasoned that the notorious excesses of martial law might well inflame the smouldering rebellion of the country.

Although not a party man himself and innocent of any political intrigue, Abercromby was accused of playing into the hands of the British parliamentary opposition, which had been condemning the violent and tyrannical proceedings of the army and magistracy in Ireland. Beresford, Clare, Foster, and Cooke took every opportunity to call for his ouster and to turn Pitt and Portland against the commander-in-chief. An agitated Beresford was astonished at Abercromby's proposal to ease the official terror: 'What is to become of us if such conduct is to go on? The country is highly exasperated. . . . Everyone sees the rebellion, the intention of overturning the constitution and murdering every man of property and loyalty . . . Full powers must be given and acted upon, and it is a joke to imagine that anything else will now answer or be submitted to.'[12]

Aware of the intrigue against him and conscious that he had lost the confidence of the principal members of Camden's cabinet, Abercromby offered his resignation. In accepting it, Camden submitted to those of his Irish subordinates who urged him to take more vigorous action in subduing sedition at home even if it might mean bypassing the laws of the realm. Reluctantly, but deprived of any consistent guidance from Pitt or Portland, the viceroy found himself accelerating the distasteful policy of coercion in Irish affairs.[13] That powerful triumvirate of the Irish government—Beresford, Clare, and Foster—led the disgruntled and alarmed Anglo-Irish gentry in demanding extreme solutions to the problems of Ireland's domestic security.

John Foster, speaker of the Irish house of commons, emerged as the

---

[10] Quoted in Lecky, *History of Ireland*, iv. 210.

[11] William Wenman Seward, *Collectanea politica* (3 vols., Dublin, 1801–4), iii. 214–15.

[12] John Beresford to Lord Auckland, 24 Mar. 1798 (PRONI, Sneyd papers, T3229/2/30).

[13] For Camden's persistent pleas for more ministerial attention to his problems, see e.g. Earl Camden to William Pitt, 10 Oct. 1797 (PRO, Chatham papers, 30/8/326/214–19).

leader and voice of this right-wing party, which enjoyed the support of the Orange Order.[14] Even though there was insufficient evidence to bring the known leaders of the conspiracy to trial, he advocated that they should be arrested. By removing the heads of the revolutionary republican movement, the government might throw the organization into such confusion as to render it ineffectual. Foster argued at a cabinet meeting that such a measure 'might possibly produce an insurrection in some part of the kingdom, but under all the circumstances the event might not be unpropitious, as it would be more in our power to quell it than if such an event happened when the enemy were off our coast'.[15] The logic of Foster's proposal was sound, if harsh. There was no question that a successful French invasion would bring about a mass rising which the British forces in Ireland would have little chance of defeating. A partial, uncoordinated, leaderless, and premature rising by the United Irishmen and their allies in the countryside might be put down swiftly and easily, in addition to offering the opportunity to break the back of the conspiracy permanently.

Again, Camden was loath to give extreme loyalists their head, but information received from the United Irish traitor Thomas Reynolds late in February 1798 convinced the viceroy that immediate action was necessary. According to Reynolds, who was a member of the Leinster directory, the underground army now numbered nearly 300,000 armed men evenly distributed (so he said) throughout Leinster, Munster, and Ulster. In March the directory would meet in Dublin to debate once again a motion to rise immediately, unassisted by the French, and this time the proposal was expected to pass.[16] Camden consequently approved Foster's proposal that the republican leaders should be arrested.[17]

On 12 March 1798 government forces under the command of Dublin's chief of police, Major Henry Charles Sirr, raided the planned meeting of the Leinster directory at the house of Oliver Bond. Fourteen delegates, together with significant, though not highly incriminating, papers were seized, and soon Emmet, MacNeven, John Sweetman, and Henry Jackson, none of whom had attended the meeting, were also apprehended. Another absentee was more fortunate. Lord Edward Fitzgerald eluded the warrant for his immediate arrest.[18]

The revolutionary movement was thrown into a state of temporary confusion. But immediately after the arrests, a new directory, consisting of five members—John and Henry Sheares, John Lawless, Sam Neilson, and the fugitive Lord Edward Fitzgerald—was formed which issued a calming

[14] A. P. W. Malcomson, *John Foster: the politics of the Anglo-Irish ascendancy* (Oxford, 1978), 72–5.

[15] Camden to Portland, 8 Feb. 1798 (PROHO 100/75/71–2).

[16] Information of Thomas Reynolds, 9 May 1798 (SPOI, Rebellion papers, 620/3/32/23).

[17] Camden to Portland, 6 Mar. 1798 (PROHO 100/75/162–9).

[18] *FDJ*, 13, 15 Mar. 1798; *BNL*, 29 Mar. 1798.

statement to the rank and file on 17 March.[19] In Lord Edward Fitzgerald the directory enjoyed the participation of a man with practical military experience. More important, however, Lord Edward offered the magic, aristocratic name of Fitzgerald to the popular movement, and with it a time-honoured tradition of resistance to English rule. A Fitzgerald at their head gave the people not only a sanction for rebellion, but also a talisman for success.

Assuming the command of about 280,000 potential insurgents, Lord Edward had no illusions that his civilian army could seriously engage the better-armed and better-disciplined crown forces in open combat. His plan was to take advantage of the element of surprise and secure a quick victory. The date for the rebellion was set for 23 May 1798. Signalled by the seizure of the Dublin–Belfast mail coach, United Irishmen in Leinster and Ulster would then rise to secure their respective counties. In addition, the plan called for the convergence on the capital of the surrounding United Irish forces of some 10,000 men, under Lord Edward's personal command. If the rebel forces could take the government unawares, they might score an early and crucial victory. With Dublin in rebel hands, the rest of the country must soon follow suit. Even if unsuccessful in securing an early victory, the insurgents in Dublin might prevent the government from sending military reinforcements to the other disturbed areas. Conversely, the scattered risings in Ulster and Leinster would tie down the local forces, ensuring that additional troops could not be sent to relieve Dublin. Thus the dispersed forces of the crown, while superior in arms and training, would be victims of the rebels' superiority in numbers.[20]

The capture of Lord Edward Fitzgerald on 19 May led the government to hope that it had finally neutralized the expected rising. With their leader seized only a few days before the insurrection scheduled for 23 May, the United Irishmen were disoriented. But did Lord Edward's capture mean that his plan for the rising would have to be postponed? Or was everything to go off as originally intended? Despite the uncertainty, the signal for rebellion was given when, on 23 May, the mail coaches from Dublin were seized. On the next day numerous parties of United Irishmen appeared in arms in the counties of Dublin, Kildare, and Meath. On 24 May Dublin was placed under martial law. Troops scoured the city in search of arms and suspected rebels. No rising materialized in the capital, owing to a lack of co-ordination and leadership. Those United Irishmen in the city still determined on resisting the government forces made their way to rebel camps in Kildare, Meath, and Wicklow. A reign of terror was let loose on

[19] Marianne Elliott, *Partners in revolution: the United Irishman and France* (New Haven, Conn., and London, 1982), 195; United Irish handbill about the arrest of the Leinster directory, Mar. 1798 (SPOI, Rebellion papers, 620/36/29).
[20] Pakenham, *Year of liberty*, 106–7.

those remaining. With Dublin secured by an increasingly confident and aggressive yeomanry, the government was able to concentrate on the scattered risings in the rest of Leinster. But then the explosion occurred in Wexford.[21]

Indeed, it was with a sense of relief that some members and supporters of the government greeted the first appearance of a United Irish insurrection. The long-promised confrontation had finally begun, and with it came a chance to deal the disaffected a final and fatal blow. 'I consider this insurrection, however distressing, as really the salvation of the country,' Cooke observed in a highly confidential letter. 'If you look at the accounts that 200,000 men are sworn in a conspiracy, how could that conspiracy be cleared without a burst? Besides,' he added significantly, 'it will prove many things necessary for the future settlement of the country when peace arises.'[22]

Unfortunately, such calm assurances about the benefits to be derived from rebellion in Ireland may have made English ministers less than sensitive to the distressed pleas of other members of the Irish administration. Pelham's successor, Castlereagh, for example, found it difficult to convey the real danger in which Irish loyalists found themselves when confronted by open rebellion in May 1798.

I understand . . . you are rather inclined to hold the insurrection cheap. Rely upon it, there never was in any country so formidable an effort on the part of the people. It may not disclose itself in the full extent of its preparations if it is early met with vigour and success; but our force cannot cope in a variety of distant points with an enemy that can elude an attack where it is inexpedient to risk a contest.[23]

The rising in Wexford had proved surprisingly formidable. Ill-armed, undisciplined, and unacquainted with fundamental military tactics, the rebels could compensate in numbers and determination for what they lacked in leadership and co-ordination. When one victory attracted hundreds of fresh recruits, the insurgents had only to hold on until the French arrived and the rebellion assumed national proportions. The government, however, was fighting against time. 'Everything depends on the first success,' Castlereagh

[21] For the rebellion in Leinster, see Lecky, *History of Ireland*, iv. 320–402; Pakenham, *Year of liberty*, 123–93, 213–317; for a close examination of the rising in Wexford, see L. M. Cullen, *The emergence of modern Ireland, 1600–1900* (London, 1981), 210–33; id., 'The 1798 rebellion in its eighteenth-century context', in Patrick J. Corish (ed.), *Radicals, rebels, and establishments* (Belfast, 1985), 91–113; id., 'The 1798 rebellion in Wexford', in Kevin Whelan and William Nolan (eds.), *Wexford: history and society* (Dublin, 1987), 248–95; Thomas Powell, 'An economic factor in the Wexford rebellion of 1798', *Studia Hibernica*, 16 (1976), 140–57; Kevin Whelan, 'Politicisation in County Wexford and the origins of the 1798 rebellion', in Hugh Gough and David Dickson (eds.), *Ireland and the French revolution* (Dublin, 1990), 83–108.

[22] Edward Cooke to William Wickham, 26 May 1798 (PROHO 100/76/289).

[23] Viscount Castlereagh to Thomas Pelham, 8 [June 1798] (Sir John T. Gilbert (ed.), *Documents relating to Ireland, 1795–1804* (Dublin, 1893), 131–2).

observed. 'It will cost much exertion to reconquer the country should the rebellion establish itself in the four provinces.'[24] The contagious insurgency in Wexford must not be allowed to infect the rest of the country. And if the French should arrive in the mean time, Ireland might well be lost. 'Even a small body of French will set the country ablaze,' warned Camden, 'and I think neither our force nor our staff equal to the very difficult circumstances they will have to encounter.'[25] While many British observers may have regarded the disturbances in Wexford as a local rising, to be easily contained and crushed by better-trained and better-equipped crown forces, the Irish government saw the situation as far more threatening. Only a quick victory would discourage further risings in other parts of the country and stave off disaster for the loyalist forces in Ireland. Only a pacified Ireland could repulse the expected French invasion.

The French failed to arrive until the flame of insurrection had died out in the late summer of 1798. But the fatal blow had been delivered when Ulster, the cradle of Irish republicanism, refused to play its part in what should have been a national insurrection. During the first week of June the rebellion in Wexford had assumed alarming proportions, but the government was encouraged to find that it was still largely confined to the southeast. The course of the rebellion, the incidence of slaughter and plunder that assumed a particularly sectarian character, allowed the government to convey the impression, sadly well-founded to some extent, that this was a peasant revolt which violated the rights of property, and, worse, a popish rebellion intent on the massacre of all protestants. Both descriptions would have a chilling effect on the United Irishmen in the north. 'Depend upon it,' a complacent General Knox reported from Dungannon on 6 June, 'the Presbyterians will not abet a Catholic plot.'[26] But on the very day in early June that *Freeman's Journal* congratulated the north, and especially Belfast, on its tranquillity and loyalty during the current crisis, the United Irishmen and Defenders of Antrim were gathering under the insurrectionary banner of Henry Joy McCracken.[27]

The road to rebellion in the north had been strewn with twists and turns as well as the obstacles of cowardice, timidity, and outright betrayal. The disarming of Ulster had delivered a serious blow to the northern republicans. The severity of the blow, and the degree to which the movement was able to recover from it, are difficult to determine. The apparent tranquillity of the north for much of the first half of 1798 could have been the result of the government's repressive policy, or the United Irishmen may have suffered only a temporary set-back. The outward peace in Ulster may have

[24] Castlereagh to Pelham, 6 June 1798 (Gilbert (ed.), Documents, 127–8).
[25] Earl Camden to Thomas Pelham, 6 June 1798 (ibid. 128–30).
[26] Gen. John Knox to Edward Cooke, 6 June 1798 (SPOI, Rebellion papers, 620/38/61).
[27] *FDJ*, 7 June 1798.

been a mere cloak for the redoubled and more disciplined efforts of the republicans. The paper strength of the organization in Ulster exceeded that of any other province on the eve of the rebellion. The hierarchy of committees functioned effectively throughout the months preceding the insurrection.

Nicholas Magin, a colonel in the United Irish military organization in Down and a recently appointed member of the Ulster provincial committee, kept the government fully informed of the movement's intentions and plans. It was Magin's contention that the United Irishmen in the north had no plans to join the insurgents of the south unless the French landed to spark a national rising.[28] Caution became the keynote of the northern organization. This caution no doubt had its roots in the bitter experience of the previous year, when Lake's troops, supported by local yeomen and Orangemen, had terrorized the republicans into passivity, if not submission.

As the movement spread to the south, and as the baton of leadership passed to Dublin, the northern societies found themselves on the fringes of an organization which they had initiated. This may have been another factor in the northern reluctance to rise as planned in the last week of May 1798. No longer leaders of the republican movement, they were wary of becoming mere followers of an uncertain and untried organization in the south. This was not simply a matter of wounded pride; it was rooted in a suspicion that the rebellion in the south was not a republican rising and, indeed, bore no relationship to the principles of non-sectarianism and popular democracy which drew Ulstermen to the standard of the United Irishmen. 'Such a change in politics [as] has appeared in this town and neighbourhood within these few days past . . . is beyond what your lordship could imagine, knowing the people,' a Belfast correspondent of the marquis of Downshire remarked on 1 June 1798. 'The stubborn and insolent republican is now become mild and gentle and wishes to put on a red coat in defence of his country.'[29] Another of Downshire's correspondents from Hillsborough reported:

It turns out to be a religious contest. The accounts of the ravages committed by the insurgents exceed belief and almost equal anything that has been done in France. It is said that at Enniscorthy in the county of Wexford every protestant man, woman, and child, even infants, have been murdered. . . . It has detached the Protestants [of the north] from a union with them [the Catholics] in their treasonable views.[30]

An oath, supposedly found among the insurgents in Wexford, was industriously circulated in the north, purportedly proving the sectarian nature of

[28] Viscount Castlereagh to William Wickham, 22 June 1798 (PROHO 100/77/180–1).
[29] James McKay to marquess of Downshire, 1 June 1798 (PRONI, Downshire papers, D607/F/192).
[30] Revd Edward Lascelles to marquess of Downshire, 4 June 1798 (ibid. D607/F/195).

the rebellion: 'I, A. B., do solemnly swear by my lord Jesus Christ, who died for me on the cross, and by the Blessed Virgin Mary, that I will burn, destroy, and murder all heretics *up* to my knees in blood.'[31] With newspapers rivalling rumour in portraying in Wexford an image of Catholic massacre and plunder equalled only by legends surrounding the rebellion of 1641, it was no wonder that many protestant United Irishmen turned their backs on the southern insurrection. They regarded it as a popish rebellion, and political principle and religious prejudice forbade them from aiding or abetting such a conspiracy.

Another reason for the decline in revolutionary spirit and initiative in the north was disillusionment with the French.[32] First, the French had mismanaged the Bantry Bay expedition by not informing the United Irishmen of its approach and by arriving in the remote south-west, where they could count on little organized assistance from the native population. Then a splendid opportunity for transforming British adversity into republican advantage had been lost when the French failed to capitalize on the mutiny of the British fleet at the Nore and Spithead in May 1797. For nearly a month the British were unable to blockade the French navy, thus leaving the door open for a successful invasion of Ireland. But the French, elated by Britain's embarrassment, nevertheless failed to exploit it.[33] Despite their repeated promises of aid, the French appeared unable or unwilling to deliver them.

The resulting lack of faith in French promises of assistance was reinforced by the growing disillusionment with the course of French republicanism. The French failed to live up to the standards that Irish republicans set for them. Most disquieting was France's treatment of those countries and territories which it had supposedly liberated. The complete subjugation of the Dutch republic, the republic of Venice, and the republic of Genoa, as well as the threats to the Swiss confederation, placed the French in the light of conquering despots fighting against the tide of national liberty.[34] Even more damaging in Irish republican eyes, however, was the rift between republican France and the republic in America.

Ulstermen were, of course, bound to America by ties of kinship, sympathy, and an affinity in their constitutional relationship to Great Britain.

---

[31] John Patrickson to marquess of Downshire, 6 June 1798 (PRONI, Downshire papers, D607/F/199).

[32] Such disillusionment was actively fostered by loyalists: see e.g. *French fraternity and French protection, as promised to Ireland and as experienced by other nations, addressed to all ranks and descriptions in this kingdom, by a friend to the people* (18th edn., Dublin, 1798), apparently a very popular pamphlet denouncing French tyranny.

[33] For these mutinies and the failed invasion attempt, see Elliott, *Partners in revolution*, 134–8; Albert Goodwin, *The friends of liberty* (London, 1979), 406–11; W. Benjamin Kennedy, 'The United Irishmen and the great naval mutiny of 1797', *Eire-Ireland*, 25/3 (Autumn 1990), 7–18; Roger Wells, *Insurrection: the British experience, 1795–1803* (Gloucester, 1983), 79–109.

[34] R. R. Palmer, *The age of democratic revolution: a political history of Europe and America, 1760–1800* (2 vols., Princeton, NJ, 1959), ii. 293–421.

America had done what the Irish were attempting to do—break the bonds subjecting them to Britain. For radical Irishmen, the sight of two great republics in France and America pointed the way for the inevitable toppling of illiberal government in Ireland. The French and Americans formed the phalanx of the future, opposed at every turn by the despotism of the past. In 1795, however, under Washington's presidency, the United States' ambassador to the Court of St James, John Jay, negotiated a controversial commercial treaty with the British. The terms of the treaty gave Britain the status of a 'most favoured nation' in American trade. This outraged the Jeffersonian republicans at home and Irish radicals and the French abroad. It appeared that the United States was establishing an informal alliance with Great Britain and betraying the republican cause in France.

Jay's treaty naturally generated a great deal of ill feeling towards America in Paris, and the immediate consequence was that American shipping became the target of French attacks. Although Irishmen denounced the treaty, they were disturbed by this French assault on a neutral power. The Americans attempted to negotiate with the French on this matter, but after initial rebuffs, the French rather highhandedly announced that their outrage could only be appeased by a large and immediate loan. The Americans were unwilling to accept such terms, but offered to negotiate a commercial treaty with the French every bit as liberal as that which they had concluded with the British. The French proved intransigent, even threatening to confiscate the property of all Americans residing in Paris unless the desired loan was forthcoming. The French were, in effect, requiring tribute from the American republic and challenging its sovereignty. Hostility on both sides was intense, and mutual declarations of war were only just averted.[35]

In Belfast especially, former revolutionaries were flocking to sign resolutions denouncing French tyranny. One observer noted the amazing change among northern republicans:

They now abhor the French as much as they formerly were partial to them, and are grown quite loyal. Last Monday the king's birthday was celebrated at Belfast with as much public rejoicing as it ever was at St James's. Not only the whole town was illuminated, but bonfires were lighted on all the adjoining hills. This could not be counterfeit. . . . It is owing to the scurvy treatment which the French have shown to the United States of America, so beloved and admired by our northern republicans. You know how enthusiastically fond they were of the Americans, and now that the latter must fly to Great Britain for protection, their Irish friends are become the warm adherents of Great Britain.[36]

---

[35] For a discussion of this deterioration in the relationship between France and the United States, see Lance Banning, *The Jeffersonian persuasion: evolution of a party ideology* (Ithaca, NY, 1978), 233–64.

[36] Quoted in Lecky, *History of Ireland*, iv. 414–15.

Disappointment with French promises of aid, disillusionment with French policies, the arrest of United Irish leaders, the repressive policies of a government enthusiastically and zealously aided by an increasingly confident and formidable yeomanry and Orange Order, and the sectarian course of the rebellion in the south—all served to dampen the revolutionary spirit of the northern republicans. Yet the resulting defections still left northern radicals in the spring of 1798 with a determined force ready to establish a non-sectarian republic in Ireland. Prominent among those who wished to take the field in support of their southern brethren was Henry Joy McCracken.

McCracken had been released from Kilmainham in December 1797 owing to the deterioration of his health. After recuperating in Belfast for a few months, nursed by his sister Mary Ann, he went to Dublin to liaise between the Ulster provincial committee and the national executive, along with the wealthy Belfast ship-broker Robert Hunter.[37] In February the northern societies were informed that they should prepare themselves for a rising. McCracken stayed on in Dublin after the arrest of the Leinster directory, assisting his old friend Sam Neilson in organizing the rebellion. In the middle of May he returned to the north to communicate the final plans for the rising, only to discover that preparations were being held up by the timidity of the Ulster leaders.[38] Preoccupied with the day-to-day needs of survival and the avoidance of detection, the United Irish organization in the north seemed to have lost sight of its strategic aims. When orders came in February to prepare for imminent rebellion, the Ulster leaders methodically went about the business, but enthusiasm for an open confrontation with the government had abated considerably in recent months. Those numerous United Irish leaders in the north who had confidently believed that the Irish people alone could break the chains which bound them in subservience to Britain had either been arrested or had fled in the face of government persecution. They were replaced by the 'foreign-aid men', the timid, cautious, middle-class leaders who, according to Hope, had far more to lose than their chains in an unsuccessful contest, and who therefore preferred to wait until the French had actually landed before they acted. When news arrived that the rising would take place before the arrival of the French fleet, though the latter was expected soon, these northern leaders were thrown into a state of confusion and indecision. The bloody course of the southern rebellion was not yet a deterrent to northern action on 23 May, the date of the projected rising. But the arrest of Fitzgerald on 19 May and the failure of any rising to emerge in Dublin encouraged the northerners to think that

[37] William McCracken to John and Ann McCracken, 9 Dec. 1797 (PRONI, McCracken papers, T1210/39); R. R. Madden, The *United Irishmen, their lives and times*, 3rd ser. (7 vols., London, 1842–5), ii. 422–3; examination of Hill Thompson, 1798 (SPOI, Rebellion papers, 620/3/32/8).

[38] Madden, *United Irishmen*, ii. 444–5.

the rebellion had been postponed. According to James Hope, 'The general of Antrim [Robert Simms] either misunderstood or knowingly misrepresented' the instructions that McCracken brought to the Ulster executive concerning the general rising.[39] Mary Ann McCracken, with characteristic charity, suggested that the Belfast directory might have misunderstood her brother by assuming that the 'first signal', the stopping of the mail coach to Belfast, 'was only one for preparation, and that it was to be followed by another giving certain knowledge of the rising in Dublin having taken place'.[40] At any rate, on 23 May the mail coach was stopped, the signal had been given, and the north did not rise.

Robert Hunter interpreted the mail-coach signal as an order to wait until Dublin was secured before launching the rising in Ulster. 'Violent young men,' among whom Hunter counted McCracken, Henry Munro, Samuel Orr (brother to the celebrated martyr William), and James Dickey, 'who had not the confidential communications, attempted to bring out the people.' Reports were received at the same time by the Ulster executive that many colonels had resolved not to rise unless there was a French invasion. Realistically appraising the situation, then, Hunter and his like-minded comrades decided that, in good conscience, they could not lead their followers to certain defeat, a defeat which would, as the counter-revolutionary terror of the last year confirmed, have only the most tragic consequences for the people of the north.[41]

On 29 May 1798 an Ulster provincial meeting was held as scheduled in Armagh. This was the first meeting to be convened after the outbreak of the rebellion in the south, and so it became the forum for an attack on the timid leadership of Simms and his colleagues on the Ulster directory. A Belfast shopkeeper, Thomas Bashford, junior, opened the assault by reviewing the directory's inaction over the last week as a betrayal of the people. Plans had been presented to the northern executive for a general rising, but the executive refused to summon the colonels to prepare for it. The mail coaches had been stopped as planned, giving the signal for the rising, but, despite repeated applications by McCracken and others, the Ulster directory had refused to act. Under the circumstances, Bashford maintained, the directory should be denounced and the provincial assembly should vote them out of office, which it subsequently did. It was then resolved that the adjutant-generals from Down and Antrim should meet the following day to draw up a general plan of insurrection for Ulster which would then be communicated to the adjutant-generals in the other northern counties. Although the general consensus of the assembly was for an immediate

---

[39] Hope, 'Autobiographical memoir', 123.
[40] Quoted in Edna Fitzhenry, *Henry Joy McCracken* (Dublin, 1936), 113.
[41] Report of Joseph Pollock on his examination of Robert Hunter, 29 Jan. 1799 (SPOI, Rebellion papers, 620/7/74/5).

rising, William Campbell, an Armagh innkeeper and host of the proceedings, was not convinced. He moved that, if there was no insurrection, the committee should meet on 24 June in Belfast. His motion was successfully opposed by his comrades, who argued that, in that case, it would be better to refrain from meeting ever again, for they should all go back to their homes and occupations and cease to deceive the people with hopes of a revolution which they themselves were unwilling to undertake.[42]

Simms was forced to call the United Irish colonels of Antrim to a meeting at Parkgate on 1 June. The meeting, though well attended, dispersed without conducting any business when it was learned that a company of dragoons was on its way to arrest them. The delegates then made their way to nearby Templepatrick to pursue their deliberations. Many expected that the final orders to rise would be given and that plans would be discussed, but they were sorely discouraged when the already beleaguered Simms announced his resignation; he refused to lead an insurrection with a doubtful outcome. A new commander had to be chosen, and delegates were sent out to canvass likely candidates. The colonels resolved to meet the next day to decide the fateful question of the rebellion. When they met again, however, they still had no commander-in-chief, a circumstance which seriously undermined their revolutionary resolve. Though their forces were numerous, these colonels contended that the organization in County Antrim was neither ordered enough nor sufficiently armed to risk battle with government troops. A heated debate ensued, but the foreign-aid men carried the day. It was resolved to wait for the ever-promised French invasion before committing the Antrim United Irishmen to the field. Their opponents roundly accused the victors of treachery to the movement and cowardice, and retired in protest from the proceedings.[43]

A few of those who had voted against the rising were returning home by way of Ballyeaston when they were stopped by a number of inferior officers anxious to learn the outcome of the colonels' meeting. 'On this being known,' Samuel McSkimin recounted,

the crowd burst forth into an open uproar, and shouts of 'aristocrats', 'despots', 'cowards', 'villains', and even 'traitors' were heard from the multitude. The unpopular leaders sought shelter from the 'pelting of the pitiless storm'. Amidst horrid threats and confusion a meeting was convened anew, at which the Belfast gentleman presided, the decision . . . was reversed, and the sovereign people declared they were appeased![44]

---

[42] Nicholas Magin's report on the meeting of the provincial committee held at Armagh, 29 May 1798 (PRONI, R. C. Lytton White papers, D714/2/23).

[43] Madden, *United Irishmen*, ii. 444–6.

[44] Samuel McSkimin, *Annals of Ulster from 1790 to 1798*, ed. E. J. McCrum (Belfast, 1906), 70.

The 'Belfast gentleman' may well have been McCracken himself, who was present at the scene. At any rate, he was appointed to command the United Irish forces and swiftly went about forming plans for the rising.

As the Ballyeaston affair suggests, rank-and-file enthusiasm for an immediate rising was in sharp contrast to the cautious timidity of many of the leaders. How strong, in fact, was the United Irish movement on the eve of the rebellion in Ulster? Official returns from Antrim and Down listed about 49,000 supporters (22,716 in Antrim; 26,153 in Down), which may or may have not included about 8,500 Defenders in the former county.[45] How many of these men actually participated in at least one engagement in June 1798? Estimates of the number of insurgents involved in the battle of Antrim range from 3,000 to 7,000, and for the battle of Ballynahinch, 5,000 to 7,000.[46] Charles Dickson adds 2,000–3,000 who arrived at Donegore Hill too late to engage in the battle for Antrim town.[47] But there were a number of other engagements before defeat in these two battles put the last nail in the coffin of the northern rebellion. As Samuel McSkimin observed: 'In almost every town, village, or hamlet in the county of Antrim, hostile movements in a greater or lesser degree took place.' He estimated that 9,000 rebels took part at the battle of Randalstown, and another 10,000 at Ballymena.[48] Furthermore, an indeterminate number of rebels rose in the Ards peninsula, and there were according to Teeling, who was there, several thousands mobilized and ready for battle in south Down.[49] The most conservative figure to be obtained from these estimates of insurgent forces at the battles of Randalstown, Ballymena, Antrim, and Ballynahinch (excluding the late arrivals at Donegore Hill) is 27,000. In Antrim alone, if we add the 8,500 Defenders to the official returns of nearly 23,000, we might conclude that 22,000 of a possible 31,500 'turned out' in 1798.[50] These figures, rough as they might be, clearly challenge the view of the United Irish organization in the north as merely a hollow shell of republican support, ravaged by Lake's campaign, and pathetically asserting itself in a disorganized frenzy of desperation and bravado. Those who were engaged in minor skirmishes, or who arrived too late for battle, or who failed to link up with the main force, or who waited, as did the men of the Mourne, to join the expected march south to Dublin, are not included in these

---

[45] For the Defender estimate, see ibid. 75.

[46] These figures are offered by Elliott, *Partners in revolution*, 206; Charles Dickson, *Revolt in the north: Antrim and Down in 1798* (Dublin, 1960), 155; Lecky, *History of Ireland*, iv. 416, 420; McSkimin, *Annals*, 78; Pakenham, *Year of liberty*, 252, 259.

[47] Dickson, *Revolt in the north*, 129.   [48] McSkimin, *Annals*, 75, 87.

[49] Charles Hamilton Teeling, *The history of the Irish rebellion of 1798* (1st edn., 1876; Shannon, 1972), 201–3.

[50] Elliott claims that about half of the organized United Irishmen rose in Antrim: see Elliott, *Partners in revolution*, 206.

estimates of insurgent strength in Antrim and Down. The numbers were
there; it was leadership and opportunity that was wanting.

So, the fact that revolutionary zeal failed to manifest itself on a sustained
and massive scale was hardly the result of organizational breakdown.
Northern enthusiasm persisted after Lake's dragooning of Ulster and even
through the confusion following the outbreak of the rebellion in the south,
but many northern militants were denied the opportunity for action by
faulty communications and their leaders' refusal to mobilize them. The hur-
ried state of preparations for the rising after the ousting of the passive
Ulster directory meant that these counties were not ready for the call to
arms when it came. Indeed, the persistence of rank-and-file militancy under
such circumstances suggests that the organization was far more successful
in producing citizens than soldiers.

Although the decision to rise had been made, the timidity of many of the
United Irish leaders was by no means counteracted. 'The greatest part of
our officers,' Hope maintained, 'especially of those we called colonels,
either gave secret information to the enemy or neutralised the exertions of
individuals as far as their influence extended. I never knew a single colonel
in the county of Antrim who, when the time for active measures came, had
drawn out his men or commanded them in that character.'[51] Simms's resignation had thrown the Antrim organization into considerable disarray, and
the arrest of William Steele Dickson, adjutant-general for County Down, on
5 June seriously undermined the readiness of the United Irishmen in that
county. 'The organisation of the north being thus deranged,' Hope recalled,

the colonels flinched, and the chief of the Antrim men, the forlorn-hope party of the
union not appearing, the duty fell on Henry J. McCracken. He sent fighting orders
to the colonels of Antrim, three of whom sent identical orders to General Nugent,
and the messenger sent to Down proving unfaithful, the people of Down had no
correct knowledge of the affairs at Antrim until they heard of the battle of the 7th
of June.[52]

The commander-in-chief's plan for the rising required all colonels of the
United Irish army to marshal their troops and simultaneously attack any
military post in their respective neighbourhoods. Then the insurgents were
to march to Donegore Hill overlooking Antrim town to join McCracken
and whatever troops he had collected in south Antrim. The attack on
Antrim would coincide with a meeting there of the county magistracy. By
this manœuvre, the rebels would seize valuable hostages in the persons of
the county magistrates and they would secure not only the northern part of
the county, but also the road to their next objective, Belfast, the capture
of which would open the way for the unification of the republican armies
of Down and Antrim. It was a well-conceived strategy which might, if

---

[51] Hope, 'Autobiographical memoir', 123–4.   [52] Ibid. 123.

properly executed, have compensated for the disarray of the United Irish organization in the north. An early success was everything, not only for its propaganda value in summoning more recruits, but also for its ability to throw the loyalist forces into confusion and shake their resolve to resist the republican advance. But as Hope ruefully observed, three of McCracken's erstwhile colonels immediately sent General Nugent copies of their leader's orders. Nugent thus prevented the magistrates from keeping their engagement in Antrim town and prepared to send reinforcements to relieve or, if necessary, to recapture the town.

On the morning of 7 June the green flag was raised in the village of Roughfort by McCracken and a band of about twenty men. They were soon joined by contingents from Ballynure and Carnmoney, and they proceeded on the road to Templepatrick, collecting more men on the way.[53] When they arrived at Donegore Hill, McCracken's men were joined by United Irish bands from further north. But the commander-in-chief must have been gravely disappointed with the troops gathered at Donegore Hill, as he counted only about 4,000 men, with the great body of Defenders absent. This was still a formidable force, to be sure, considering the disorganization into which the movement had been thrown in the last weeks, but it was woefully short of expectations. Of course, hundreds of United Irishmen were engaged elsewhere in the county, and about 2,000–3,000 arrived at Donegore too late to participate in the battle. As the rebels gazed out from their lofty height at Donegore, however, they were encouraged to see smoke rising in the direction of Randalstown. The promised rebellion was apparently well under way.

McCracken's marching orders included the instruction to seize Randalstown as well as Antrim. Early on the morning of 7 June the United Irishmen and some Defenders from the surrounding parishes gathered together under the leadership of Samuel Orr and a man named George Dickson. As usual, a detachment of the Toome yeomanry stationed at Randalstown had been forewarned of the insurgents' intentions, but, outnumbered, they failed to repulse the rebel advance which poured into the town simultaneously from the directions of Ballymena, Ahoghill, Portglenone, and Toome. Attesting to the fact that the Defenders had never been fully assimilated into the United Irish organization, the Catholic insurgents fought under banners of green cloth tied to pike shafts, bordered with white or yellow and displaying a yellow cross. At least one banner carried the words, 'Remember Armagh'. The Presbyterian United Irishmen marched under green flags, some of them ornamented with the harp without a crown. At first, the Defenders and United Irishmen hesitated as they disagreed over which body should lead the advance, but they soon reached

---

[53] For the rising in Co. Antrim, see Dickson, *Revolt in the north*, 127–36; Pakenham, *Year of liberty*, 248–55.

the compromise that they should both march together. Under this formidable assault, the yeomanry retreated to the Randalstown market-house while the rebels occupied neighbouring buildings. The antagonists proceeded to fire on one another, but with little advantage to either side. McSkimin caustically observed that,

judging from the firing kept up during this conflict, never were combatants less disposed to deeds of blood. Seldom did any of either appear in sight; the muzzles of the guns were merely seen, and they were fired off either by those protected by the window jambs or who lay squatted on the floor. . . . The contents of their guns rarely descended lower than the roof of the adjoining house, so that if any person was killed or wounded, they had themselves to blame.[54]

This rather desultory combat had continued for about forty minutes when a woman, perhaps impatient with the lackadaisical course of the battle, set fire to the market-house. The yeomen immediately cried out their surrender, but since the stairs to the ground floor were in flames, they relied for their rescue upon the insurgents themselves, who rushed ladders to the soldiers' assistance. Three yeomen lost their lives in the fire, but the entire incident, with rebels rescuing yeomen, was in marked contrast to the bitter and vengeful struggles taking place in the south.[55]

With Randalstown secured, the rebel leaders ordered a small contingent to proceed to Toome bridge, but they were hastily turned back by news that government troops from Derry were on their way to recapture Randalstown. The main body of the Randalstown victors marched on to Antrim, under the command of Samuel Orr, to join McCracken. A smaller force was left behind to keep the town in rebel hands, but during the celebrations that ensued, the Catholics and Presbyterians soon fell into drunken disagreement among themselves. The Presbyterians happily toasted victory to the Irish union, while the Defenders rather churlishly drank success to the 'true Defenders', meaning themselves. Dissensions within their ranks, compounded by news of approaching government troops and the defeat of McCracken at Antrim, alarmed the rebels at Randalstown, who soon evacuated the town and sought the relative safety of their homes.[56]

Risings took place in east Derry as well. In Maghera, about 5,000 rebels gathered to take the town on the night of 7 June. In Garvagh a partial rising took place, but when the leaders discovered that there were more troops in the garrison than expected, they deserted, leaving their followers adrift and discouraged. Similarly, the men of Kilrea were ready to rise, but their chief joined the yeomen on the eve of battle and informed them of the insurgents' plans, thus thwarting the rebel effort in that neighbourhood. Those Derrymen who were still determined to make the effort sent a messenger to McCracken asking for guidance. Should they concentrate their

[54] McSkimin, *Annals*, 75–6.   [55] Ibid. 76.   [56] Ibid. 77.

efforts in their own county, or should they proceed to join the main rebel force at Antrim? Come to Antrim with all speed was the desperate reply. On the way, however, accounts reached the Derry contingent that McCracken had been defeated, and the rebels, uncertain how to proceed under the circumstances, disbanded and returned home.[57]

Ballymena, ten miles to the north of Donegore Hill, was another important strategic centre for the United Irish forces. At about two o'clock in the afternoon of 7 June the rebels attacked the town, drove the defending troops into the market-house, and, as in Randalstown, smoked them out and accepted their surrender. A committee of public safety was appointed to keep the peace in the town, and though some loyalist shops were plundered, the United Irishmen acted with a restraint and order that was to characterize the northern rebels.[58] Similar risings took place in other parts of the county, and by the evening of 7 June, virtually all of Antrim except for the south-east was in rebel hands or under immediate threat of falling to them. Though sedition had always been rife in Belfast and Carrickfergus, the strong presence of large local garrisons kept the inhabitants in order, and those who sought to join the rebels took great pains to elude the watchful guards of the two towns.

The decisive battle, however, took place at Antrim, which, if captured by the insurgents, would have prepared the ground for an assault on Belfast, the junction of the Down and Antrim rebel armies, and the opening of the way for a march on Dublin. On the morning of 7 June General Nugent informed the commander of the Antrim garrison to expect a rebel attack. The garrison consisted of perhaps 150 regular troops, yeomen, and civilian volunteers. Just as McCracken's forces entered the town, however, a vanguard of Nugent's promised reinforcements, a party of about 150 mounted dragoons, galloped into the town. A pitched battle ensued in which the cavalry came off worst, losing about fifty men. The tide appeared to be turning in the rebels' favour, and the dragoons began their retreat. Just at that moment Samuel Orr led his Randalstown men into the town. Confronted by the retreating dragoons, Orr's men thought that they were being attacked; they panicked and broke ranks. Half an hour later the rest of Nugent's reinforcements arrived, armed with artillery, and the rebels were quickly routed.[59]

McCracken returned to the rebel camp at Donegore Hill, hoping desperately that reinforcements would greet him. But the news of his defeat travelled quickly, and those who arrived late to the battle rapidly dispersed when they saw the course that it was taking. On the rebel side, the casualties had been light. Of the several thousand who had taken part in the battle, less than a score actually fell in combat. On the loyalist side, perhaps

[57] Ibid.   [58] Dickson, *Revolt in the north*, 137–9.
[59] McSkimin, *Annals*, 78–81; Madden, *United Irishmen*, ii. 451–7.

sixty were killed or wounded.[60] While the rebels lost few in the fighting itself, those unlucky enough to be captured by the victorious loyalists found themselves victims of brutal revenge, in marked contrast to the rebels' own treatment of captured loyalists. Suspected rebels were hunted down and shot on sight. Their bodies were gathered together in carts and buried in unmarked mass graves, and little attention was given by the work detail as to whether their cargo was alive or dead. One story had it that a yeoman officer, on seeing such a gruesome cart-load, called out: 'Where the devil did these rascals come from?' To his great astonishment, a feeble voice from the cart responded: 'I come frae Ballyboley.' But he was buried, alive, along with the rest.[61]

The loyalist victory at Antrim effectively sealed the defeat of the rebellion in the north, though this was not immediately apparent to the antagonists. Much of County Antrim remained in rebel hands, and Down was yet to rise. General Nugent still faced the serious problem of roving rebel bands in much of Antrim. He chose to use his main force to secure Belfast and prepare for the expected rising in Down rather than to scatter his scarce troops in isolated and costly operations in the countryside. Taking advantage of the shocked northern reaction to the sectarian features and counter-terror of the southern insurrection, Nugent wisely appealed to what the historian Thomas Pakenham calls the 'property instinct' of the inhabitants of the wealthy county of Antrim. He offered republicans in arms the chance of amnesty, which, if not accepted immediately, would be followed by the shooting of rebels on sight and by indiscriminate burnings. The leaders of the insurrection could expect to face courts martial, but the rank and file would be allowed to go home unmolested.[62] Nugent's policy was very much in the spirit of his former commander-in-chief, Abercromby; indeed, Nugent had already employed this policy of leniency, tempered with severe reprisals for leaders, when he had rooted out sedition among the soldiers and militiamen at Blaris camp in the previous year.[63] The current commander-in-chief, Lake, the darling of the reactionary wing of the ascendancy, considered the only deterrent to further rebellion to be wholesale executions, and, as a consequence, the mopping-up process in the south took years.

Nugent's policy proved remarkably effective. He had dispersed the Antrim rebellion just in time to free his troops to contend with his next major crisis—the rising in Down. With Dickson's arrest immediately before the date set for the Ulster rebellion, the rebel army in Down found itself without a leader. Two men were designated to assume Dickson's command; the first to accept would be appointed to lead the Down insurrec-

[60] Pakenham, *Year of liberty*, 254.
[61] Robert M. Young, *Ulster in '98: episodes and anecdotes* (Belfast, 1893), 68.
[62] Pakenham, *Year of liberty*, 255–6.   [63] See Ch. 6.

tion. The luckless winner of this prize was a prosperous linen draper in Lisburn, Henry Munro. A member of the established church and a freemason, Munro had held no prior post in the United Irishmen's underground army.[64] But his own inexperience was shared by many of his subordinate officers, for, along with Dickson, the whole network of colonels in Down had been arrested on Magin's information, leaving the rebel army there in almost total disarray. William Fox, commander of the rebel forces from the Ards, recalled that the arrest of officers would merely have been embarrassing if the next in rank had filled the office of his incarcerated superior:

but in general the arresting of a colonel threw the whole battalion into disorder and, in the moment of embodying, proved of infinite disadvantage, for instead of the forces meeting at any point in collected and organised bodies, they met rather more by accident than design—and they were in no better order than *a mere country mob*. And when thus assembled without any military subordination, a great deal more time would have been necessary to have organised them and reduced them to anything like a military body than the whole of the time they were in arms.[65]

The Down rebellion was scheduled to coincide with the rising in Antrim, but on 3 June an express arrived announcing the original decision of the Antrim colonels to await the French before committing their troops.[66] Though this decision was almost immediately overturned at Ballyeaston, McCracken's message to the United Irishmen in Down was never received. On 5 June Dickson was arrested, and on 6 June a messenger finally notified the Down committee that the rising was set for the following day. With such little notice, the Down republicans could hardly prepare themselves— even if their officers had been forthcoming. But on 9 June the first action took place at Saintfield. The battle itself was indecisive, but when the garrison was recalled to Belfast, the insurgents occupied the town, sparking off risings in the surrounding countryside. Newtownards fell to the rebels, but the local yeomanry successfully defended Portaferry. These were, in effect, mere skirmishes, for both sides were preparing for a great and decisive confrontation at Ballynahinch.

Munro established his camp outside the village of Montalto, on the estate of the liberal whig peer Lord Moira, and summoned the United Irishmen from Saintfield and the Ards to meet him there. Fox was disgusted at the disarray of the rebel camp, and his men grumbled at the sleeping arrangements provided for them. This was no trivial matter, for the greatest concern of the rebel leaders was to prevent the defection of their

---

[64] For Henry Munro, see R. R. Madden, *Antrim and Down in '98* (Glasgow, n.d.), 227–47.

[65] William Fox, 'A narrative of the principal proceedings of the republican army in the county of Down during the late insurrection' (SPOI, Rebellion papers, 620/4/41).

[66] For the rebellion in Co. Down, see Dickson, *Revolt in the north*, 145–55; Pakenham, *Year of liberty*, 257–64.

followers.[67] From their camp, they could see a trail of smoke coming from the direction of Belfast, marking the approach of Nugent's army, which was burning suspected rebel houses along the way. The time for decision was at hand, and the rebel leadership was divided. Munro counted about 7,000 men under his command, but only a small minority had firearms. The northern part of the county, including the entire Ards peninsula, was almost completely in rebel hands. Much support could be expected in the southern half of Down. With the approach of Nugent's army, Munro had to decide whether to risk everything in an open confrontation with highly armed and disciplined crown forces at Ballynahinch or to save his army for a more advantageous opportunity. William Fox urged him to delay a battle, arguing that the hastily summoned republican army was ill-equipped to meet such a formidable government force. The rebel army must play for as much time as possible before engaging in battle.[68] But Munro possessed that fatal flaw of adventurism shared by so many other United Irish field commanders. 'Few men were better fitted for the active duties of the field,' Charles Teeling generously remarked of Munro, 'but those qualifications so desirable in a leader were more than counterbalanced by a romantic love of glory and a mistaken feeling of honour, which impelled him to reject more temperate counsels when opposed to that thirst of fame which formed the leading passion of his breast.'[69] Munro decided to meet Nugent's forces head on, and he occupied Ballynahinch on 12 June.

Meanwhile, Nugent was marching from Belfast, meeting no resistance along the way. At their approach to Ballynahinch on the afternoon of 12 June, Nugent's troops encountered a body of rebels at Windmill Hill, the advance guard of Munro's forces. They were soon dislodged, and the government troops left one unfortunate insurgent hanging from the windmill as a gruesome reminder of the fate accorded to the disloyal. Nugent then decided to rest his exhausted troops, and proceeded to set up his artillery against the town and the camp at Montalto. His plan was to attack at dawn.

Another crucial decision faced Munro. The discipline of the crown forces broke that evening when the troops decided to celebrate the minor skirmish at Windmill Hill as if it were a great victory. With the soldiers drunk and unprepared, some of Munro's officers urged that he should take advantage of the situation and attack Nugent's vulnerable army in the middle of the night. 'A council of war was assembled,' Teeling recalled,

the voice of the people declared for *instant* action; the commander-in-chief alone opposed it. The discussion was warm and animated,—the best spirit prevailed amongst the troops,—the proudest feelings had been roused by the bold exertions of

[67] Fox, 'Narrative of proceedings' (SPOI, Rebellion papers, 620/4/41).
[68] Ibid.   [69] Teeling, *History of the Irish rebellion*, 132.

the day [the taking of the town of Ballynahinch], and those feelings had not yet subsided. The ammunition was insufficient for tomorrow, but ammunition was not wanting for a night attack, for the pike and the bayonet were more efficient.[70]

But Munro remained adamant in his resistance to such a plan. First, he argued that his force was too undisciplined to make a night assault, but, more important, he maintained that such an attack would be inconsistent with his own sense of honour and that of the cause of the United Irishmen. Such lofty sentiments did not go down well with men who were risking their lives in serving under Munro's command, and the result was that many hundreds deserted the camp in protest and disgust. This included a body of some 700 Defenders, who also accused Munro of sectarian bias when he proposed that they should lead the advance the next morning. At dawn on 13 June the remaining rebels entered Ballynahinch. But despite desperate fighting on the rebel side, the raw republican forces were decidedly outmatched by the well-disciplined government troops. Nearly 400 rebels were left dead in the streets, the greatest defeat yet suffered by the United Irish army in the north. Found among the dead were the bodies of two women dressed in green silk who had carried the rebel standards. Apparently the town prostitutes, they had been called the goddesses of liberty and reason.[71]

Nugent followed up his victory by offering the same terms of amnesty to the Down insurgents as those set for the rebels in Antrim. All were to go free if they peacefully laid down their arms. Only the leaders had to account for their actions before a court martial. Those who refused to accept the government's terms joined with another body of insurgents in central and south Down, but the rebellion had effectively been suppressed, and even the most dedicated soon realized the futility of their cause.

Both McCracken and Munro were tried before courts martial, found guilty, and executed for their role in the Ulster rebellion; thirty-two other northern leaders also received and suffered the death penalty for their insurrectionary activities. Among them were two Presbyterian ministers, the Revd James Porter of Grey Abbey and the Revd Archibald Warwick of Kircubbin. Numerous others were convicted of treason, but were allowed to exile themselves. Although the north under Nugent's command did not suffer the full ravages of counter-revolutionary terror inflicted by Lake in the south, the weeks following the Ulster insurrection were a source of tragedy to countless families. Undisciplined and vengeful bands of yeomen often ignored their general's orders to offer clemency to the rebels. Suspects were burned out of their homes.[72] The courts martial themselves provided a forum for the exercise of personal vendettas as well as a means of bringing

[70] Ibid. 135–6.   [71] Pakenham, *Year of liberty*, 263–4.   [72] Ibid. 324–5.

United Irish leaders to justice.[73] 'At this period,' Hope recalled, 'confidence was driven back to the narrow circles of well-tried acquaintance, and every stranger was met with suspicion.'[74]

The magnitude of the tragedy in terms of the loss of life and property was severe enough, but a further source of bitterness in the north was the failure of the United Irish leadership to assert itself when needed. On 15 June 1798 the *Belfast News-Letter* reported that the northern rebellion had been entirely suppressed.[75] Two weeks later it announced: 'It is a common saying among the folk of the Ards that nobody will ever prevail on them *to go catch cannon balls on the points of pikes and pitchforks again*.'[76] The taunt that the 'Dissenters of the north began the business and in the time of need were the first to abandon it', circulated through Antrim and Down— bitter gall to the defeated forces of McCracken and Munro.[77]

Defeat could not be attributed solely to the failure of the north to exert itself effectively as a consequence of treachery or timidity on the part of the leadership. True, the United Irishmen were ill-prepared for the conflict in terms of their small stockpiles of arms and ammunition. Much, however, had been expected of the militiamen sworn to the union. Had the rebels proved more successful, they might well have commanded the allegiance of many government troops in time, but as it was, the militia stood loyal to the crown, sometimes overzealously so. The much-lauded union of Catholic and protestant, the hallmark of United Irish strategy, failed to materialize. At Randalstown and Ballynahinch, United Irishmen and Defenders became divided by suspicion and mutual distrust. As the Ballynure regiment of United Irishmen was making its way to join McCracken on the eve of the rebellion, an incident took place which seemed to highlight the fundamental cleavage between Catholic and Presbyterian aims. Larry Dempsey, a deserter from the 24th Dragoons, a Catholic native of Munster, held a position of command. Overwhelmed with enthusiasm and pride as he carried out his office, riding at the front of the line on horseback and waving a sword, Larry forgot himself as he attempted to embolden his troops: 'By J——s, boys, we'll pay the rascals this day for the battle of the Boyne!' His predominantly Presbyterian followers, profoundly shocked by the utterance, froze in uneasy suspicion. A brother officer reprimanded Dempsey for his tactless outburst, but the words were the talk of the battalion until they arrived at Donegore Hill and had other business with which to occupy their minds.[78] James Dickey, a Crumlin attorney who commanded a rebel force in County Antrim, reportedly exclaimed shortly before his execution in

---

[73] For these courts martial, see SPOI, Rebellion papers, 620/2–3.
[74] Hope, 'Autobiographical memoir', 130.   [75] *BNL*, 15 June 1798.
[76] *BNL*, 29 June 1798.   [77] Hope, 'Autobiographical memoir', 131.
[78] McSkimin, *Annals*, 74–5.

Belfast that 'he knew well that had the *north* been successful, *they* would
have had to fight the battle over again with the Catholics of the *south*.'[79]

Another source of rebel disillusionment was the failure of the French to
arrive when expected. When the promised assistance came, in August 1798,
it was a story of too little, too late. Humbert's landing at Killala rallied
thousands of Irishmen from Connacht, and they made a desperate but
valiant march towards Dublin before they were finally defeated, in
September, at Ballinamuck in County Longford by overwhelming forces
under the command of the new viceroy and commander-in-chief, Lord
Cornwallis. At one point, Humbert hoped to rendezvous with the United
Irishmen of Ulster, but he received word that the rebellious spirit had been
effectively quelled in the northern province.[80] Those who had taken up
arms with such disastrous results only months before could not be induced
to risk themselves again. In the following October the rest of the expeditionary force attempted unsuccessfully to land in Donegal. Theobald Wolfe
Tone was on board one of the ships intercepted, and though he was a com-
missioned officer in the French army, he was tried and found guilty of treason in Dublin. He cheated an ignominious death on the scaffold by taking
his own life in his gaol cell.[81]

One of the most infrequently asked questions, and certainly the most
difficult to answer, is why those United Irishmen in Ulster who rallied to
McCracken and Munro turned out at all, especially given all the barriers to
participation and the disillusionment with the republican cause which had
already set in by the eve of the rebellion. We have already discussed at
some length the reasons for the reluctance of middle-class United Irish leaders to come forward at the appointed time. The failure of many of the rank
and file to appear can also be attributed to this loss of nerve on the part of
the leadership and to the resulting confusion and disarray which beset the
northern organization. The remarkable thing, however, was that, under
such adverse circumstances, at least 27,000 men in Antrim, Down, and east
Derry actually took part in one or more engagements with government
forces.

One must look at insurrectionary participation as constituting a series of
concentric circles around a corps of committed ideologues. The United Irish
movement in Ulster had, from the beginning, enjoyed enthusiastic—and,
indeed, militant—rank-and-file support in the villages and countryside of
Antrim and Down. The size of this circle of undeterred militants is impossible to determine, but in most cases it proved to be the nucleus around
which the less committed rallied, those whose motives were something less

---

[79] *BNL*, 24 July 1798.
[80] For the rising in Connacht, see Pakenham, *Year of liberty*, 336–84.
[81] For Tone's arrest, trial, and death, see Marianne Elliott, *Wolfe Tone: prophet of Irish
independence* (New Haven, Conn., and London, 1989), 386–402.

than to establish a democratic, secular republic. These local leaders, who may or may not have held official leadership positions in the United Irish organization, were frequently regarded with respect and admiration by their neighbours. As they asserted themselves in the republican cause, they were able to call on the allegiance of their groups of admirers, who thus constituted the second circle of United Irish participation. He 'would stand by Captain [Hugh] Boyd "till death"', William McCarter was heard to exclaim as he rallied to the rebel standard at Ballymoney.[82]

But if ideological conviction or personal loyalty accounted for the first two of our concentric circles of insurrectionary participation, the third can most properly be called the circle of self-interest. This took a variety of forms. First, with wild rumours rife throughout the countryside, there was no way of knowing the actual state of the country during the critical weeks of late May and early June 1798. The sight of many of their friends and neighbours preparing for battle may have persuaded many less enthusiastic villagers that the speedy success which had long been promised by United Irish leaders was finally at hand. If victory was certain, it would be better to share in that triumph and in the spoils that would accrue from it. Patrick Smith, a prosperous farmer from Islandmagee, attempted to rally recruits by telling them that the people had been victorious everywhere once they had revolted against their despotic rulers. Smith, it should be noted, only went a little way with his recruits. When he was elected their commander, he pleaded a sudden illness and returned home.[83] Their numbers may have seemed formidable to the men marching on the road to Donegore Hill or Ballynahinch, and promises that the militia would join them, or that the French would shortly arrive, greatly encouraged them. In addition, the participants knew that something would be done with the land to be confiscated from recalcitrant loyalists and the church. The first in line when such a redistribution occurred would be those soldiers active in the republican cause. Munro implied as much in his proclamation on 12 June, when he called for the non-payment of rent to 'disaffected landlords'.[84]

A more immediate motive of self-preservation explained the participation of another group of insurgents. The records of the courts martial which followed the rebellion contain the oft-repeated claim that the defendant had been coerced into joining the rebels. William Colman and William Neilson of Ballycarry explained that they had been working peaceably in the fields when a body of rebels came upon them and thrust pikes into their hands.[85]

---

[82] Court martial of John Doghill, 24 June 1798 (SPOI, Rebellion papers, 620/2/8/10).

[83] Court martial of William Colman and William Neilson, 25 June 1798 (ibid. 620/2/9/16).

[84] Proclamation of Henry Munro (PRONI, McCance papers, D272/73/463).

[85] Court martial of Colman and Neilson, 25 June 1798 (SPOI, Rebellion papers, 620/2/9/16).

James Moore of Glenahoe was found guilty of threatening to kill those who did not join his brother's regiment of insurgents.[86] Although the plea of coercion cannot be taken too seriously, considering that the defendant was under threat of the lash, transportation, or even execution, there is still reason to believe that, in some cases, this really was the case. It was even maintained that all who had to be forced to join the rebels would be put in the front lines during the battles, making direct coercion unnecessary in many cases.

Inevitably, assemblies of large numbers of people often attract the unstable, the violent, and those seeking a chance for plunder or revenge. Thomas Bunburry Isaac, a gentleman from Holywood, maintained that George Wilson, the son of one of his own tenants, interrupted him as he was trying to dissuade the people from joining the insurgents. 'It was your day,' Wilson threatened Isaac. 'I'll have mine now.'[87] On the whole, however, such violent motives were not very prominent among the rebels. The record of the Ulster insurgents was almost untarnished by cases of plunder or personal violence. Many gentlemen and farmers in the area, it is true, were forced to give up their arms and money to the rebels, but they were usually given requisition orders to be redeemed after the rebellion.

Curiosity was another factor in participation. The movement of so many thousands could not escape unnoticed by the rural and village population. James Patterson and Thomas Watt were maybe fortunate in that, deciding to join the rebels at Ballymoney, they arrived too late; the insurgents had already marched towards Ballymena. Their curiosity was nevertheless satisfied, and Patterson and Watt returned home.[88]

It would seem that the dominant motives for turning out were loyalty to the cause or to their comrades and the expectation that the rebellion would prevail. The mass defections after each defeat discouraged the optimistic, who might have expected that their mere appearance in arms would induce the loyalist forces to think better of the contest. The battles at Ballynahinch and Antrim were in sharp contrast to the faction fights that had provided almost a source of rural entertainment for the population. Few expected a protracted campaign. Pride, bravado, and the hope of making their fortune brought many men to the battlefield, but the battlefield proved to be a most disabusing experience. Where were the leaders? Where were the thousands of comrades who had been promised? Where were the arms and ammunition? Why did the militia not join them? When were the French to arrive? An unsatisfactory answer to all these crucial questions persuaded many to return to their homes.

The curious, the faint-hearted, the disillusioned—all defected, if they

---

[86] Court martial of James Moore, 24 June 1798 (ibid. 620/2/8/4).
[87] Court martial of George Wilson, 25 July 1798 (ibid. 620/2/8/9).
[88] Court martial of Andrew Morton, 11 July 1798 (ibid. 620/2/8/10).

could, before the moment of battle. The ideologically committed resolved
to take their stand, as they had promised to do by a solemn oath of loyalty
to the cause. But many others charged down Donegore Hill or Montalto
for less lofty reasons. Quite simply, many were drunk. To keep their troops
hopeful about the outcome, many United Irish leaders supplied them liberally with liquor.[89] One leader, finally convinced that he would only be leading men to death, tried to persuade his followers to return home, but they
were too intoxicated to heed his advice.[90]

The desertions by their leaders, the defections of so many rank-and-file
members, and the subsequent jostling at the courts martial to prove one's
own innocence at the expense of a comrade inspired a thoroughly disillusioned James Orr, 'the bard of Ballycarry', to write his bitter and sardonic
'Donegore Hill'. After describing the break-up of the rebel camp, Orr
caught the mood of general disillusionment:

> What joy at hame our entrance gave!
> 'Guid God! is't you? fair fa' ye! —
> 'Twas wise, tho' fools may ca't no brave,
> To rin or e'er they saw ye.'

> 'Aye wife, that's true without dispute,
> But lest saunts fail in Zion,
> I'll hae to swear —— forc'd me out;
> Better he swing than I, on
> Some hangin' day.'[91]

One problem remained for the government after the untidy mess of rebellion had been effectively cleared: what was to be done with the eighty-odd
state prisoners lodged in Dublin gaols? Informers such as Magin and
McNally refused to come forward in public court to condemn their old
friends. Chagrined, the government knew that it could not secure convictions against the great majority of these suspected traitors. Even the arrest
of the Leinster provincial committee in March 1798 had not produced
sufficient evidence to warrant bringing its members to trial. One witness
did finally agree to come forward—Thomas Reynolds—but his testimony
would convict only three of the prisoners, Oliver Bond, John McCann, and
William Byrne. In addition, there was enough evidence to indict John and
Henry Sheares. In July 1798 these unfortunate brothers were the first of the
prisoners to be tried, found guilty, and executed for high treason.
Convictions of Bond, McCann, and Byrne followed.[92] At this point the

---

[89] See e.g. court martial of William Boyce, 9 July 1798 (SPOI, Rebellion papers, 620/2/9/8).

[90] Court martial of Hugh Boyd, 6 July 1798 (ibid. 620/2/8/10).

[91] D. H. Akenson and W. H. Crawford, *Local poets and social history: James Orr, bard of Ballycarry* (Belfast, 1977), 39–40.

[92] See William Ridgeway, *A report of the proceedings in cases of high treason at a special commission of oyer and terminer held in and for the county and city of Dublin in the month of*

prisoners opened negotiations with the government, but, unfortunately, they came too late for Byrne and McCann, who were executed before any agreement was reached. The prisoners offered to give full details of the United Irish movement in Ulster and elsewhere without implicating any individual by name. In return, they asked for permission to emigrate. Bond's life was saved when a pact was signed between the government and the seventy-eight remaining prisoners.[93]

The written and oral statements of Emmet, MacNeven, O'Connor, Bond, and Neilson set forth the goals and principles of the leaders of the revolutionary movement in the most unambiguous terms. They strove for an independent, secular, democratic Irish republic. Since physical force was the only means of securing this goal, it had been adopted as official policy in 1796, and that same year the United Irishmen had concluded an alliance with France for military assistance. The leaders blamed themselves for the failure of the rebellion. Had they only been able to restrain their forces until the French landed, or had they at least co-ordinated a simultaneous general insurrection, their fate might have been different.[94] For MacNeven, this capitulation to the government was the 'best service' that the prisoners could 'perform to save the country from the cold-blooded slaughter of its best, its bravest, its most enlightened defenders'.[95]

But it was a sorry ending to the great events promised by the Irish Jacobins. The United Irish movement clung tenaciously to life in the north, but its lack of popular support no longer made it a formidable threat to the established order.[96] Soon to prosper in their adopted countries of France and America, the former leaders left behind them an estimated 30,000 dead.[97] Setting aside the terrible loss of life and property, the chief consequence of the great rebellion was the act of union. Except for Robert Emmet's last brief gasp in the streets of Dublin in 1803, the democratic and republican ideals of the United Irishmen ceased to be a major force in Irish politics until the emergence of the Fenians more than half a century later.[98]

July 1798 (trial of the Sheares brothers) (Dublin, 1798); id., *A report of the trial of John McCann upon an indictment for high treason* (Dublin, 1798).

[93] Pakenham, *Year of liberty*, 325–31.   [94] *Rep. secret comm.* 306–21.

[95] William James MacNeven, *Pieces of Irish history illustrative of the condition of the Catholics of Ireland* (New York, 1807), 179.

[96] For the activities of the United Irishmen after the rebellion of 1798, see Elliott, *Partners in revolution*, 341–64.

[97] Pakenham, *Year of liberty*, 17. While Pakenham has estimated that 30,000 met their deaths in the several rebellions of 1798, Teeling, a partisan observer to be sure, suggested that the death-toll might be calculated, 'whether in the field or on the scaffold, by the hand of torture or the pestilence of the prison, at the appalling number of *a hundred thousand men!*' (Teeling, *History of the Irish rebellion*, 294).

[98] For the best treatment of Emmet's rising, see Elliott, *Partners in revolution*, 282–322.

Conclusion

EARLY Irish republicanism bore little resemblance to its later separatist incarnations. It is true, as Gearoid Ó Tuathaigh has written, that 'the concept of a *republic* as the quintessential expression of Irish separatism originated with the United Irishmen'.[1] Yet, as we have seen, the movement itself cannot be dismissed simply as separatist and anti-English. Republican ideals animated the United Irishmen, and when government policies made it clear that these ideals could no longer be expressed within the existing constitutional framework, the radicals adopted the goal of a separate republic as a final strategy. And as a strategy, this goal was required to secure French assistance. What is clear is that there was much improvisation in United Irish mobilization. In 1793 hopes were raised that Catholic emancipation alone would reap a reform along republican principles. In 1795 Fitzwilliam's viceroyalty raised the possibility that reform could come from above, from Pitt and the British ministry itself, and purge Ireland of its more onerous oligarchic and illiberal impediments to good government. The last refuge of the patriot was the threat of revolution, and the willingness to back that threat by enrolling the lower classes and allying with the French.

Oliver MacDonagh has accused this revolutionary nationalism which the United Irishmen bequeathed as being 'almost empty of positive content'.[2] And it is certainly true that there was much that was negative about United Irish ideology, especially seen through the writings of Theobald Wolfe Tone. The Irish republicans did view English influence as the bane of Ireland, but they defined this influence as ministerial tampering with the Irish parliament, as—not surprisingly, given the roots of the United Irishmen—the whig patriots had also defined constitutional injustice in Ireland. Parliamentary reform could provide a measure of popular influence to offset British and ascendancy control. When this seemed unattainable many United Irishmen did turn to separation, which must be considered as a positive goal which would liberate Ireland for new commercial opportunities.

MacDonagh also characterizes the republicans as negative for lacking a

---

[1] Gearoid Ó Tuathaigh, *Ireland before the famine, 1798–1848* (Dublin, 1972), 29.
[2] Oliver MacDonagh, *States of mind: a study of Anglo-Irish conflict, 1780–1980* (London, 1983), 75.

specific social and economic programme.[3] This conclusion is somewhat at variance with Jim Smyth's contention that recent historians, myself included, have perpetrated a 'new, inverted, misreading, or anti-myth', which diminishes the social radicalism of his 'men of no property' by insistence on the bourgeois, conservative tendencies of the United Irishmen.[4] He describes them as 'pre-socialist revolutionaries' who developed a 'radical-populist critique' of late eighteenth-century Irish politics and society.[5] I have argued that the radical populist elements of United Irish propaganda were largely instrumental, designed to secure a mass following. This is not to deny that there were social radicals among the leaders, or that segments within the mass following were not genuinely animated by radical expectations—and, indeed, forced the United Irishmen to acknowledge traditional social and economic grievances. Russell and McCracken, to be sure, sympathized greatly with the plight of the poor. But the United Irish social agenda carried only three items—economic liberalism, political liberalism, and education.[6] All three placed the onus for social improvement on the individual, in a society which would offer fair competition and equal opportunity. Still, rank and file members and Defenders may have been less beguiled by this promise of a liberal paradise, and the United Irish leaders recognized as much when they inserted a rather instrumental populist rhetoric in their pronouncements, referring to land redistribution, for example. Relief from tithe, taxes, and high rents, however, were as much a part of the liberal agenda as its embodiment of traditional popular aspirations. It is anachronistic of both MacDonagh and Smyth to dismiss late eighteenth-century liberalism as inherently negative or conservative.

The liberalism which the United Irishmen were articulating was not a positive programme of economic and social change. It argued for trade without restraints, for the removal of irksome civil disabilities, freeing individuals to succeed, and rewarding them for merit and achievement— revolutionary aspirations. The United Irishmen, in today's parlance, were anti big government. It is a negative view, though not necessarily a surly one. In the context of the late eighteenth and nineteenth centuries, the United Irishmen were, as R. F. Foster has described them, 'modernizers'.[7]

Indeed, the United Irishmen represented the forces of a struggling eighteenth-century radical whiggism which emerged triumphant in

---

[3] Ibid.

[4] Jim Smyth, *The men of no property: Irish radicals and popular politics in the late eighteenth century* (New York, 1992), 165.

[5] Ibid. 169.

[6] For United Irish pronouncements on the need for a national system of education, see e.g. William Drennan, *A letter to his excellency Earl Fitzwilliam, lord-lieutenant, etc., of Ireland* (Dublin, 1795); Thomas Addis Emmet, Arthur O'Connor, and William James Macneven, *Memoire, or detailed statement of the origin and progress of the Irish union* (Dublin, 1798), 47–8.

[7] R. F. Foster, *Modern Ireland, 1600–1972* (London, 1988), 270.

nineteenth-century liberalism. The theatre that encompassed this development, however, was not Ireland, but the United Kingdom. The inclusive, secular, national consciousness forged by Tone, Drennan, Neilson, and their colleagues in Dublin and Belfast in the early 1790s collapsed before it had ever neared its goal. Throughout the course of the following centuries the Irish national identity was increasingly defined in exclusive Gaelic and Catholic terms. Irish protestants, particularly those radical Dissenters in Ulster who felt threatened by what they saw as an illiberal, intolerant, popish menace, retreated from the principles of 1791 into a closer identification with Great Britain. They were further encouraged by the prosperity which blessed Ulster as a result of the economic union with England.

The union of Catholic and Dissenter which gave rise to the United Irish movement in the 1790s was based on a common hatred of the Anglo-Irish ascendancy. But each sect hated the ascendancy for different reasons. The Catholic peasant felt such dominance most immediately through a landlord whom he regarded as a member of an alien and conquering race. The middle-class Dissenter resented the institutions which upheld a landed élite. The act of union represented the first small step in undermining the political dominance of the ascendancy, but one which was noted with approval by a number of United Irish republicans. By reducing the Irish parliamentary delegation by two-thirds, the union at the very least eliminated some of the most corrupt features of the representation system. As Archibald Hamilton Rowan remarked to his father: 'In that measure I see the downfall of one of the most corrupted assemblies I believe ever existed.'[8] As the liberalism espoused by the United Irishmen emerged triumphant in Great Britain in the nineteenth century, Ulster radicals found even more reason to become reconciled to the union. The Ulster protestant became loyal to the union with Britain, but it was, and is today, a conditional loyalty, recalling the Lockian contractualism of the United Irishmen.[9]

The petty-bourgeois social base of United Irish activism readily identified with the democratic republican ideology of this advanced whiggism. But the necessary alliance with the Defenders and the peasantry debased the purity of the republican and liberal coinage and contributed to the desecularization of the movement. The United Irishmen compromised their avowed non-sectarianism by exploiting and exacerbating confessional hostility and contradicted their economic individualism by making vague promises of social and economic transformation. Their uneasiness with these allies and

---

[8] Archibald Hamilton Rowan, *The autobiography of Archibald Hamilton Rowan*, ed. William H. Drummond (1st edn., 1840; Shannon, 1972), 340.

[9] For the conditional loyalty of past and present Ulster unionists, see David W. Miller, *Queen's rebels: Ulster loyalism in historical perspective* (Dublin, 1978); Padraig O'Malley, *The uncivil wars: Ireland today* (Boston, 1983), 133–203.

their distaste for the compromises made to secure them pushed the United Irishmen into a strategic dependence on France.

The United Irishmen possessed a real genius for disseminating their ideas. In catering to popular tastes, however, they naturally highlighted the oppression engendered by traditional grievances such as high rents and taxes and the deeply resented tithe. They directed their ire at the source of this oppression—a landed élite and its dependants which had christened itself the protestant ascendancy. Despite the efforts of United Irish leaders to analyse ascendancy misrule in terms of the triumph of political corruption over civic virtue, it was inevitable that the Catholic peasantry would regard their burdens in sectarian and nationalist terms—as the cruel impositions of a protestant and alien race.

The United Irishmen professed to represent a united nation, united against self-serving landowners and their British backers. Thus they were obsessed with numbers, and the quest for recruits took precedence over ideological conversion. This raises two points of relevance to subsequent republican movements. First, republican ideology assumed an indivisible nation, but Ireland was divided not only along confessional lines, but by class, region, and economic pursuits. Urban artisans and rural peasants may have found common ground for their hostility to the ascendancy, yet they came to this ground for different reasons. The United Irishmen became a mass movement because they were skilled propagandists who could highlight injustice in Ireland and appeal to each aggrieved party separately. But we should see this movement not as an indivisible assertion of the public will, but rather as a political party in the modern liberal tradition, a collection of interest groups sharing some generalized beliefs, animated by the same enemies, but pursuing their own specific agendas. So, middle-class United Irishmen saw themselves taking centre stage in the political arena of a new Ireland, Defenders hoped for the resurgence of Catholic Ireland, and lower-class republicans sought relief from rents, tithes, and taxes. But because the United Irishmen clung to an eighteenth-century conception of the nation as unified, they underestimated the extent to which class and religion could pull the nation apart. Like subsequent nationalists, they overestimated their ability to forge a unified nation. It was not sufficient merely to call Ireland a nation.

What was required was to define a culture which supported and united that imagined community of the nation. This raises the second point of relevance to the republican nationalist tradition. The United Irishmen were adept and assiduous propagandists, and I have argued that their propaganda exercises must be seen as self-defining. They did seek to refashion political culture in Ireland. But the bedrock that informed their efforts was republican in the classical sense: the elevation of civic virtue. Citizenship, with all its rights and all its responsibilities, was what the United Irishmen were after in political terms. In social, religious, and economic terms, they sought the rights of individuals. Their ideology was, above all, inclusive and universal. It is one of the more attractive features of the movement.

Yet a nation is a self-defined entity which is both particular and exclusive. Exclusion is based on deviance from the history, tradition, and culture, however broadly defined, of that nation. One is born into a nation, or one might be adopted into a nation. Citizenship, for the United Irishmen, however, was the bond which held individuals together, and citizenship was a universal right of all adult men. It is interesting to note that, while the United Irishmen were attempting to construct a political culture based on civic humanist and liberal principles, other Irishmen were asserting the rich culture of a historic Irish nation. While some United Irishmen like Thomas Russell and Whitley Stokes were involved in the late eighteenth-century Gaelic revival, the movement itself remained, at best, mildly supportive but, in fact, uninterested. Similarly, a distinctly Irish literature written in English was making advances in the late eighteenth and early nineteenth centuries, with representation by United Irishmen and such sympathizers as William Drennan, William Hamilton Drummond, and Thomas Moore. Certainly, the pages of the United Irish press were open to such endeavours, yet it would be overstating the case to say that the republicans were in the forefront of the construction of an enduring nationalist literature, nor did they have a monopoly in its construction.

Tom Dunne tends to dismiss what he calls the 'bland bourgeois propaganda' of the United Irishmen as being either alien or irrelevant to the mass of the people.[10] In one respect, his indictment is well aimed. When all is said and done, the United Irish failed to leave deep ideological footprints in the sand. Their brand of liberal republicanism failed to survive the rebellion of 1798. They proved unable to construct a secular political culture which emphasized civic rights and duties and was capable of withstanding the heady resurgence of sectarianism in Ireland from the late 1790s, a resurgence to which the United Irishmen contributed, but from which they ran, at least metaphorically, as they watched the course of the rebellion with horror from their gaol cells. Elements of United Irish liberalism certainly did find their way into subsequent nationalist movements, constitutional and republican. But how could they not? Liberalism was the ideology of the modernizers, the middle class whose support was so crucial to the success of these movements. *Paddy's resource* or Porter's *Billy Bluff and the squire* may have constituted a literary legacy of sorts, but it seems, although this question certainly requires investigation, that the imprint of United Irishmen was very slight indeed until consciously reproduced and adapted by Thomas Davis, the Fenians, Patrick Pearse, and the rest.

[10] Tom Dunne, 'Popular ballads, revolutionary rhetoric and politicisation', in Hugh Gough and David Dickson (eds.), *Ireland and the French revolution* (Dublin, 1990), 145.

In the long run, United Irish ideology and propaganda may have had only a tenuous and heavily mediated impact on the construction of an Irish nationalist culture, but the immediate achievements of the radicals should not be dismissed as bland or even bourgeois. The *Northern Star* and the *Press* were the most heavily subscribed papers in Ireland in the eighteenth century, and neither paper can be described as bland. But if, as Dunne implies, the United Irishmen should have been concerned with tapping into rural and Gaelic culture, these papers were undoubtedly irrelevant and ineffectual. The appeal, however, was to the middle classes and the artisans, to the inhabitants of the towns and their environs, which is exactly the audience to which the United Irishmen intended to address their appeal. It was an English-based cultural appeal which succeeded best in the more English-influenced parts of Ireland. Their efforts at political education were impressive and, judging from membership returns and official reaction, effective, though ephemeral. Just as the United Irishmen thought that they could easily bridge the religious chasm in Ireland, so, too, they naïvely underestimated the cultural gap.

As ideologues and politicizers, the United Irishmen were hardly original, drawing heavily as they did on British and Irish precedents, though they took such precedents to an extreme. But as mobilizers, their like had not been seen in the British Isles. It is no mean feat to create a mass-based secret society. In their organization the United Irishmen sought to meld republican theory with insurrectionary practice—to make citizens as well as soldiers, and they were remarkably successful in doing both. One can see many features of the modern political party in this organization. But the principle of representative democracy, however, gave way to autocratic management by the provincial and national directories. The organizational flaws and the social and sectarian fears which were raised as the United Irishmen emerged as a mass movement contributed powerfully to its failure. Informers and spies easily breached the walls of United Irish secrecy. Given that so many recruits joined the movement because of self-interest or fear, it is hardly surprising that they should have defected once United Irish fortunes began to sink.

The French alliance enhanced United Irish chances of success, but it also undermined the strategic flexibility of the movement, forcing the republicans to wait upon events. Moreover, United Irish devotion to revolutionary France precluded any possibility of a junction between the disappointed and frustrated moderate whiggism of Grattan's party and the middle-class radicals. The Irish whigs had, of course, become a spent force in parliament by 1797, when they walked out in protest against intransigence on the part of the administration on the questions of reform and emancipation. Abhorring the Jacobin and Francophile United Irishmen, the whigs were isolated from both the left and the right of the Irish political spectrum. Had the whigs been able to put themselves at the head of a popular movement in the 1790s, the subsequent history of Ireland might have been quite different. The United Irishmen courted whig support, to be sure, but not at the price of sacrificing their democratic republican principles.

The United Irishmen were frustrated not only by the strategic inflexibility imposed on them by their French alliance, but also by the determination of the government to confront the radicals at every turn. Each United Irish tactical innovation was effectively countered by the administration. When the United Irishmen sought to ride the Trojan horse of the Volunteers to mobilize public support, the government suppressed the Volunteers. When the radicals attempted to use representative conventions to apply pressure on the legislature, parliament outlawed conventions. When the United Irishmen hoped to undermine the loyalty of the militia, the government responded with exemplary executions. And, finally, when republicans succeeded in choking the normal judicial channels employed to bring United Irishmen to justice, the government adopted extraordinary legal powers.

One question lingers over every discussion of the United Irish movement. Freed of the bondage of the French alliance and able to respond quickly and effectively to the changing limits of their mobilization, were the republicans strong enough to cast off the yoke of the ascendancy by themselves? A rising early in 1797 might have had the best chance of success. United Irish strength had probably reached its limits in Ulster by that time, but revolutionary resolve had yet to be undermined by Lake's military repression. It would have been a provincial rising, but since the forces of loyalism were not yet ready to suppress it, it might well have sparked a national rising. Yet, one reason for the United Irish strength early in 1797 was precisely the French demonstration, at Bantry Bay in the previous December, of their willingness to assist them. Indeed, the possibility of French assistance made a mass United Irish movement possible. The middle-class radicals would have been very reluctant to mobilize the lower classes if they had been unable to count on the French to help them pre-empt a possible social revolution.

While the United Irishmen waited for their French allies to appear, loyalists were able to strengthen their own position. Severe government repression, aided by the Irish militia and yeomanry, forced the submerged dissensions and weaknesses of the republican movement to the fore. The United Irishmen were, after all, anything but united. The class and sectarian tensions which were exacerbated by United Irish propaganda and recruitment methods and by their alliances with the lower orders and the French not only weakened the mass movement internally, but provoked mass hostility as well. Because the republicans attempted to be all things to all people, subsequent generations have been free to interpret them as they wish. The United Irishmen, it has been said, represented one link in the chain of resistance to British oppression. The United Irishmen were nationalists who united Catholics and protestants under the common name of Irishmen. Or the union promoted by enlightened Presbyterians was betrayed by a fanatic, vengeful Catholicism which reared its ugly head in Wexford, demonstrating at last the fundamental inability of protestant aspirations for liberty to take root in priest-ridden Catholic Ireland. The legacy of the United Irishmen, however interpreted, has proved as divisive for later generations as the practice of this so-called union did in the 1790s.

APPENDIX

United Irish Social Composition

HAVING collected the names of several thousand United Irishmen directly implicated in the rebellion, or actively involved in its preparation in Dublin and Ulster between 1795 and 1798, I have identified the occupations of 1,731. The method was simple but crude. Every time I encountered a name of a United Irishman in the newspapers, in magistrates' reports, in arrest lists, or even in secondary sources, I made out an index card, adding data as I found it.

One important qualification must be made concerning this evidence. These names were culled mainly from newspaper reports of arrests and assizes as well as from information supplied to the government by magistrates and informers between 1795 and 1798. Those named in these sources tended to be the activists of the movement, the 'deep, intriguing politicians' whose conduct attracted the attention of the authorities. A significant but indeterminate group remains unrepresented in the sample—all those victims of martial law who, on suspicion of involvement in treasonable or seditious activity, were sent aboard the tenders and from there to serve in the fleet. Many undoubtedly came from the lowest social class among the United Irishmen, a group without sufficient influence or status to secure certain legal privileges. The magnitude of this group is particularly elusive. Lord Carhampton, when pacifying Connacht in 1795, reportedly sent more than 1,000 suspected Defenders to the fleet.[1] A larger figure may have been seized in Ulster during the period of martial law under General Lake. By June 1797, nearly 200 suspected United Irishmen had been sent aboard the tenders lying off the coast of Derry, but this number excludes those who were 'permitted' to volunteer for naval service.[2]

Furthermore, the sample as collected is biased towards the middling classes. One reason for this is the greater scrutiny that these elements received from the authorities. But additionally, for Dublin in particular, I consulted the *Gentleman's and citizen's almanack* of 1795 and its directory of Dublin lawyers, doctors, and merchants to ascertain the careers of those United Irishmen for whom I had discovered no occupation. Thus it has proved easier to identify middle-class United Irishmen by occupation than their lower-class peers. Nevertheless, the sample presented here should

---

[1] W. E. H. Lecky, *A history of Ireland in the eighteenth century* (5 vols., London, 1898), iii. 420.

[2] Philip Corby to Robert Marshall, 22 June 1797 (SPOI, Rebellion papers, 620/31/138).

prove a valuable indicator of the social composition of those United Irishmen who were most active in, and therefore most committed to, the republican cause.

In Tables 5.6, 5.8, and 5.10, where the focus is on social status, I have divided the 1,731 United Irishmen who have been identified by occupation into eleven categories: (1) gentlemen, current or former military officers, barristers, and solicitors; (2) schoolmasters and Dissenting or protestant ministers; (3) Roman Catholic priests; (4) merchants, manufacturers, and shopkeepers; (5) farmers; (6) physicians, surgeons, and apothecaries; (7) publicans and innkeepers; (8) artisans, weavers, and tradesmen; (9) clerks; (10) labourers, apprentices, and servants; and (11) a miscellaneous category including such diverse occupations as civil servants, smugglers, artists, and fishermen. If groups 1–7 in Table 5.6 are regarded as belonging to the upper and middle classes, they account for 54.9 per cent of all United Irishmen identified in the total sample.[3] Of course, class is an imprecise measure of analysis when dealing with late eighteenth-century social movements, and certain of the categories employed here are admittedly broad. But, if anything, at least in terms of the sample, this figure of nearly 55 per cent errs on the side of caution. Many of the participants listed in the category of artisans, weavers, and tradesmen were indeed quite prosperous and independent and could hardly be described as plebeian or working class. Yet the sources do not permit a division of this category according to status within the trade.

The sample may also be biased towards Dublin and Belfast, the two centres of radical activity, once again reflecting the middle-class bias in the sample as well as the greater concentration of the sources on these two towns. Table A.1 presents an urban–rural breakdown of United Irish participation. Even when rural insurgents are isolated from urban activists, the data confirm the argument in Chapter 5 that the United Irishmen tended to appeal most strongly to groups within the commercial and industrial sector in Ireland.

The United Irishmen boasted a membership of half a million out of a population of five million, and if occupations could be established for all these participants, it would no doubt call into serious question the numbers presented here. But, recognizing the limits of my sampling procedure, I have chosen to focus on the activist core of the movement, those who did invite the attention of the authorities. While I would not wish to make any claims for the scientific basis of my sample, it should be noted that the results tend to be supported by qualitative evidence. The United Irishmen did appeal strongly to the middle classes. They were better organized and more numerous in commercial and industrial centres. And the numbers and

[3] The inclusion of farmers here may appear questionable, but these farmers were usually described as either 'comfortable' or 'substantial'.

proportions put forward, while statistically problematic, nevertheless offer an indication of the tendencies of United Irish participation.

Tᴀᴇˇ. A.1. *Urban–rural breakdown of United Irish participation*

Sector	Dublin and Belfast		Rural Ulster		Total	
	No.	%	No.	%	No.	%
Agriculture	13*	1.4	187	23.5	200	11.6
Commerce and industry	765	81.6	409	51.5	1,174	67.8
Professional	131	14.0	176	22.2	307	17.7
Other	28	3.0	22	2.8	50	2.9
TOTAL	937	100.0	794	100.0	1,731	100.0

*Includes gentlemen and neighbouring farmers active in Dublin.
Source: Appendix.

SELECT BIBLIOGRAPHY

MANUSCRIPT SOURCES

Belfast, Linenhall Library
  Joy papers
Belfast, Public Record Office of Northern Ireland
  Abercorn papers (T2541).
  Annesley papers (D1503).
  Belfast Chamber of Commerce minute-book (D1857/1/AB/1).
  Bruce papers (T3041).
  Caldwell papers (T3541).
  Caledon papers (D2433).
  Castlereagh papers (D3030).
  Clarke papers (D1108/B).
  Dobbs papers (D162).
  Downshire papers (D607).
  Drennan letters (T765).
  Duffin papers (T965, D729).
  Fitzgibbon papers (T3287).
  Forbes papers (T3391).
  John Galt's diary (D561).
  Gosford papers (D1606).
  Grey/Ponsonby papers (T3393).
  Groves papers (T808).
  Hort papers (D1634).
  Immigrants' list, 1802–14 (T1011).
  Lake and Hewitt papers (Mic. 67).
  Lenox-Conyngham papers (D1449).
  Lowry papers (D.1494).
  R. C. Lytton White papers (D714).
  Macartney papers (D572).
  McCance papers (D272).
  McCracken papers (T1210).
  John Macky's diary (T925).
  McPeake papers (T3048).
  Montgomery papers (T1638).
  Perceval Maxwell papers (T1023).
  Pilson papers (D365).
  Potts–Lemon correspondence (T1012).
  Records of the Antrim presbytery (T1053).
  Robb papers (T1373).
  Roden papers (Mic. 147).
  Rogers papers (T2685).

A. H. Rowan's notebook (T939).
Sharman Crawford papers (D856).
Sneyd papers (T3229).
Stanhope (Pitt) papers (T3401).
D. Stewart papers (D1759).
Stewart of Killymoon papers (D3167).
Tennent papers (D1748).
Belfast, Ulster Museum
Revd Samuel Barber papers (H4).
Andrew Morrow MS (018).
Dublin, National Library of Ireland
Blaquiere letters (MS 877).
F. S. Bourke collection (MS 9870).
Dobbs letters (MS 2251).
Hartnell papers (MSS 2763–5).
Kilmainham papers (MSS 1205–7, 1386).
Knox (Lake) papers (MS 56).
Lord-Lieutenants' correspondence (MS 886).
Melville (Dundas) papers (MS 54A).
Musgrave papers (MSS 4156–7).
Townshend letters (MS 394).
Dublin, Public Record Office of Ireland
Frazer papers.
Dublin, Royal Irish Academy
Burrowes papers (MS 23 K 53).
Charlemont papers (MS 12 R 14–21, 26).
Daniel O'Connell's diary, 1795–1802 (MS 12 P 13).
Dublin, State Paper Office of Ireland
Rebellion papers.
State of the country papers.
Westmorland correspondence.
Dublin, Trinity College Library
Hope papers (MSS 7253–6).
Madden papers (MS 873).
Russell correspondence (MS 868).
Sirr papers (MS 869).
London, British Library
Auckland papers (Add. MSS 34452–4).
Thomas Grenville papers (Add. MS 41855).
Halisbury papers (Add. MS 56367).
Hertford papers (Egerton MS 3260).
Holland House papers (Add. MSS 51682–3).
Huskisson papers (Add. MS 38759).
Pelham letter-book, 1795–7 (Add. MS 33113).
Pelham misc. state papers on Ireland (Add. MSS 33118–19).
Pelham papers (Add. MSS 33100–6).
Percy (Dromore) papers (Add. MSS 32335, 34756).

Wellesley papers (Add. MS 37308).
Windham papers (Add. MSS 37873–8).
London, National Army Museum
  Nugent papers.
London, Public Record Office
  Chatham papers (30/8/323–31).
  Colonial Office papers (CO 906/1).
  Home Office: general letter-book (HO 122/3–4).
  Home Office: king's letter-book (HO 101/2).
  Home Office: papers relating to Ireland (HO 100/31–81).
  Home Office: correspondence, military (HO 50/29).
  War Office papers (WO 1/612).
Maidstone, Kent, Kent County Archives Office
  Pratt papers.

PARLIAMENTARY PAPERS

The debate in the Irish house of peers on a motion made by the earl of Moira, Monday, February 19, 1798 (Dublin: J. Milliken, 1798).
Journals of the house of commons of the kingdom of Ireland (19 vols., Dublin, n.p., 1613–1800).
The report of the secret committee of the house of commons, with an appendix (Dublin: n.p., 1798).

CONTEMPORARY NEWSPAPERS AND PERIODICALS

Belfast News-Letter
Drogheda Journal
Dublin Magazine and Irish Monthly Register
Faulkner's Dublin Journal
Freeman's Journal
Gentleman's and Citzen's Almanack (Dublin)
Londonderry Journal
Northern Star
Press
The Times (London)

PUBLICATIONS OF THE HISTORICAL MANUSCRIPTS COMMISSION (GREAT BRITAIN)

The manuscripts and correspondence of James, first earl of Charlemont (2 vols., London: Eyre and Spottiswoode, 1891, 1894).
The manuscripts of J. B. Fortescue, Esq., preserved at Dropmore, 14/5 (5 vols., London: Eyre and Spottiswoode, 1894).

WORKS BY CONTEMPORARIES AND PRINTED DOCUMENTARY SOURCES

BARTLETT, THOMAS, 'Select documents, XXXVIII: Defenders and Defenderism in 1795', *Irish Historical Studies*, 24/95 (May 1985), 373–94.

BERESFORD, JOHN, *The correspondence of the right hon. John Beresford*, ed. William Beresford (2 vols., London: Woodfall and Kinder, 1854).

BINNS, JOHN, *Recollections of the life of John Binns* (Philadelphia: Parry and McMillan, 1854).

BIRCH, REVD THOMAS LEDLIE, *Letter from an Irish emigrant to his friend in the United States* (New York: n.p., 1798).

BRADY, REVD JOHN, *Catholics and Catholicism in the eighteenth-century press* (Maynooth: Catholic Record Society, 1965).

A brief account of the trial of William Orr of Farranshane in the county of Antrim, to which are annexed several interesting facts and authentic documents connected therewith (Dublin: J. Chambers, 1797).

BURK, JOHN, *The trial of John Burk of Trinity College for heresy and blasphemy before the board of senior fellows, to which is added his defence, containing a vindication of his opinions, and a refutation of those inquisitorial charges, in which he shews that his opinions are perfectly consonant to the spirit of the gospel* (Dublin: n.p., 1794).

BURKE, EDMUND, *The correspondence of Edmund Burke, 1794–6*, viii (Sept. 1794–Apr. 1796), ed. R. B. McDowell (Chicago: University of Chicago Press, 1969).

—— *Reflections on the revolution in France*, ed. and introd. Thomas H. D. Mahoney (Indianapolis and New York: Liberal Arts Press, 1955).

[BYRNE, J.], *An impartial account of the late disturbances in the county of Armagh, containing all the principal meetings, battles, executions, whippings, etc., of the Break o' Day Men and the Defenders in the year 1784 down to the year 1791, with a full and true account of the nature of the rising of both parties* (Dublin: n.p., 1792).

A candid and impartial account of the disturbances in the county of Meath in the years 1792, 1793, and 1794, by a County Meath freeholder (Dublin: N. Kelly, 1794).

CAREY, W. P., *An appeal to the people of Ireland by W. P. Carey, late proprietor of the 'National Evening Star' and intended proprietor of the 'New Evening Star'* (Dublin: n.p., 1794).

CASTLEREAGH, VISCOUNT, *Memoirs and correspondence of Viscount Castlereagh, second marquess of Londonderry* (4 vols., London: Henry Colburn, 1848–9).

COIGLEY, REVD JAMES, *The life of Revd James Coigley, an address to the people of Ireland, as written by himself during his confinement in Maidstone gaol* (London: n.p., 1798).

CORRY, JOHN, *Odes and elegies, descriptive and sentimental, with 'The patriot', a poem* (Newry: R. Moffet, 1797).

The country book-club: a poem (Dublin: Z. Jackson, 1790).

Defence of the subcommittee of the Catholics of Ireland from the imputations attempted to be thrown on that body, particularly from the charge of supporting the Defenders, published by order of the subcommittee (Dublin: H. Fitzpatrick, 1793).

DE LATOCNAYE, *A Frenchman's walk through Ireland, 1796–7*, trans. John Stevenson (Belfast: McCaw, Stevenson, and Orr, 1917).

DICKSON, WILLIAM STEELE, *A narrative of the confinement and exile of William Steele Dickson, DD, formerly minister of the Presbyterian congregation of Ballyhalbert and Portaferry in the county of Down* (Dublin: J. Stockdale, 1812).

—— *Three sermons on the subject of scripture politics* (Belfast: n.p., 1793).

DRENNAN, WILLIAM, *A letter to his excellency Earl Fitzwilliam, lord lieutenant, etc., of Ireland* (Dublin: J. Chambers, 1795).

—— *Letters of Orellana, an Irish helot, to the seven northern counties on a more equal representation of the people in the parliament of Ireland* (Dublin: T. Chambers and T. Henry), 1785.

The Drennan letters, ed. D. A. Chart (Belfast: HMSO, 1931).

DRUMMOND, WILLIAM HAMILTON, *Hibernia: a poem, part the first* (Belfast: Northern Star Office, 1797).

—— *The man of age: a poem* (Belfast: n.p., 1797).

The duty of armed citizens at this awful period examined (Dublin: n.p., 1797).

EDWARDS, R. DUDLEY (ed.), 'The minute book of the Catholic Committee, 1773–92', *Archivium Hibernicum, or Irish Historical Records*, 9 (1941), 3–172.

EMMET, THOMAS ADDIS, O'CONNOR, ARTHUR, and MACNEVEN, WILLIAM JAMES, *Memoire or detailed statement of the origin and progress of the Irish union, delivered to the Irish government by Messrs Emmett, O'Connor, and M'Nevin, together with the examinations of these gentlemen before the secret committees of the houses of lords and commons in the summer of 1798* (Dublin: n.p., 1798).

FITZWILLIAM, WILLIAM WENTWORTH, 4th earl, *First letter: a letter from Earl Fitzwilliam, recently retired from this country, to the earl of Carlisle, explaining the causes of that event* (2nd edn., London: G. G. and J. Robinson, 1795).

—— *Second letter: a letter from Earl Fitzwilliam, who recently retired from Ireland, to the earl of Carlisle, explaining the causes of that event* (3rd edn., London: G. G. and J. Robinson, 1795).

French fraternity and French protection, as promised to Ireland and as experienced by other nations, addressed to all ranks and descriptions in this kingdom, by a friend to the people (18th edn., Dublin: J. Milliken, 1798).

A full report of the trial at bar in the court of king's bench, in which the right hon. Arthur Wolfe, his majesty's attorney general, prosecuted, and A. H. Rowan, Esq., was defendant, on an information filed ex-officio against the defendant for having published a seditious libel (Dublin: W. McKenzie, 1794).

A full report of the trial at bar in the court of king's bench, of William Drennan, MD, upon an indictment charging him with having written and published a seditious libel, with the speeches of counsel and the opinions of the court at large (Dublin: J. Rea, 1794).

GEBBIE, JOHN H. (ed.), *An introduction to the Abercorn letters (as relating to Ireland, 1736–1819)* (Omagh: Strule Press, 1972).

GILBERT, SIR JOHN T. (ed.), *Documents relating to Ireland, 1795–1804* (Dublin: Joseph Dollard, 1893).

GRATTAN, HENRY, *Memoirs of the life and times of the rt. hon. Henry Grattan*, ed. Henry Grattan, his son (4 vols., London: Henry Colburn, 1842).

GURNEY, JAMES, *The trial of James O'Coigly, otherwise called James Quigley, otherwise called James John Fivey, Arthur O'Connor, Esq., John Binns, John Allen, and Jeremiah Leary for high treason under a special commission at Maidstone in Kent on Monday the twenty-first and Tuesday the twenty-second days of May 1798* (London: M. Gurney, 1798).

HOWELL, THOMAS BAYLEY, and HOWELL, THOMAS JONES, *A complete collection of state trials and proceedings for high treason and other crimes and misdemeanours* (34 vols., London: Hansard, 1811–26).

JOY, HENRY, *Belfast politics, or a collection of the debates, resolutions, and other proceedings of that town in the years 1792 to 1793* (Belfast: H. Joy, 1794).

—— *Historical collections relative to the town of Belfast from the earliest period to the union with Great Britain* (Belfast: George Berwick, 1817).

KNOX, ALEXANDER, *Essays on the political circumstances of Ireland written during the administration of Earl Camden, with an appendix containing thoughts on the will of the people* (Dublin: Graisberry and Campbell, 1799).

LAWLESS, JOHN, *The Belfast politics enlarged, being a compendium of the political history of Ireland for the last forty years* (Belfast: D. Lyons, 1818).

LAWLESS, VALENTINE (Lord Cloncurry), *Personal recollections of the life and times, with extracts from the correspondence, of Valentine, Lord Cloncurry* (Dublin: James McGlashan, 1849).

LOCKE, JOHN, *The second treatise on government*, ed. Thomas P. Peardon (Indianapolis: Bobbs-Merrill, 1952).

MCDOWELL, R. B., 'The proceedings of the Dublin Society of United Irishmen', *Analecta Hibernia*, 17 (1949), 3–143.

—— 'Select documents: United Irish plans of parliamentary reform, 1793', *Irish Historical Studies*, 3/9 (Mar. 1942), 39–59.

MACNEVEN, WILLIAM JAMES, *Pieces of Irish history illustrative of the condition of the Catholics of Ireland, of the origins and progress of the political system of the United Irishmen, and of their transactions with the Anglo-Irish government* (New York: Bernard Dormin, 1807).

MCNEVIN, THOMAS, *The leading state trials in Ireland from the year 1794 to 1803, with an introduction, notes, etc.* (Dublin: James Duffy, 1844).

MCSKIMIN, SAMUEL, *Annals of Ulster from 1790 to 1798*, ed. E. J. McCrum (Belfast: James Cleeland, 1906).

The martyr of liberty: a poem on the heroic death of Lawrence O'Connor, executed at Naas in Ireland on a charge of high treason, September 7th, 1796 (Dublin: n.p., 1798).

MUSGRAVE, SIR RICHARD, *Memoires of the different rebellions in Ireland from the arrival of the English; also, a particular detail of that which broke out the XXIIId of May, MDCCXCVIII, with the history of the conspiracy which preceded it* (3rd edn., 2 vols., Dublin: R. Marchbank, 1802).

NEWELL, JOHN EDWARD, *The apostacy of Newell, containing the life and the confessions of that celebrated informer, his reasons for becoming and so long continuing one, his exposure of government and their plans against the lives and liberties of the people, his correspondence with some of the most celebrated characters of the present administration, written by himself* (London: n.p., 1798).

[O'CONNOR, ARTHUR], *A view of the present state of Ireland, with an account of the origin and progress of the disturbances in that country, and a narrative of the facts addressed to the people of England by an observer* (London: J. S. Jordan, 1797).

The oppression of tithe exemplified, or a review of a late contest between conscientious scruple and ecclesiastical exaction, as exhibited in a number of publications in the 'Northern Star', which are now collected into a pamphlet at the desire of many respectable persons who are not subscribers to the paper (Belfast: Belfast Printing Office, 1797).

Paddy's resource, being a select collection of original and modern patriotic songs, toasts, and sentiments compiled for the use of all firm patriots (Philadelphia: T. Stephens, 1796).

PAINE, THOMAS, *Rights of man*, ed. and introd. Henry Collins (Harmondsworth, Middlesex: Penguin Books, 1976).

PORTER, REVD JAMES, *Billy Bluff and Squire Firebrand, or a sample of the times, as it appeared in five letters, with a selection of songs from 'Paddy's resource'* (1st edn., 1796; Belfast: n.p., 1812).

POWELL, JOHN (ed.), *Statistical illustrations of the territorial extent and population, rental, taxation, finances, commerce, consumption, insolvency, pauperism, and crime of the British empire* (London: n.p., 1827).

RIDGEWAY, WILLIAM, *A report of the proceedings in cases of high treason at a special commission of oyer and terminer held in and for the county and city of Dublin in the month of July 1798* (trial of the Sheares brothers) (Dublin: J. Exshaw, 1798).

—— *A report of the trial of John McCann upon an indictment for high treason* (Dublin: J. Exshaw, 1798).

—— *A report of the trial of Patrick Finnerty, upon an indictment for a libel, before the hon. Judge Chamberlain and the hon. Baron Smith* (Dublin: J. Exshaw, 1798).

ROWAN, ARCHIBALD HAMILTON, *The autobiography of Archibald Hamilton Rowan*, ed. William H. Drummond (1st edn., 1840; Shannon: Irish University Press, 1972).

RUSSELL, THOMAS, *Journals and memoirs of Thomas Russell, 1791–5*, ed. Christopher Woods (Dublin: Irish Academic Press, 1992).

—— *A letter to the people of Ireland on the present situation of the country* (2nd edn., Belfast: Northern Star Office, 1796).

—— and SAMPSON, WILLIAM, *Review of the lion of old England, or the democracy confounded, as it appeared from time to time in a periodical print, with additions and amendments by the reviewers* (Belfast: Northern Star Office, 1794).

[SAMPSON, WILLIAM], *Advice to the rich by an independent country gentleman, pointing out the road to security and peace* (Dublin: n.p., 1796).

—— *A faithful report of the second trial of the proprietors of the 'Northern Star' at the bar of the court of king's bench on the 17th of November, 1794, on an information filed ex-officio by the attorney general for the insertion of the Society of United Irishmen's address to the Volunteers of Ireland on the 19th December 1792, by a barrister* (Belfast: n.p., 1795).

—— *A faithful report of the trial of Hurdy Gurdy at the bar of the court of king's bench, Westminster, on the 28th day of May 1794, on an examination filed ex-officio by the attorney general, by a barrister* (Belfast: J. Rabb, 1794).

—— *A faithful report of the trial of the proprietors of the 'Northern Star' at the bar of the court of king's bench on the twenty-eight of May 1794, on an information filed ex-officio by the attorney general for the insertion of a publication of the Irish Jacobins of Belfast on the fifteenth of December 1792, by a barrister* (Belfast: n.p., 1794).

[SAMPSON, WILLIAM], *Memoirs of William Sampson, an Irish exile, written by himself* (London: Whittaker, Treacher, and Arnot, 1832).

SAMPSON, WILLIAM VAUGHAN, *Statistical survey of the county of Londonderry* (3rd edn., Dublin: Graisberry and Campbell, 1802).

Selections from the papers of the London Corresponding Society, 1792–1799, ed. and introd. Mary Thale (Cambridge: Cambridge University Press, 1983).

SEWARD, WILLIAM WENMAN, *Collectanea politica, or the political transactions of Ireland from the ascension of George III to the present time* (3 vols., Dublin: A. Stewart, 1801–4).

Society of United Irishmen of Dublin, established November IX, MDCCXCI: 'Let the nation stand' (proceedings), (Dublin: n.p., 1794).

SWEETMAN, JOHN, *A refutation of the charges attempted to be made against the secretary to the sub-committee of the Catholics of Ireland, particularly that of abetting the Defenders* (Dublin: H. Fitzpatrick, 1793).

TEELING, CHARLES HAMILTON, *The history of the Irish rebellion of 1798 and sequel to the history of the Irish rebellion of 1798* (1st edn., 1876; Shannon, Ireland: Irish University Press, 1972).

TONE, THEOBALD WOLFE, *Life of Theobald Wolfe Tone*, ed. William Theobald Wolfe Tone (2 vols., Washington, DC: Gales and Seaton, 1826).

The trial of Revd William Jackson (Dublin: J. Exshaw, 1795).

LATER WORKS: BOOKS

ADAMS, J. R. R., *The printed word and the common man: popular culture in Ulster, 1700–1900* (Belfast: Institute of Irish Studies, Queen's University of Belfast, 1987).

AKENSON, DONALD HARMON, and CRAWFORD, W. H., *Local poets and social history: James Orr, bard of Ballycarry* (Belfast: PRONI, 1977).

ALTICK, RICHARD D., *The English common reader: a social history of the mass reading public, 1800–1900* (Chicago: University of Chicago Press, 1957).

ANDERSON, BENEDICT, *Imagined communities: reflections on the origin and spread of nationalism* (London: New Left Books, 1983).

APPLEBY, JOYCE, *Capitalism and a new order: the republican vision of the 1790s* (New York and London: New York University Press, 1984).

ASHCRAFT, RICHARD, *Revolutionary politics and Locke's two 'Treatises of government'* (Princeton, NJ: Princeton University Press, 1986).

ASPINALL, ARTHUR, *Politics and the press, c.1780–1850* (London: Home and Van Thal, 1949).

BAILYN, BERNARD, *The ideological origins of the American revolution* (Cambridge, Mass.: Harvard University Press, 1976).

BANNING, LANCE, *The Jeffersonian persuasion: evolution of a party ideology* (Ithaca, NY, and London: Cornell University Press, 1978).

BARKLEY, JOHN M., *A short history of the Presbyterian church in Ireland* (Belfast: Presbyterian Church in Ireland, 1960).

BARTLETT, THOMAS, *The fall and rise of the Irish nation: the Catholic question, 1690–1830* (Savage, Md.: Barnes and Noble, 1992).

—— and HAYTON, D. W. (eds.), *Penal era and golden age: essays in Irish history, 1690–1800* (Belfast: W. & G. Baird, 1979).

BECKETT, J. C., *The Anglo-Irish tradition* (Ithaca, NY: Cornell University Press, 1976).

—— *The making of modern Ireland, 1603–1923* (New York: Alfred A. Knopf, 1973).

—— *Protestant dissent in Ireland, 1687–1780* (London: Faber and Faber, 1948).

BLUM, CAROL, *Rousseau and the republic of virtue: the language of politics in the French revolution* (Ithaca, NY, and London: Cornell University Press, 1986).

BONWICK, COLIN, *English radicals and the American revolution* (Chapel Hill, NC: University of North Carolina Press, 1977).

BOYCE, D. GEORGE, *Nationalism in Ireland* (Dublin: Gill and Macmillan, 1982).

BOYLAN, HENRY, *Theobald Wolfe Tone* (Dublin: Gill and Macmillan, 1981).

BREWER, JOHN, *Party ideology and popular politics at the accession of George III* (Cambridge: Cambridge University Press, 1981).

BROWN, TERENCE, *The whole protestant community: the making of a historical myth* (Field Day pamphlet 7; Belfast: Dorman, 1985).

BURKE, JOHN F., *Outlines of the industrial history of Ireland* (Dublin: Browne and Nolan, 1920).

CANNON, JOHN, *Parliamentary reform, 1640–1832* (Cambridge: Cambridge University Press, 1973).

CLARK, SAMUEL, *Social origins of the Irish land war* (Princeton, NJ: Princeton University Press, 1979).

—— and DONNELLY, JAMES S., jun. (eds.), *Irish peasants: violence and political unrest, 1780–1914* (Madison, Wis.: University of Wisconsin Press, 1983).

CONE, CARL B., *The English Jacobins: reformers in late 18th-century England* (New York: Scribner's, 1968).

CONNOLLY, S. J., *Priests and people in pre-famine Ireland, 1780–1845* (Dublin: Gill and Macmillan, 1982).

CORISH, PATRICK J., *The Catholic community in the seventeenth and eighteenth centuries* (Dublin: Helicon, 1981).

—— (ed.), *Radicals, rebels, and establishments* (*Historical Studies*, 15; Belfast: Appletree Press, 1985).

COUGHLAN, RUPERT J., *Napper Tandy* (Dublin: Anvil Books, 1976).

CRAWFORD, W. H., *Domestic industry in Ireland* (Dublin: Gill and Macmillan, 1972).

CROKER, T. CROFTON, *Popular songs illustrative of the French invasions of Ireland* (London: T. Richards, 1845).

CRONIN, SEAN, *Irish nationalism: a history of its roots and ideology* (Dublin: Academy Press, 1980).

CULLEN, L. M., *The emergence of modern Ireland, 1660–1900* (London: B. T. Batsford, 1981).

DALY, MARY E., *Social and economic history of Ireland since 1800* (Dublin: The Educational Company, 1981).

DICKINSON, H. T., *Liberty and property: political ideology in eighteenth-century Britain* (London: Weidenfeld and Nicolson, 1977).

DICKSON, CHARLES, *Revolt in the north: Antrim and Down in 1798* (Dublin: Clonmore and Reynolds, 1960).

DICKSON, DAVID, *New foundations: Ireland, 1660–1800* (Dublin: Helicon Limited, 1987).

DICKSON, DAVID, WHELAN, KEVIN, and KEOGH, DÁIRE (eds.), *The United Irishmen: republicanism, radicalism, and rebellion* (Dublin: Lilliput Press, 1993).

DOBSON, C. R., *Masters and journeymen: a prehistory of industrial relations, 1717–1800* (London: Croom Helm, 1980).

DOYLE, DAVID NOEL, *Ireland, Irishmen, and revolutionary America, 1760–1820* (Dublin and Cork: Mercier Press, 1981).

DUNN, JOHN, *The political thought of John Locke: an historical account of the argument of the two 'Treatises of government'* (Cambridge: Cambridge University Press, 1969).

DUNNE, TOM, *Theobald Wolfe Tone, colonial outsider: an analysis of his political philosophy* (Cork: Tower Books, 1982).

ELLIOTT, MARIANNE, *Partners in revolution: the United Irishmen and France* (New Haven, Conn., and London: Yale University Press, 1982).

—— *Watchmen in Sion: the protestant idea of liberty* (Field Day pamphlet 8; Belfast: Dorman, 1985).

—— *Wolfe Tone: prophet of Irish independence* (New Haven, Conn., and London: Yale University Press, 1989).

FAOLAIN, TURLOUGH, *Blood on the harp: Irish rebel history in ballad (the heritage)* (Troy, NY: Whitson Publishing, 1983).

FITZHENRY, EDNA, *Henry Joy McCracken* (Dublin: Talbot Press, 1936).

FITZPATRICK, W. J., *'The sham squire' and the informers of 1798, with jottings about Ireland a century ago* (3rd ed., Dublin: M. H. Gill, n.d).

FOSTER, R. F., *Modern Ireland, 1600–1972* (London: Allen Lane, Penguin Press, 1988).

GARVIN, TOM, *The evolution of Irish nationalist politics* (Dublin: Gill and Macmillan, 1981).

GIBBON, PETER, *The origins of Ulster unionism: the formation of popular protestant politics and ideology in nineteenth-century Ireland* (Manchester: Manchester University Press, 1975).

GILL, CONRAD, *The rise of the Irish linen industry* (1st edn., 1925; Oxford: Clarendon Press, 1964).

GOODWIN, ALBERT, *The friends of liberty: the English democratic movement in the age of the French revolution* (London: Hutchinson, 1979).

GOUGH, HUGH, and DICKSON, DAVID (eds.), *Ireland and the French revolution* (Dublin: Irish Academic Press, 1990).

HAIRE, J. L. M. (ed.), *Challenge and conflict: essays in Irish Presbyterian history and doctrine* (Antrim: W. & G. Baird, 1981).

HEWITT, JOHN, *The rhyming weavers and other poets of Antrim and Down* (Belfast: Blackstaff Press, 1974).

HONE, J. ANN, *For the cause of truth: radicalism in London, 1796–1821* (Oxford: Clarendon Press, 1982).

HONT, ISTVAN, and IGNATIEFF, MICHAEL (eds.), *Wealth and virtue: the shaping of political economy in the Scottish Enlightenment* (Cambridge: Cambridge University Press, 1983).

HUNT, LYNN, *Politics, culture, and class in the French revolution* (Berkeley, Calif.: University of California Press, 1984).

HUTCHINSON, JOHN, *The dynamics of cultural nationalism: the Gaelic revival and the creation of the Irish nation state* (London: Allen and Unwin, 1987).

INGLISS, BRIAN, *The freedom of the press in Ireland, 1784–1841* (London: Faber and Faber, 1954).

Ireland after the union: proceedings of the second joint meeting of the Royal Irish Academy and the British Academy, London, 1986, introd. Lord Blake (Oxford: Oxford University Press, 1989).

JACOB, MARGARET, *Living the Enlightenment: freemasonry and politics in eighteenth-century Europe* (Oxford: Oxford University Press, 1991).

—— and JACOB, JAMES (eds.), *The origins of Anglo-American radicalism* (London: George Allen and Unwin, 1984).

JACOB, ROSAMUND, *The rise of the United Irishmen, 1791–4* (London: George C. Harrap, 1937).

KEE, ROBERT, *The green flag: a history of Irish nationalism* (London: Weidenfeld and Nicolson, 1972).

KENNEDY, LIAM, and OLLERENSHAW, PHILIP (eds.), *An economic history of Ulster, 1820–1940* (Manchester: Manchester University Press, 1985).

LATIMER, W. T., *Ulster biographies relating chiefly to the rebellion of 1798* (Belfast: James Cleeland, William Mullan and Son, 1897).

LECKY, W. E. H., *A history of Ireland in the eighteenth century* (5 vols., London: Longmans, Green, 1898).

LEPPER, JOHN HERON, *Famous secret societies* (London: Sampson, Low, Marston, and Co., n.d.).

LYNCH, JOHN, *The Spanish American revolutions, 1808–1826* (2nd edn., New York: W. W. Norton, 1986).

MCANALLY, SIR HENRY, *The Irish militia, 1793–1816: a social and military history* (London: Eyre and Spottiswoode, 1949).

MCCARTNEY, R. L., *Liberty and authority in Ireland* (Field Day pamphlet 9; Belfast: Dorman, 1985).

MCCORMACK, W. J., *Ascendancy and tradition in Anglo-Irish literary history from 1789 to 1939* (Oxford: Oxford University Press, 1985).

MCCRACKEN, J. L., *The Irish parliament in the eighteenth century* (Dublin: Historical Association, 1971).

MACDERMOT, FRANK, *Theobald Wolfe Tone and his times* (Tralee: Anvil Books, 1968).

MACDONAGH, OLIVER, *States of mind: a study of Anglo-Irish conflict, 1780–1980* (London: George Allen and Unwin, 1983).

MCDOWELL, R. B., *Ireland in the age of imperialism and revolution* (Oxford: Clarendon Press, 1979).

—— *Irish public opinion, 1750–1800* (London: Faber and Faber, 1944).

MACKENZIE, NORMAN (ed.), *Secret societies* (New York: Collier Books, 1967).

MCNEILL, MARY, *The life and times of Mary Ann McCracken, 1770–1866: a Belfast panorama* (Dublin: Allen Figgis, 1960).

MADDEN, R. R., *Antrim and Down in '98* (Glasgow: Cameron, Ferguson, n.d.).

—— *The history of Irish periodical literature from the end of the 17th to the middle of the 19th century, its origins, progress, and results, with notices of remarkable persons connected with the press in Ireland during the past two centuries* (2 vols., London: T. C. Newby, 1867).

MADDEN, R. R., *Literary remains of the United Irishmen of 1798 and selections from other popular lyrics of their times, with an essay on the authorship of 'The exile of Erin'* (Dublin: James Duffy, 1887).

—— *The United Irishmen, their lives and times*, 3rd ser. (7 vols., London: J. Madden, 1842–5; 12 vols., New York: Catholic Publication Society of America, 1916).

MALCOMSON, A. P. W., *John Foster: the politics of the Anglo-Irish ascendancy* (Oxford: Oxford University Press, 1978).

MILLER, DAVID W., *Queen's rebels: Ulster loyalism in historical perspective* (Dublin: Gill and Macmillan, 1978).

MITCHISON, ROSALIND (ed.), *The roots of nationalism: studies in northern Europe* (London: John Donald, 1980).

MOODY, T. W., and VAUGHAN, W. E. (eds.), *A new history of Ireland*, iv. *Eighteenth-century Ireland, 1691–1800* (Oxford: Clarendon Press, 1986).

O'BRIEN, GERARD, *Anglo-Irish politics in the age of Grattan and Pitt* (Dublin: Irish Academic Press, 1987).

—— (ed.), *Parliament, politics and people: essays in eighteenth-century Irish history* (Dublin: Irish Academic Press, 1989).

O'CONNELL, MAURICE R., *Irish politics and social conflict in the age of the American revolution* (Philadelphia: University of Pennsylvania Press, 1965).

O'DONNELL, PATRICK, *The Irish faction fighters of the 19th century* (Dublin: Anvil Books, 1975).

O'MALLEY, PADRAIG, *The uncivil wars: Ireland today* (Boston: Houghton Mifflin, 1983).

Ó TUATHAIGH, GEAROID, *Ireland before the famine, 1798–1848* (Dublin: Gill and Macmillan, 1972).

PAKENHAM, THOMAS, *The year of liberty: the story of the great Irish rebellion of 1798* (London: Granada, 1978).

PALMER, R. R., *The age of democratic revolution: a political history of Europe and America, 1760–1800* (2 vols., Princeton, NJ: Princeton University Press, 1959).

POCOCK, J. G. A., *The ancient constitution and the feudal law: a study of English historical thought in the seventeenth century. A reissue with a retrospect* (Cambridge: Cambridge University Press, 1987).

—— *The Machiavellian moment: Florentine political thought and the Atlantic republican tradition* (Princeton, NJ: Princeton University Press, 1975).

—— *Virtue, commerce, and history: essays on political thought and history, chiefly in the eighteenth century* (Cambridge: Cambridge University Press, 1985).

POWER, T. P., and WHELAN, KEVIN (eds.), *Endurance and emergence: Catholics in Ireland in the eighteenth century* (Dublin: Irish Academic Press, 1990).

ROBBINS, CAROLINE, *The eighteenth-century commonwealthman: studies in the transmission, development, and circumstances of English liberal thought from the restoration of Charles II until the war with the thirteen colonies* (New York: Atheneum, 1968).

ROGERS, REVD PATRICK, *The Irish Volunteers and Catholic emancipation, 1778–1793* (London: Burns, Oates, and Washington, 1934).

ROYLE, EDWARD, and WALVIN, JAMES, *English radicals and reformers, 1760–1848* (Lexington, Ky.: University of Kentucky Press, 1982).

SCHAMA, SIMON, *Citizens: a chronicle of the French revolution* (New York: Alfred A. Knopf, 1989).

SENIOR, HEREWARD, *Orangeism in Ireland and Britain, 1795–1836* (London: Routledge and Kegan Paul, 1966).

SHAW, PETER, *American patriots and the rituals of revolution* (Cambridge, Mass.: Harvard University Press, 1981).

SIBBETT, R. M., *Orangeism in Ireland and throughout the empire* (2 vols., Belfast: Henderson, 1914–15).

SMITH, E. A., *Whig principles and party politics: Earl Fitzwilliam and the whig party, 1748–1833* (Manchester: Manchester University Press, 1975).

SMYTH, JIM, *The men of no property: Irish radicals and popular politics in the late eighteenth century* (New York: St Martin's Press, 1992).

STEWART, A. T. Q., *The narrow ground: aspects of Ulster, 1609–1969* (London: Faber and Faber, 1977).

THOMAS, KEITH, *Religion and the decline of magic* (New York: Scribner's, 1971).

THOMIS, MALCOLM I., and HOLT, PETER, *Threats of revolution in Britain, 1789–1848* (London and Basingstoke: Macmillan Press, 1977).

THOMPSON, E. P., *The making of the English working class* (New York: Vintage Books, 1963).

WALL, MAUREEN, *The penal laws, 1691–1760* (Dundalk: Dublin Historical Association, 1976).

WELLS, ROGER, *Insurrection: the British experience, 1795–1803* (Gloucester: Alan Sutton, 1983).

WHELAN, KEVIN, and NOLAN, WILLIAM (eds.), *Wexford: history and society. Interdisciplinary essays on the history of an Irish county* (Dublin: Geography Publications, 1987).

WILLIAMS, GWYN A., *Artisans and sans-culottes: popular movements in France and Britain during the French revolution* (New York: W. W. Norton, 1969).

WILLIAMS, T. DESMOND (ed.), *Secret societies in Ireland* (Dublin: Gill and Macmillan, 1973).

WOOD, GORDON S., *The creation of the American republic, 1776–1787* (New York: W. W. Norton, 1972).

WOODBURN, REVD JAMES BARKLEY, *The Ulster Scot: his history and religion* (London: H. R. Allenson, 1915).

YOUNG, ROBERT M., *Ulster in '98: episodes and anecdotes* (Belfast: Marcus Ward, 1893).

ZIMMERMANN, GEORGES-DENIS, *Songs of Irish rebellion: political ballads and rebel songs, 1780–1900* (Hatboro, Pa.: Folklore Associates, 1967).

LATER WORKS: ARTICLES

BARTLETT, THOMAS, 'An end to moral economy: the Irish militia disturbances of 1793', *Past and Present*, 99 (May 1983), 41–64.
—— 'Indiscipline and disaffection in the armed forces in Ireland in the 1790s', in Patrick J. Corish (ed.), *Radicals, rebels, and establishments* (Belfast: Appletree Press, 1985), 115–34.

BEAMES, M. R., 'The Ribbon societies: lower-class nationalism in pre-famine Ireland', *Past and Present*, 97 (Nov. 1982), 128–43.

BIGGER, FRANCIS JOSEPH, 'Rural libraries in Antrim', *Irish Book Lover*, 13/4 (Nov. 1921), 47–52.

CHRISTIANSON, GALE E., 'Secret societies and agrarian violence in Ireland, 1790–1840', *Agricultural History*, 46 (1972), 369–84.

COLLEY, LINDA, 'Whose nation? Class and national consciousness in Britain, 1750–1830', *Past and Present*, 113 (Nov. 1986), 97–117.

COMERFORD, R. V., 'Patriotism as pastime: the appeal of Fenianism in the mid-1860s', *Irish Historical Studies*, 22/87 (Mar. 1981), 239–50.

CULLEN, L. M., 'The cultural basis of modern Irish nationalism', in Rosalind Mitchison (ed.), *The roots of nationalism: studies in northern Europe* (London: John Donald, 1980), 91–106.

—— 'The political structures of the Defenders', in Hugh Gough and David Dickson (eds.), *Ireland and the French revolution* (Dublin: Irish Academic Press, 1990), 117–38.

—— 'The 1798 rebellion in its eighteenth-century context', in Patrick J. Corish (ed.), *Radicals, rebels, and establishments* (Belfast: Appletree Press, 1985), 91–113.

—— 'The 1798 rebellion in Wexford: United Irishmen organisation, membership, leadership', in Kevin Whelan and William Nolan (eds.), *Wexford: history and society. Interdisciplinary essays on the history of an Irish county* (Dublin: Geography Publications, 1987), 248–95.

CURTIN, NANCY J., 'The Belfast uniform: Theobald Wolfe Tone', *Eire-Ireland*, 20/2 (Summer 1985), 40–69.

—— 'Symbols and rituals of United Irish mobilisation', in Hugh Gough and David Dickson (eds.), *Ireland and the French revolution* (Dublin: Irish Academic Press, 1990), 68–82.

—— 'The transformation of the Society of United Irishmen into a mass-based revolutionary organisation, 1794–6', *Irish Historical Studies*, 24/96 (Nov. 1985), 463–92.

—— 'The United Irish organization in Ulster, 1795–8', in David Dickson, Dáire Keogh, and Kevin Whelan (eds.), *The United Irishmen: republicanism, radicalism, and rebellion* (Dublin: Lilliput Press, 1993), 209–21.

—— 'Women and eighteenth-century Irish republicanism', in Margaret MacCurtain and Mary O'Dowd (eds.), *Women in early modern Ireland* (Edinburgh: Edinburgh University Press, 1991), 133–44.

DONNELLY, JAMES S., jun., 'Hearts of Oak, Hearts of Steel', *Studia Hibernica*, 21 (1981), 7–73.

—— 'Irish agrarian rebellion: the Whiteboys of 1769–76', *Proceedings of the Royal Irish Academy*, 83C/12 (1983), 293–331.

—— 'Propagating the cause of the United Irishmen', *Studies*, 69/273 (Spring 1980), 5–23.

—— 'The Rightboy movement', *Studia Hibernica*, 17–18 (1977–8), 120–202.

—— 'The Whiteboy movement, 1761–5', *Irish Historical Studies*, 21/81 (Mar. 1978), 20–54.

DUNNE, TOM, 'Popular ballads, revolutionary rhetoric and politicisation', in Hugh Gough and David Dickson (eds.), *Ireland and the French revolution* (Dublin: Irish Academic Press, 1990), 139–55.

ELLIOTT, MARIANNE, 'The "Despard conspiracy" reconsidered', *Past and Present*, 75 (May 1977), 46–61.

—— 'The origins and transformation of early Irish republicanism', *International Review of Social History*, 23/3 (1978), 405–28.

—— 'The United Irishman as diplomat', in Patrick J. Corish (ed.), *Radicals, rebels, and establishments* (Belfast: Appletree Press, 1985), 69–89.

GARVIN, TOM, 'Defenders, Ribbonmen, and others: underground political networks in pre-famine Ireland', *Past and Present*, 96 (Aug. 1982), 133–55.

GIBBON, PETER, 'The origins of the Orange Order and the United Irishmen: a study in the sociology of revolution and counter-revolution', *Economy and Society*, 1 (1972), 134–63.

HILL, CHRISTOPHER, 'The Norman yoke', in *Puritanism and revolution: studies in interpretation of the English revolution of the seventeenth century* (New York: Schocken Books, 1964), 50–122.

HILL, JACQUELINE, 'The meaning and significance of "protestant ascendancy", 1787–1840', in *Ireland after the union: proceedings of the second joint meeting of the Royal Irish Academy and the British Academy, London, 1986*, introd. Lord Blake (Oxford: Oxford University Press, 1989), 1–22.

—— 'National festivals, the state, and "protestant ascendancy" in Ireland, 1790–1829', *Irish Historical Studies*, 24/93 (May 1984), 30–51.

—— 'The politics of Dublin corporation, 1760–1792', in David Dickson, Dáire Keogh, and Kevin Whelan (eds.), *The United Irishmen: republicanism, radicalism, and rebellion* (Dublin: Lilliput Press, 1993), 88–101.

—— 'The politics of privilege: Dublin corporation and the Catholic question, 1792–1823', *Maynooth Review*, 7 (Dec. 1982), 17–36.

JONES, MERVYN, 'Freemasonry', in Norman MacKenzie (ed.), *Secret societies* (New York: Collier Books, 1967), 128–51.

KELLY, JAMES, 'The genesis of "protestant ascendancy": the Rightboy disturbances of the 1780s and their impact upon protestant opinion', in Gerard O'Brien (ed.), *Parliament, politics and people: essays in eighteenth-century Irish history* (Dublin: Irish Academic Press, 1989), 93–127.

KENNEDY, LIAM, 'The rural economy, 1820–1914', in Liam Kennedy and Philip Ollerenshaw (eds.), *An economic history of Ulster, 1820–1940* (Manchester: Manchester University Press, 1985), 1–61.

KENNEDY, W. BENJAMIN, 'The Irish Jacobins', *Studia Hibernica*, 16 (1976), 109–21.

—— 'The United Irishmen and the great naval mutiny of 1797', *Eire-Ireland*, 25/3 (Autumn 1990), 7–18.

—— ' "Without any guarantee on our part": the French Directory's Irish policy', in Lee Kennett (ed.), *The consortium on revolutionary Europe, 1750–1850: proceedings, 1972* (Gainesville, Fla.: University of Florida Press, 1973), 50–64.

KRAMNICK, ISAAC, 'Republican revisionism revisited', *American Historical Review*, 87/3 (June 1982), 629–64.

MACDERMOT, FRANK, 'Arthur O'Connor', *Irish Historical Studies*, 16/57 (Mar. 1966), 48–69.

McDOWELL, R. B., 'The age of the United Irishmen: revolution and the Union, 1794–1800', in T. W. Moody and W. E. Vaughan (eds.), *A new history of Ireland*, iv. *Eighteenth-century Ireland, 1691–1800* (Oxford: Clarendon Press, 1986).

McDowell, R. B., 'The Fitzwilliam episode', *Irish Historical Studies*, 16/58 (Sept. 1966), 115–30.

—— 'The personnel of the Dublin Society of United Irishmen, 1791–4', *Irish Historical Studies*, 2/5 (Mar. 1940), 12–53.

Maguire, W. A., 'Lord Donegall and the Hearts of Steel', *Irish Historical Studies*, 21/84 (Sept. 1979), 351–76.

Miller, David W, 'The Armagh troubles, 1784–95', in Samuel Clark and James S. Donnelly, jun. (eds.), *Irish peasants: violence and political unrest, 1780–1914* (Madison, Wis.: University of Wisconsin Press, 1983), 155–91.

—— 'Presbyterianism and "modernization" in Ulster', *Past and Present*, 80 (Aug. 1978), 66–90.

Moody, T. W., 'The political ideas of the United Irishmen', *Ireland To-Day*, 3/1 (Jan. 1938), 15–25.

Murphy, Sean, 'Charles Lucas and the Dublin election of 1748–9', *Parliamentary History*, 2 (1983), 93–111.

—— 'The Dublin anti-union riot of 3 December 1759', in Gerard O'Brien (ed.), *Parliament, politics and people: essays in eighteenth-century Irish history* (Dublin: Irish Academic Press, 1989), 49–68.

O'Connell, M. R., 'The American revolution in Ireland', *Eire-Ireland*, 11/3 (1976), 3–12.

—— 'Class conflict in pre-industrial society: Dublin in 1780', *Duquesne Review*, 9/1 (Autumn 1963), 43–55.

Ó Loinsigh, Séamus, 'The rebellion of 1798 in Meath', *Riocht na Midhe: Records of the Meath Archaeological and Historical Society*, 4/2–5 (1968–71), 33–50, 3–28, 30–54, 62–75.

Pocock, J. G. A., 'Radical criticisms of the whig order in the age between revolutions', in Margaret and James Jacob (eds.), *The origins of Anglo-American radicalism* (London: George Allen and Unwin, 1984), 33–57.

Powell, Thomas, 'An economic factor in the Wexford rebellion of 1798', *Studia Hibernica*, 16 (1976), 140–57.

Robertson, John, 'The Scottish Englightenment at the limits of the civic tradition', in Istvan Hont and Michael Ignatieff (eds.), *Wealth and virtue: the shaping of political economy in the Scottish Enlightenment* (Cambridge: Cambridge University Press, 1983), 137–78.

Sheehy, Edward, 'Tone and the United Irishmen', *Ireland To-Day*, 2/12 (Dec. 1937), 37–42.

Shulim, Joseph I., 'John Daly Burk: Irish revolutionist and American patriot', *Transactions of the American Philosophical Society*, NS 54/6 (1964), 1–60.

Smyth, James, 'Dublin's political underground in the 1790s', in Gerard O'Brien (ed.), *Parliament, politics and people: essays in eighteenth-century Irish history* (Dublin: Irish Academic Press, 1989), 93–127.

—— 'Popular politicisation, Defenderism and the Catholic question', in Hugh Gough and David Dickson (eds.), *Ireland and the French revolution* (Dublin: Irish Academic Press, 1990), 109–16.

Smyth, P. D. H., 'The Volunteers and parliament, 1779–84', in Thomas Bartlett and D. W. Hayton (eds.), *Penal era and golden age: essays in Irish history, 1690–1800* (Belfast, 1979), 113–36.

STEDMAN-JONES, GARETH, 'Rethinking Chartism', in *Languages of class: studies in English working-class history, 1832–1982* (Cambridge: Cambridge University Press, 1983).

STEWART, A. T. Q., '"A stable unseen power": Dr William Drennan and the origins of the United Irishmen', in John Bossy and Peter Jupp (eds.), *Essays presented to Michael Roberts* (Belfast: Blackstaff Press, 1976), 80–92.

STEWART, JOHN HALL, 'The Irish press and the French revolution', *Journalism Quarterly*, 39/4 (1962), 507–18.

SYNDERGAARD, REX, 'The Fitzwilliam crisis and Irish nationalism', *Eire-Ireland*, 8/2 (1973), 34–41.

THOMPSON, E. P., 'The moral economy of the English crowd in the eighteenth century', *Past and Present*, 50 (Feb. 1971), 76–136.

TOHALL, PATRICK, 'The Diamond fight of 1795 and the resultant expulsions', *Seanchas Ardmhacha (Armagh Diocesan Historical Society)*, 4 (1957), 19–50.

VANCE, NORMAN, 'Celts, Carthaginians, and constitutions: Anglo-Irish literary relations, 1780–1820', *Irish Historical Studies*, 22/87 (Mar. 1981), 216-38.

WALL, MAUREEN, 'The rise of a Catholic middle class in eighteenth-century Ireland', *Irish Historical Studies*, 11/42 (Sept. 1958), 91–115.

—— 'The United Irish movement', *Historical Studies*, 5 (1965), 122–40.

WALZER, MICHAEL, 'Puritanism as revolutionary ideology', *History and Theory*, 3/1 (1963), 59–70.

WHELAN, KEVIN, 'Politicisation in County Wexford and the origins of the 1798 rebellion', in Hugh Gough and David Dickson (eds.), *Ireland and the French revolution* (Dublin: Irish Academic Press, 1990), 156–78.

WOODS, C. J., 'The place of Thomas Russell in the United Irish movement', in Hugh Gough and David Dickson (eds.), *Ireland and the French revolution* (Dublin: Irish Academic Press, 1990), 83–108.

YOUNG, ROBERT M., 'Edward Bunting's Irish music and the McCracken family', *Ulster Journal of Archaeology*, 4/3 (Apr. 1898), 175–8.

UNPUBLISHED MATERIAL

MONAGHAN, JOHN J., 'A social and economic history of Belfast, 1790–1800', MA thesis (Belfast, 1936).

STEWART, A. T. Q., 'The transformation of Presbyterian radicalism in the north of Ireland, 1792–1825', MA thesis (Belfast, 1956).

INDEX